PRAISE FOR *CONSTRUCTIVE CONFLICTS: FROM EMERGENCE TO TRANSFORMATION*

"*Constructive Conflicts* by Bruce W. Dayton and Louis Kriesberg is a new classic. It is an indispensable synthesis of what we know about conflicts and how they can be approached constructively. Their new tagline, *From Emergence to Transformation*, captures well the dynamism that invites responsibility. Conflicts are not a given, something that 'just happens.' They are the product of human choices and trends, complex interactions that must be understood and responded to with commitment, competence, and compassion. This sixth edition is a jewel, a must-read for any scholar, student, and practitioner open to seek what is possible and good for all." **— Andrea Bartoli, president, Sant'Egidio Foundation for Peace and Dialogue**

"This new edition of a standard-setting work in the field of conflict studies brings the authors' insights into contact with some of the most salient recent developments and challenges in the field. Using fresh cases and a reconfigured approach to grasping conflict roots, the authors stimulate much-needed reflection while remaining grounded in the vast literature of conflict studies. The addition of updated cases and new study questions at the conclusion of each chapter enables readers to apply the book's concepts to today's world." **— Chester A. Crocker, emeritus professor, Georgetown University**

"Louis Kriesberg and Bruce Dayton have helped us to understand and untangle the complex web of conflict ever since their first seminal book came out in 1998. Its lessons about the transforming harmful and destructive relations into constructive ones are ever more important for our polarized world. An essential book for today's students, activists, and policy makers." **— Pamela Aall, American University; and senior advisor, Conflict Prevention and Management, United States Institute of Peace**

Constructive Conflicts

From Emergence to Transformation

Sixth Edition

Bruce W. Dayton and Louis Kriesberg

ROWMAN & LITTLEFIELD
Lanham • Boulder • New York • London

Executive Acquisitions Editor: Michael Kerns
Assistant Acquisitions Editor: Elizabeth Von Buhr
Senior Marketing Manager: Ami Reitmeier

Published by Rowman & Littlefield
An imprint of The Rowman & Littlefield Publishing Group, Inc.
4501 Forbes Boulevard, Suite 200, Lanham, Maryland 20706
www.rowman.com

86-90 Paul Street, London EC2A 4NE

British Library Cataloguing in Publication Information Available

Library of Congress Cataloging-in-Publication Data Available

ISBN 978-1-5381-6099-2 (cloth) | ISBN 978-1-5381-6100-5 (paper) |
ISBN 978-1-5381-6101-2 (ebook)

Contents

Figures and Tables

FIGURES

TABLES

Preface and Acknowledgments

Conflicts are the ultimate interdisciplinary puzzle. They are manifest at every level of social interaction, are driven by multiple dynamics, and manifest in different ways at different times. The goal of this book is to demystify these processes so that those who care about transforming conflicts can make better choices about where to begin and how. Over eleven chapters we seek to help explain why large-scale conflicts emerge, escalate, de-escalate, become settled, and often emerge again in new forms.

Much has changed in the world since *Constructive Conflicts* was first published in 1998. Populism has emerged in opposition to globalization and liberal international norms. Consolidated democracies in Europe and the Americas have come under threat by internal division and right-wing authoritarianism. The migration of people across the globe has accelerated in response to war, failed governance, environmental collapse, and financial failure. New social media platforms have upended the way that people communicate their concerns and make sense of the world, often providing new spaces for vitriol and conspiratorial thinking. And debates over politics—who gets what, when, and how—have become increasingly polarized and destructive. Many feel despondent and even hopeless in the face of these developments. Fortunately, knowledge about how to constructively manage conflicts has accelerated during this time as well. Conflict analysis and transformation has become a major field of investigation, replete with case studies, skills training, and proven mechanisms to limit destructive escalations.

In this sixth edition of *Constructive Conflicts*, we have reorganized our chapters, added up-to-date content and cases, and more deeply explored three core skills to the constructive conflicts approach: negotiation, mediation, and dialogue. We incorporate new insights about human conflict from the fields of neuroscience throughout the book. We also have altered several of our frameworks for conflict analysis to help the reader more easily apply our ideas to the cases they care about. Each chapter now ends with a set of discussion questions that can be used individually or within a classroom setting to explore key concepts and ideas more personally and deeply. We have also changed the subtitle of our book, which previously was *From Escalation to Resolution*, to *From Emergence to Transformation*. This was done in recognition of the full lifecycle of large-scale social conflicts and the fact that conflicts rarely end; rather, they become transformed. Finally, Lou, who for the past fifty years has pioneered the study of social conflicts, has stepped into the second author position and Bruce has assumed the first author position.

We thank the students and their instructors who used earlier editions for comments and questions that helped improve this sixth edition. We are also indebted to current and former colleagues at the School of International Training, where Bruce serves as Associate Professor and Director of the CONTACT Peacebuilding Program, and the Maxwell School of Syracuse University, where Lou serves as Maxwell Professor Emeritus of Social Conflict Studies. Among them are John Ungerleider, Paula Green and Tatsushi Arai, Margaret Hermann, and Robert Rubinstein. We appreciate the keen design work of Abigail Dayton and Harry Dubke who are responsible for making many of the figures found throughout the book. Finally, deep appreciation to Rebecca Stefan Dayton and Paula Freedman for their unending support, editing, and insightful advice.

Part I

CONFLICT ANALYSIS AND CONFLICT THEORY

Chapter One

The Constructive Conflicts Approach

People often see conflicts in a negative light, as situations to be avoided, suppressed, or resolved as quickly as possible. And that is no wonder. At the individual level, conflict episodes cause the body to release adrenaline and cortisol, hormones that are associated with stress and impulsive action, and that in the long term are associated with anxiety and depression. At the group level, conflicts can trigger the worst in human behavior—aggression, dehumanization, oppression, and war—at great cost to lives, property, and human development.

Yet there is another side to conflicts. For all the harm that they can cause, conflicts—whether at the interpersonal, intergroup, or international level—also provide avenues for new understanding between people and groups, for improving relationships, and for creating new structures and processes that help communities live together in better ways. Without conflicts, desired changes may not occur. In short, conflicts can be varyingly *constructive or destructive*, a force for greater equity and understanding or a force for societal disintegration.

Understanding how conflicts move in one direction, or the other, is the topic of this book. Over the following eleven chapters, we examine the strategies that can be used to minimize the destructiveness of large-scale conflicts—including civil and interstate wars, labor-management cleavages, environmental and business struggles, ethnic and racial struggles, among others—and to transform them for significant mutual benefit. We present examples of diverse strategies and tactics so that persons studying and coping with large-scale social conflicts can learn about conflict episodes that have avoided extreme coercion or violence and which have resulted in the advancement of the interests of most parties impacted.

PLAN FOR THE BOOK AND INTENDED AUDIENCE

The following chapters are organized into four sections. Chapters 1 and 2 focus on conflict analysis, how conflicts differ and can be classified, and the theoretical debates about what drives conflict between people and groups. Chapters 3 to 5 focus on the emergence of conflict and the strategies available for adversaries to wage their struggle. Chapters 6 and 7 focus on processes of conflict escalation and de-escalation. Chapters 8 to 10 focus on mediation, negotiation, and post-conflict outcomes. A brief concluding chapter considers the monumental challenges currently facing human communities and how the constructive conflicts approach might help us to navigate them successfully. Throughout each of these chapters we share vignettes and cases illustrating the constructive conflicts approach. Each chapter ends with a list of discussion questions to help the reader consider the ideas presented in more detail.

Our book is intended for three audiences. First, for readers who are simply curious about conflict processes and want to better understand why some conflicts are constructive while others are highly destructive. Second, for laypeople and students who want to know how to act so that the conflicts that they care about—whether at the community, national, or international level—can be managed more effectively and with better outcomes. Third, for those devoting a significant part of their professional lives to mitigating destructive conflicts and seeking to achieve more just, sustainable, and satisfying conflict outcomes. This final group includes those that work in community groups, governmental or nongovernmental organizations, international organizations, or philanthropy.

CONFLICT DEFINITIONS

Conflict is defined in diverse ways by different people. Lewis Coser, for example, defined conflict as "a struggle over values and claims to scarce status, power and resources in which the aims of the opponents are to neutralize, injure or eliminate their rivals."[1] Ramsbotham, Woodhouse, and Miall defined conflict as "the pursuit of incompatible goals by different groups."[2] Pruitt and Rubin defined it as "a perceived divergence of interest, or a belief that the parties' current aspirations cannot be achieved simultaneously."[3] To Rioux and Redekop, conflict is "an antagonistic relationship between two or more parties over intractable divergences regarding what is mutually significant to the parties involved."[4] Others, such as John Burton, have distinguished conflicts from disputes, suggesting that conflicts arise from deep-seated problems that resist resolution while disputes revolve around short-term disagreements that are amenable to negotiation.[5]

In this book we adopt the following definition for conflict: *Conflicts occur when two or more persons or groups manifest the belief that they have incompatible objectives*. Nearly every word in that definition needs elaboration. "Two or more" means that the persons involved in a conflict view each other as adversaries in trying to achieve their goals. "Persons or groups" include individuals and organizations that claim to represent larger collectivities such as governments, classes, ethnic communities, or other identity groups. "Manifest" means that members of at least one of the contending groups engage in visible conduct attempting to change the other side's behavior in ways that bring it closer to their objectives, for example, by organizing a protest march, by boycotting businesses, by participating in a work stoppage, by launching a missile strike, or by cutting off communication. Finally, "belief that they have incompatible objectives" means that members of one or more of the parties think that another party impedes some of their goals.

SIX FOUNDATIONAL IDEAS

Throughout the various editions of this book, we have come back repeatedly to six foundational ideas that guided our thinking about the possibilities of more constructive approaches to conflicts: conflicts are inevitable and essential, conflicts can be waged constructively or destructively, conflicts are dynamic, conflicts are socially constructed, conflicts are interconnected, and all conflicts can be transformed. Each of these foundational ideas is examined in the following.

Conflicts Are Inevitable and Essential

There is nothing inherently wrong with conflict situations. To the contrary, conflicts between people and groups are natural and inevitable aspects of social interaction. They alert us to the underlying tensions that exist in every social relationship, give us a pathway to change the status quo, and can even improve relationships between adversaries, friends, family members, and coworkers, when constructively managed. Without conflicts, exploitive hierarchies would remain unchallenged, communities would remain stagnant, relationships could not mature and develop, and the problems confronting groups, organizations, and nations would never be considered, debated, and solved. Words are said, arguments are launched, lawsuits are issued, and wars are waged as a signal of deeper incompatibilities that cannot be sustained. In this way, we can see that all conflicts have the *potential* of being functional in the sense that they can serve as a pathway to needed change when social, political, and economic relationships become strained and unjust.

Such thinking is not new to this book. It has guided contemporary scholarship on conflict studies since the emergence of peace and conflict studies as a distinct academic discipline in the 1950s and 1960s.[6] Recognizing the functional elements of conflict also has intellectual roots in various philosophical traditions of social change, growth, and progress, such as Dualism, Dialectics, Hegelianism, Marxism, and Enlightenment traditions. Each of these traditions sees human change as resulting from clashes between competing or contradictory forces, whether the forces of Yin and Yang in ancient Chinese philosophy, a thesis and antithesis in the Hegelian tradition, or the dialectics of Marxism.

Conflicts Can Be Waged Constructively or Destructively

If one accepts the certainty and necessity of social conflicts, it follows that the most important question facing us is how to wage the inevitable conflicts that we face in ways that are more constructive and less destructive. In other words, if conflict is an inevitable feature of social and political relationships, and if it can serve to improve relations and alert people to underlying tensions, the goal for conflict management should not be to create a conflict-free world, but rather to help people find ways to fight that harm fewer people and result in settlements that are relatively fair and enduring.

Figure 1.1 shows some of the available choices available to partisans in a fight. The figure illustrates that there are far more means to achieve a desired change than most partisans are usually aware of. Fighting can involve direct violence, or an attempt to change things via nonviolent social movements, enlisting the help of an intermediary, yielding, persuading, mediating, or eliminating contact altogether.

Skilled conflict managers know how to choose among the different tools, and across different contexts, to nudge conflicts in constructive directions. Consider the analogy of a carpenter's tool belt. In carpentry there is a tool for nearly every job or problem. Successful carpenters do not choose the same tool from their belt no matter what the job. Instead, they will choose a tool that is most likely to aid in the long-term integrity of the piece being crafted. So too in conflict transformation the goal is to help those in a fight to understand that multiple tools exist to navigate their conflict. Use of some tools in some contexts will damage relationships, lead to outcomes that are unfair, and plant seeds that will guarantee the reemergence of the conflict later. Other tools are more likely to facilitate ongoing communication, lead to creative problem-solving, and yield outcomes that are fair and satisfactory to all stakeholders.

Two important caveats are important to consider when considering Figure 1.1. First, we do not claim that conflicts are either waged wholly construc-

Figure 1.1. Conflict Management Toolkit

tively or wholly destructively. Social conflicts can be both, with periods where great harm occurs interposed with periods of collaboration and mutual accommodation.[7] Partisans in a fight are continually making choices about what ends to seek and what means to adopt to those ends. Moreover, partisans may adopt different conflict management tactics at different points in time, some constructive and some destructive. We explore these ideas in detail in chapters 4 and 5.

Second, a determination of whether a conflict being waged constructively or destructively is ultimately a subjective one. For example, pacifists argue that the use of direct physical violence during a conflict can never be justified or viewed as constructive. As Martin Luther King argued, "violence begets violence." Others disagree, arguing that violence is both tactically necessary and morally justified in cases of great oppression by an unyielding adversary. Readers of this book will have their own opinion on such matters. In our own view, the singular use of violence to achieve a desired change is usually a flawed strategy, both tactically and ethically. From a tactical perspective extreme coercion by one side in a conflict invites the use of extreme coercion by the other side. That, in turn, leads to a "spiral of escalation" where both parties end up further away from their goals and underlying interests. Ethically, violence is difficult to justify given the wide array of other usable and less destructive conflict management strategies available to partisans in a fight. Violence is the bluntest of instruments for conflict management; relying on it signifies a failure of imagination and creativity. Of course, we recognize that in some situations, such as an unprovoked attack by an adversary with malicious intent, responding to violence with violence may be the only short-term avenue available for survival.

Our own formula for assessing destructive and constructive conflicts is based on an analysis of three aspects of a conflict. First, the *ends* being sought by partisans, that is the goal or destination that is being sought by the parties. Second, the *means* partisans use to get achieve these goals, namely their conflict strategies and behaviors. Third, the *outcomes* of a particular episode of conflict. Table 1.1 summarizes some of the major distinctions we make between constructive and destructive ends and means. Readers should note that the variables we use to classify a conflict and constructive or destructive are on a continuum. Few conflicts are wholly on one side or the other, and adversaries involved in most major conflicts will vacillate between the extremes at different points of contention. Details of each approach, and explanations of why they are adopted, are found later in the book.

Table 1.1. Elements of Destructive and Constructive Conflicts

	Destructive	*Constructive*
Ends Sought	Victory over Capacity to control Marginalization of opponents	Victory with Capacity to integrate Inclusion and accommodation of opponents
Means Used	Reliance on violence and extreme coercion Stereotype and dehumanize opponents Construct barriers to communication and interaction	Reliance on persuasion and reward Respectful attention Humanize opponents and build superordinate identity Institutionalize opportunities for interaction
Outcomes	None, or if achieved grievances remain Zero-sum High cost to lives, property, treasure, and quality of life	Outcome reached that is deemed acceptable by all parties Mutual gains Low cost to lives, property treasure, and quality of life

Conflicts Are Dynamic

Third, social conflicts are never static; they are fluid and move through various stages as partisans adopt new strategies, develop different perspectives, achieve some objectives, and fail to achieve others, or as the composition of the contending groups or the environment in which they are operating changes. A diagram of the potential sequence of stages is shown in Figure 1.2.

The series of arrows directed at the circle indicates that preconditions for many latent conflicts exist, from which a conflict emerges, escalates, de-escalates, becomes settled, and finally results in outcomes that either terminate the conflict or become the basis for new forms of contention, thus repeating the cycle. How the previous stage is enacted heavily influences the next stage and is partly determinant of whether the conflict can be viewed as constructive or destructive. We call this diagram the *Conflict Transformation Cycle* to note that wide-scale social conflicts are rarely resolved. Instead, they are transformed from one state to another and in either a constructive or destructive direction.[8]

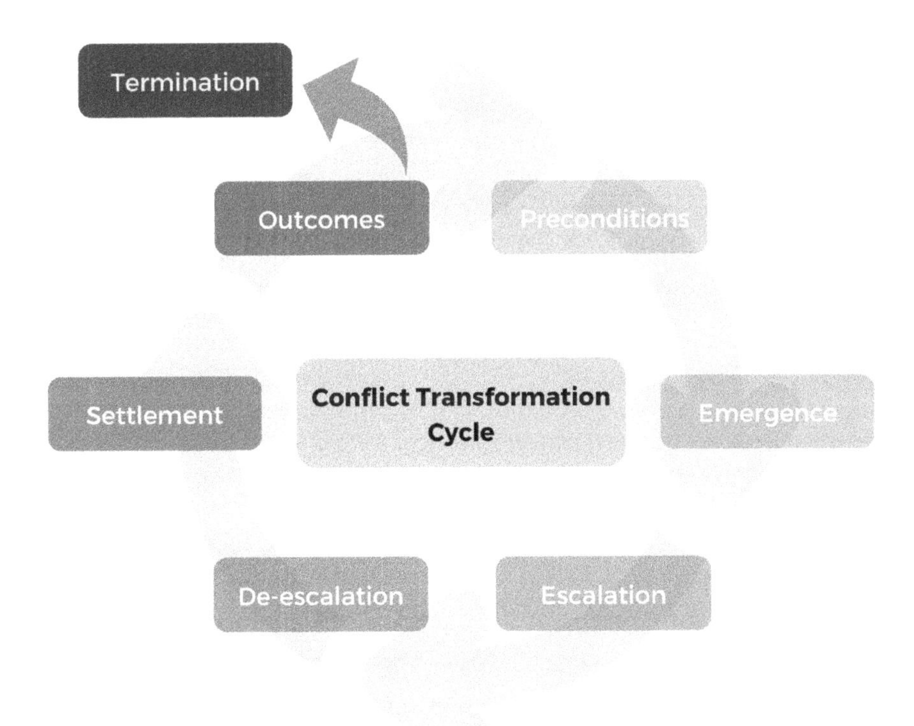

Figure 1.2. Conflict Transformation Cycle

Preconditions

Before a conflict emerges, its preconditions exist. These preconditions could include inequalities between persons or groups, decision-making systems that favor some voices over others, other power imbalances, emotional wounds, discordant worldviews and ideologies, or incompatibilities in what people or groups want. Peace and conflict scholars are far from unified in which of these preconditions offer the most explanatory power when it comes to understanding where social conflicts "come from." Work in behavioral neuroscience, for example, has revealed intriguing evidence that genetic and epigenetic forces combine to play a significant role in predisposing some people to psychopathologies associated with violence, trauma sensitivity, assertion, and other ancillaries of social conflicts.[9] Other researchers downplay the genetic significance of social conflict, focusing instead on the contribution of structural violence, social-psychology, and other exogenous forces. We examine this fascinating debate in chapter 2, classifying different ideas about the sources of conflict from across various traditions and disciplines.

Emergence

Not all potential conflicts emerge into visible fights. Conflicts only emerge when at least one potential adversary acts on the belief that its goals are incompatible with those of an adversary. That act can take countless forms: a teacher yelling at a student, a boycott, a march, building a wall, a legal filing, physical violence, or the declaration of war. Often the emergence of a conflict is triggered by a specific event. These might include an act of violence, new policies that restrict rights of groups, a natural disaster, or any other event that reveals incompatible objectives among different individuals and groups. The outbreak of the COVID-19 pandemic in 2020, for instance, triggered conflicts around the world related to the tension between personal liberty versus government mandates related to public health practices, such as mask wearing, social distancing, and the closing of businesses and schools. Triggering events alone are not enough to lead to conflict emergence. They require a ripe set of preconditions, often related to structural inequality, differences in identity among stakeholders, and incompatible goals. The processes of conflict emergence are examined in chapter 3.

Escalation

An escalating stage is reached when the adversaries begin to actively pursue their incompatible goals. Escalation can proceed gradually or sharply depending on the choices made by those involved in a conflict. For example, when adversaries have similar levels of power and when each chooses to wage their conflict using coercive tactics, conflicts are likely to escalate quickly. This dynamic is sometimes called a spiral of escalation, meaning that each coercive step taken by a stakeholder makes it more likely that their adversary will respond in kind. When the contending sides have an equal amount of coercive and defensive power such escalations are unlikely to resolve quickly as victory by one side over the other is unlikely. On the other hand, in asymmetric conflict situations, in which the weaker party quickly capitulates to a more powerful foe, the escalation phase can end quickly—at least in the short term. The various ways a conflict may be pursued are discussed in chapters 4 and 5, and the processes of escalation, including choices that tend to limit destructive escalations, are examined in chapter 6.

De-escalation

Conflicts not only escalate; they also de-escalate after a brief or sometimes exceedingly long period of time. A protracted conflict often has many escalating and de-escalating episodes of varying magnitude. Some appear tantalizingly close to a period of de-escalation only to return to a highly escalated state. Such was the case with the breakthrough between Israeli and Palestinian negotiators that resulted in the Oslo Peace Accord in 1993, which was followed by successive events that re-escalated tensions, including the assassination of Yitzhak *Rabin* by a right-wing Jewish student in 1995, the second Intifada in 2000, and subsequent acts of widespread violence and fragile ceasefires between Israel and Hamas in 2014 and 2021. Other conflicts de-escalate quickly after both sides reach what has been called a ripe moment or hurting stalemate; a situation where the parties conclude that they cannot reach their goals through unilateral attempts to defeat the other side and when a better option for waging their fight more collaboratively emerges.[10] De-escalatory dynamics are reviewed in chapter 7.

Settlement

Settlement of conflicts occur through both negotiated and non-negotiated means and can be formal or informal. Moreover, sometimes a conflict ends for less discernable reasons. The UPSALA Conflict Database, for example, classifies the termination of war in one of three ways: victory by one side over the other, a negotiated settlement, or low activity, which denotes a reduction of violence to a level below which the conflict is classified as a war. Interestingly, low activity, or what has elsewhere been called the withering away of a conflict, accounts for sizable portions of terminations. In one recent study of civil war terminations between 2002 and 2013, low activity accounted for close to 50 percent of terminations, followed by negotiated settlements at close to 30 percent, followed by victory by one side over the other.[11] We explore both negotiated and non-negotiated settlements in chapter 8.

Outcomes

Conflict settlements usually produce outcomes that change the dynamics between adversaries. Sometimes adversaries in a conflict may be unhappy with the settlement achieved. It may be viewed by one side as unfair, the result of coercion, or as an affront to their dignity. In these cases, which result in what can be called an *unstable* peace, the settlement achieved creates an outcome that makes it more likely that one or both sides will renew their fight at a later day. One often-cited example is that of the Treaty of Versailles, which was signed in June 1919 to mark the formal end of World War I. That treaty held Germany responsible for the outbreak of World War I and sanctioned it by demanding territorial compensation, demilitarization, and reparations payments. This settlement is often credited for incentivizing the militarization of Germany and the rise of the Third Reich in the run up to World War II. At other times, the settlement of one phase of a conflict may transform it toward a *stable* peace. Adversaries may have learned to communicate in more effective ways, institutionalized forms of ongoing conflict management may have been created, agreements may have been forged that allow for more inclusivity over decision making and distribution of things of value. For instance, after two decades of contentious and sometimes violent struggle between labor and management in the United States during the 1920s and 1930s, the federal government created the War Labor Board, which was charged with mediating and arbitrating industrial disputes.[12] This, and other efforts to institutionalize collective bargaining as a form of dispute resolution among unions and management, is often credited with helping the United States avoid the escalation of class-based struggle to the level of widespread violence or revolution.

Critically important to recognize, regardless of the specific outcome, is that conflicts rarely end; rather they are transformed from one state to another. The outcome of one fight produces the preconditions for the emergence of a new one that is either more or less constructively waged. Conflict outcomes and transformation sequences are explored in detail in chapter 10.

Conflicts Are Socially Constructed

Conflicts are waged not just with protests, fists, or guns, but also through narratives. These are socially constructed.[13] Each side enters a conflict with understandings that reflect their own experiences and positionality. Stakeholders tell their own distinct stories about what happened and why, who is to blame, and what is to be done. The more complex the situation, the more likely these stories will deviate in significant ways: one person's terrorist is another's freedom fighter, a police officer may alternately be viewed by different people as a public servant or an oppressor, nuclear energy is alternatively framed as technological marvel or an existential threat to human health and the natural world. Such pronouncements are inseparable from the positionality of the viewer.

The book *Side by Side: Parallel Histories of Israel-Palestine*, written jointly by Israelis Dan Bar-On and Eyal Naveh and Palestinian Sami Adwān, illustrates this point beautifully.[14] In it the authors show how history books written by Palestinian and Israeli scholars and read by generations of school children tell fundamentally different stories about common historical events. By placing the text found in the Palestinian history books side by side with the text found in Israeli history books, the authors reveal that our narrative reconstruction of historical events differs to such an extent that it is almost as if each side is telling stories about completely different events.

This is not to say that there is no truth when it comes to social conflicts. Atrocities are committed, words are uttered, threats are made and carried out, and policies are enacted that have devastating and lasting impacts on real people. These cannot be denied, although partisans often try to do so. But in the end, every event that humans experience as individuals or within groups is interpreted through a subjective point of view—a framework of understanding impacted by one's culture, social class, relative power, racial and ethnic identity, life experiences, gender identification, birth order, and a plethora of other variables that distort and shape our view of conflict situations. Conflicts are thus framed in ways that fit our preexisting conceptions of the world.[15]

Accepting this premise is uncomfortable for many people of strong conviction. It is far easier to believe that we alone have been blessed with an ability to see things as they truly are. However, admitting that we are as much prisoners of our own time, space, and positionality as are our adversaries does not mean we must let go of our convictions; rather, it means that we recognize that tolerance for different ideas are hallmarks of well-functioning societies. As the late Jerome Bruner asserted in his book *Acts of Meaning*:

> I take open-mindedness to be a willingness to construe knowledge and values from multiple perspectives without loss of commitment to one's own values. Open-mindedness is the keystone of what we call a democratic culture.[16]

That the meaning given to events are socially constructed has serious implications for conflicts of all types, particularly in this age of so-called fake news. When stakeholders cannot agree on how to define a problem, or even if it exists, little room remains to develop shared and successful strategies for bringing about a needed change. And when independent voices are no longer trusted, storytelling about what is happening and why fractures, conspiracies thrive, and destructive conflicts are nurtured. Worse, partisans become untethered from any sources of information that do not reflect their preconceptions of the world. In extreme cases dissenting voices are eliminated from the public discourse, as occurred in Russia with the criminalization of any speech contradicting the government's official narrative of its military invasion into Ukraine in March 2022.

The discourse over the COVID-19 pandemic and the use of vaccines to control it is another case in point. Policies have been difficult to develop, and resistance to public health mandates have been significant due to contradictory narratives, high levels of distrust, and political polarization. The COVID-19 response exists in what has been called an *infodemic*, defined by the World Health Organization as *too much information including false or misleading information in digital and physical environments during a disease outbreak.*[17] Infodemics exist within nearly all intense social debates, increasingly so as social media platforms proliferate and bad actors seek to spread disinformation to foment conflicts.[18] The hallmarks of infodemics are confusion, mistrust, fear, conspiratorial beliefs, and resulting actions that usually make a problem worse. While difficult, strategies can be adopted to counter infodemics and related problems. These are explored in subsequent chapters on conflict de-escalation and settlement.

Conflicts Are Interconnected

Social conflicts are interconnected over time and space.[19] Thus one or more side in a conflict may view their current conflict as a renewal of a prior conflict, waged years, decades, or even centuries in the past. Skilled movement leaders often capitalize on historical grievances to rally constituents and build support for a cause, a practice often called *memory activism*, which has been observed across numerous conflict zones including Serbia, Israel and Palestine, and Eastern Europe.[20] In these cases, historical memories of suffering, defeat, or glory are packaged into emotional and compelling stories that can trigger in-group solidarity, out-group hatred, and a thirst for revenge.

Many conflicts are also nested in larger-scale conflicts. The struggle between the Syrian government and antigovernment rebel movements is embedded in a larger regional conflict involving Turkey, Iraq, Iran, Saudi Arabia, and others. That regional conflict is, in turn, embedded in an even larger global conflict over the nature and scope of international intervention that involves still other players, such as the United States, China, and Russia, as well as multilateral organizations such as OPEC and the United Nations. In addition, each adversary is likely to be simultaneously engaged in conflicts with more than one other adversary.

All Conflicts Can Be Transformed

The belief that some social conflicts are intractable—eternal and nonsolvable—has been central to thinking in peace and conflict studies for many years. Conflicts may be considered intractable when six conditions are present: critical resources are at stake, unilateral victory by one side over the other is impossible, stakeholders commit themselves to a set of unyielding positions, opponents are viewed as an existential threat, structural inequalities privilege some parties over others, and self-other conceptions revolve around dehumanizing narratives of one's opponent. For such conflicts, which include those between Catholics and Protestants in Northern Ireland and Islamic separatists and the Indian government in the Kashmir Valley, it may seem that conflict transformation is impossible.

For even the most intractable conflicts, however, it is conceivable for someone, somewhere, to do something that helps to transform the conflict in a positive direction, if only modestly. For instance, large-scale conflicts usually involve diverse actors including nongovernmental organizations and nonprofit groups; stakeholders at the local, national, or international level; financial organizations; social networks; and other stakeholders, each of which offers and avenue for conflict transformation. Therefore, when the official representatives of antagonistic sides of a conflict are unwilling to communicate directly with each other about possible settlements, it may be possible for members of unofficial communities to act. For example, during the height of the civil war in Sri Lanka members of the diaspora *Sinhalese* and *Tamil* living abroad were able to conduct informal dialogues with each other that led to meaningful connections and understandings not possible in their home country.[21] Similarly, in the United States several civic organizations and nonprofits are currently working within communities separated by political ideology to overcome what has been called the red-blue divide between Republican-leaning and Democratic-leaning citizens. The civic group, Better Angels, for example, has formed a network of Republicans and Democrats that promote dialogue, debate, and collaborative events, the creation of mutually beneficial economic projects, and the building of social and support networks.[22]

VARIETIES OF CONFLICTS

Conflicts differ in six important and consequential ways: the type of issue in contention, the domain in which it is occurring, the stakeholders who are impacted, the characteristics of the adversaries, the nature of their relationship, and the means used by those stakeholders to wage their struggle. Those interested in taking action to contain or de-escalate a conflict will benefit from careful analysis of each.

Issues in Contention

Adversaries wage conflicts over two kinds of matters: interests and values. Thus, they may quarrel about resources, assets, or capabilities that they each want to have and believe how much they have must be at the expense of the opponent. These resources include material such as land, money, oil, and water. Similarly, they may quarrel over social resources, such as their prestige, or their power to make decisions independent of the desires of others. Adversaries may quarrel as well over the values that each side holds dear. These become matters in contention when one side insists on the inherent superiority of its values that another party finds objectionable or when members of one group insist that others adopt their values, as can occur in proselytizing efforts for religious beliefs or political ideologies.

Conflicts that are waged over things are, in general, more negotiable, and more easily managed constructively, than conflicts waged over beliefs and values. This is because things can be divided but beliefs and values cannot. Arguing about the price of an item for purchase rarely results in violence. The purchase price may leave one side less satisfied than the other but does not normally compromise their sense of self-worth or meaning, nor does it upend their belief system. Arguments over the value of human life or choice—which are central to family planning and reproductive rights—by contrast, are non-negotiable. They are seen as fundamental values that cannot be bargained away. In such situations compromise is often impossible, positions easily become hardened, stereotyping and dehumanization of advisories is common, and a loss by one side to the other is more likely to be seen as an existential threat.

A close examination of issues in contention helps conflict analysts to make better choices about what kind of conflict mitigation techniques to use. If a conflict is over distributable things, then straightforward conflict mitigation techniques such as interest-based negotiation, finding trade-offs, and encouraging compromise may succeed. For conflict over values, additional conflict transformation techniques are nearly always required. These range from, among others, separating the parties so they cannot damage each other, engaging them in deep dialogue about self and other to transform attitudes, and developing new conflict narratives that emphasize superordinate identities over parochial ones. We discuss several of these options in chapter 8.

Of course, the most difficult conflicts are those that involve both distributable things and deep underlying differences in values and beliefs. For example, conflict among teachers, parents, and school administrators over resources devoted toward STEM training versus funding for the arts is not simply a matter of negotiating a budget. Rather, such a conflict also involves contested values regarding the purpose education and the role schools should play in child development. Conflict transformation efforts in such situations are challenging. They require doing more than one thing at the same time, or perhaps sequencing conflict interventions to address multiple conflict drivers at different times (e.g., start by exploring differences in worldviews and building understanding, and only then transitioning to negotiating budget allocations).

Domain

A review of popular writing about conflicts illustrates a tendency of academics and consultants to group conflicts according to the domain in which a struggle is occurring. Hence, entire literatures, conferences, and trainings are devoted exclusively to subfields as interpersonal conflict management, labor-management relations, public policy conflicts, organizational conflicts, identity conflicts, intrastate conflict and civil war, and international conflict. Such classifications are helpful to the extent to which different of conflict management techniques may be required in different domains. For example, collaborative governance in the domain of public policy dispute management or nonprovocative defense in the domain of international conflict.[23]

One danger here is that teachers often abandon efforts to expose students to "the field" of conflict studies broadly construed and instead narrow the focus of study to more manageable proportions, such as the study of war, postconflict reconstruction, interpersonal dispute resolution, or collaborative governance. Such an approach would lead students to believe that violent international conflicts have nothing to do with interpersonal disputes, that labor-management conflicts are wholly different from environmental conflicts, and that alternative dispute resolution is relevant only within a domestic political context. In short, by "tribalizing" our field we are, perhaps unwittingly, teaching students those comparisons *across* various conflict domains and settings is less valuable than comparisons *within* each domain and setting. We strongly disagree.

Stakeholders

Conflicts can also differ according to the parties, or stakeholders, involved. For example, imagine a conflict over water distribution in a fragile ecosystem that is experiencing a prolonged drought. Stakeholders in such a conflict could include farmers, ranchers, homeowners, environmental advocates, local business associations, land rights activists, and town, county, and federal land management agencies. Each of these groups may have contrasting interests when it comes to water use, and each stand to be positively or negatively impacted by water distribution and conservation decisions. In addition, some stakeholder groups may be highly mobilized and regularly participate in actions designed to influence the course of the conflict. In other cases, a stakeholder group may participate little, or not at all, in conflict processes.

During a conflict analysis, each stakeholder group can be "mapped" in a way that reveals their relative power and their relationships. One common mapping technique is to visually depict each stakeholder group as a circle in the case of primary disputants or square in the case of a secondary stakeholder group. Circles and squares are large or small in proportion to the analyst's assessment of the relative power of each. Lines are then drawn between each group to illustrate the nature of their relationship; solid lines, for instance, indicate an ongoing relationship, dashed lines indicating an existing but dormant relationship, broken lines as indicating an active conflict, dual lines indicating a formal alliance, and so on. An example of a conflict map, as applied to the current conflict in Yemen, is shown in Figure 1.3. It shows the variety of stakeholders active in that conflict and the relationship between them.

Conflict maps, such as the one in Figure 1.3, help the analyst see potential pathways to constructive conflict transformation if, for example, the primary conflicting parties have existing or dormant relationships with the same secondary stakeholder group. For this reason, a conflict setting with a complex array of stakeholder groups and a complicated set of intersecting relationships can be easier to intervene in than one with few stakeholders and relationships. Under such conditions, multiple points or entry may be available to the conflict manager. When primary disputants cannot be engaged, secondary disputants often can be.

Characteristics of Adversaries

Stakeholders that perceive themselves to be in a conflict and mobilize for a fight are known as adversaries. Two general features of adversary groups have implications for how destructively or constructively they engage in their conflict: the adversary's self-other conceptions and the clarity of the adversary's social boundaries.

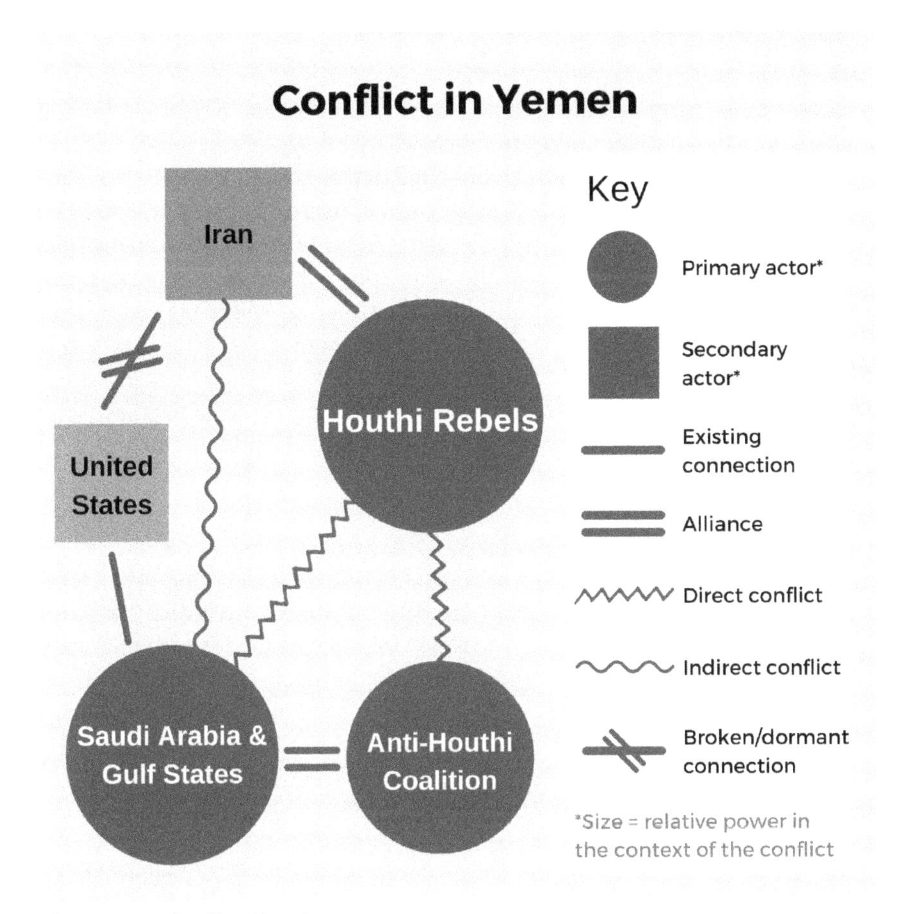

Figure 1.3. Conflict Mapping

Self-Other Conceptions

Adversaries often tell stories about their opponent that rely on stereotypes, tropes, and negative attributions. At the same time adversaries tend to tell stories about their own group that emphasize their virtuous qualities and that defend aggressive actions as necessary steps to protect freedom, dignity, or other essential qualities. For example, if my child gets into a fight at school I may rush to the conclusion that she must have been bullied, picked on, or was acting in self-defense. "My child is not a bad person," I declare, "she was simply put in a circumstance where she committed a bad act!" But when someone outside of our group commits a bad deed, we tend to attribute that behavior to their innate qualities. They did the bad deed, we say, because they are a bad person. Meanwhile, members of the other group are doing the same thing, justifying their own bad acts as circumstantial dynamics but the bad acts of their adversary as an innate part of that other group's character. Social psychologists call this dynamic attribution bias and have found that it characterizes the outlook of groups everywhere.[24]

A relatively benign example can be found in the context of sporting events, where the hometown fans may celebrate the qualities and virtues of their team while chastising the qualities of the visiting team or taunt and disparage the character of a particularly disliked star on the opposing team. A more destructive example is found in cases of organized violence, where conceptions of the other are so heinous and opponents are so dehumanized as to justify acts of brutality against them, a well-known example being the characterization of Tutsis by Hutu-affiliated radio stations as *inyenzi*, or "cockroaches," and *inzoka*, or "snakes," in the run-up to the Rwandan genocide of 1992.[25]

Boundary Clarity

The social boundaries of parties in a conflict vary in clarity and permeability and can also impact the relative constructiveness or destructiveness of a conflict. Sometimes boundaries between ethnic groups, for example, may be sharp and sustained by law and custom that restricts communication and movement across ethnic borders. This was the case in the Southern United States during the years of the Jim Crow laws and in South Africa during the years of apartheid. In both cases racial groups were legally segregated. In other times and places, as in cosmopolitan cities, the boundaries between many ethnic groups may be vague and the realms of life governed by ethnic designation more limited. Indeed, increasingly now, many people have multiple national identities and even dual citizenship, they appreciate multicultural experiences, and they value diversity of opinion and experience as a source of social capital.

In general, clear, and strong boundaries between adversaries contributes to the destructiveness of a conflict. Without opportunities for interaction, adversaries are freer to stereotype opponents and advocate for policies that distribute things of value unequally or conflict tactics that rely on coercion. On the other hand, regular interaction among adversaries can improve the constructiveness of a conflict. An entire subfield of conflict transformation, for instance, is based on what is called the "contact hypothesis," which holds that intergroup interactions diminish prejudice between those groups, under specific conditions.[26]

That is not to say that regular interaction is always constructive. For example, peacekeeping—the act of inserting neutral observers between armed groups so they cannot fight—illustrates how lack of contact can, at times, be a constructive approach to conflict management. It allows adversaries to cool off, creates room for diplomatic channels to evolve, and breaks the cycle of violence and revenge.[27] Thus highly escalated conflicts may, at times, benefit from boundaries between adversaries whereas emerging and settled conflicts may benefit from more robust and ongoing opportunities for interaction.

Relations between Adversaries

Adversaries involved in a conflict may be integrated and mutually dependent upon each other. They may share greater or lesser degrees of similarities in identities, values, and interests. They may be more or less symmetrical in the resources that they can control relative to each other. Variations these dimensions greatly affect how a conflict is waged and transformed. Four variations in the social relationship between and among conflict adversaries are particularly interesting to consider: (1) whether the relationship is a one-off interaction or an ongoing one, (2) their shared history, (3) the degree to which they are integrated with each other, and (4) the degree of power asymmetry between them.

One-off or Ongoing Interaction

A one-off relationship is one where the parties to the conflict will only interact once. Once the conflict is settled, the adversaries are unlikely to see each other again. Economic transactions often are one-off. The buyer and seller interact around the price of an item but once their business is concluded they are unlikely to interact again. Conflicts that take between individuals or groups that will regularly interact with each other in the future, such as family members, workers and managers, and political parties in a parliamentary system, are, by definition, ongoing.

Conflicts embedded within an ongoing relationship can be variably easier or harder to navigate. On the one hand, the ongoing relationship may make it more likely that conflict management has become institutionalized, that the parties to the conflict have a deeper understanding of each other, and that they have an incentive to preserve good relations since they are always interacting under what has been called the "shadow of the future."[28] Collective bargaining between unionized workers and management is an example. This form of labor-management relations institutionalizes a set of rules about the negotiation process that are institutionalized, predictable, and recognized as serving the long-term stability of the organization that both sides belong to. On the other hand, poorly managed conflicts in the context of an ongoing relationships can become much more destructive when one or both sides become aggrieved. Neither side can extract themselves from the relationship, but past wounds become the impetus for retaliation and rapid escalation.

One-off relationships are similarly complex. Since adversaries only interact once they may have little incentive to preserve good feelings and may resort to confrontation, dirty tricks, and manipulation to achieve their interests. At the same time, when such conflicts become destructive the impacts are likely to be contained to a particular time and place, making destructive escalation less likely.

Shared History

Adversaries may have a history of past antagonistic relations, including one-sided oppression, bloody suppression, or genocidal attacks. Those past experiences and the memories of them influence the interpretation of current actions and future options, making cooperation and even interaction impossible. In contrast, adversaries may share a history of being closely integrated or allied against a common enemy. In both cases, past histories are not permanent and unchanging. Past events are subject to new interpretations as ways of thinking change and as the groups with varying interpretations change their relations, as the external environment changes, as new conflicts emerge, and as people change the stories that they tell about each other. For example, relations between the United States and Japan are generally considered to be stable. Each country shares close economic ties with the other, close military and security cooperation, and a relatively similar set of interests regarding the geopolitics of the Pacific Rim. In recent decades past, however, the United States and Japan were locked in a bloody war with each side claiming the other posed an existential threat to its survival.

Integration

Integration refers to the degree of engagement and interdependence the parties normally have with each other. At one extreme, the parties may be so interdependent that neither could survive without the other, or for each to achieve what it wants, cooperation with the other is desirable or even necessary. Under these circumstances, conflicts are often about how to best cooperate and work together. At the other extreme, the adversaries may be almost wholly independent of each other, each party normally functioning with little exchange or other kind of interaction with the other.

Generally, integration between adversaries helps constrain them from destructive escalation. Each party is inclined to avoid disrupting mutually beneficial relations and try to quickly settle disputes that emerge. Thus, one of the main pillars of the so-called liberal peace thesis is that peace is more likely when states are tied together through common economic policies, which are overseen by established multilateral institutions. In such contexts, it is argued that states, particularly democratic ones, will be more likely to cooperate with other members of the international community and be less inclined to confrontation and destructive conflict with each other.[29] This logic was central to the formation of the European Union in 1993 and its predecessor the European Steel and Coal Community in 1951. After two bloody continental wars, Europeans came to believe that the integration of economic, political, and cultural systems would create significant "functional interdependence" which would reduce the probability of future conflict.[30]

Power Asymmetry

Power relations are generally regarded to have great relevance for analyzing conflicts, but the notion of power has much conceptual ambiguity. The term *power* sometimes refers to a social system's capacity to accomplish an agreed-on task, but often it refers to the relationship between groups within a system in which one group directs the other.[31] Given the attention in this book to conflicts, the latter meaning is more pertinent. Power refers here to a person's or group's ability to induce another party to act as the power wielder wishes, even (but not necessarily) against the resistance of those others. That ability may rest on actual or threatened negative sanctions (coercion). But it may also rest on the use of positive sanctions (the provision of benefits). Power may also rest on the sense of identity that the subordinates share with those exercising power, finding their persuasion convincing.[32]

Power asymmetry comes in many forms.[33] One basis for asymmetry is a person's or group's ability to threaten or impose negative sanctions, which may include physical coercion and the denial of needed resources. Asymmetry also rests on the ability of one party to use positive sanctions to ensure compliance by the other party, creating dependency of the subordinate party. Asymmetry also arises by one side's control over interpretations of what is happening in a relationship between the dominating and dominated groups. This control may be carried out in the way ideas are expressed and communicated, as exemplified by totalitarian regimes' control of information.

When all these forms of domination are combined, the dominant party (whether an ethnic group, ruling class, or political party) may be regarded as a hegemon.[34] Moreover, when inequalities become part of the everyday norms and procedures of politics, commerce, and cultural expression there exists a situation of what is called structural violence.[35] Under such conditions one group overwhelmingly enjoys privileges and advantages not afforded to other groups and these advantages are widely maintained and enforced by societal institutions. Currently, for example, the United States is in the throes of a national reckoning with what activists call structural racism, the systemic effort to maintain institutions, laws, and economies that overwhelmingly benefit white Americans.

Control, however, is rarely total, even in the most hegemonic of organizations or societies. Some resistance is always possible, and the dominating party may take that into account in the extent to which it imposes sanctions or takes advantage of its superior position. It may constrain itself from being overly exploitative, fearing a rise in resistance. Such was the case with many of the colonial powers, which often granted limited control to local leaders to better control potential opponents.

Power wielders are obeyed in many social settings because they are regarded as having the right to give orders; authority is accorded them because of the office they hold and the way they came to occupy the office. Legitimacy, however, is never unlimited and may be withdrawn by the followers when they believe the basis for it has been violated. Herein lies the great power of nonviolent resistance when masses of people stop deny legitimacy to office holders. What appears to be an all-powerful hegemon may collapse in short order in the face of mass protests, noncooperation, work stoppages, and ridicule.

Means of Conflicting

Conflicts can also be distinguished by the means that the adversaries use to achieve their objectives. These range from mediation to negotiation to electoral politics to armed struggle to mass protest (means of conflicting are discussed extensively in chapters 4 and 5). More than one means can be used at the same time.

Two inter-related dimensions of the means used in conflicts are especially important for understanding constructive conflict: the degree of regulation and the severity of the conflict methods. Regulation entails rules about how a conflict should be pursued and procedures for reaching decisions to settle a dispute. Such rules exist in all societies, but they vary in in their degree of institutionalization; that is, the extent to which they (1) have been internalized by the participants; (2) are expressed in tradition, formal writing, or some other embodiment external to the participants; and (3) are enforced by sanctions.[36] These rules may be quite effective in governing conflict conduct, but they tend to be more effective when participants engaged in a conflict agree about the rules and believe the rules are legitimate. Certainty of punishment if rule violations are committed also increases the likelihood of compliance. Organizations or systems that lack an overarching authority that can set the rules and police them are more prone to unruly conflict than those organizations or systems that have such an authority. This is clearly of importance in the international system, in which UN resolutions are often not enforced due to the constraints of national sovereignty that are sanctioned within the UN Charter itself.[37]

When disputes are highly institutionalized, they are often not even regarded as conflicts. For example, in long-established democratic societies, the issue of which political party will control the government for a coming term may be popularly discussed using the metaphors of military campaigns, but they also are spoken of as sporting contests. The selection of high political officials is conducted according to generally accepted rules, and analysts and participants think of them as contests rather than as conflicts.

Choice about means of conflicting is directly related to the degree of injury suffered by adversaries. The injuries may be equally shared or, more likely, greater harm is endured by one of the parties than another. The injuries may result from violent or nonviolent coercion, such as firing guns, burning buildings, imposing economic sanctions, or excluding certain groups from political participation.

Sometimes the harm done during a struggle is unintentional or even self-inflicted. Preparing for struggle, for example, exacts costs in resources ordinarily used for consumption or investment. The self-harm can also be more direct, as when military preparations result in accidental deaths or injuries. In waging the Cold War between the United States and the Soviet Union, for example, the development of nuclear weapons and their testing and production caused great environmental damage resulting in extensive illness in the former Soviet Union and to a lesser degree in the United States.[38] Similarly, troops returning from military campaigns often suffer from psychological trauma and face great difficulty in reintegrating into society.

Severity of injury also includes harm done to those not engaged in the conflict, such as the civilians in a city suffering "collateral damage" and those who flee to avoid being killed. Such injuries result from military fighting, riots, and revolutionary struggles. Sometimes the harm done to noncombatants is intentional, meant to dry up support for the combatants, to drive people of the other side away, or to commit genocide. In many recent violent conflicts, more noncombatants than combatants have been killed.[39]

Another important aspect of severity is the negative emotions held by each side toward the other. Conflict parties vary in how strongly their members feel hatred toward their adversary, and how many of them have such feelings. Conflict parties also vary in their beliefs about their adversaries. Sometimes many of their members think that their opponents are inferior humans or not fully human, with destructive consequences, notably in the Holocaust and in the treatment of native peoples around the world by European colonialists.

COMBINATIONS CONSTITUTING DESTRUCTIVENESS AND CONSTRUCTIVENESS

It is the combination of characteristics reviewed earlier that determines the extent to which a conflict becomes a highly destructive or a highly constructive struggle. In general, destructiveness increases as the scale of the conflict expands, with increased numbers of adversaries participating, when self-other conceptions are characterized by stereotypes and negative attributions about the other, when opportunities for interaction among conflicting groups are scarce, when fundamental values and worldviews are at stake and each side sees the other as presenting an existential threat, and where significant structural inequality privileges some groups over others. Moreover, destructive forms of contention tend to flourish where few institutionalized mechanisms for dispute resolution are available to disputants or when institutionalized forms of dispute management are viewed as favoring some groups over others. In these cases, marginalized groups may abandon benign forms of contention and adopt more destructive conflict management tactics. Authorities may, in turn, adopt repressive tactics to maintain order and suppress dissent or overt conflict, resulting in what has been called a "negative" peace.

Constructive conflict management, in contrast, tends to thrive where significant functional interdependence exists among stakeholders and where multiple opportunities for interaction help to undermine stereotypes and support the humanization of opponents. Systems with relatively fair access to decision making and more egalitarian forms of exchange also aid in constructive approaches to conflicts, as do systems that are relatively homogeneous, with members sharing overlapping identities and histories.

The good news is that none of these variables is static. Careful conflict analysis will always reveal pathways through which conflict managers can transform any conflict, even the highly intractable ones. Such pathways may be only modestly impactful in cases where destructiveness is heightened, but strung together over time small steps may lead to large changes. Often conflict transformation requires multiple people doing multiple things over longer periods of time. The key is to choose interventions that are based on a careful assessment, that target specific conflict drivers, and that are realistic and measurable.

SUMMARY AND DISCUSSION QUESTIONS

This chapter explored the meaning of conflict, the pivotal ideas that guide our own thinking about constructive conflict transformation, and some of the ways that people can analyze conflicts to predict their destructive trajectory and reveal avenues for constructive interventions. Readers are encouraged to explore the ideas presented in this chapter further by thinking about and discussing the following questions.

1. Everyone has their own philosophy about conflicts; that is, why they emerge, how to manage them, and what role they play in relationships, in social settings, and in politics. What is your own conflict philosophy? What are the important people or events that have shaped your view, and how/why has it has changed over the years?
2. Identify a conflict with which you are familiar. Who are the stakeholders, what incompatibility exists between or among them, and how that incompatibility has become visible?
3. Apply the variables reviewed in the last part of this chapter (varieties of conflicts) to a conflict of interest to you. What does your analysis reveal? How does your analysis help you think about a potential intervention that might push the conflict in a more constructive direction?
4. Using Figure 1.3 as a guide, draw a map of the conflict you identified in question 2. What does the map reveal about potential pathways to conflict transformation?
5. Think about a conflict that is important of interest to you. Using Figure 1.2, the Conflict Transformation Cycle, as a guide, identify the stage that conflict is currently in. What kinds of conflict interventions might be possible or impossible in this stage of the conflict's lifecycle that might not be possible during other stages?

Chapter Two

Preconditions

Three Perspectives on the Origin of Conflicts

Conflicts between people and groups do not mysteriously come into being out of nothing. Rather, each is a product of a set of underlying preconditions that combine to facilitate the emergence of a conflict at a particular point in time. In this latent stage of conflict all that is missing to animate the potential conflict is a necessary triggering event, be that a sudden and dramatic event, the emergence of a new leader, or another kind of shock.

What preconditions are most important to consider is, however, a matter of vigorous theoretical debate. Are human beings hardwired for conflict? Is strife, competition, and violence part of our evolutionary journey and biological make up? Or is conflict between individuals and groups—whether constructively or destructively waged—mostly a matter of socialization, cultural forces, and structural arrangements about how to distribute the things we value? Such questions are more than just theoretical; they are foundational to decision making about how to manage the conflicts we care about. For example, if one believes that conflict between groups results from a lack of exposure to each other or miscommunication, then our pathway to constructive conflict management lies with dialogue, engagement, and dismantling our fear of the other. If, on the other hand, one believes that evolutionary pressures have molded human beings into a competitive and self-interested species, then the pathway of constructive conflict management lies with devising rules of behavior and political structures that protect the group against the acts of selfish individuals.

The field of conflict studies is far from unified on these matters. Particularly intense is the debate between deterministic schools of thought, which consider conflictual and altruistic behavior as being "hardwired" within human physiology, and indeterminist schools of thought, which posit that most conflict behavior results from learned behaviors and specific kinds of political and economic contexts. Historically, conflict studies focused largely on the latter set of explanations. Indeed, the fields of sociology, political science, and anthropology are primarily centered on the way in which cultural, social, economic, and political systems interact to either facilitate constructive or destructive forms of conflict. More recently, however, advances in neuroscience have led to renewed interest in what is sometimes called the sociobiology of conflict.

In this chapter we examine various preconditions related to the emergence of constructive or destructive conflicts. These preconditions can be roughly divided into three categories. First are preconditions that focus on endogenous forces: impulses and behaviors that are fundamental to human nature and relatively fixed. Second are preconditions related to sociocultural relations, including socialization, cultural norms and values, and social relations between members of a community. Third are preconditions that focus the features of the system setting in which potential adversaries operate, including rules, norms, and policies for managing conflicts and distributing things of value. Readers should note that none of these traditions are mutually exclusive. Endogenous and exogenous preconditions of conflict interact with each other. The task of the conflict analyst is to determine how those interactions take place, and which preconditions are most salient to any given conflict. A summary of each of these perspectives is found in Table 2.1. It is followed by a more detailed overview of each perspective.

Table 2.1. Conflict Preconditions

	Endogenous Forces	*Sociocultural Relations*	*System Attributes*
Focus	Genetic and epigenetic determinants of human behavior. Basic needs. "Hardwired" cognitive and emotional response. Personality.	Social and cultural factors that shape the behavior of individuals and groups.	Institutionalized rules, norms, policies, and procedures that determine how things of value are distributed and how disputes are managed.
Examples	Release of adrenaline and cortisol during high-stress events, which increases impulsivity. Expressions of love, solidarity, and collaboration.	Socially constructed conflict narratives that dehumanize or stereotype an adversary. Superordinate cross-cutting identities.	Voting rights restrictions targeting a specific ethnic, racial, or other identity group. Constitutional protection of minority rights.
Dynamism	More static	Somewhat dynamic	Dynamic

ENDOGENOUS FORCES

Popular thought frequently attributes conflicts among humans to fundamental characteristics of our biological and psychological nature, suggesting our helplessness in stopping or controlling these antagonisms. From this point of view social conflict and social collaboration are influenced to a significant degree by evolutionary forces that have shaped the cognitive, neurological, and behavior traits of primates since the Eocene Epoch nearly fifty million years ago and *Homo sapiens* for over three hundred thousand years ago. Distinct lines of research in the human nature school include genetics and epigenetics, unconscious impulses, human needs, personality, and cognitive processing.

Genetic and Epigenetic Features

Human temperament is generally accepted to have a significant—albeit complex—genetic component, estimated by some scientists to be between 40 and 60 percent.[1] Some individuals are temperamentally shy, extroverted, excitable, or agreeable. During interpersonal conflicts such differences can be highly consequential, with some individuals more likely to wage conflicts more competitively, others to wage them more collaboratively, and others to avoid conflicts altogether.

At the group level, evolutionary biologists speculate that natural selection across the past tens of millions of years has favored a genetic propensity toward both selfish and altruistic behavior within primate—and more recently human—communities. Both traits appear to have evolutionary advantages, selfishness for survival of an individual *within* a group, and altruism for the cohesiveness and survival *of* the group. E. O. Wilson explains it this way:

> Individual selection is the result of competition for survival and reproduction among members of the same group. It shapes instincts in each member that are fundamentally selfish with reference to other members. In contrast, group selection consists of competition between societies, through both direct conflict and differential competence in exploiting the environment. Group selection shapes instincts that tend to make individuals altruistic toward one another (but not toward members of other groups).[2]

From this point of view both cooperative behavior as well as selfish behavior is hardwired into the human condition. Each provides functional advantages and thus favored in evolutionary development.

Yet human behavior is not determined solely by a fixed genome. Also important are environmental-genetic—also known as epigenetic—interactions, such as adverse life experiences, that modulate gene expression by "turning on" some neural pathways and closing off others. Epigenetic interactions appear to be most consequential during the prenatal and early childhood period when the brain is undergoing rapid development and neural circuitry is being swiftly established. For example, recent research has found that fetuses that experience prolonged periods of stress during the first trimester of pregnancy are at greater risk of manifesting physical aggression and other conduct disorders later in life.[3] Similarly, animal and human studies have shown that adverse events during prenatal and early childhood shape neural development in a way that impacts emotional regulation and aggression and can trigger the emergence of antisocial personality disorder.[4] Exposure to traumatic events is likewise predictive of a difficulty in regulating the body's conflict system. A 2015 study by Marusak and colleagues found that trauma-exposed youth were unable to dampen prefrontal cortex activity and engage the amygdala-pregenual cingulate needed to regulate emotional conflict.[5] In contrast, children who have not experienced traumatic events and are raised within supportive environments tend to exhibit more prosocial behavior.

Other research has examined behavioral similarities between humans and our closest relatives, chimpanzees (*Pan troglodytes*) and bonobos (*Pan paniscus*), in an effort to uncover common genetic dispositions.[6] For example, territoriality is to be found in a variety of animal species and thus a "territorial imperative" may be attributed to humans, including gang turf battles, jurisdictional disputes between government officials and citizens in religious communities, as well as border wars between sovereign states.[7] Similarly, research on status ranking in small, established groups among many primate species found ranking in all the groups.[8] This is expressed by overt threats and physical attacks among the species most distant from humans.

Among humans and our genetically closest primates, expressions of deference are exhibited subtly, and the dominant animals quietly perform control and service functions. This indicates that humans establish dominant relationships not purely by threats and physical violence but by contributions to the group, for which they receive deference. Therefore, traits and behaviors such as altruism, a well-developed sense of morality, collaboration, and providing aid to those in need appear to have a genetic basis as well. Each of these behaviors has helped bands of people to survive and, as Samuel Bowles and Herbert Gintis argue, are favored by natural selection at the level of human groups.[9]

Unconscious Impulses

Some psychological theories about conflict link unconscious impulses to aggression. The most familiar of these was pioneered by Sigmund Freud and others working in the psychoanalytic tradition. Freud viewed the human psyche as containing three parts: the ego, the id, and the superego. Each plays a distinct function in human behavior, with the id, the most primitive part of the mind, containing instinctual urges such as sexual satisfaction, aggressive instincts, and the gratification of all basic human needs without regard for social impacts. Freud proposed that the id is present at birth, an innate part of human biology, and guides human behavior at infancy. The ego and superego develop over time; the superego provides the individual with a moral conscience and the ego acts as a "mediator" between base desires and moral action.[10]

Contemporary research has found little scientific evidence to support many of Freud's claims. Nonetheless, Freud's central premise that human experiences and behaviors are in part driven by forces outside our conscious awareness has become central to modern psychotherapy. Indeed, today it is well understood that individuals use numerous unconscious defense mechanisms to protect them from anxiety, unacceptable thoughts, and unacceptable feelings. For example, some people may resolve their feelings of guilt about being ambivalent toward their parents by idealizing authority figures and directing their hostile feelings toward out-groups.[11] This is the basis for the large body of research about the authoritarian personality, which posits that some individuals are more likely than others to follow commands from authority figures, even if it those commands run contrary to established humanitarian values. Others may unconsciously displace their anger about a person they depend on by striking out at a vulnerable scapegoat with less status and authority and who has no relationship to the source of the anger—a dynamic called displacement, and one familiar to those who have studied the rise of nativism in the United States, Europe, and elsewhere. The frustration may even be turned inward to self-blame.

In both cases the "primitive" parts of the human psyche are controlled by reactive impulses that may cause harm to the self and other. From this perspective, the most dangerous members of any community are those whose superego and ego never fully developed. Such individuals appear incapable of controlling their impulses, containing their aggression, or exhibiting empathy. An extreme example would be an individual classified as having an antisocial personality disorder, a condition characterized by egocentricity, incapacity for love, lack of remorse or shame, a grandiose sense of self, poor self-control, and the capacity to use charm and intelligence to manipulate others.[12] When such individuals assume leadership positions, often at the head of populist movements, the results can be particularly disastrous.[13]

Basic Needs

A third posited endogenous precondition of conflict is that all humans have a set of underlying human needs that drive behavior, including those related to hostility and cooperation. Maslow, for example, proposed that all humans have five types of needs: physiologic, safety, love, esteem, and self-actualization. These needs are hierarchically organized so that only when base level needs are met will the individual move to higher order needs satisfaction. Research has shown that Maslow's needs positively correlate to a subjective sense of wellbeing among individuals in different areas of the world.[14] Maslow's work has also been critiqued on two grounds: cross-cultural validity and unidimensional linearity.[15] Whether these five needs are universal and exhaustive is thus an open question.

Among contemporary conflict writers, John Burton has extended Maslow's thinking by emphasizing the necessity by all humans to satisfy a core set of human needs if a conflict is to be prevented.[16] He posits eight needs endemic to human beings: a need for response, a need for security, a need for recognition, a need for stimulation, a need for distributive justice, a need for meaning, a need for rationality (and to be seen as rational), and a need for control. Where basic human needs are frustrated, individuals will seek to satisfy them, even against great odds and in cases of sure defeat. As with Maslow's hierarchy, Burton appears to base his theory on the belief that basic human needs are inherent in human nature; that is, essential for human development. For example, the human need to live in personal physical security, without threat of physical harm. Like Maslow, Burton's work has been criticized for being overly deterministic and for denying cultural variation among human groups.

Personality

Personality theory, popularized in psychological and leadership studies, sees conflictual and cooperative behavior as a function of one's innate personality. One dominant line of research suggests that all human beings vary in personality in five core ways: neuroticism, extraversion, openness to experience, agreeableness, and conscientiousness.[17] Studies have found that these traits are heritable, with genetics accounting for roughly 50 percent of variance of those in the study.[18] In 2005 a team of researchers measured the personality scores of individuals from forty-nine different cultures to see if this "Five Factor Model" held across different cultures. Their findings suggested that it did, with variation in the distribution of personality scores in each culture studied differing only slightly.

Among political psychologists there has been a parallel effort to identify traits that characterize the behavior of political leaders. Margaret Hermann's leadership trait analysis method, for instance, suggests that all political leaders vary in three predictable ways: their openness to information, their sensitivity to external constraints, and whether they are motivated to solve problems or take care of relationships. Accommodative leaders, for example, respect constraints imposed on them, are open to information that may contradict their point of view, and seek to maintain good relationships. Expansionistic leaders, in contrast, are closed to receiving information that disconfirms their beliefs, challenge constraints imposed upon them, and focus on solving problems, not maintaining relationships. Differences in traits appear to influence the conflict management and problem-solving techniques leaders use to navigate the political environment, sometimes in dramatic ways. A comparison of the last three U.S. presidents—Obama, Trump, and Biden—seems to bear out such claims. President Trump regularly challenged constitutional constraints placed upon the presidency and would regularly deny information that was contradictory to his goals, to the point of triggering a near constitutional crisis in the United States at the end of his term in office. Obama appeared to be more cautious leader, seeking incremental rather than dramatic change, staying focused on problems, and approaching policy challenges analytically; to the point, his critics claimed, of inaction. Biden appears to share many of Obama's predilections, although his focus on attending to relationships and openness to compromise are notable.

Social-Psychological Response

A fourth perspective from the endogenous school concerns cognition. Many cognitive psychologists claim that the human brain is "hardwired" at birth to categorize objects, people, and groups. This capacity to see patterns and sort them into meaningful categories aids survival because it allows infants to distinguish between, for instance, a house cat and a lion, sunlight versus a fire, their mother versus someone else's mother. That we are wired to create patterns out of chaos is, in and of itself, not conflict triggering. However, research in social psychology has shown that just as humans categorize objects, they also categorize people by defining who is "like me" (in-group) and who is "not like me" (out-group). Indeed, if person A was to sit in a room with people from around the world, they would immediately, and instinctually, separate others into "like me" and "not like me" categories.[19]

The tendency to differentiate among people, coupled with the need to view the in-group in a positive light, is further postulated to lead to in-group favoritism and out-group bias. Individuals tend to denigrate the motivations and capabilities of outside groups to elevate the perceived merits of their own group.[20] This process helps to maintain in-group cohesion and cooperation among group members but also serves as a driver of conflict with other groups. One example is stereotyping, a fixed, overgeneralized belief about members of an out-group where all individuals of that group are assumed to share a narrow range of traits and behaviors, often ones that paint them as "less than" the in-group. In the West, for instance, a common stereotype is that Afghan men are tribal, violent, and traditional and Afghan women submissive, silent, and dominated.[21]

Dynamism and Endogenous Forces

Genetic preconditions of conflict are static variables. They change only slowly as environmental pressures favor some genes over others and random mutations in DNA become widespread. For conflict managers, therefore, focusing on the genetics makes little practical sense. Absent unthinkable efforts to selectively cull human populations of individuals with traits deemed to be conflict-enhancing, there is little we can do.[22] Basic human needs, personality, and human cognition is likewise resistant to rapid change. We can study them, and use them to predict where conflict will manifest and what kind of personality types tend to be conflict prone, but they are generally assumed to be relatively fixed in nature. Epigenetic forces, however, are more amenable to change. It is possible to reduce the amount of stress on pregnant mothers caused by poverty or to remove young children from a war zone, where their developing brains are subject to extreme anxiety. It is also possible to provide safe and nurturing environments where young children can learn and grow. Such steps will certainly impact neural development for the better, although it is likely beyond our capacity to accurately measure how much.

One additional point about the dynamism of human nature is important to note. There has been steady scientific progress toward the selective editing of human genes since the human genome project first sequenced the entire human *DNA* in 1990. Today, the gene-editing tool CRISPR can be used to edit the genes within embryos to select traits deemed desirable. Such research is highly controversial because genetic therapies create permanent changes to the genome, which are passed down to future generations.

Currently, the use of genetic engineering is limited, and it is largely confined to research dedicated to eliminating such genetic diseases as cystic fibrosis and muscular dystrophy. However, within a short period of time it is likely that gene editing technologies will be improved and widely used. This raises the possibility that genetic characteristics of humans not related to disease will be targeted in the future, some of which will be related to temperament. The revolutionary impact that such technologies will have on human societies and human conflict is hard to overstate. How such technologies are developed and applied will have profound implications for the evolution of our species for generations to come.

SOCIOCULTURAL RELATIONS

Some endogenous approaches to conflict, which focus on fixed traits and basic human nature, have been harshly criticized. Many critics have expressed concern that sociological explanations of conflict provide cover for scientific racism and harken back to nineteenth-century justifications of colonialism grounded in social Darwinism.[23] Others have pointed to a lack of evidence for genetic causation when it comes to violence. In 1989, a distinguished international group of geneticists, anthropologists, psychologists, biochemists, and other researchers summarized the state of scientific knowledge about the causes of violence and war in the Seville Statement. The statement was endorsed by the UN Educational, Scientific, and Cultural Organization and was subsequently endorsed by many scientific and professional associations. The statement concludes that "it is not scientifically correct to say that war or any other violent behavior is genetically programmed into our human nature," or "that in the course of human evolution there has been a selection for aggressive behavior more than for other kinds of behavior."[24]

A widely embraced alternative to the endogenous school is the sociocultural school. Culture is a set of shared practices, beliefs, and norms that are core to the way a group makes meaning out of the world. Socialization is the interactive processes through which individuals acquire these practices, beliefs, and norms. The sociocultural relations perspective, therefore, considers how learned systems of meaning, expression, and beliefs can serve as a precondition of conflict or collaboration.

Socialization and Culture

A large body of evidence indicates that different patterns of socialization may make persons and groups prone to conflict or cooperation. Socialization occurs primarily through an infant's and a child's experience with parents, but also with siblings and other kin, with peers, and with institutions such as schools, churches, and the mass media.

Compelling evidence suggests that children whose rearing had been warm, affectionate, and loving are well prepared for cooperative relations later in life.[25] Open expression of affection toward children and close father-child relations foster the development of skills that are beneficial for nonviolently resolving conflicts. Evidence also suggests that nurturing environments—those that minimize exposure to stressful and destructive events, that promote prosocial and self-regulatory behavior, and that monitor and restrict opportunities for antisocial behavior—prevent most mental, emotional, and behavioral disorders.[26]

On the other end of the spectrum, considerable research supports the idea that harsh socialization of the young produces aggressive adults who are prone to engage in overt conflict.[27] Harsh socialization includes severe physical punishment and emotional deprivation. The connection between such experiences and later tendencies for aggression and violence may be explained by learning theory, encompassing imitation, modeling, and reinforcement. If a group relies on aggression and power to solve disputes, then it is likely that members of that new members to that group will emulate and pass on that behavior.

In many societies those individuals identified as male tend to be socialized in such a way makes them more prone to aggression. The Spanish term "macho," for example, is widely used to refer to a particular sense of masculinity, which stresses bravery and sensitivity to challenges of honor. Differences between men and women in these regards result from socially constructed combinations of inborn, socialization, and situational factors. We note here that some of these differences may occur in some societies because of confused male identity.[28] This pattern can happen when males grow up in a male-dominated society with fathers who are distant; therefore, boys develop very strong bonds with their mothers, which they must break to meet expectations of proper male behavior. To sever those ties may be frustrating, and furthermore the way to do so may require behavior that is regarded as "masculine": tough, strong, and prideful.

Some observers argue that the patterns of child rearing and other experiences of socialization when shared by society members tend to produce an enduring national character, which may include traits of aggressiveness.[29] For example, during World War II some U.S. and British analysts reasoned that the German national character was authoritarian. Germans were obedient to those above and arrogant to those below. After the war, however, the profoundly changed German policies and relations with the United States and allied governments contributed to the rejection of such attributions of an unchanging German national character.

Attempts have been made as well to generalize cultural approaches to negotiation and dispute resolution. Some cultural approaches to dispute management appear to be more confrontational, others more avoidant, others egalitarian.[30] Moreover, cultural approaches to communication differ in the way nonverbal cues are used to convey meaning, the use of space to communication, understandings of time, and the appropriateness of touch. Significant differences often complicate cross-cultural negotiations and may serve as an important precondition of conflict escalation. For example, Raymond Cohen, who has written extensively about culture and conflict, used cultural analysis to reveal how variation in Israeli and Egyptian understandings of violence, retribution, and vendetta have been an ongoing barrier to effective problem solving between the two countries.[31]

Understanding cultural impacts on conflict has also been advanced by the work of Geert Hofstede, who along with his colleagues identified six primary dimensions of cultural difference: power difference, individualism, masculinity, uncertainty avoidance, long-term orientation, and low versus high context. This work has been built on by a multiyear project to study of cross-cultural interaction among leaders and managers called the Global Leadership and Organizational Behavior Effectiveness research program (GLOBE).[32] GLOBE has advanced the idea that leaders and managers from different countries cluster into ten different cultural groups, including Anglo, Eastern European, Germanic European, Confucian Asia, and other cultural subtypes. Each cluster has been shown to have unique ways of understanding and exhibiting norms related to, among others, gender egalitarianism, collectivism, and performance.

While it is tempting to generalize about the preconditions of conflict found in culture, it is important as well to note that culture is never uniform and never unchanging.[33] Regional, class, organizational, gender, and other subcultures always exist, and every person has a unique variation. Some individuals conform to generalizations about their culture, while others will not. Moreover, as circumstances change, so does the culture.

Differences in Values and Beliefs

Dissensus, the lack of consensus about what is desirable, is another precondition of conflict. This occurs when one party insists that the other agree with its preferences or believes that the other party threatens its way of life. Dissensual conflicts arise from differences between religions, cultures, worldviews, values, and lifestyles. They are particularly powerful preconditions of conflict when the issue at stake involves multiple and diverse stakeholders who are separated by identity, worldview, and status.

The idea that differences in values and beliefs are preconditions to conflicts is consistent with the work of many contemporary analysts who emphasize that reality is socially constructed. People use language and other symbolic systems to define and give meaning to their experience.[34] The meaning conveyed by these sociocultural systems becomes an organizing force in the lives of people. It allows them to understand and navigate their world. When an individual's or group's meaning system is threatened by the behavior or values of other individuals or groups, or by broader changes to social and political systems, significant conflicts often result.[35] For instance, in recent years changes in social norms related to sexuality, gay marriage, the role of religion in public life, and access to abortion has animated white evangelical Christian identity and activism. Increasingly, evangelical Christians see themselves as being in an existential struggle with the secular left. Author and radio talk show host Eric Metaxas, for example, said during the 2016 election cycle that: "In all of our years, we faced all kinds of struggles. The only time we faced an existential struggle like this was in the Civil War and in the Revolution when the nation began. . . . We are on the verge of losing it as we could have lost it in the Civil War."[36] Such attitudes make it more likely that believers will contend in ways that are more extreme and destructive.

The people in the world, in each society, or in any social systems, however, are not homogeneous in their values and beliefs. Having varying perspectives or backgrounds engenders different visions of reality and of right. Such differences can also have profound effects on how stakeholders define a problem and what options seem viable at any point in time. One source of such diversity is the varying experiences that different generational cohorts have in their formative years.[37] Persons who come to political maturity while their country is suffering a severe depression or a major war develop enduring orientations from that historical experience, setting off their generation from others. Succeeding generations develop a distinctive set of concerns, beliefs, values, and, sometimes, even identities. Intergenerational differences in collective mentalities are a frequent source of authority-challenging youth movements and other dissensual conflicts.

Differences among people in their views of themselves and of the social world they live in are the source of conflict only if certain other beliefs are also held. Thus, if members of a group are indifferent to the religious convictions of another group or think the convictions are simply harmless, no conflict will arise. If, however, one or more sets of people feel that the other's religious views are morally outrageous, then an underlying conflict exists. The outraged persons are likely to want to change the views and/or behavior of those holding such improper convictions. Or suppose that a group of people is so convinced of the virtue and validity of its views that it considers it urgent that others accept its views and learn the truth and so gain salvation. Certainly, political and religious revolutionary movements, on gaining control in one country, have often set out to proselytize and spread the good news to peoples in other countries. This has been true of advocates, for example, of the Russian, Cuban, and Iranian revolutions. Ideological proselytizing often is mixed with advancing economic interests and political domination of a powerful state, as appears to be the case in some programs to spread American democracy in the Middle East and elsewhere in the world.[38]

Differences in worldviews or values may also foster misunderstanding, conflict escalation, and conflict perpetuation without the adversaries' awareness. Thus, disputes about environmental issues such as desirable land use or responding to global warming may be exacerbated by underlying differences in ways of thinking about nature, God, scientific knowledge, the role of humans in the natural world, and economic progress.[39] In these cases, individuals may hold incompatible ideas about what future humans should be aspiring to, and whether human societies should be maximizing personal freedom and the production of wealth, or living within the bounds of what nature can provide.

Both consensual and dissensual factors are often varyingly intertwined as sources of conflicts and their escalation or transformation. Consider the renewed struggle of women for greater equality in the United States. For many women and men, the struggle was and is largely about equal work opportunities and equal pay for equal work. Yet disputants in the struggle for greater gender equality frequently also differ in their evaluation of characteristics associated with masculinity and femininity. Thus some people feel that in business at least, it is good to be aggressive, dominating, competitive, stoic, risk taking, and physically tough. Those people label such characteristics masculine and assume that men possess them naturally. They further assume that feminine characteristics must be the opposite of masculine and that women are or should be feminine; it then follows that women are less highly regarded in a workplace that is considered competitive.

Feminists in the women's liberation movement do not concur with these values and beliefs.[40] Some argue that such stereotypical characterizations of male and female roles constrain and limit both men and women, forcing them to be less than they might otherwise be. The liberation of women from the restricted social role they learn and must play would also liberate men from their circumscribed masculine role. Other feminists agree that there are differences in the way men and women tend to think, feel, and act, but they invert the masculine evaluations. The feminine emphasis on human relationships, openness to emotional expressiveness, and aversion to hierarchy are esteemed by these partisans.

Integration

The degree to which possible adversaries are socially integrated might be expected to increase or decrease their likelihood of competing and fighting one another, thus serving as another important precondition of conflict. After all, parties that have nothing to do with each other do not fight each other; conflict is a way of relating. The previous discussions suggest that integration between parties who are relatively equal and whose differences are small tends to make severe conflicts unlikely. On the other hand, integration between parties who are relatively unequal, who are markedly different, and who are divided by their claims to scarce and valued resources tends to generate grievances.[41]

Insofar as one or more parties can easily leave the relationship, the chances of conflict are reduced. The would-be antagonists then have options other than fighting. In some circumstances, everyone in each adversary unit may be able to leave and establish new relationships; this is typically the case in competitive market relations. Often, while individuals may leave, the units themselves cannot survive without continuing their relationship; this is the case, for example, in labor-management relations in a corporation. And sometimes the individuals constituting the unit find it almost impossible to leave; this is the case, for example, with prison inmates and sometimes for members of ethnic groups living alongside each other.

Finally, groups in any long-term relationship each have their own narratives about that relationship. Their narratives about past experiences help provide a context and a way of interpreting current inequalities and differences. If a group of people believes that in the past it has been exploited or humiliated by another, the group is likely to interpret current undesirable circumstances as a continuation of old injustices, be less willing to accommodate, and even seek retribution.

Specialized Roles

Finally, for large-scale conflicts, groups, organizations, and societies are differentiated, with members playing specialized roles, which often include defense of the systems' members from external attack. The status and resources of the incumbents of those roles depend greatly on the perceived size of the threat and their success in countering it. Consequently, they have an interest in proclaiming a great external threat, and perhaps even in provoking it to enhance their status, and control over resources.

This reasoning underlies the warnings about the dangers of the military-industrial complex, as expressed by President Dwight D. Eisenhower in his 1961 farewell address.[42] There has been much literature on the way the military establishments, defense industries, political leaders, and other groups on antagonistic sides advance their interests by helping to sustain and even intensify military threats and engagements.[43] Scholarly research on these matters has been steadily expanding since the 1960s, but there is not a parallel growth in political debate about the dangerous effects of the military-industrial complex upon foreign policy choices in the United States and many other countries.[44]

Dynamism and Sociocultural Dynamics

Sociocultural preconditions of conflict are, in general, somewhat dynamic. Many patterns of socialization are deeply ingrained into the human psyche and difficult to change. Enculturation on such issues as sexuality, morality, freedom, and conformity begin at birth. Once established they are reinforced through overt and covert messages in the media, from educators, and through art, ritual, and political and legal regulation, as well as through rituals. This is not to say they are unchanging. Profound shifts in attitudes about same-sex marriage, sexual harassment, diversity and inclusion, and racial integration have occurred across a matter of decades, at least in some areas of the world. For example, a recent Pew Research poll found that support for same sex marriage in the United States grew from 31 percent in 2004 to 61 percent in 2019.[45] Moreover, nonconforming individuals continually reshape sociocultural norms through collective action and education. In the past two decades, for instance, gender has increasingly been viewed as a social construction, opening room for new nonbinary identities to emerge among many individuals. Of course, all efforts to redefine sociocultural values and norms are resisted by dominant voices and institutions, which itself is a trigger of conflict. Sociocultural change rarely occurs without pushback.

SYSTEM ATTRIBUTES

Just as conflict emerges within the confines of human nature, so too do they emerge in the confines of the system in which they occur. Among the many attributes of a system that serve as a precondition for constructive or destructive conflicts are five dynamics: the degree of structural inequality, institutional procedures in place for members to manage conflicts, functional interdependence, the consistency and stability of the system, and the degree to which the system is characterized by a scarcity of resources.

Structural Inequality

Social systems are characterized by varying degrees of laws, rules, and norms of conduct, which are established and reinforced by the formal and informal institutions of that system. For example, in the classroom students may be expected to raise their hand before being invited to speak, in the courtroom procedural rules dictate the way that evidence is presented, in most countries a one language is selected as the official language of the land, and among states the principle of state sovereignty guides conduct. Each of these ideas, rules, and norms make up the structure of the system; that is, comprise the "girders and beams" established and reinforced by societal institutions that constrain the agency of the individuals and groups that move about in that system. Just as the way a house is constructed determines the way that individuals can move through a living space, so too the underlying social, cultural, economic, and political construction of every social system constrains how people can move about, who has access to the benefits of that system and who does not, and who is privileged and who is not. Moreover, in every system the set of rules and norms established are enforced to one degree or another by the institutions of those systems, whether they be courts, schools, fathers or mothers, teachers, police officers, judges, generals, religious leaders, or banking regulators.

Every system, from large to small, contains some elements of structural inequality. In many classrooms teachers are allowed to talk whenever they like while students must raise their hands. In most family systems parents enjoy decision-making rights not afforded to children. In some patriarchal societies men enjoy the ability to own property, drive vehicles, and vote while women cannot. In most countries, natural-born citizens have rights that noncitizens, migrant labor, or illegal aliens do not. On the international stage countries with powerful economies and armies set rules of economic exchange and intervene in the affairs of other countries to advance their own interests while less powerful countries have little agency in this regard.

When structural inequalities are both visible and pervasive, a system will often convulse in conflict as those with few privileged seek redress. Examples include the wars of colonial liberation that occurred around the world in the 1960s and 1970s, the suffrage movement in the early 1900s, the Civil Rights Movement in the 1960s, land claims conflicts by indigenous peoples in North America, South Africa's anti-apartheid movement, and the struggle for migrant workers' rights. In each of these cases structural inequality served as a powerful precondition of overt conflict, solidifying group solidarity and serving as a rallying point for action. The racial justice movement in the United States and Europe serves as a contemporary example. Black people and their allies have increasingly pushed against institutions and structures that have maintained advantages for white people and have led to unequal outcomes in health, economic wellbeing, and justice. Such disparities provide compelling proof that racial identity significantly determines how well one does in life.[46]

Not all structural inequalities result in overt conflict, even if they clearly advantage some and disadvantage others. Students rarely revolt in the classrooms because rules dictating conduct and grading are generally accepted. Children rarely seek emancipation from their parents because cultural norms, economic dependency, and the legal status of minors makes such action either unthinkable or extremely difficult. Even in highly stratified and authoritarian societies where structural inequalities are extreme, such as North Korea, the instruments of state control may not afford those who are oppressed with the ability to manifest their grievances through social movements, work stoppages, boycotts, or violence. Dissent in these societies is immediately stifled with those speaking out against structural inequalities imprisoned or killed.

Individuals in such situations often have fatalistic views of the suffering they endure, believing it is God's will or due to immutable forces. Additionally, structural inequality may be unexamined due to pervasive social and cultural norms, examined previously. We don't speak out against what we cannot see, nor do we speak out against what we perceive to be a natural order. In this regard the debate over what is right or just is ultimately subjective and relative to the time and place occupied by the observer.[47] Such systems may be free of overt forms of conflict, but they exist in a state that Johan Galtung has famously called a "negative peace." Peace, in other words, is more than simply an absence of overt violence. It also requires structural conditions that nurture the full development of all individuals.

Institutionalized Means for Conflict Management

All social systems have mechanisms in place that help individuals resolve the disputes and conflicts that arise between and among them. These range from actual or ritualized warfare, to restorative justice practices, to highly developed legal systems with complex rules for evidence and the determination of culpability. Family, classroom, and workplace practices also adopt conflict-management practices that are either explicitly or implicitly understood and adopted by members. Human resources departments in most organizations, for instance, have developed processes for employee grievances or disputes over work conditions, compensation, and sexual harassment. Colleges rely on student handbooks and course syllabi lay out rules for conduct, plagiarism, grading, grade appeals, and what it means to be a student in good standing. Organizations with unionized workers nearly always have detailed agreements between labor and management about procedures for hiring and termination, wage increases, and promotions. Collectively all such arrangements are powerful predictors of whether communities will be resilient to destructive conflicts or susceptible to them.

Conflicts tend to be resolved constructively and more quickly when dispute processes are (1) well developed and understood by all community members, (2) deemed to be relatively fair and accessible (i.e., applied in the same way to all members), and (3) institutionalized to a degree that they have become routinized elements of day-to-day social relations. When these three conditions are met, community members are more apt to accept outcomes, even if those outcomes put them on a "losing" side.

Democratic forms of social order are particularly advantageous in this regard. This idea is the basis of numerous theories of social conflict including the so-called liberal peace thesis popular among many proponents of liberalism.[48] Democratic practices such as free and fair elections, checks and balances among branches of government, independent judiciaries, civilian control of militaries, and rights related to speech, assembly, and protest make it less likely that members will use violence when they don't get their way. Data on political violence confirms this, indicating that consolidated democracies have less internal political violence than semidemocracies and that pairs of democratic states are less likely to engage in interstate conflict than other types of states.[49] In a consolidated democracy, individuals will vote, protest, boycott, and contest conflicts in court but, in general, will not resort to revolution as long as they feel judgments rendered are fair and just. John Mearsheimer has attributed this to five forces: a balance of power among competing factions, cross-cutting ties across disparate groups, well-established bureaucracies that are insulated from politics, economic interdependency, and a nationalism born of shared narratives and faith in the integrity of the state.[50]

Even democratic countries, however, are subject to backsliding. If a sufficiently large group of people lose faith in the integrity of a system's dispute management procedures, conflict escalation and violence often follow. A good example is the January 6, 2021, riots that engulfed the U.S. Capitol in the aftermath of the 2020 presidential election in which Donald Trump was defeated by Joe Biden. Many of those who participated in the storming of the capital reported a loss of faith in fairness of the political system, claiming that the election was stolen and that shadowy forces were manipulating the U.S. political system. Some leaders even believed that that they could overturn the election, committing an insurrection. Of course, many other factors reviewed in this chapter contributed to this violence as well, including manipulation by a charismatic leader, economic dislocation, and loss of status by the aggrieved.

Some systems have few institutionalized procedures to manage conflicts whatsoever. Within international politics, for instance, the lack of a global government to set the rules and enforce them creates significant structural insecurity. Under these conditions, states may feel the need to protect themselves by increasing their military and economic capabilities. Of course, every other state in the system is doing the same, resulting in a spiral of escalation, called in international relations the "security dilemma," which is discussed in detail in chapter 6. As Thomas Weiss notes, despite the existence of numerous multilateral organizations, the most powerful nations on earth still appear to struggle for dominance in a rule-free environment, only abiding by multilateral edicts when it suits their interest.[51] Where rules and norms of conflict management are absent, disputes are managed through an ad hoc process and often become contests of relative power.

Functional Interdependence

Everything else being equal, insofar as members of different groups or societies are interconnected through shared institutions and economies, they tend not to fight with each other.[52] It is the also the foundation of some approaches to international peace that seek to integrate countries into common markets, common cultural practices, or common political entities. One of these is the functional school of thought popularized by David Mitrany in the aftermath of World War II.[53] Mitrany, and those that followed him, believed that the key to international peace is to build technical and intergovernmental organizations to enhance the cooperation of state actors. Once bound together, states will be less likely to fight, if for no other reason than to protect their self-interest.

The European Union is a good example of functionalism at work. Founded in the years after World War II, EU members believed that by building shared political and economic systems a shared prosperity would evolve that might protect members of the block from outbreak of a third World War. Of course, functional ties do not always ensure peace. For example, Russia invaded Ukraine in 2022 despite its economic interdependency with European energy markets. Clearly the potential loss of the European energy market was not sufficient to thwart the Russian attack on Ukraine.

Functional interdependence does not only occur in international politics. It also characterizes all social relations. Family members, for instance, are often dependent on each other for specialized childcare tasks, income generation, and home maintenance. Labor and management are functionally independent in that both sides require the other to perform its function for the firm to be successful. While functional interdependence among these entities generally leads to stability and constructive conflict management, exceptions occur when structural oppression, cultural norms, or external shocks are present. These variables are explored elsewhere in this chapter.

Consistency and Stability

The various elements of a social system are never wholly consistent and stable. Rapid change of any social system places strains on its members and can serve as a precondition to conflict. Change never occurs at the same rate for all components of a system; consequently, some components inevitably lag others. Traditional attitudes may not keep up with new circumstances or various segments of the system may develop differences in interests and values, which create new potential conflicts. This is true in communities where swift changes in population due to the entry of people from another part of the metropolitan area, country, or region of the world generate the basis for conflicts.[54]

Some analysts regard social change that moves a society out of equilibrium as a condition leading to revolution.[55] For such reasons, societal transition from authoritarian rule to a democratic political order is often accompanied by intensified conflicts and violence, as has become evident in North Africa and the Middle East since the Arab Spring protests erupted in 2011.

Finally, abrupt political, economic, or ideological changes in one part of the global system can contribute to conditions that help generate large-scale conflicts. For example, a revolutionary regime generally alters the surrounding international system as it tries to create social and political space for itself. The probability of conflicts increases as other regimes see threats in the new situation or opportunities to settle old scores. The collapse of a large social system is another kind of abrupt change that generates grounds for numerous new conflicts, as occurred in Eastern Europe and the former Soviet Union after 1992.

Scarcity

Underlying conflicts tend to exist where potential adversaries view themselves as being in a zero-sum relationship; that is, when gains or losses are perceived by one side to be directly proportional to the losses and gains of the other. Zero-sum conflicts are most likely to appear in a social system where the resources its members seek are scarce and the system is small and closed. When the system includes many parties in addition to the possible adversaries and when system members interact readily with nonmembers, much of what the adversaries want may be obtained from others within the system or from people outside, and disputes do not erupt. Consider even a desired resource such as the income of two groups, one of which is employed by the other. The two sides would be in a zero-sum relationship if they constituted the entire system. But if they are producing a product for sale to customers, they might cooperate to pass on costs to the customer or produce a more attractive product and win additional customers, thus increasing the amount of income they have to distribute between them. Income also may be regarded as a symbol of relative status, and not simply as an amount of money needed to purchase goods. In that case, income relative to some other group's income is what is significant. If potential adversaries compare their incomes to each other and to no one else they are in a zero-sum situation; the more one has relative to the other, the less the other has.

Reframing a conflict so it is not viewed as a zero-sum circumstance is a way to transform the relation from a conflictual to a cooperative one. Working together to expand the pie can allow all sides to larger slices of the pie. Reframing from a zero-sum to a mutual gains mindset is examined when we discuss negotiation, mediation, and dialogue later in this book.

Scarcity also has a material basis, as in the availability of clean water, arable land, petroleum, and many other resources. Competition for such resources is an important basis for interethnic as well as interstate conflicts. For example, declines in potable water as well as available river water for energy production and agriculture has triggered conflicts between upstream and downstream users in the Nile basin; between Turkey, Iraq, and Syria in the Euphrates-Tigris basin; and between China and Laos in the Mekong basin. Such conflicts are likely to grow in scope and intensity in the years to come. In 2018 the UN World Water Development Report predicted that by 2050 nearly six billion people in the world will be affected by water scarcity, a prediction that does not bode well for the emergence of conflict in poor and arid regions of the world in the near term.[56]

Dynamism and System Attributes

The system attributes reviewed earlier are relatively dynamic and thus important targets for those interested in addressing the preconditions of conflicts. Structural inequalities, for example, are grounded in policies and laws that are amenable to change. Of course, in some systems these changes are easier to achieve if, for instance, individuals are able to choose their leaders, freely express their discontents, and communicate with one another through a free and open media. In authoritarian systems such activities are much more difficult and often deadly.

Functional interdependence is possible to build and is, as an example, a feature of many peacebuilding programs that have sought to build economic ties between conflicting parties in Israel and Palestine, South Sudan, Guatemala, and El Salvador.[57] System stability and consistency is somewhat less dynamic, but dramatic changes to the underlying preconditions of conflict do occur as a result of external shocks, often to the detriment of constructive conflict management. Finally, recourse scarcity is the least dynamic variable reviewed previously. As long as the availability of a resource is fixed and essential to human flourishing, little can be done to decrease the likelihood that an ongoing scarcity will trigger a conflict. Conflict emergence is less likely if new technologies, such as water desalinization, reduce the scarcity or if alternative resources can be found.

SYNTHESIS

Endogenous forces, sociocultural dynamics, and system attributes are three distinct theoretical frameworks that help us to understand where conflicts *come from*. They are, however, best considered as complementary rather than as competing approaches, interacting with each other in nearly every situation. To borrow an example from human biology, being tall or short is a function of natural selection; that is, the genes we inherited from our biological parents that provided their ancestors with an evolutionary advantage in their environmental setting. But height is also a function of regular access to nutritious food, which is determined by political and economic policies and one's good or bad luck in being born into a community that enjoys structural advantages or does not. Finally, sociocultural beliefs and values determine whether and how being tall or short "matters" within a particular community.

A simple way of conceptualizing the interconnection between human nature, systemic, and sociocultural preconditions of conflict is shown in the Venn diagram shown in Figure 2.1. This diagram illustrates that while each precondition is distinct, each interacts and blends as well.

As an example, take the ongoing conflict between nomadic herdsmen and indigenous farmers in Nigeria, which is emblematic of multiple land use conflicts around the world. In this case, nomadic herdsmen from northern Nigeria have moved south in search of pasture for their animals because of

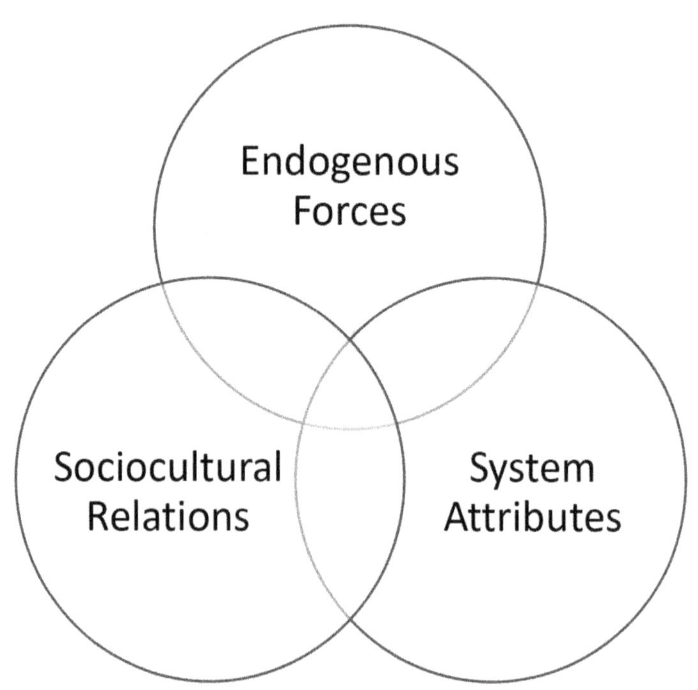

Figure 2.1. Intersection of Three Schools of Thought on the Origin of Conflicts

drought. There they have clashed with southern farmers with violence leading to the death of over twenty-five hundred people and the displacement of sixty-two thousand others between 2016 and 2018.[58]

How is a conflict analyst to understand this conflict, and what preconditions might have helped us to predict its emergence? From the human nature perspective, the conflict might be viewed as an outgrowth of the basic human needs for water, food, security, and identity. If any of these is denied, we can expect those seeking them to contend with until their need is satisfied. So too we can implicate other features of human nature, including the territorial imperative and genetic predispositions to in-group altruism and out-group competition. From a system attribute perspective, we might speculate that the Nigerian government's failure to put into place country-level procedures for managing conflicts between herders and farmers has left stakeholders with no institutionalized means to resolve their disputes. Absent these, violence becomes more likely. Similarly, structural inequalities related to the power of herders and farmers to influence land use policy is also relevant. Finally, from a sociocultural perspective one might point to the fact that the nomadic herding community is largely Muslim and the farming community to the south is largely Christian. Thus what may appear to be an environmental conflict over basic needs has an additional level of complexity related to identity, with each stakeholder being shaped by narratives about the other that are rooted in historical animosity, stereotypes, and fear. Each set of conditions impacts others. Of course, this is only a cursory overview of what is a very complex conflict involving multiple other preceding conditions as well. But it illustrates the idea that human nature, systemic forces, and sociocultural forces all interact with each other, shaping the field upon which conflicts can emerge, escalate, de-escalate, and become settled.

Finally, analysts should be aware that the saliency of each component to conflict emergence will vary from case to case. For some conflicts, sociocultural factors may be more prominent while for others systemic factors or factors related to endogenous forces will be more prominent. Specifically, sociocultural factors are likely to be less significant preconditions when accounting for conflicts among clearly bounded adversaries, with enduring relationships, and who function within the context of shared rules and norms. In these situations, shared narratives, values, and norms are likely to bind members of the community together, making conflict emergence less likely. On the other hand, impulses and behaviors related to human nature may offer greater explanatory power for conflicts that emerge during crisis events, where high threat, short time, and great uncertainty make careful deliberative decision making close to impossible. Good conflict analysis considers the context of the situation.

SUMMARY AND DISCUSSION QUESTIONS

This chapter has explored preconditions of conflict related to three forces: endogenous forces, the sociocultural context, and the attributes of the system. Each of these perspectives offer unique insights about where conflicts come from, but each also interact with the others, creating unique variation that makes every conflict unique. The job of the conflict analyst is to learn how to unpack these interactions so that they can better predict when a conflict will emerge, and how to respond if it does. Readers are encouraged to explore the ideas presented in this chapter further by thinking about and discussing the following questions.

1. Conduct a self-scan of your own underlying temperament and conflict style. What makes you unique in this regard? To what degree do you believe your tendencies are a product of your own internal nature, the sociocultural context and events that shaped your life, and the attributes of the system in which you live? How has this constellation of forces impacted what you see, feel, and do in conflict situations?
2. Working in a group, think together about a large-scale conflict that is of interest to all. Using the various preconditions of conflict presented in this chapter as a framework, discuss which precondition(s) best explain why that conflict emerged and why.
3. Scan your local community, looking for variation in the variables presented in this chapter. Based on this analysis, predict what conflicts are likely to occur in the future, between whom, and over what?

Part II

CONFLICT EMERGENCE AND CONFLICT STRATEGIES

Chapter Three

Emergence

Countless numbers of conflicts might occur in the world at any time, yet most potential conflicts never emerge. It may be that potential adversaries never interact, that essential resources remain plentiful, or that a triggering event that could spark a fight simply does not occur. It may be as well that highly destructive conflicts are relatively rare because human beings are, for the most part, a cooperative social species and the benefits of harmonious relations often outweigh the benefits of conflictual ones.

Yet large-scale social conflicts do sometimes occur and at times become highly destructive. While multitudes of factors can reasonably be correlated with conflict emergence, four conditions must be minimally present.[1] The first condition is that members of at least one of the parties to the emerging conflict identify themselves as an entity separate from others they identify as opponents. Second, members of at least one of the parties must feel they have a grievance. Third, at least one of the parties must formulate goals to change another group's behavior so that the grievance will be reduced. Fourth, members of the aggrieved party must believe that they can indeed bring about the desired change in the antagonist. These four conditions—identity, grievance, goals, and a belief that redress is possible—are highly interdependent. Thus, the conceptions of who we are, what aggrieves us, who is responsible, and what can be done about it all interact. We explore each of these dynamics in the following.

IDENTITY

For every individual, developing a sense of identity—*an abiding sense of the self and of the relationship of the self to the world*—is an essential part of becoming a person.[2] Without a conception of who we are in relation to the world, life would be unnavigable, confusing, and likely short. Identity provides individuals with a road map for prescribed behaviors, a context for decision making, and a way to make meaning out of social relationships and life events.[3] It also provides a vehicle for group belonging, a basic human need that is key to the survival of individuals and groups.

Everyone holds many identities, some of which are nested in each other. These may be as broad as "woman" or "Buddhist" or as narrow as being the youngest child in a family. Some identities are relatively fixed and unchanging, for instance, older people cannot become young, and people born in South Korea can never truthfully claim they were born somewhere else. Other identities are acquired and then lost as individuals navigate their life. For example, at varying times in life an individual may become a student, a resident of a particular city, or an employee at a particular company.

Collective identity occurs when groups of people coalesce around the shared narratives, history, rituals, and cognitions of a particular group, or as Snow and Corrigall-Brown put it, "a shared and interactive sense of we-ness and collective agency."[4] Thus we may speak of ourselves as being Jewish, Black American, Japanese, Southern Baptist, Eastern Orthodox, straight, or transgendered. In each case, the implication is that we share a set of common experiences and legacies, core beliefs, and practices with all other members of that group.

Individuals hold multiple identities that together provide them with a relatively unique outlook on the world. The salience of one of these identities over others often depends on the context. A Ghanaian may be much more aware of her identity as a person from Ghana while traveling abroad in Norway than she would be traveling in Ghana. Similarly, a woman walking down a dark street late at night may be more aware of her gender identity than a man in a similar circumstance. Researchers have thus speculated that the salience of one identity over others increases when an individual comes under threat for holding that identity, be that a threat of violence, discrimination, or even unwanted attention.[5]

The identities we adopt, and those that are imposed upon us, can either facilitates social, political, and economic mobility or inhibit it. For example, in most societies people who are blind have less agency to traverse a communal space than do individuals capable of sight. The built environment was simply not created with their needs in mind. The interplay between power, social position, and identity has thus become a large topic of research in the social sciences and an important object of inquiry among social justice activists.[6]

A strong sense of a collective identity is often implicated in conflict emergence.[7] Ethnic, ideological, or religious identities serve as a basis for mobilization and organization, the source of grievance, and the glue that sustains collective action.[8] For example, the Islamic State (IS) has successfully coopted the notion of jihad to provide its fighters with a shared identity and purpose, in this case defending Islamic lands from infidels and apostates. Those recruited to the jihadi cause by IS are attracted to the meaning and belonging offered by that group's brand of jihadist identity.[9] For many recruits, Jihadi provides such individuals with self-esteem, a broad and simplified narrative through which to understand complex social and political forces, and a belief that their life has significance.[10] Similarly, the rioters that attacked the U.S. Capitol building on January 6, 2021, were not just contesting an election—they were also seeking to protect their sense of what America is and should be. Political scientist Robert Pape found, for instance, that a fear that the rights of minority groups and immigrants in America were superseding the rights of white people was the main motivation for action among the nearly four hundred people arrested after the capitol riots.[11] Many of the rioters were thus engaged in much more than a protest; instead, they were participating in a premeditated act of rebellion meant to preserve an imagined way of life that they feared was being lost.

When core identities come under threat, mobilization is swift and often aggressive. Compromise is unthinkable, and a loss to opponent is more than just a temporary setback; rather, it is an existential threat to the system of meaning that gives life shape and significance.

Internal Characteristics and Identities

Four internal characteristics tend to facilitate the development of collective identities and serve as precursors to conflict emergence: homogeneity, ease of communication, clear boundaries, and organizational potential.

Homogeneity of Members

Group homogeneity tends to facilitate communication and to foster a sense of solidarity and shared fate. If sufficient, it provides an important impetus for conflict mobilization. French speakers of Quebec, for instance, tend to share religion and class position within a particular region of Canada. This, in turn, facilitates a strong Quebec identity and has led to mobilization for Quebec autonomy or independence. Group heterogeneity, on the other hand, can inhibit in-group solidarity and make it less likely that members will mobilize for a fight. For example, in the United States, the ethnic heterogeneity of U.S. workers has hampered their class solidarity and their mobilization for trade union membership or for class-conscious political parties.[12] The high degree of occupational differentiation also hinders working-class solidarity.[13]

Similarly, women's solidarity as a conflict group opposing men is also handicapped by their heterogeneity. Not only are women diverse in terms of ethnicity, region, and occupation, but in many societies their marital status and their husbands' occupational positions have great importance for them as well.[14]

Ease of Communication

A sense of common identity is highly dependent upon the ease of communication among members. Factors affecting ease of communication include the members' number, proximity, social and technical skills, sharing of a common language, and the social and nonsocial links among them.

Increased opportunities for effective communication among members of potential conflict groups can increase the feeling of dissatisfaction and the belief that a grievance can be reduced. To illustrate, prior to the October 1917 Russian Revolution, the increasing concentration of workers in very large factories supported the growth of proletarian solidarity. Although the industrial proletariat was small, "it was disproportionately concentrated both in large-scale industrial enterprises and in major industrial centers."[15] This facilitated communication, mobilization, and organization and so contributed to the emergence of militant-organized opposition to the czar, and ultimately to the October Revolution. Such cases have led many authoritarian governments to seek ways to limit communication among potential opponents. One can surmise, for example, that China's adoption of security laws granting the government the authority to exert sovereignty over cyberspace and to cut public access to some Western social media platforms and the internet during public security emergencies is driven by a fear of domestic dissatisfaction to its rule.[16]

The accessibility of global information networks has also had profound consequences for mobilizing collective identities. In recent years, new media outlets with a global reach, such as Telemundo, Al Jazeera, and the Xinhua News Agency, for example, have been established to report on and frame global events. Thus, today immigrants can maintain ongoing connections with their homeland and sustain various degrees of dual national identity.[17] Thus too, social movements struggling to defend human rights, protect the environment, or promote good working conditions can more easily mobilize across national borders.[18] Globalized communication structures also facilitate the formation of and actions by transnational extremist organizations within ungoverned areas of the world.[19] One example is the Amaq News Agency, which has been linked to the Islamic State of Iraq and the Levant and is regularly used to announce operations by that organization.

Clear and Stable Boundaries

Insofar as the social boundaries of population categories are clear and unchanging, their members tend to develop a sense of solidarity and common fate. For example, members of a caste, as in India, are more likely to think of themselves as having a shared identity and fate than are members of a social class, whose boundaries are permeable. Of course, whether a social category is highly homogeneous or not depends on the boundaries used by an analyst or by the members themselves. Therefore, the distribution of these characteristics may radically shift when the boundaries change, as people in a territory secede or are incorporated within another country.

Organizational Potential

The nature of a group's organizational capacities greatly affects the likelihood that the group will become mobilized as a collectivity. The more highly integrated and interdependent are the members of a potential group, the more likely are they to see themselves as a collectivity with common interests. Miners, for example, are vitally interdependent in their work activities and historically have had a high sense of solidarity compared with other occupational groups. Such solidarity is reinforced by other factors, such as isolation, concentration of residency, and high risk.

Social movement networks linking persons and small groups often have high organizational potential. Such networks facilitate communication and the creation of shared identities, giving certain issues salience. They are also crucial in mobilizing people, galvanizing a feeling of dissatisfaction, and in creating the belief that their dissatisfaction can be alleviated by their efforts.[20] This is illustrated by the rise of the U.S. Civil Rights Movement against segregation in the U.S. South. The movement rested upon the local churches and other already-existing organizations and the interpersonal channels linking the people with those institutions.[21] Similarly, in Iran in 1979, mosques were important centers for the mobilization of the people who mounted the revolution against the government. Finally, in the United States evangelical Christian megachurches have mobilized conservative voters in a similar fashion, often using sophisticated data mining techniques to connect evangelical voters to preferred candidates and causes.[22]

In the contemporary age of rapid communication and movement of goods and people, transnational networks linking small groups in many parts of the world can come together to wage large continuing campaigns. It is now possible for small groups of individuals with a clear message, committed followers, and technological know-how to organize and direct large-scale protests in a matter of days. This is evident in the mobilization of public protests throughout the world in recent years, such as the 2017 Women's March on Washington; rallies mobilized by Extinction Rebellion throughout Europe and the United States in 2019, 2020, and 2021; and successive waves of protests COVID-related public health restrictions throughout France, Germany, and Austria in 2020 and 2021. Each protest harnessed social media platforms to spread information, mobilize participation, and coordinate logistics quickly and efficiently.[23]

Such trends appear to be increasing as the accessibility of social media platforms improve. A 2019 Pew Research Center report on the use of social media in the United States revealed that 72 percent of American adults utilize some form of social media. That number was only 5 percent in 2005, the year after Facebook went live.[24] Newer social media platforms are rapidly expanding as well. According to the BBC, TikTok, one of the fastest growing social media apps in the world, and its sister app Douyin—which is available in China—now have an estimated two billion downloads worldwide, with over eight hundred million active global users. The reach of such platforms is unprecedented in human history. In 2019 the Pew Research Center estimated that five billion people worldwide owned mobile devices, half of which included smartphone technology able to connect to various apps and social media platforms.

Adversary Relations and Identities

In defining themselves, groups also define others. Indeed, all groups establish a sense of "who they are" by emphasizing how they are not like others. As discussed in chapter 1, people are generally inclined to evaluate their own group as superior to others to build self-esteem.[25] Indeed, the mere act of randomly separating people into different groups and putting those groups into competition with each other often triggers a dynamic known as in-group favoritism and out-group bias.[26] This social-psychological tendency toward ethnocentrism may contribute to "us" against "them" thinking in intergroup relations.[27]

On its own, us-them thinking may not trigger large-scale conflicts. Indeed, members of one people often find members of another interestingly different and enjoy their music, food, or other traditional products. Additionally, social psychological research indicates that positive attachment to one's country—patriotism—is separate from feelings of national superiority—nationalism.[28] However, when identity differences are joined by structural inequalities between groups, or the oppression of one identity group by another, then conflict emergence and intensification may result.[29] Interestingly, however, there are cases where under long-term domination, many members of the dominated group may internalize the evaluations of those who dominate them or their place in the social hierarchy.[30] The result may be self-hatred and self-denigration, which then inhibits challenging the system of domination.

In some cases, identity-based conflicts are relatively latent, but emerge because of an external attack. For example, nationalist identification often emerges in the face of coercive treatment by foreign armies. When Japanese troops invaded China in 1937, they took ruthless action against the entire rural population, arousing intense anti-Japanese feelings among the peasants.[31] That invasion and subsequent occupation raised the Chinese peasants' sense of citizenship and their interest in building and strengthening an independent Chinese state.

Changing Identities

Identities, because they are socially constructed, do change. For example, in the United States, "LGBTQIA" identity is a relatively recent creation, and the "white race" has expanded over the years to include Jews and others previously excluded groups, such as people of Italian heritage.[32] These identity shifts often significantly affect the outbreak of a conflict and help determine whether its course will be constructive or destructive. Thus, broad country identities may dissipate and the organizations that sustain them weaken so that religious or ethnic identities become more salient. This happened in the late 1980s for many people in Yugoslavia. Their identifications as communists and as Yugoslavs were undermined, and old ethnic and religious identities became more prominent, leading to the breakup of Yugoslavia and the creation of multiple separate states starting in 1991.

A sudden rise in migration can also lead to the emergence of previously less-salient nationalistic identities. Mass migration occurring in societies undergoing disorienting rapid change or a deterioration of living standards is particularly likely to precede conflict emergence. In these cases, feelings of frustration build and may be directed at vulnerable migrant groups who are viewed as nonmembers.[33] This process helps account for the rise of Nazism in Germany, as high inflation and the worldwide depression worsened socioeconomic conditions and reduced many people's status and living conditions. It also helps to explain the recent rise of nativist thinking that paralleled the election of Donald Trump in the United States, Boris Johnson in the United Kingdom, Hungarian Prime Minister Viktor Orbán, as well as other right-wing populist leaders around the world. In each case populations vulnerable to economic dislocations caused by globalization have made immigrants and refugees the objects of their frustrations, sometimes in violent ways. Such channeling is not inevitable; it depends on the repertoire of possible responses and the alternatives presented by leaders. After all, the economic depression of the 1930s did not result in a fascist regime in the United States or in most other countries.

GRIEVANCE

The condition that receives most analytic and popular attention in explaining the emergence of a conflict is the grievance felt by at least one adversary. Contending groups usually account for their entering a conflict by referring to the injustices they suffer.[34] A sense of grievance arises from internal, relational, and contextual factors. Factors from all these sources combine to account for the content and the strength of the grievance.

Internal Developments and Grievance

Discrepancies between attainments and expectations have been the subject of much research in conflict studies and are generally viewed to have three major sources. First, members of a society or a segment of the society experience a decline in what benefits they have had for a long time and had expected would continue. The decline may be due to an economic recession, or it may be due to a decline in autonomy, territorial control, or respect and deference from others. Second, improving conditions produce the expectation of continuing improvement; consequently, when attainments decline, or simply stop rising, people are disappointed and feel aggrieved. This has been used to explain the outbreak of the French Revolution and many other major social convulsions.[35] In these cases the gains won by some groups may also be seen by others as losses in status, power, or other benefits. Consequently, newly aggrieved groups sometimes struggle to regain what they believed they had rightly enjoyed. Such may help explain why white working-class males are less supportive of the racial justice movement in the United States than are other social and racial groups.[36] The third source of discrepancy between expectations and attainments are rising expectations, which may occur for several reasons. One reason is that people learn, for example, from the mass media, that others have much more of what they also want. The ever-greater exposure of deprived people to knowledge of the lives of the advantaged in the world tends to raise their expectations. For example, shortly after World War II, some analysts argued that traditional societies would undergo modernization as people in underdeveloped countries discovered what was available in economically advanced countries.[37] However, many countries failed to grow economically and did not keep pace with the economic growth of the developed countries. This resulted in the emergence of conflict among societies that "missed out" on expected gains.

Changes in expectations relative to attainments do not, however, always lead to overt conflict. Poor conditions may be made endurable by promises of improvements in the or sacrifice in the name of a glorious future. It is also plausible that if conditions have been improving, people are able to absorb a setback with less bitterness. Under other circumstances, a new deprivation may be interpreted as a personal failure that induces guilt or self-hate so that no outwardly directed efforts at redressing the grievance are taken. Finally, the partial improvement of conditions may be sufficient to satisfy rather than arouse appetites. For example, many immigrants have found U.S. working conditions much better than their previous conditions, and therefore they are more satisfied than their U.S.-born children and other U.S. workers.[38]

Relationship Developments and Grievance

A good way to begin considering how the relationship between adversaries affects their members' sense of grievance is to examine inequalities in class, status, and power. Differences in class position, in status ranking, and in relative power are to be found in some degree within all social systems, and such differences are likely sources of grievances. Class differences are based in the labor, capital, and other markets and affected by government tax and welfare policies. They are indicated by variations in income, wealth, and other measures of economic well-being. People also vary in their ranking in status hierarchies. Thus, in many societies some people are accorded high regard due to their familial origins as aristocrats, while others are looked down upon due to their lowly origins. Variations in prestige and deference also may be accorded based on their occupations, educational level, ethnicity, religious adherences, lifestyles, or other qualities that are ranked according to culturally agreed-upon standards.

There is much empirical data, as well as theoretical reasoning, regarding the relationship between inequalities and grievances. Survey data from many societies do indicate that persons with low occupational status or at low economic levels tend to be dissatisfied as measured by responses to several kinds of questions.[39] Similarly, occupational studies generally find that the lower the prestige, income, or work autonomy of an occupation, the more likely are its incumbents to be dissatisfied and want to leave it.[40] Furthermore, low rank in different dimensions, like education and income, has a cumulative negative effect.

Dissatisfaction, however, is not always directly expressed in conflict or even a sense of grievance for several reasons. One is that people who rank low on a consensually valued dimension are socialized to think poorly of themselves and wish to avoid identifying themselves in terms of that dimension; consequently, the resulting weak solidarity interferes with collective recognition of dissatisfaction. In addition, severely deprived persons tend to be preoccupied with day-to-day efforts at coping rather than developing a shared sense of grievance. For example, a study in nine countries found that workers, compared with middle-class respondents, were less likely to identify with persons of their own nation who were not of their own class and less likely to identify with members of their own class in other countries.[41] Accommodation to severe deprivation can even take the form of suppression and denial of hostile feelings and lead to placating and ingratiating behavior toward those of higher rank.

Another difficulty with the idea of simple deprivation as an explanation of grievance is that in many struggles, the party that initiates the pursuit of a contentious goal is relatively advantaged, not disadvantaged. It is often the stronger, the richer, or the higher-status groups that seek more of what they already have from those who have less. Perhaps they do so because they can, but it also may be that by their standards, they feel that they not only deserve their high rank, but that they deserve even more wealth, deference, and power. Their grievance, if we may call it that, derives from their claim that they are due even more than they already have. It may be as well that relatively advantaged groups develop a grievance out of a fear that others will challenge and displace them. One example is efforts by republican legislatures in several U.S. states to restrict access to voting in the wake of Donald Trump's loss to Joe Biden in the presidential elections. In the first half of 2021 alone, fourteen states enacted twenty-two new laws that restrict access to the vote.[42] Many of the enacted provisions are likely to disproportionately impact democrat-leaning and relatively disadvantaged constituencies such as Blacks, low-income communities, and immigrants. Common provisions include restrictions on early voting, stringent new voter ID laws, limits to "drive through voting," and restrictions on voter outreach. In each case it a appears that a more powerful and advantaged group is motivated by the fear of losing status.

Studies have been made to specify the effects of different kinds of rank incongruence. Thus, some evidence supports the idea that persons ranked high on ascribed dimensions (e.g., ethnicity) or dimensions that are considered investments (e.g., education) but low on achieved or reward dimensions (e.g., income or occupational status) may be called "under-rewarded." They tend to experience failure and feel disappointment and anger. On the other hand, persons ranked low on ascribed or investment dimensions and high on achieved or reward dimensions would tend to feel successful and contented, and some may even feel guilt and obligated to assist the less advantaged.

Although there is evidence that rank inconsistency has effects, certain considerations limit its utility in explaining the emergence of large-scale unregulated social conflicts.[43] First, rank inconsistency may not uniformly contribute to feeling dissatisfied because under some circumstances persons may use their low rank as a standard of reference. Second, for some people at least, being high in certain hierarchies would compensate for being low in others. For example, university professors generally have lower incomes than other professionals with a terminal degree, yet their educational status undercuts their sense of class grievance. Finally, for collective action to emerge in large-scale conflicts, grievances must be experienced collectively.

Besides the antagonistic interests arising from inequalities, possible adversaries often are interdependent and share positive bonds, interests, and identities. The invigoration of such positive ties tends to inhibit feeling aggrieved, while their deterioration contributes to rising salience of dissatisfactions. One important positive aspect of the relationship between potential adversaries is the extent to which their members hold common identities. The loss of such a common identity creates the space for secondary antagonisms to become primary ones, as happened to many people in the former Soviet Union who suffered the loss of shared identity as supporters of communism and as Soviet citizens.

Another positive aspect of a relationship is the extent to which the potential adversaries share a common goal and work together cooperatively to attain it. This typically is a major cohesive force in social life. Within industrial organizations, for example, workers and managers collaborate to produce products that will be marketed to earn money for the organization, which is shared with owners and others, to varying degrees. Shared goals are based on consensus, on the similarities in values and beliefs that people have. Cooperative activities may also be aided by dissensus when people differ in what they enjoy doing and therefore complement each other's work.

The degree to which members of potential adversary groups have ties that crosscut their lines of cleavage is another positive aspect of relations we must consider. These ties include interpersonal bonds or alliances against third parties. Thus, persons with friendships across possible conflict-group boundaries are less likely to construe potentially contentious issues between the groups antagonistically.

Finally, the degree of mutual affection between potential antagonists is another positive aspect of a relationship. As Lewis A. Coser writes, "The closer the relationship, the greater the affective investment, the greater also the tendency to suppress rather than express hostile feelings."[44] In short, changes in the relative balance between cooperative and antagonistic aspects of the relationship are crucial to the emergence of a social conflict. A deterioration of positive bonds and activities, as well as an increase in negative ones, contributes to the outbreak of a conflict.

Increasing inequalities between potential adversaries tend to arouse a sense of grievance among the relatively disadvantaged, and the changes that make one party appear to benefit at the expense of another are particularly pertinent.

Changes in the Social Context and Grievance

The social context within which potential adversaries interact often changes in ways that enhance the partisans' sense of grievance. Those changes not only become possible sources of deprivation, but also help provide the criteria by which circumstances are judged to be unsatisfactory and unjustified.

The sociocultural conditions discussed in chapter 2, which could be the source of dissatisfaction, are not static, and changes in the social and physical environment often result in groups feeling aggrieved. Thus increased immigration tends to alter the demographic balance among ethnic, cultural, religious, and class categories. Some people in the host country may regard these immigrants as threatening their own economic position or political power and oppose their entry. This is more likely when economic conditions are worsening. For instance, the influx of war refugees from Syria, Afghanistan, and North Africa into Europe since 2014 have occurred when many European countries experienced generally stagnant economic conditions, a trend made worse with the economic shutdown of many industries due to the COVID outbreak of 2020. In the wake of these economic challenges some countries or specific political groups within them, have resisted resettlement efforts on the grounds that new migrants would take away jobs from native citizens.

Changes in the global economy are a source of strain within and among societies and trigger conflict emergence. Shifts in investments, trade patterns, and labor flows often exacerbate inequalities and thereby provide the grounds for grievances. The background to the eruption of violence in Chiapas, Mexico, on January 1, 1994, the day the North American Free Trade Agreement took effect, is illustrative.[45] The state of Chiapas, on Mexico's southern border, has long been characterized by extreme inequality between privileged landowners and impoverished indigenous peoples. Changes in the 1980s and early 1990s worsened the conditions of the poor indigenous Mayan communities. Some of these changes were related to transnational developments and the Mexican government's economic liberalization policies, including the end of land reform and of price supports for agricultural products. Land pressures also increased because of migration into the area. At the same time, the Catholic bishop Samuel Ruiz and some priests in Chiapas preached liberation theology, criticizing the policies that further impoverished the poor. Many indigenous resistance groups were organized, and support grew for the emerging Ejército Zapatista de Liberación Nacional.

Prevailing ways of thinking and communicating provide the language in which deprivations are articulated. They vary among organizations, societies, and civilizations and change from one historical period to another. The commonly shared sentiments and social norms may be expressed in the discourses of religion and spirituality, of class struggle, of ethnic and other communal traditions, of individualistic psychology, or of innumerable other discourses. They include various standards about core values, be they personal freedom, social equality, collective self-determination, or stable order.

In the 1960s and 1970s, in the United States and elsewhere in the world, social equality was highly valued and groups that had been relatively disadvantaged believed they deserved remedial social action. Even those who were not disadvantaged generally regarded the demands as legitimate. Since then, however, there are signs of backlashes and of renewed importance given to individual rights. The view that individuals should maximize and retain their gains from the marketplace became more prevalent and legitimate. The widespread economic recession that began in 2008 reduced the confidence in the workings of unfettered markets, a trend that repeated with the COVID downturn of 2020. To a certain extent this tension between individual liberties and broader collective responsibilities is inherent in every social system. This tension continues today in much of the world, as the rights of collectivities and the appreciation of multicultural social systems come into conflict with individual freedoms.

Finally, standards may be raised by the actions and words of authorities recognized by the partisans in a conflict. For example, the 1954 U.S. Supreme Court decision in *Brown v. Board of Education*, which declared segregated schools unconstitutional, was made unanimously by the most authoritative interpreters of the fundamental law of the country. That decision reinforced and raised the expectations of Blacks throughout the United States, as well as undercut the legitimacy of defenders of racial segregation.[46]

Structural characteristics of the social system in which possible adversaries interact also affect the rate of conflicts within the system. Studies of international conflicts, for example, examine the incidence of wars as related to different alliance structures and economic relations in the world system. Thus status inconsistency can be regarded as a system characteristic, assessing the degree to which the countries in the world are inconsistent in military expenditures, economic strength, and prestige.[47] High-rank disequilibrium might be conducive to international conflict since national leaders would seek to alter that status quo. On the other hand, high disequilibrium might contribute to international crosscutting ties, while high consistency would reinforce lines of cleavage and make international conflict more likely.

Empirical studies for the years 1946 to 1964 found that the incidence of wars correlated moderately with the degree of status inconsistency. But a replication, covering the years 1950 to 1980, did not find this relationship.[48] Perhaps this is explained by the greater global dominance of the United States in the earlier period and a greater dispersal of power during the later years. Thus during the earlier period the strong hegemonic capabilities of the United States and the deep political cleavage of the Cold War meant that status inconsistency tended to be related to the struggle between the hegemon's group and the challenging group. In the later period, status consistency would be more indicative of fundamental cleavages in the international order.

FORMING CONTENTIOUS GOALS

For a conflict to become overt, one group must attribute a grievance to the actions or stance of another group and develop goals that will eliminate the source of the grievance. Although contentious goals are infinitely various, three major dimensions of goals determine if a conflict emerges along a constructive or destructive trajectory. First is the degree to which the change sought is toward greater integration or toward greater separation. The second dimension is the magnitude of the changes being sought. The left-right continuum is the third dimension to be usefully considered.

Generally, as conflicts emerge adversaries may seek to mitigate it by either integrating or separating. Goals to achieve greater integration include attaining equal opportunities for educational and occupational positions, becoming assimilated, imposing conformity, or converting the other side. At the opposite extreme, goals to achieve greater separation include autonomy, independence, or the expulsion or destruction of the adversary. The scale of the change sought depends on the degree of integration or separation that already prevails.

The magnitude of the changes sought may be small, such as modifications in allocating resources or altering the policies being implemented by the adversary. These reform goals are often of an aggregate rather than a collective character. That is, the goals pertain to opportunities for members of the quasi group as individuals, rather than for the group. At the other extreme, a revolutionary change in who has the authority to make allocations may be the objective. These goals often have a relatively collective character, as when a transformation is sought so that new groups or classes come to dominate. In between the extremes are goals to reform relationships, alter policies, or change leaders. Leaders of an ethnic minority, for example, may seek increased representation by its members in policymaking. Even a coup by a military junta taking over the highest government offices from another junta (regarded as a palace revolution) often does not entail a radical change in the society. In a sense, the magnitude of the change sought is a function of the discrepancy between the goals of the adversary camps. The greater the difference between their goals, the more radical each side's goals will be regarded by their opponent.

Finally, the left-right dimension is a frequently discussed variation in goals. Seeking to restructure the relationship or change the policy between social strata is generally considered "left" insofar as the objective is to increase equality in economic well-being, social status, and political power.[49] Another characterization of this dimension stresses who is making claims on whom. Thus, when the disadvantaged make claims against those who have relative advantage, their objectives are considered leftist. When members of the dominant group seek to maintain or enhance their position, their objectives are regarded as rightist or even reactionary.[50]

Certainly, the nature of the goals being pursued has implications for the course of a conflict. For example, conflicts about the allocation of resources are relatively amenable to compromise, especially when the resources are sufficient and divisible. This is typically the case in consensual disputes. Some consensual conflicts, however, involve radical restructuring of the adversary relationship and are not easily settled. As when a revolutionary group seeks to end private ownership of large agricultural estates, such goals are unitary and not easily divisible.[51]

Dissensual conflicts are often about issues that each side views as requiring significant changes by the adversary and are relatively difficult to settle via compromise. This is typically the case when one party tries to convert the other to its way of believing. However, a group's goal, for example, to attain greater autonomy for its members to practice their religion, is more amenable to negotiation.

A group's goals incorporate mental constructs of desired future conditions and usually are embedded in a set of ideas about the partisans' plight and what can be done about it. These goals and ideas are varyingly shared and deeply held by group members. They also are varyingly well articulated, sometimes being only implicit and inferred from indirect verbal expressions and from conduct. Thus, E. J. Hobsbawm observes that the classical city mobs, acting before they had access to formal political processes, manifested ideas in their actions.[52] Mob participants expected to achieve something, assumed that the authorities would be responsive to their actions, and directed their activities selectively against the rich and powerful. The focus here is on sustained intergroup struggles and adversaries with explicit goals, often formulated by leaders.

Membership Characteristics and Goals

Three aspects of a group's membership that impact the formation of contentious goals are leadership, culture and social system, and the members' grievances. Leaders of a conflict group play a primary role in formulating contentious goals. Discontent may be widespread among the members of a quasi-group but be dormant and festering. A leader, to mobilize followers for a struggle, must convince them that their grievances are attributable to the actions of other people. Leaders explain that view and help formulate the specific demands whose satisfaction would reduce or even end their grievance. Leaders holding offices of authority generally have advantages in making persuasive arguments. Thus, explanations by government or church officials tend to be accorded credence by those recognizing their legitimacy.

The leaders' assertion that a particular group is the cause of their grievance is often contested, particularly by those who are blamed. Indeed, feelings arising from internal sources may be displaced on some scapegoat, as in the case of attributing conspiracies to vulnerable minority groups, but also to elite groups, or external foes.

Government officials who attribute responsibility for a problem to a foreign power can usually count on the loyalty of their constituency in accepting the attribution. An extensive review of the U.S. public's response to foreign policy crises concludes, "It appears that, almost regardless of prior attitudes of the public, regardless of the popularity of the president and regardless of how well [or poorly] the president handles the crisis, a large proportion of the population will support him."[53] This is illustrated by the degree of support President George W. Bush was able to rally for a preemptive war against Iraq in 2003, despite the wide range of critics noting the lack of evidence of an imminent threat.[54] It is also evidenced by President Donald Trump's effort to blame the outbreak of the COVID-19 pandemic directly on the country of China though use of the phrases "the China virus" and the "Kung flu." In the weeks after Trump began to reference the virus in such terms, public opinion toward Asian Americans became more hostile as evidenced by the percentage of hashtags labeled "#covid19" or "#chinesevirus" that contained anti-Asian sentiments.[55] Such a dynamic, sometimes called the "rally around the flag" effect, is particularly pronounced during the peak of a crisis and tends to dissipate in intensity as the crisis ebbs.[56]

The task for would-be leaders of opposition groups is more difficult. They must rely more on charisma or use their legitimate authority based in a subunit of the social system whose leadership they would challenge. For example, Martin Luther King Jr. drew on his authority as the minister of the Dexter Avenue Baptist Church in Montgomery, Alabama, in helping to arouse and mobilize the Blacks of Montgomery to carry out the bus boycott initiated in 1955; he drew on his broader charisma to arouse the widening general support.[57]

In addition to leadership, culture and social context are additional aspects of a group's membership affecting the formation of goals. Which goals seem convincing depend in part on the experiences and belief systems of an adversary group's members. Thus, members who believe that they previously improved their condition by formulating goals that blamed others for their unsatisfactory conditions and also changed the others' conduct are likely to replicate that formulation. Thus, advocacy groups that have made gains by nonviolent demonstrations directed at elected government officials are likely to try such methods again.

Conversely, having formulated and pursued goals that were unsuccessful in the past discredits those goals from being pursued in the future. The goal is then reformulated, becoming more reformist and attainable, but sometimes becoming more extremist and radical; in the Middle East, changes in goals of Palestinian, Israeli, Islamic, and Arab groups illustrate both kinds of changes. At times, however, advocates on both sides argue that the goal had not been attained simply because it had not been pursued with sufficient vigor and persistence. Such differences in interpretation are often debated within each contending party.

Sociocultural and psychocultural qualities within a latent group help shape the emergence of contentious goals, as noted in chapter 2. These are usually relatively stable features of a quasi-group. Therefore, the formulation of a contentious goal requires new developments, which mesh with the established sociocultural and psychocultural tendencies.

Furthermore, the emergence and character of a contentious goal is greatly affected by the grievance to be redressed. By considering how different types of grievances affect the formulation of goals, we can resolve some of the apparent contradictions about the importance of different sources of discontent.

People who feel they are generally deprived or who suffer further deterioration of their condition tend to support more radical goals than do people with status inconsistency or whose improving conditions were halted. During the Great Depression of the 1930s, voices calling for radical change emerged within the U.S. labor movement. When economic conditions later improved, however, trade union members advocating more reformist goals regained influence.

The direction of goals, whether to the left or right, toward increasing or decreasing inequalities, also depends on the nature of the discontent. Even moderately deteriorating conditions for those who had been well-off dispose them to favor goals that restore previous inequalities. Thus, reactionary political movements have drawn disproportional support from such persons. Persons with ascribed or investment statuses that are higher than their achieved or reward statuses, such as persons with high ethnic ranking and low incomes, tend to support conservative or reactionary goals, while persons with over-rewarded kinds of inconsistencies, such as persons with low ethnic standing but high incomes, tend to support more egalitarian aims.[58]

The pattern of status inconsistency affects the content of contentious goals in other ways. People are inclined to raise themselves along the dimensions in which they have relatively low status and therefore tend to challenge those who are above them on those dimensions. This challenge helps shape their goal. Thus persons with low ethnic and high occupational and income levels try to raise the status of their ethnicity by campaigns against prejudice directed at their ethnic group. Jewish Americans organized effective organizations to wage such campaigns and as Arab Americans have become more numerous and prosperous, they have similarly organized.[59]

Contexts and Goals

The prevailing ways of thinking within the social environment also help channel the formulation of goals, pointing at who is to blame and what they must do to rectify the injustice. Thus in some eras and civilizations economic forces and class struggles are widely thought to be the predominant forces shaping social relations. Consider that in many parts of the world during much of the twentieth-century Marxist analyses of domestic and international relations were widely used to account for the injustices people experienced and to point to solutions. With the evident failures, immense social costs, and final collapse of the Soviet Union, Marxist analysis was widely discredited. The capitalist class was less often seen as the oppressor and a strong government less often regarded as a necessary counterforce.

For several decades, starting in the mid-1970s, the take-home pay of many U.S. workers declined; increasingly, families needed two earners to compensate for this decline.[60] Responsibility for the declining disposable income was variously attributed. Some people pointed to decreased worker productivity due to worker incompetence and laziness, to managerial shortsightedness and greed, to out of control executive salaries, or to the diversion of research and development investment into military projects. Others blamed the government for increasing taxes to support government bureaucrats, unnecessary military expenditures, giveaways to those who shirk working, or corruption and waste. Still others pointed to increasing competition within the U.S. economy by the growth of women's participation in the labor force and by new waves of immigration. Others emphasized the increasing globalization of the economy, pitting U.S. workers against the lower-paid workers in less economically developed countries; this was framed either as the necessary working of impersonal market forces or the machinations of international corporations.

Clearly, the nature of the goals formulated by members of an adversary group will be quite different depending on which combination of explanations they choose. Some of the variations in goals are presented and argued within the context of the institutionalized political system. Others fall outside of politics, erupting into the severe social conflicts of particular concern here. For example, in much of the world, for many decades grievances had become politicized and attributed to the persons who exercised power, particularly state power, rather than to impersonal social forces or to immoral conduct.[61] In the 1970s, women's oppression also came to be explained in terms of patriarchal thinking, differential control of resources, and state power.[62]

Politicization has often been combined with ideologies of a universalistic nature, such as Marxism, liberalism, and realism, which are universalistic in their applicability and in their openness, with believers trying to convince everyone to share their beliefs. Recent decades have seen a renewed attraction of more particularistic ideologies. This may have been partly a response to the impersonality of universal ideologies and to their failures to satisfy felt needs relating to communal and moral concerns. The attraction of particularistic ways of thinking is evident in the emphasis on ethnicity and some kinds of religious fundamentalism. Members of ethnic and religious communities celebrate their own ways and experiences, and some of them impose significant restrictions on persons who do not come from their community.

Nationalism combines ethnic and other communal identities with political claims, including having an independent state, and nationalism has long been an important influence in the formulation of contentious goals. Revolutionary challenges to a government can be aided by cloaking them in nationalistic claims. For example, a government may be charged with being the instrument of foreign powers; this has been the message of many revolutionary movements. This charge contributed to the mobilization of Iranian resistance to Shah Mohammad Reza Pahlavi, his government's collapse, and the coming to power of Ayatollah Ruhollah Khomeini in 1979.[63] Also, when the Soviet Union invaded Afghanistan in 1979 to maintain a Marxist-secular government there, the Afghan resistance flourished, drawing on nationalist and religious convictions.[64] Similar resistance has often occurred countering U.S. interventions in Latin America, the Middle East, and elsewhere.

The social environment helps each conflict group determine who its adversary is, and so influences its goals. Thus, the visibility and the vulnerability of different groups in a society make them more or less likely adversaries. Some groups, such as governments, are likely targets since they presume to be responsible for a wide range of social and economic as well as political conditions. Other groups, such as ethnic minorities, may be vulnerable to attack and available to be blamed for grievances arising from many sources. For example, traditions of anti-Semitism have made Jews such targets at various times in history.[65]

Another important aspect of the social context is the extent to which a social system appears to be closed and contracting. Insofar as potential adversaries regard themselves to be in a zero-sum situation, they formulate goals to redress their grievances in those terms. There may be predispositions, based on experience, for some groups of people to view their world as a limited one.[66] Conversely, experiencing expanding opportunities tends to dampen the belief that contending parties are in a zero-sum relationship. This tendency is exemplified by the reduced incidence of wars among European states when their colonial empires were expanding elsewhere.[67] In the nineteenth century, the United States' expanding economy and open frontier offers another example. Those conditions probably reduced the sense that people were living in a zero-sum society. Conversely, the economic stagnation of many African and Middle Eastern countries, even at the beginning of the twenty-first century, contributes greatly to the internal wars there.

Third parties and their possible evaluations also significantly influence the goals adversaries formulate. Contending groups often consider the reactions of such third parties to gain their support or lessen their opposition, and this sometimes gives a reason to moderate the goals to rally wider support.[68] The increasing globalization of the world tends to foster the engagement of more external parties in more conflicts; thus, domestic conflicts are becoming increasingly internationalized.

Importantly, the degree and form of institutionalized conflict regulation strongly affects the formulation of goals, particularly their lessened radicalism. Units that are part of a larger system with legitimate means of reaching collective decisions tend to construct reformist goals. Democracies provide mechanisms for resolving conflicts and help moderate the goals of various ethnic and other communal groups. The United Nations and other international organizations increasingly provide the venues for global and regional decision making on contentious matters.

Finally, the globalization of the world itself helps shape the formulation of goals, locating responsibility for grievances at the global level. Thus, environmental problems, such as climate change, are increasingly viewed as requiring global policies. In addition, the growth of economic integration and multinational corporations raises issues of control that cannot be managed at the national level.[69] Furthermore, the growth of international governmental bodies such as the International Monetary Fund, the World Bank, and the World Trade Organization locates power at the global level in regard to matters of widespread impact.[70] Partly as a result of these developments, as well as technological advances, transnational social-movement organizations proliferate and formulate goals to affect the conduct of each other and of multinational corporations and international governmental organizations.[71]

Adversary Relations and Goals

Adversaries significantly affect each other's goals. A potential conflict group may formulate objectives that in some ways mimic those of its opponent or develop ones that magnify the differences. An illustration of the former process may be seen in the formation of Zionist goals in response to the intensified persecution of Jews in Russia toward the end of the nineteenth century. Zionists aimed to establish a national home and have a social and economic life like the Russians and others among whom they lived, emphasizing productive labor, especially on the land. This was one kind of response to persecution and the denial of the right to own land and to farm. If they could not be accepted as Russians or Germans because they were Jews, then as Jews they would have their own country. When Zionism began to focus on Palestine, under British mandate, Palestinian nationalism, in turn, was aroused and was strongly affected by Palestinians' experience with Zionism and the establishment of Israel.[72]

The demands one party makes on another are also shaped by the structure of their relations with each other. For example, an analysis of agrarian revolutions demonstrates how certain agricultural relations generate revolutionary or reform goals. Noncultivators derive their income from the ownership of the land and the cultivators earn their income in the form of wages, as migratory workers. Revolutionary nationalist movements are likely to erupt in such migratory estate systems, and often did in colonial areas. Of course, certain other conditions must exist for such movements to emerge. For instance, if the migratory workers return to village subsistence holdings when the harvest ends, traditional tribal or peasant leadership can provide the resources needed for organization and workers have the time they need to collectively mobilize. Traditional village authorities will join the migratory laborers in the revolutionary nationalist movements "only when their own economic base of support is being ended by the same estate system that is exploiting the poor laborers."[73] This resulted in the rise of revolutionary movements in Vietnam and in Angola during the 1950s and 1960s.

The leaders and intellectuals who seek to formulate a goal for their group often do so considering the goal's utility not only for mobilizing their group, but also for influencing the adversary. If members of the enemy side can be induced to question the morality and justice of their position, then the chances of arousing feelings of guilt or shame, acts of defection, and readiness to yield will increase. Consequently, aims are often formulated in terms shared with the opponent—values such as justice, freedom, or equality, as when leaders of national independence movements lay claim to the rights of a people to rule themselves.

Finally, the attractiveness of pursuing a particular goal is affected by the group's feelings toward the adversary. If one group hates another, it will derive extra pleasure by pursuing an aim that humiliates its adversary. Vengeance can be sweet. The gratification from extracting retribution, however, may lead a group to pursue goals that become self-defeating or inflict self-losses. On the other hand, if positive feelings are strong enough, a goal may be chosen that minimizes the harm to the opponent, even if it fails to maximize the group's own benefits. The result may be mutually beneficial in the long term. For example, the transformation in South Africa, in the early 1990s, was managed with less destructiveness than many anticipated because the primary adversaries set goals that allowed each side to gain or retain minimal safeguards.[74]

BELIEVING REDRESS IS POSSIBLE

The fourth condition to be present for a conflict to emerge is the belief by at least one party's members that they can act to change an adversary and/or the adversary's conduct, thereby attaining more of what they want. Analysts of social conflicts increasingly recognize the importance of attaining this condition. This recognition reflects the change in emphasis in theories about the emergence of social movements. For many decades, the strain, alienation, or dissatisfaction experienced by some population groups was used to explain the rise of a social movement or revolutionary challenge. Beginning in the 1960s, such theories drawing from ideas about collective behavior were superseded by theories stressing how groups mobilize resources to seek redress for their grievances.[75] Discontent is taken for granted, but the ability to change conditions that are unsatisfactory explains the rise of challenging social movements. Even terrible conditions may be endured without contention if those who suffer them believe that they cannot correct the behavior of those they hold responsible.

The availability of legitimate and credible means of seeking redress provides alternatives to coercive contention. Within many societies, electoral politics or a judicial system may seem effective, which may keep the kinds of struggles examined in this book from emerging. Members of an adversary group come to believe that they can improve their unsatisfactory conditions by changing their antagonist when they believe either that their capabilities have grown stronger or that the capabilities of those they would change have weakened. Such new beliefs follow changes within the adversaries, changes in their social context, or changes in the relations among the adversaries.

Membership Characteristics and Redress

Among the many features of a potential group that contribute to its members' sense that they can act to reduce their grievances, two are particularly noteworthy: changing capabilities and leadership.

As members of a potential adversary group improve their conditions, their dissatisfaction may be expected to decline. But their improved conditions also tend to give them resources that prompt them to believe that their conditions can be improved even more. The earlier discussion of status inconsistency generating grievances is relevant here. If people have high ranks along particular dimensions, they are likely to have some resources that give them reason to believe they might raise their low rankings. On the other hand, research findings also indicate that status inconsistency does not always result in contentious behavior but may instead subject people to inconsistent claims and directives.[76] This would diminish the belief that unsatisfactory conditions could be corrected, and that dampens recognizing dissatisfaction. Furthermore, the discomfort of some kinds of rank inconsistencies may be expressed in anxiety, which also interferes with believing that unsatisfactory conditions can be improved.[77]

Leaders play a major role not only in shaping an identity, developing a sense of grievance, and formulating a conflict goal, but also in convincing their constituents that they can achieve their goals. This in part depends on offering an analysis of the opposing sides' relative weakness, claiming the sympathy of those not yet engaged in the struggle, and finally stressing their own significant resources.

Goals differ in the time needed to attain them. Leaders can help develop a long-term strategy with a sequence of subgoals, starting with relatively immediate and attainable ones that then provide the basis for reaching larger goals. For a conflict organization to mobilize support and sustain itself, the succession of goals must be closely related to the group's capacities relative to its opposition. Particularly for emerging conflict organizations, the formulation of short-term attainable goals is important in building confidence and gaining more support.[78] If the organization is to persevere and win its larger goals the immediate goals should be feasible and if reached should not end the sense of grievance.

Leaders also play an important role in attracting allies, forming coalitions of diverse interests.[79] This may be done by promising future benefits after victory, by offering side payments, and by appealing to shared values and interests. Those coalitions enable a conflict to be undertaken with a prospect of victory, and they also shape the goals of the conflict. For example, after the Iraqi invasion of Kuwait in August 1990, U.S. President George H. W. Bush was able to quickly construct a coalition including nearly all the Arab governments and the permanent members of the UN Security Council. This gave international legitimacy and the capability of threatening and waging a land war from Saudi Arabia. It also put constraints on the conflict; the coalition probably could not be held together for long without decisive action, and a goal limited to driving the Iraqi forces from Kuwait.

Leaders often try to convince their followers that they have the capability to wage a successful struggle by pointing to the past when they had what they now propose to achieve. For example, an ethnic leader may argue that in the past members of their ethnicity were much more advanced than the barbarian peoples around them. In addition, leaders often argue that the opposition is weak and getting weaker while their side is strong and getting stronger. Leaders agitate, then, not only by trying to increase their followers' discontent, but also by raising the hope that this can be changed, and by their own efforts. That seems paradoxical. To emphasize how exploited and victimized people are seems to contradict their possibility of bettering themselves. One solution to the paradox is to use the power of weakness. Desperation can engender determination and recklessness; having little, there is little that can be withheld from those who appear weak. Thus, Karl Marx and Friedrich Engels, in the *Communist Manifesto*, exhorted the workers of the world to unite in struggle, since "The proletarians have nothing to lose but their chains. They have a world to win."[80]

The task is often easier for leaders of a group with considerable resources in some arenas but dissatisfied in certain other arenas. An economically advantaged community may believe it can use its resources to gain more political autonomy and so not be required to share its resources with the disadvantaged of the larger society. Thus, in Spain the two regions with particularly strong movements for autonomy have long been Catalonia and the Basque country; both regions have been relatively advanced economically.[81]

Contexts and Redress

Various aspects of the adversaries' context affect a potential party's belief that it can change another group and so better its condition. For one, successes by other groups in making improvements against opposition provide models of what might be accomplished by struggle. They also may contribute to reinforcing belief in the efficacy of means of struggle, such as nonviolent resistance. Thus, surges of reliance on nonviolent action have followed significant applications, as occurred in Eastern Europe in 1989 and in North Africa and the Middle East in 2010 and 2011.

The social context includes people who are not clearly members of the adversary parties. They are an audience that the partisans address, pointing to the inequities they suffer to justify their action and to win support. Some members of that audience may be drawn into the struggle, and as they are, the conflict expands. An aggrieved party may seek redress, therefore, if its members believe their cause can be made visible and will win sympathy and support from persons not yet engaged in the struggle. This external audience can include various types of parties, including influential elites and opinion shapers, corporations, or nongovernmental organizations with a global reach.

Outsiders sometimes take the initiative in entering an emerging conflict situation. They tend to enter to help those with whom they feel linked by class, religion, ethnicity, ideology, or other interests or identities. They often help provide the means to sustain the struggle and so fuel the fight. For example, Ilham Tohti, an economist and member of the Uyghur minority community in China, has been a frequent and vocal critic of the Chinese government's treatment of the Uighur people in the Xinjiang region of Northwest China. Imprisoned for sedition for life in 2014 by the Chinese government, Tohti's work, and his cause, have received wide recognition by international nongovernmental organizations such as Amnesty International. In 2019, Tohti was nominated for the Sakharov Prize for Freedom of Thought, awarded annually by the European Union for individuals or groups who have dedicated their lives to the defense of human rights and freedom of thought. Among others nominated for the prize in 2019 were Restorers, a group of student app developers from Kenya, Russian opposition politician Alexei Navalny, and gay rights activist Jean Wyllys.

Adversary Relations Redress

A conflict is often initiated when members of a group with a grievance perceive that their opponent is relatively weak. An opponent may reveal such weakness in several ways. It may act inconsistently, hesitantly, and incompetently, and show disunion and lack of conviction in its own positions. That may give credence to the view that a deterioration of conditions is due to that party's failures, which also indicates its vulnerability to pressure. Thus, analysts of revolutions generally agree that one of the immediate causes of revolts is the appearance of uncertainty and of self-doubt among the authorities. This may be signaled by verbal signs of panic and by defections. Such signals invite more radical goals, if they indicate that fundamental restructuring of authority relations rather than reforms is needed and are becoming possible.

Changes in the relative power of potential antagonists are often the prelude to conflict emergence. For example, analyses of the great revolutions of France, Russia, and China reveal that the state in each case had been strained beyond its capacity by its international ventures.[82] More recently, numerous analysts have argued that the United States' extensive foreign policy commitments and disastrous foreign adventures in Iraq and Afghanistan, coupled with its eroding global economic dominance, has subjected it to bold challenges from other states or nonstate actors in the international community.[83]

Finally, it should be noted that a powerful group believing that it has overwhelming dominance may exploit that dominance and so provoke strong resistance from the exploited, subordinated, or vulnerable party. Consequently, extreme acts of repression may fail to be effective, convincing groups previously unengaged in a struggle that they have no alternative but to resist and resort to desperate methods. That can set the stage for a destructive conflict escalation.

SUMMARY AND DISCUSSION QUESTIONS

A conflict emerges when members of one or more potential antagonistic parties develop a shared identity, generate a sense of grievance, form a goal to change another party to reduce the grievance, and finally believe that they can bring about that change. These four conditions are highly interdependent, affecting each other as a struggle emerges.[84] Each is necessary, but none is sufficient alone; furthermore, various combinations of different levels of each can result in the initiation of a conflict. Together, they provide the impetus for at least one side to move against another, igniting a struggle.

It is important to remember, however, that most potential conflicts do not become manifest, and of those that do, most are managed using means regarded by the participants as legitimate. Often conflicts do not emerge because individuals find other means of coping with the inequalities and the differences that they find unsatisfactory. Seeking to escape from the relationship they find punishing, they emigrate, they divorce, or they quit their jobs. People also resist by using barely conscious ways to express their discontent. For example, in disliked employment relations, employees may arrive late, be absent, work slowly, or act ineptly. Individuals also frequently try to escape the unsatisfactory conditions by seeking personal advancement. Some curry favor with those with authority who can give them what they want. Others work hard, acting as they think their superiors want them to act. In some situations, as well, people may deny that anyone else is responsible for their unsatisfactory conditions and see no way out. They think their predicament is a matter of fate, luck, or God's will. Indeed, a culture of fatalism is often implicated in understanding why the oppressed and unhappy do not rebel.

When conflicts do emerge, the characteristics of the identity, grievance, goal, and method used to redress the grievance greatly affect how destructive the conflict becomes; as those characteristics change, so does the destructiveness of the conflict as it moves through its trajectory. This analysis has wide-ranging implications for reducing conflict destructiveness. The multiplicity of factors and processes that account for identities, grievances, goals, and means of struggle indicate that many ways exist for partisans and intermediaries to restructure a conflict so that it is waged more constructively. Individuals and groups can, for instance, inhibit the development of intensely antagonistic identities by arranging for regular interaction among potentially conflicting identity groups. They may ameliorate the grounds for severe grievances by creating institutionalized structures deemed by community members as fair to make distributional decisions. They may avoid goals that cast a fight in zero-sum terms, instead devising goals that are more likely achieved through integrative solutions resulting from collaboration. They may adapt more cognitively complex views on the origins and drivers of the conflict, thus diverting the formulation of goals that attribute responsibility for the grievance to a single "other."

Each of the possibilities suggested here can be adopted when individuals and groups wish to prevent conflict emergence. A final note, however, is that partisans at times may not want to prevent a conflict from emerging. In some instances, justice is served, and liberty is won, if a conflict is allowed to emerge and escalate. In these cases, which will be examined in the following chapters, the eruption of conflict may be inevitable. Here too, however, attention to constructive rather than destructive strategies will avoid new injustices and new denials of freedom and are more likely to inhibit the development of a destructive cycle of conflict.

Readers are encouraged to think about and discuss the following questions to deepen their understanding of this chapter.

1. Proving a negative is always difficult. It is, in general, easier to explain why something did happened than why it did not. Despite this difficulty, it is interesting to imagine why certain potential conflicts that seem like they should have emerged, have not. Identify one of these situations either from your own life or within broader societal relations in your community or country. Which of the factors examined in this chapter best explain why that potential struggle has not occurred? What lessons from that case could you carry forward to other cases?
2. With the discussion of collective identity presented in this chapter in mind, explore your own identity. Which, if any, of your identities are "organic," that is, unchanging and assigned at birth? Which of your identities are temporary, that is, a product of context, space, and time? How do these identities situate you in the world, providing you with advantages, disadvantages, or access? How are they implicated in the emergence of conflict?
3. Spend some time writing down all the identities that determine who you are in relation to the world. Then form a pair with another person you do not know very well. Before speaking to them, write down all the identities that you would ascribe to that person. They will do the same for you. Then share your lists. What do you notice about how your list of your own identities differs from the list that your partner developed about you? What does this exercise help you to understand about identity-based conflicts, stereotyping, and the potential of conflict transformation?
4. Consider a case of social conflict that you are familiar with. Examine the case using the identity, grievance, goals, and redress framework presented in this chapter. What factors not explored in this chapter might you add to your analysis to further explain the conflict's emergence?

Chapter Four

Alternative Conflict Strategies

Coercion, Reward, and Persuasion

A conventional understanding among many observers of conflicts is that injurious coercion is needed to induce an adversary to change against its will. Apply enough pressure, so the logic goes, and one's adversary will eventually yield. Without doubt coercion sometimes does result in getting an adversary to capitulate. This is evidenced by the ability of repressive regimes to stifle political opposition, the victory of one side over another during war, the successful use of strikes by laborers to force management to comply with their demands, and threats of physical violence between community members. Other times, however, the use of coercion to defeat an adversary results not in their capitulation but in a heightened devotion to their cause. This appears particularly true for dissensual conflicts, those where existential issues, group identity, or core values and worldviews are at stake. In these cases, injurious coercion seems to strengthen the cohesion and willingness to fight on the part of the attacked group. Coercion has other costs as well. Coercive strategies can damage relationships, psychologically and physically harm groups and individuals, lead to cycles of revenge that may be difficult to escape, and often lead to outcomes that are temporary and unstable.

In this chapter we argue that it is always possible for one or both sides to choose less violent and less coercive conflict strategies that are more likely to result in constructive forms of conflict transformation. For instance, one side may promise future benefits to an opponent if the opponent yields much of what it seeks. Or one party may try to convince its adversary that to provide what it requests would be in the adversary's own true interests. Such non-coercive inducements are often combined with some coercion, but often the coercion is limited and not necessarily destructive of positive future relationships between the adversaries.

CHOOSING STRATEGIES

A contending party's choice of conflict strategy is often a product of trial and error and generally shifts over time. Stakeholders to a conflict frequently adopt more than one strategy at the same time or use different strategies at different times as the conflict matures and the context changes. Moreover, since every conflict is interlocked with many others, a group within one contending party is likely to use different strategies with various antagonists, within and outside its camp, and with parties that have diverse stakes in the conflict.

Often, a party's selection of a conflict management strategy does not entail consciously considering alternatives whose likely effectiveness is assessed, or their costs weighed, before being selected. At times, a tactic may be used simply because it appears to be the only reasonable one available, a similar strategy worked in the past, or because so many resources have been dedicated to the current strategy that changing course seems unthinkable.[1] Sometimes conflicts are highly institutionalized, and the adversaries mutually agree to employ one mode of conflict management, as occurs in cultures with norms regarding duels, feuds, strikes, judicial proceedings, and so on. Other times the parties disagree about what mode is being used; one side may proclaim it is engaging in respectful petition or protest, while the other regards the conduct as an unlawful threat to authority and violently represses it. No single party wholly determines how a struggle is conducted; rather, the adversaries jointly shape their mode of struggle.

Whatever the circumstances, alternative conflict strategies are always conceivable. Identifying them and understanding why they were or were not chosen is critical if we are to learn to wage conflicts more constructively.

COERCION, REWARD, AND PERSUASION

To examine the adoption and the consequences of different conflict modes, it is useful to consider three primary kinds of inducements available to conflicting parties: coercion, reward, and persuasion.[2]

Coercive Inducements

Coercion is a major element of the struggles examined in this book. It refers to actions, including symbolic ones, that injure or threaten to injure the adversary. Coercive inducements include efforts to intimidate and deter the opponent or to force the opponent to comply with the demands made by the coercer. The cessation of coercive action, then, is conditional on the opponent's compliance.

One significant difference in the form that coercion can take is between threatened and actualized coercion. Coercion is generally threatened before being applied, in the hope that the threat will suffice. In foreign policy the idea of a "red line," for instance, is often used as a warning to an adversary about what actions would result in a severe consequence. For example, U.S. presidents have often proclaimed that the use of chemical weapons by a regime against its people is a red line that, if crossed, would lead to some form of retaliation.[3] Another important distinction lies between violent and nonviolent coercion. Violent coercion refers to threatened or actual direct physical death or injury to people or destruction of part of their valued material world. Nonviolent coercion, on the other hand, refers to actions that do not physically harm an adversary but, rather, induce a change though means such as sit-ins, boycotts, noncooperation, or strikes.[4]

The magnitude of coercive inducements varies greatly, but not along a single dimension. A high level of coercion is evident when force is used to change the conditions of the target group. At the most extreme this would include, for instance, widespread violent attack on members of an opposing partisan, as in cases of war. More typically, coercion is used against only some members of the opposing sides, thus weakening and intimidating enough of the other side so that the entire body is obliged to comply. This would include attacks against the other side's leading figures, as happen in January 2020 when a missile fired by a U.S. drone killed top Iranian General Qasem Soleimani and nine other individuals as they were traveling by convoy nearby the Baghdad International Airport.[5] Violent coercion also includes police repression of opposition figures and torture or disappearances of political activists.

Nonviolent coercion, such as boycotts or economic sanctions, is generally considered to be of lower magnitude than violent coercion.[6] For instance, a threat may be made to withhold payment or services on which the other party depends, as often occurs in labor-management disputes. In valued personal relations, the mere expression of disapproval or anger is also an example of nonviolent coercion.

For threats of coercion to be effective they must appear credible to the threatened. That means the party making the threat must seem capable and willing to execute it. For example, a government threatening warfare must build and maintain a powerful military force that is perceived by the other side as having a capability to inflict serious harm and the readiness to bear the costs of the likely counter blows. Thus, in international politics many countries counter an adversary by building up such military capabilities that an external attack would be unthinkable to its foe for fear of retaliation, a strategy known as deterrence.[7] Carrying out a threat can have high costs, both in terms of exercising the coercion and suffering the consequences of retribution. Failing to follow through with a threat, when compliance is not won, is also costly, damaging future credibility with constituents as well as external adversaries and allies. Such risks deserve consideration by adversaries before making threats.

Finally, coercion can be an uncertain and imprecise means of inducing an adversary to change. In large-scale conflicts trying to induce the leaders of the adversary to change may involve subjecting their constituents to massive violent coercion Horrific arial bombardments of cities such as London, Berlin, Hamburg, Dresden, and other cities during World War II, for instance, killed tens of thousands of civilians. Similarly, Russia's policy of indiscriminate destruction of civilian infrastructure across portions of Ukraine in 2022 resulted in the death thousands and the displacement of millions. Such coercion seeks to undermine the willingness of an opponent to fight on. In reality, however, coercive tactics such as these often turn counterproductive as the initially wavering constituency rallies to support their leadership against the outside attacker. Such was the case in Ukraine where Russian attacks solidified in-group solidarity and strengthened the hand of President Volodymyr Zelensky to organize an effective Ukrainian resistance and an international alliance to counter Russia. The use of broad and unselective coercion, then, tends to widen the conflict, add to its destructiveness, and sometimes prolong it. Finally, the resulting animosities and destruction severely hampers the attainment of mutually agreeable relations afterward.

Rewards as Inducements

Rewards as a form of inducement are commonly used but are relatively neglected in thinking about social conflicts. In child rearing and learning generally, an extensive body of theory and research indicates the value of using rewards rather than punishments when seeking to alter the behavior of another.[8] For example, positive behavior recognition therapies with adolescents tends to support self-esteem, cultivate moral reasoning, and build prosocial behavior.[9] This principle is also observable in large-scale conflicts. For example, negotiations concluded between Iran and the five permanent members of the UN Security Council over Iran's nuclear program in 2015 promised normalized diplomatic and economic relations in exchange for Iran's compliance with technology restrictions and external nuclear oversight. Although dismantled by the Trump administration in 2016, the Biden administration again has turned to positive sanctions to induce Iran to come back to the negotiation table, so far with no success. Positive sanctions such as these are more likely to be used and to be effective in the closing stages of a conflict than during a period of escalation or of intense antagonism. That is because offers of benefits while a conflict is being waged with great coerciveness tend to be regarded with suspicion by the recipient.[10] In these cases, initial measures, such as an exchange of prisoners on each side, may be an initial, albeit less dramatic, way of signaling the possibility of eventually normalizing relations. These types of interim steps designed to gradually build trust are often called confidence-building measures.

Rewards come in many forms and may include money, land, or promises of access to occupational positions. In addition, rewards may involve less tangible offers, such as approbation or status recognition. President Donald Trump's diplomatic meetings with North Korean Chairman Kim Jong-un in Singapore in 2018 and the demilitarized zone and in Hanoi in 2019, for example, provided the North Korean leader with a degree of international legitimacy and standing that he apparently craved. Kim was the first North Korean to meet with a sitting U.S. president, a concession that the Trump administration believed would pave the way for a negotiated agreement to reverse North Korea's nuclear weapons program.

As is true for negative sanctions, the recipients of positive sanctions vary in susceptibility. Certain individuals or factions within the opposing side in large-scale conflicts are more likely to obtain the benefits than are others. Hardliners within opposing sides may fear they will lose influence and power if a mutual de-escalating accommodation is reached. In addition, at times one faction may choose to accept positive inducements while another faction steadfastly refuses them, leading some to call those that refuse peaceful overtures "spoilers" of peace processes.[11] Often benefits may be covertly offered to the leaders of the opposing side, knowing that exposed acceptance would be regarded as corruption or treason. In collective bargaining situations, some agreements are considered "sweetheart contracts" because they offer little to the workers and imply that the union negotiator has received side payments from the management.

Over time rewards can be part of a powerful strategy for constructive conflict transformation. Labor relations in the North America and Europe is an instructive example. In the nineteenth and twentieth centuries, class conflict erupted between workers and the owners of the industries where the workers were employed, sometimes leading to confrontations, many of which were violently suppressed. Yet gradually in most of these countries, governments began to implement social welfare policies and laws to protect workers, largely with the acquiescence of the dominant economic class. Members of the wealthy class in those countries saw that the stability of the society so purchased would be to their benefit as well as to the workers' benefit. In part this recognition was the result of coercion, but also of the persuasive efforts of the workers and their middle-class allies to show that solidarity between workers could not be violently suppressed.

Persuasive Inducements

Persuasive inducements are efforts to influence an opponent by normative arguments, facts, or appeals designed to alter the other side's feelings or perceptions of the conflict.[12] Since conflicts arise and persist only because adversaries believe they have incompatible goals, persuasion can play a significant role in their emergence, escalation, and transformation.

Persuasive inducements are sometimes difficult to assess because antagonists rarely acknowledge that the enemy has convinced them of anything. Nevertheless, persuasive inducements have clear transforming effects. This is evident in the past four decades, during which the advocates of same-sex marriage have overcome resistance to bring about immense changes in marriage equality in much of the world. This struggle, which has relied heavily on persuasive inducements, has produced a profound social-cultural transformation that continues to spread. Pew Research Center polling in 2004, for example, revealed that most Americans opposed same-sex marriage by a margin of 60 percent to 31 percent. Since that time support for same-sex marriage has grown rapidly with 2019 Pew polling revealing that most Americans (61 percent) support same-sex marriage, while 31 percent oppose it. Changing attitudes about marriage equality are due to several overlapping forces. These include the 2015 Supreme Court ruling in *Obergefell v. Hodges* legalizing gay marriage nationwide, strong support for same-sex unions among young people, increasing interpersonal contact with gays and lesbians, a rise in overall level of education, and an overall decline in religiosity.[13]

Persuasive efforts are likely to be more effective at the initial stages of conflict emergence before mutual mistrust has intensified. At this point the parties to the conflict are more likely to have cross-cutting ties and open channels of communication. During the highly escalated phase of a conflict persuasive inducements are much less likely to succeed because avenues for interaction have closed, coercive inducements dominate, and hostile intergroup narratives dominate. Later, as a conflict enters a de-escalating phase, persuasive inducements may be renewed as one or both sides try to convince the other that their common interests should be given higher priority. The resulting reframing of the conflict marks its transformation and may be aided by a mediator's redefinitions and restructuring.[14]

Persuasive inducements vary widely in content, depending on who is trying to influence whom, what the issues in contention are, and the stage the struggle has reached. Such efforts may be couched in appeals to shared values about justice, fairness, or freedom where the other side is urged to concede what is being sought. Persuasive inducements may also be applied by other parties with a stake in the fight or even by intermediary groups, some of whom may try to convince the adversaries that they have common or complementary interests and that those interests would be well served by making what previously had been regarded as concessions.[15]

Adversaries who become convinced that they have a common enemy have a reason to moderate or even settle their conflict with each other and form a coalition to confront their shared enemy. One of the adversaries may persuade the other of the salience of this shared antagonist, or an intermediary may try to persuade two antagonists about the dangers from a third party. It is also possible that the adversaries become convinced that they have an opportunity for mutual gain by cooperation. Finally, the adversaries may be persuaded to recognize they share a problem that can best be overcome by their joint efforts. Thus, although labor unions and environmental organizations often are in contention, pitting interests in jobs against protecting the environment, collaborative alliances sometimes are made between them. This is happening currently with the BlueGreen Alliance, a partnership between labor unions and environmental organizations in the United States that seeks to promote clean energy economy, economic opportunities, and the reduction of the threat of climate change. In the case of this alliance, a mutual interest in good jobs, a resilient infrastructure, and fair trade provides room avenues for environmental-business collaboration across multiple fronts.[16]

A contending party may also seek to persuade their opponent that what it wants does not endanger that opponent's interests. As noted previously, advocates of marriage equality have long argued that same-sex couples were merely asking for the same constitutional rights already enjoyed by heterosexual couples. In announcing the historic Supreme Court ruling for a constitutional guarantee of the right to same-sex marriage in the United States, Justice Kennedy noted that the plaintiffs were simply seeking "equal dignity in the eyes of the law."

Finally, persuasive inducements may provide information to convince the opponent that agreement would be advantageous to them. The information is likely to be expressed as predictions of future losses or foregone gains if the other side does not change as desired. Predictions of future losses, generally called warnings, foretell terrible consequences, but only if those matters are not under the persuader's control. If they are, the predictions are regarded as threats. For example, leaders of a protesting organization may point out that if they fail to get what they seek, another leadership or a rival organization will take over and be even more hostile. Information may also come in the form of forecasting future benefits if the opponent changes and agrees to concede; for example, other groups would praise them. If what is predicted is under the control of the party making the predictions, it is a promise; when it is not, it has been called a mendation.[17]

In conflict relations, partisans often say that actions speak louder than words. Indeed, appeals, arguments, and information frequently are more convincingly conveyed by the contending party's behavior than by what it says. The gestures, policies, and dozens of other kinds of actions by members of a contending party are observed and interpreted by the other side and provide credibility to the words uttered. We cannot fully separate persuasive inducements from other kinds of inducements. In any mode of waging a conflict, positive and negative sanctions tend to be combined with persuasive efforts. Thus, in a war, psychological techniques are used to encourage enemy soldiers to surrender.[18] During the East-West Cold War, each side used various propaganda methods to undermine support of the other's leadership. In the American struggle against the Islamic State and other radical Islamic groups, persuasive efforts are widely recognized as vital to deny those groups support from mainstream Muslims.

STRATEGIES AND MODES OF STRUGGLE

Coercive and noncoercive inducements are combined in many ways to during a conflict. They may be short-term tactics such as a protest march or long-term strategies such as a guerrilla war. What strategies are relied upon at any time is a product of the conflict environment, that is, the relative power and leverage each side holds, levels of public support, leadership, commitment to the cause, capacity to wage the struggle, and the involvement of external actors in the fight.

Often, long-term strategies incorporate many tactics conducted in sequence. In the twenty-year struggle against the Taliban in Afghanistan, for example, the United States regularly vacillated between the use of overwhelming coercive force and the use of negotiation and positive inducements to achieve its interests, often combining the two. Even after the U.S. military departed Afghanistan, diplomats continued to use a combination of threats of withholding future aid and promises of political recognition to influence Taliban decision making. Meanwhile, of course, the Taliban were cycling among different strategies as well, even using different strategies with different kind of opponents. For instance, as it became clear to the Taliban in 2020 that the United States intended to withdraw from Afghanistan, they continued their strategy of violent confrontation when it came to Afghan government forces but adopted a strategy of cooperation with the Americans to secure their departure from Kabul in August and September 2021.

Many modes of conflict management revolve around a familiar set of methods, beliefs, and practices that are repeated over time. These can be thought of as social constructs. Adversaries may agree, for example, that a particular action is part of "collective bargaining," a form of conflict management between labor and management where unions negotiate contracts with employers to settle issues related to pay, benefits, health and safety provisions, and other terms of employment. They then share certain expectations about what the other side will do, and both feel constrained not to act outside the mutually understood rules. Similarly, legal systems are collectively enacted to provide procedures by which many disputes and conflicts are conducted and settled within a society.

Institutionalized Conflict Regulation

Since social conflicts are omnipresent, every social system has contrived ways to manage them.[19] Within all societies, there are rules for conducting and settling conflicts that become institutionalized over time. The judicial system in most countries implements regulations regarding disputes between individuals and/or corporate entities. The decision makers in these systems tend not to be the disputants themselves, but authorities such as judges, juries, or heads of religious or political organizations. Adversaries generally pursue and resolve conflicts by their own actions within the confines of such institutionalized regulations, as when conflicts between developers and environmentalists are conducted by the parties according to laws regarding zoning, wetland protection, and endangered species. Sometimes institutionalized modes of conflict management become so ingrained that the conflicts being managed are regarded as games more than as fights. In democratic societies, some more than others, electoral politics may be so habitual and so well regulated that contesting political parties are not regarded as being in a social conflict, except metaphorically. By the definition used in this book, however, they are in conflict.

Degree of Regulation

As previously noted, rules often govern many aspects of adversarial conduct, which can be true even for conflicts waged with deadly violence. Thus, in many societies quarreling men have fought duels in which careful protocol was followed that might result in a death.

Wars, too may be quite limited, as were European wars between about 1640 and 1740 when contending sides mutually agreed to cease fighting to gather the harvest, compared with the relatively unlimited wars of the prior two centuries.[20] However, with the establishment of large armies of conscripts at the end of the eighteenth century and the development of mechanized war fighting in the nineteenth and twentieth centuries, the scale of wars, the capabilities of killing people, and the deaths inflicted upon civilians grossly increased, reaching extreme levels in World War I. More war horrors followed. In response to the horrors of World War I, World War II, and the large-scale killings in internal wars and genocides, numerous treaties, international resolutions, and other efforts were made during the twentieth century to prevent and restrain particular ways of killing people. These treaties and understandings have been widely accepted, and they have been largely observed.[21] For example, since the dropping of two atom bombs in 1945, neither nuclear nor bacteriological weapons have been employed in warfare. Chemical weapons have generally not been used since World War I. Three exceptions are notable: in 1988 during the Iraqi Iranian war, Saddam Hussein used chemical weapons on Kurdish citizens of Iraq; during the Syrian civil war, government forces deployed chlorine, sarin, and mustard gas against civilian and military targets in 2014 and 2018; and chemicals were used as a defoliating agent by U.S. military forces in the war in Vietnam.

The content of rules governing conflict engagement is crucial. International norms regarding human rights and democracy have influenced the rules established in countries that are in transition away from authoritarian control.[22] The rules often help provide safeguards for individual and group security and procedures to challenge the privileges of the dominant political party, class, ethnicity, or other groups. Many international governmental and nongovernmental organizations are influential in helping establish such rules, including the Organization for Security and Cooperation in Europe, the UN Development Programme, and the European Union.

The term "conflict regulation" refers to the rules that govern the contending parties' conduct in a dispute. But rules that are unilaterally imposed cannot be regarded as regulations, nor are policies that allow one party to violently suppress another and that are used as a mask for partisan struggle. Authentic regulation exists insofar as the contending parties recognize each other's legitimacy and regard the rules governing their conflict as legitimate. Moreover, the existence of a government exercising control in a country does not in itself ensure the protection of human rights for the people in that country. Many of the worst atrocities in modern human experience have been conducted by government leaders against their own people, claiming legitimate authority and promising a future utopia; this is epitomized by the imprisonment and killing of millions of people by the totalitarian regimes of the Soviet Union headed by Joseph Stalin, of Nazi Germany headed by

Adolf Hitler, of the People's Republic of China led by Mao Zedong, and of the Cambodian Khmer Rouge headed by Pol Pot.[23]

Degree of Institutionalization

The existence of legitimate sanctions to punish violations and sanctions to reward compliance are crucial elements of the institutionalization of regulations and their maintenance.[24] Sanctions that may be employed by officials, religious leaders, charismatic leaders, or friends include punishments such as fines or incarceration and rewards such as social acclaim or the promise of everlasting life in heaven. Rules embodied in written form or orally transmitted beyond one generation take on an independent quality that helps maintain and foster adherence to them. Persons accorded the authority to do so may codify these rules, making the rules less vulnerable to differing interpretations by contending parties. Institutionalization is increased when all the adversary parties as well as the other members of their social system internalize the pertinent regulations.[25] When the rules are internalized through socialization and other social learning, people generally police themselves and anticipate feeling guilty or ashamed if they violate the rules.

Bases of Regulation and Institutionalization

The fundamental factor underlying the content of the rules governing conflict behavior and the institutionalization of the rules is prior recurrent practices. Repeated actions come to be expected and deviations become not only violations of these expectations, but also illegitimate.[26] The social logic for such codification is compelling: the way things are done is the way they should be done because that is the way they have been done. In the advanced consolidated democracies such as Sweden, Iceland, and New Zealand, for example, it would be unthinkable for a political party that loses an election to take up arms to prevent the prevailing party from assuming office. Yet in many areas of the world, including most recently the United States, such practices do occur, often with regularity.[27]

The adversaries' anticipation of continuing relations fosters regulation of conflicts, while the absence of expected ongoing relations removes the incentive for regulatory compliance. Furthermore, insofar as the contending parties expect that they will have recurrent conflicts, they tend to develop shared understandings about how they should each pursue their goals, and other ways of fighting come to be regarded as wrong.[28] It follows that those patterns of conflict behavior that are stable and expected to remain stable tend to become institutionalized.

Several aspects of the relationship between the contending parties greatly affect the development of rules regarding their conflict behavior. Insofar as the parties are integrated with each other and have a shared culture, their conflict behavior will be regulated, while great separation and autonomy hampers conflict regulation. The level of inequalities between the adversaries also affects the regulation of their conflict behavior, but in contradictory ways. On the one hand, insofar as the parties are equal, rules governing their conflict behavior will be more equitable and adherence to them will be more acceptable to all parties. On the other hand, insofar as some parties have greater resources to shape the rules, those rules tend to serve their interests. Furthermore, the likelihood that rules will be enforced is greater when it appears to be in the interest and capability of persons to enforce them. Consequently, not only do the rules themselves tend to serve the interests of those who are dominant in the social system, but also those rules that particularly favor the dominants are the ones most likely to be enforced. Systems with a high degree of institutionalized privilege afforded to those with power are often condemned as unjust by subordinated people and analytically are deemed to exhibit "structural violence."[29]

The characteristics of the contending parties also affect the development of conflict rules and their institutionalization. Thus the culture of a party affects the likelihood that some procedures and not others will be considered legitimate and amenable to institutionalization. Many of the Catalan people in Spain, for example, think of themselves as "deal makers" who have always tended to negotiate about issues in dispute. They offer that as an explanation for their successful negotiated achievement of regional autonomy.[30] More generally, in Western societies disputants in a controversy tend to have internalized expectations that disputes only have winners and losers, and their contentious behavior is guided by that expectation. In many traditional societies, and often in Asian cultures, generally the goal is to restore harmonious relations between the contending parties, and participants and intermediaries have internalized those expectations so that conflict becomes a search for resolutions that will enable the parties to resume coexistence in reasonable tranquility. Such broad cultural generalizations should not be overdrawn; there are individual and group variations within every culture. Furthermore, cultural patterns change over time and vary in different circumstances.[31]

The structure of governance within a social system also profoundly affects the content and institutionalization of conflict rules. In all social systems legitimate agents of an overarching social system seek to impose rules governing conflict between constituent contending parties. Such efforts are most successful in situations where governance bodies collaboratively fashion rules, have the capacity to enforce them, and enjoy legitimacy in the eyes of the affected social groups. Where these conditions are absent, social systems may suffer from fragmented, decentralized, or ineffective modes of conflict management. For example, at the international level supranational institutions have increasingly used international treaties and institutions to manage spheres of social, political, economic, and military affairs, notably evident in human rights violations. The establishment and functioning of the International Court of Justice, ad hoc tribunals, and the International Criminal Court are illustrative of that trend.[32] However, in a world where state sovereignty is a major legal norm, supranational institutions often lack the capacity to enforce the principles that they champion. The International Court of Justice, for example, has no ability to force states to appear before it nor can it force states to submit to its judgments. On the other hand, those who violate laws within countries that have well-developed legal systems can be compelled by local or state authorities to conform to the institutionalized rules.

Globalization, in its many dimensions, not only helps in ameliorating large-scale conflicts, but also unleashes and exacerbates such conflicts. Groups from different societies that lack shared understandings encounter each other and generate intense antagonisms with few shared rules about how to handle the consequent conflicts. The reaction of some Muslim Salafists to Western influence can spur efforts to revitalize a radical Islam transnationally.[33] Consequently, international networks, such as the Islamic State, can emerge, whose members, based on their own self-reinforcing understandings, can feel justified in extreme attacks against alien others.

Finally, the kind of issues in contention profoundly affects the degree to which conflict behavior is controlled by institutionalized regulations. For example, conflicts in which the contending parties do not think their vital interests or fundamental identities are at stake tend to be relatively susceptible to institutionalized regulation. Also, some contentious issues seem relatively divisible, which makes them more amenable to negotiated resolution.

ILLUSTRATIVE STRATEGIES

To illustrate how coercive, rewarding, and persuasive inducements may be combined in various ways to constitute a strategy of struggle, we discuss four sets of strategies that employ different combinations of inducements. The strategic approaches are nonviolent actions (Nv), terrorist actions (Tr), coengagements (Ce), and problem-solving meetings (Ps) (Figure 4.1).

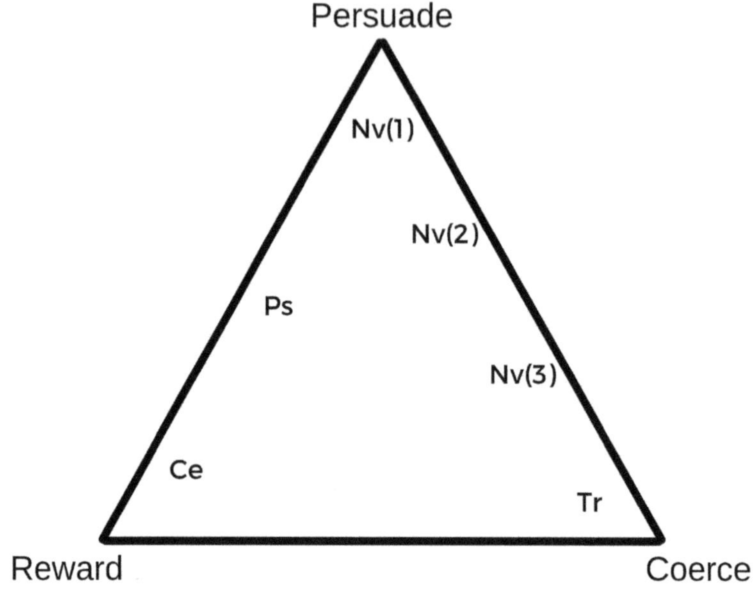

Figure 4.1. Strategies Combining Inducements

Nonviolent Actions (Nv)

Nonviolent actions are often used to bring about and to resist political, cultural, economic, and other major changes.[34] Sometimes participants in these nonviolent efforts, and often the resisting authorities, have resorted to violence as well. Participants in large-scale struggles employ a variety of nonviolent actions, combining different degrees of coercion, persuasion, and reward.[35] For example, a demonstration in which protesters march, distribute information, and carry banners expressing their views is largely an effort at persuasion. By publicizing a cause, and illustrating a commitment to it, demonstrators are seeking to persuade their audience to see that cause in a new light. Many such actions would be located about the point "Nv(1)" in Figure 4.1.

More typically, nonviolent action refers to activities that have larger and more severe coercive components. This includes withholding purchases, goods, or services, as in boycotts and strikes—located at point "Nv(2)" in Figure 4.1. Such actions are often intended to communicate how important the goal is to those making the claim and are usually executed in compliance with institutionalized rules. The effort of the Boycott, Divestment, Sanctions (BDS) movement is a case in point. Organized by Palestinians and supported by a network of international activists, BDS seeks to draw attention to oppressive Israeli policies toward Palestinian communities and to encourage people and governments to boycott select Israeli-produced goods, divest in Israeli companies, and put implement economic sanctions on the state of Israel. The BDS strategy appears to have had some success at impacting attitudes among targeted populations. A recent University of Maryland poll found that close to half of those polled (49 percent) in the United States said they have heard about BDS at least "a little." Of those individuals, 26 percent said they supported the movement, 26 percent were neutral, and 47 percent opposed it.[36]

Other nonviolent actions are based on noncompliance to laws that the challengers regard as unjust, such as laws upholding segregation between ethnic communities. Such noncompliance can be carried out in ways that disrupt or prevent those who practice segregation from doing so—located at point "Nv(3)" in Figure 4.1. This was the case with battles to desegregate public accommodations in the U.S. South, waged by civil rights organizations during the early 1960s. Their actions had coercive components but embodied persuasive elements as well, since they were conducted in a manner to avoid hurting the people whose actions they sought to change, even at the cost of enduring violence themselves. The actions were presented as demonstrating the importance of ending segregation. The demonstrators expressed their view of segregation as immoral, but their demonstrating was done without hate and with the promise that once the segregated practices were ended, mutual benefits would follow.

Practitioners of nonviolent actions usually represent their efforts as not solely coercive since they seek to persuade opponents of the mutual benefits in changing their objectionable conduct. The opponents are told, for example, that they will better satisfy their own value commitments to their country or to God.

Mohandas Gandhi developed a comprehensive approach to principled nonviolence in the struggle he led for the independence of India from Great Britain.[37] His approach, termed *satyagraha*, or "truth force," has been influential throughout the world. Three concepts are fundamental in satyagraha: truth, nonviolence, and self-suffering. For Gandhi, truth is God; it is an end we seek, but since we cannot know absolute truth, its pursuit excludes the use of violence. Nonviolence does not imply the negative action of not harming, but positive love, of doing good to the evildoer. It does not mean acquiescence to the wrong, but resistance to the wrongdoer, even if that does injure the wrongdoer. Self-suffering means a willingness to endure suffering, not out of weakness but out of courage to refrain from violence even when it is possible to use violence. It is directed at moral persuasion.

Other advocates and practitioners of nonviolent action argue for its use on pragmatic grounds, asserting it is more effective, more durable, and less costly in human life than violent conflict strategies. A well-known 2011 study of nonviolent versus violent change movements has shown, for instance, that nonviolence tactics succeed, or partially succeed, at achieving objectives more often than do violent tactics.[38] Of course conflict analysts recognize that in actual struggles, violent actions often occur in conjunction with nonviolent behavior.[39] Different organizations within each side may use alternative and often complementary nonviolent means, the mixture changing within the course of a conflict. Even within a single movement, different factions may adopt fundamentally different strategies to bring about desired change, as evidenced by the activities of Provisional Irish Republican Army's paramilitary and political wings during the 1970s, 1980s, and 1990s.

Whether principled or pragmatic, some features of nonviolent actions tend to foster constructively waged rather than destructively waged struggles. Certainly, the adversary tends to be less dehumanized by the process; indeed, nonviolent action often appeals to the empathy and reasonableness of the adversary. It can even garner respect from the adversary, often a goal of a people who have been viewed as inferior. As Martin Luther King Jr. wrote in 1963 about the civil rights struggle, "The Negro's method of nonviolent direct action is not only suitable as a remedy for injustice; its very nature is such that it challenges the myth of inferiority. Even the most reluctant are forced to recognize that no inferior people could choose and successfully pursue a course involving such extensive sacrifice, bravery, and skill."[40]

Nonviolent action often gains effectiveness by attracting support and allies who are impressed by the demonstration of commitment and the lack of generalized threat such action seems to convey. This may be seen in trade union organizing and strike efforts. For example, in the 1960s, Cesar Chávez effectively mobilized consumer boycotts against grapes to support the strike efforts of the National Farm Workers Association.[41]

In international relations, economic sanctions are increasingly used and regarded as a nonviolent form of coercion. The suffering imposed on the general population and the limited effectiveness of sanctions have led to proposals to employ narrowly targeted or "smart" sanctions.[42] Targeted sanctions are directed at decision makers and include freezing of financial assets, arms embargoes, flight bans, and travel bans. Smart sanctions have been a favored tool of the West to coerce authoritarian regimes into complying with international norms or resolutions to mixed effect. Many have argued, for instance, that economic oil and financial sanctions on Iran throughout the Bush and Obama administrations paved the way to Iran's agreeing to the July 2015 Joint Comprehensive Plan of Action with the P5+1 group, led by the United States, an agreement that was scuttled by the Trump administration in 2018.[43]

Others contend that even smart sanctions are often too blunt, easy to bypass in the complicated world of international finance, and still may incur grave humanitarian costs.[44] As with all international economic sanctions, their effectiveness depends on a number of factors, one of which is adaptation by a broad cross-section of the international community.[45] The more fundamental factor affecting the impact of sanctions is the intended goal and what the target of the sanctions believes is the goal. If the targeted group believes the goal is its elimination, it will resist what it regards an existential threat and not yield to the demands of the sanctioning parties.

Terrorist Actions (Tr)

Since the attacks in the United States of September 11, 2001, and the ensuing efforts by the U.S. government to counter terrorist attacks, a great many people have tried to account for terrorism and propose ways to respond to it. Yet there is no universal agreement even about defining terrorism. Persons identifying with the targeted people generally use the term "terrorism" pejoratively to condemn certain antagonistic actions by an enemy and to justify strong countermeasures. Such usage is relevant for understanding the course of many large-scale conflicts, but it hampers comprehensive analyses of the phenomenon.

The solution taken here is to start with a broad definition of terrorist actions, and then distinguish different aspects of such actions, which various groups use to label certain actions as terrorist. A broad definition is acts or threatened acts of violence in order to create fear and compliant behavior in a victim or audience for some collective purpose.[46] Terrorism so defined fits in the coercion corner of Figure 4.1: Tr(1). Various groups use qualities of such acts to further delimit what they judge to be "terrorism," including qualities of the act, its target, the perpetrator, and the context of the actions.

For many people, to be designated terrorist, the actions must be unusually gruesome and frightening. This may mean not just killing someone, but also desecrating the body and exhibiting the result. Thus, when the Ku Klux Klan (KKK) acted to restore white domination of Blacks in the U.S. South after the Civil War, KKK members publicly lynched Black Americans. Bodies were left hanging from tree limbs and were sometimes mutilated.[47]

We must consider which kinds of violent behavior are so outrageous and terrifying that significant numbers of people regard them as terrorist. Obviously, what people regard as abhorrent and beyond the conventional limits depends on their normative standards. The capacity of humans to commit atrocities and still believe they are acting properly certainly helps propel conflicts destructively.

Terrorism is also defined according to the targets of the action. Violent attacks on noncombatants are widely regarded as terrorism. For instance, the Center for International Development and Conflict Management, at the University of Maryland, defines terrorism as "the intentional targeting of civilian, noncombatant populations."[48] This view is so widespread that violence directed against ordinary citizens and particularly children is likely to be counterproductive for the perpetrators' cause. Particularly if an individual or small group commits such actions, they and their cause often are discredited, as happened after the bombing of the federal building in Oklahoma City on April 19, 1995.

On the other hand, a wide variety of military actions, such as shelling, bombing, setting booby traps, or planting landmines, if directed against other combatants, tend not to be regarded as terrorist, even if many noncombatants are the victims. In contemporary warfare, rules have been established to limit civilian casualties and ill treatment of combatants, but violations of those rules, for example, by killing or starving prisoners, tend to be regarded as crimes or atrocities, but not terrorism.

For many groups, however, the target alone does not always distinguish violence as terrorist. Thus, even when noncombatants have been subjected to bombing in their homes and workplaces, and deprived of life-supporting necessities, those who order or commit the acts claim that they are defensive and are necessary to end a war quickly and therefore save lives. Terror bombing of population centers in Europe and Japan were prevalent during World War II and regarded by their perpetrators as legitimate, even if regrettable. Not surprisingly, the people in the societies subjected to those actions tended to regard the actions as terrorism.

Furthermore, the very notion of who is or is not a combatant is not always clear. Thus, when the naval vessel USS *Cole* was attacked in the harbor at Aden, Yemen, on October 12, 2000, and seventeen sailors were killed, the U.S. government and public regarded the action as a terrorist attack even though the target was military. This characterization of the attack was made because the al Qaeda network led by Osama bin Laden conducted the action.[49]

Perpetrators of targeted killing of noncombatants sometimes justify their conduct by arguing that they are merely reciprocating such atrocities committed by the enemy or that the so-called victims are actually combatants. For example, immediately after the 9/11 attacks, a senior al Qaeda operative, who helped plan the attacks, Ramzi bin al-Shibh, defended them by denying that they were terrorist attacks:

> They are legally legitimate, because they are committed against a country at war with us, and the people in that country are combatants. Someone might say that it is the innocent, the elderly, the women, and the children who are victims, so how can these operations be legitimate according to sharia? And we say that the sanctity of women, children, and the elderly is not absolute. There are special cases. . . . Muslims may respond in kind if infidels have targeted women and children and elderly Muslims [or if] they are being invaded [or if] the non-

> combatants are helping with the fight, whether in action, word, or any other type of assistance, [or if they] need to attack with heavy weapons, which do not differentiate between combatants and non-combatants.[50]

The same complexities confound definitions of domestic terrorist actions. Governments usually regard violent attacks on police, soldiers, public officials, or civilians by organized opposition groups as terrorist actions. However, such groups, waging a revolutionary or secessionist struggle, regard themselves as conducting a legitimate fight and using necessary violence. Noteworthy examples of such organizations include the Liberation Tigers of the Tamils in Sri Lanka, the Kurdistan Workers' Party of the Kurds in Turkey, and the Basque Fatherland and Liberty of the Basque in Spain.[51] Increasingly, such distinctions are also relevant in the United States, where various extremist groups associated with white nationalism promote unfounded conspiratorial ideas—such as the grand replacement theory and fears of a white genocide—to justify domestic violent extremism.[52]

Often governments resort to widespread arrests and even imprisonment, torture, assassinations, and "disappearance" of presumed opponents. This may be done to prevent or to suppress challenging organizations. Such government actions are often conducted covertly and sometimes through nonofficial militia groups. Such operations are generally regarded as "state terrorism," such as those carried out some years ago by assassinations and disappearances of citizens in Argentina, Guatemala, and Chile. In the latter two countries, the terrorism was conducted by military regimes that seized power after democratically elected governments were overthrown with the covert assistance of the U.S. Central Intelligence Agency as part of the struggle against Soviet communism.[53] Terrorism also includes the massive killings, labor-camp incarcerations, and torture by "internal security" forces within Hitlerite Germany and the Stalinist Soviet Union.

States also sometimes support and provide havens for organizations waging revolutionary or liberation struggles within other countries. The organizations may be too weak to wage large-scale violent or nonviolent campaigns in those other countries, but the support enables them to conduct occasional terror attacks. This was the case made during the Cold War in support of Soviet and U.S. covert conduct. It is also the case where a country provides a haven for organizations attacking military and civilian targets in a neighboring country. Pakistan, for instance, was criticized throughout the twenty-year U.S. occupation of Afghanistan for providing haven for the Taliban, and al Qaeda before them, within the Federally Administered Tribal Areas of Pakistan's Northwest Frontier Province.

Another standard used to characterize violence as terrorist is the nature of the perpetrator. A defining feature of a state is that it holds a monopoly on legitimate violence. By this logic, when agents of the state commit violence under orders from above, they are engaging in warfare or police action, which cannot be classified as terrorism. This is evident in the definitions of terrorism adopted by various U.S. government agencies.[54] The definition used by the Central Intelligence Agency is contained in Title 22 of the U.S. code, Section 2656f(d):

> The term "terrorism" means premeditated, politically motivated violence perpetrated against noncombatants by subnational groups or clandestine agents, usually intended to influence an audience.

Nongovernmental actors, however, sometimes challenge the very legitimacy of a state. If they view a state as illegitimate, then the state's use of violence is illegitimate, and their acts are criminal. The authority of a state may be diminished in another way. Members of an organization operating transnationally or citizens of another country can more readily reject obedience to the government of the country in which they are carrying out violent attacks.

Some individuals or groups may commit terrifyingly violent acts that are generally not regarded as constituting terrorism. This is the case, for example, for criminal gangs who terrorize people from whom they extort money. It is also true for individuals who are suffering severe mental illness and violently attack political figures.

Finally, the context of the violent actions also can affect whether the actions are regarded as terrorist. One aspect of the context is the degree of transparency shown by the persons committing the action. Some violent actions are covert, and the agents conducting the action deny carrying it out. This makes it difficult to understand what goals are being pursued or how the conflict might be settled. The mystery of who committed the violent activities often contributes to their terrifying quality. This was true with the appearance of anthrax spores in the U.S. mail in October 2001. Furthermore, persons engaging in covert operations generally can act with little accountability and few constraints on perpetrating atrocities.

Another aspect of context is the degree to which the violence is part of a wide array of other methods of struggle. It may be incidental in a large-scale struggle in which various nonviolent methods are also being used, in which case it is less likely to be regarded as terrorist, while if it is the primary method of conducting a conflict, it is likely to be labeled terrorist.

Sometimes terrorism is conducted as if the perpetrators seek to persuade the targeted opposition of the depth of their feelings and the strength of their convictions. That may also enhance the intimidating character of the action, signaling that such actions will persist and cannot be prevented. Terrorist acts carried out by people who complete suicide in the process are an extreme example of such demonstrations of commitment and are honored by some people in whose name they die.[55]

The extent to which the violent actions are carried out with the ultimate purpose to negotiate an agreement with the adversary is an additional aspect of the actions' context. Violent actions may even be used to gain the attention of the inattentive. A cause is being announced, and indeed, an audience is gained as people try to understand why such actions are taken. Various terrorist actions, then, may combine different degrees of coercive and persuasive inducements, Tr(2). Sometimes, however, terrorism seems hardly instrumental and not calculated to win concessions. Rather, it appears intended to punish the other side for its past wrong deeds. Insofar as the terrorist actions are punishing and revengeful, they may stiffen the enemy's resolve rather than achieve any desired change. Indeed, the terrorist acts may be largely expressive for some of the perpetrators. These qualities of terrorism tend to make struggles in which it is used more intractable and destructive.

Certainly, terrorism has existed throughout human history, even as its character and frequency have varied. In the twenty-first century, however, several new conditions provide new opportunities for nonofficial as well as official organizations to conduct terrorist activities. First, technological developments provide particularly effective and frightening ways to kill people. Not only have explosives become more powerful and delivery systems more precise, but also weapons of mass destruction, including nuclear, chemical, and biological weapons, have proliferated. Second, the rapid means of communication and transportation make transnational organizations able to function effectively and make organizations that are structured as a network rather than in a hierarchical form increasingly feasible, which makes their incapacitation more difficult. Moreover, global communication systems enable information and images to spread rapidly throughout the world, increasing the impact of a terrifying event anywhere. Third, the growing social and political integration of the world facilitates the movement of peoples and the ease of foreign people to fit into different societies. Finally, the growing integration of the global economy increases its vulnerability to widespread disruption by an attack at one junction point.

In short, terrorist actions vary immensely and there is no consensus about which actions deserve that label. Often, adversaries in intense conflicts attach the label terrorism to the other side's violent deeds. Although the discussion of terrorism in this book gives particular attention to nonstate perpetrators, violent deeds against noncombatants committed by government agents are not to be ignored.

Coengagements (Ce)

Rewards are typically employed to help settle and transform conflicts and to prevent the eruption of destructive conflicts. They are often components of strategies to establish an ongoing relationship in which the opposing sides engage in activities that promise shared benefits. These strategies include co-optation, corporate codetermination, collaboration, and political power sharing, and are often part of a broad strategy in waging a conflict and sustaining a postsettlement accommodation.

Phillip Selznick influentially used the term "co-optation" in his analysis of the Tennessee Valley Authority (TVA).[56] Soon after President Franklin D. Roosevelt's inauguration in 1933, the federal government established a public corporation to undertake a multipurpose river valley development program to produce electricity and provide water for irrigation. Groups and interests that might have opposed some of the developments were invited to participate in policymaking and became supporters of the TVA. Similar strategies to involve stakeholders in policymaking processes are now widely used by regulatory authorities and are credited with reducing public policy conflicts and instances of post facto litigation.[57]

Various forms of co-optation can be discerned in diverse settings. In some regards, programs undertaken in the United States under the Economic Opportunity Act of 1964 are illustrative. As part of the government's War on Poverty, the act authorized community action programs.[58] Urban disorders and riots had begun to erupt, partly in conjunction with the Civil Rights Movement. The community action programs were to stimulate local communities to mobilize resources in a coordinated attack on poverty and to do so by including the poor to participate to the "maximum feasible" extent. Indeed, poor persons did participate in the many local programs to alleviate poverty that were undertaken. Nevertheless, discontent rose and urban riots occurred widely in the late 1960s. The authors of the 1968 Kerner report on civil disorders noted the demand for greater grassroots engagement in directing the programs affecting low-income neighborhoods and racial ghettos. They concluded, "meaningful community participation and a substantial measure of involvement in program development is an essential strategy for city government."[59]

For many persons, co-optation has bad connotations, implying that a group seeking to improve its conditions abandons their aims, or settles for very little, and joins the dominant view. Co-optation may also refer to the actions of a group's leadership, who soften their demands and derive personal benefits from the dominants. Indeed, a dominant group may make concessions to win acquiescence in the future. Certainly, co-optation takes many forms and can have contradictory consequences. In general, there are risks of forgoing greater gains that might be achieved by further struggle rather than securing the gains already won by institutionalizing them.[60]

Within industrial organizations, efforts to ameliorate labor-management strife have included formal systems of worker engagement in management.

For example, in the Federal Republic of Germany after World War II the trade unions sought codetermination, that is, worker representation in each company's board of directors and executive committee.[61] This was achieved in 1951 in the coal and steel industries, and 1972 legislation extended worker representation to all companies with at least five workers.

Collaboration is a more informal process between relatively independent parties jointly developing rules and structures to govern their relations and decision making. This process is increasingly being adapted within and among governmental and corporate organizations about issues they must manage interdependently. Indeed, most public policy problems can no longer be solved without coordination across multiple government agencies, business interests, and other stakeholder groups. In response, the field of "collaborative governance" has emerged within the discipline of public administration to illuminate the ways that multistakeholder problem solving and best occur.[62]

Finally, one or another power-sharing arrangement may be instituted to settle and transform conflicts in a society rent by fighting along ethnic, religious, or language lines. Power sharing is a governance system that ensures representation of diverse groups in policymaking and in administrative institutions, particularly in the police and military services.[63] For example, in South Africa in 1994, the first elections in which people of all races could vote, major opposition parties were guaranteed that they would have a seat in the government and in the cabinet, for a transitional period, and would hold parliament seats proportional to their numbers in the population.

In Northern Ireland, the process of reaching a power-sharing arrangement acceptable to the major parties with a stake in the conflict between the Protestant and Catholic communities is illuminating.[64] In 1968, the Catholic minority began a civil rights campaign against discrimination and for equality. The Royal Ulster Constabulary, the police of the Protestant-controlled government, forcefully broke up the peaceful demonstrations, which were also attacked by Protestant vigilante groups. The Irish Republican Army, which had been dormant, began to organize to defend the Catholic community and raised the old demand to reunite the island of Ireland. Thus, the struggle intensified and the British government suspended the Protestant-controlled governing body and imposed direct rule from London. The British were unable to sustain a tentative power-sharing government when Protestant workers led a general strike. Then, in 1985 the British and Irish governments agreed to work together and this helped transform the conflict. Although violent fighting between armed groups continued, negotiations also continued and some agreements were reached, but did not endure. Finally, a comprehensive settlement, the Good Friday Agreement, was achieved in April 1998 and gradually implemented with many stops and starts. The agreement consisted of three strands: proportional representation and power sharing in the North, a linked ministerial council between the assembly and Ireland, and British-Irish ties, consisting of a British-Irish council and a standing intergovernmental conference.

Problem-Solving Meetings (Ps)

The final strategy selected for particular attention here is engagement in meetings to exchange information to solve what may be regarded as a shared problem. This is an important mode of conflict resolution, but also a way to wage a conflict constructively.[65] The essential features of the problem-solving mode are that members of the contending parties discuss the nature of their problem and their possibly shared responsibility; they propose various solutions and consider ways to implement the mutually preferred solutions. The participants recognize the concerns of each other and seek ways in which those can be addressed in a mutually acceptable settlement. In this approach, adversaries are not viewed as unitary actors whose leaders are the only significant policymakers. As Harold H. Saunders writes, "The power of citizens is most fully realized and demonstrated in the capacity to build and change relationships."[66]

Problem solving is typically tried at an early stage of a conflict and at various points when the parties in conflict are seeking to de-escalate it. As with the strategies of nonviolent action and terrorist actions, problem solving may be carried out by official agents of the contending parties or by other members of the adversary camps. Unlike the previously discussed strategies, however, intermediaries often participate in problem solving, for example, as facilitators or mediators. Further, problem solving involves a joint decision-making process, rather than a unilateral imposition. Over the past forty years, many problem-solving conflict-resolution methods began expanding greatly. They include informal and formal exchanges and dialogues, as well as mediated problem-solving negotiations, nongovernmental oranizations spanning ethnic and other fault lines, and workshops facilitated by intermediaries. They have expanded, particularly because of experience with ethnic and other communal conflicts within one country and in protracted conflicts between countries. For example, facilitated workshops have been conducted with Catholics and Protestants from Northern Ireland, members of various religious communities in Lebanon, Greek and Turkish Cypriots, Jewish Israelis, and Arab Palestinians, among others.[67]

Even workshops among persons who lack authority to bind their respective parties may contribute over time to the de-escalation and resolution of a conflict. Nongovernmental agencies may help inform influential people on each side about the concerns of their adversaries. The understandings and options generated may become vitally relevant when the circumstances have changed and an opportunity for official de-escalating efforts arises. Sometimes the people with workshop experience become part of the official problem-solving negotiations.[68]

In traditional competitive negotiations, in contrast, each party usually seeks to maximize its gain, often at the expense of the other side. Such negotiations usually involve an exchange of persuasive inducements, directed at changing the other side's position. Although the negotiations sometimes include promises of benefits to the other side in exchange for benefits received, overall, each side takes a hard line, insisting on as much as it thinks it may get and threatening coercive consequences if it does not. Traditional negotiations may be accompanied by coercive actions, as when union-management negotiations are conducted while the union members are on strike. We discuss different forms of negotiation in detail in chapter 9.

In problem-solving negotiations, efforts are made to understand the interests or needs of the other side and to discover possible solutions that maximize all the parties' goals. Mutual benefits result. Coercive inducements are minimized, but the negotiating parties may both anticipate losses if their search for mutual gain fails. Such problem-solving negotiations are located at point "Ps" in Figure 4.1.

A problem-solving mode is more likely to be used in domestic conflicts than in international conflicts. For example, it may be seen even in attempts to find accommodations among peoples with ethnic, linguistic, religious, and other communal differences within a single society. Often, the efforts include negotiations among representatives of the different communities to find a constitutional formula to solve the problem they face. This may be seen in the negotiations leading to the transition of power in South Africa from a white-ruled country to one organized based on equality in political rights of all peoples.[69] The problem-solving approach has also been advocated and utilized in labor-management relations and in regard to environmental issues.[70] Problem-solving methods are increasingly employed in international conflicts by nongovernmental organizations, but also by officials in conjunction with mediation undertaking, which are explored later in this volume.

SUMMARY AND DISCUSSION QUESTIONS

This chapter explored three different strategies that partisans in a conflict can adopt as they seek to change the behavior of their opponents: persuasion, reward, and coercion. In most large-scale conflicts stakeholders choose different strategies at different times, thereby opening new pathways to either more constructive or more destructive forms of conflict transformation. Readers are encouraged to explore the ideas presented in this chapter further by thinking about and discussing the following questions.

1. Using Figure 4.1 as a guide, identify additional strategies that you have observed stakeholders using in conflict situations and "place them" in the triangle. Consider (or explain if you are working in a group) why you placed the strategy where you did within the triangle.
2. Recall a conflict situation that you experienced where you used each of the three types of inducements presented in this chapter—reward, coercion, and persuasion—to change the behavior of your opponent. How successful was that strategy, and what explains its impact or lack of impact? How might you have changed strategies to engender a different outcome?
3. Explore a case of a large-scale conflict using the ideas presented in this chapter. What strategies were used by adversaries in that case? What caused adversaries to adopt the strategies they used? What forces might have led them to adopt more constructive strategies?

Chapter Five

Adopting Conflict Strategies

The previous chapter examined three approaches used by people and groups in conflict to change the behavior of their adversary: coercion, reward, and persuasion. In this chapter we examine why adversaries choose certain approaches over others at different points during a conflict. We are particularly interested in exploring why partisans in a conflict sometimes adopt less coercive modes of contention, which preserve relationships and open possibilities for joint gains. To answer this question, we focus on five variables of interest: conflict style, partisan goals, the internal characteristics groups involved in a fight, their relationship, and the social context in which they are operating.

CONFLICT STYLE

One's choice of conflict strategy is frequently assumed to be a matter of personality. Some individuals appear to have an aversion to overt conflict, others to relish in competition and debate, and others still seem to have a knack for managing conflicts with others in more harmonious ways. Figure 5.1 presents one way of categorizing such differences. It suggests that ever individual has their own conflict style that varies along two dimensions: concern for oneself and concern for the relationship.[1] A low concern along both dimensions would be expressed by a conflict-avoidance approach. For these individuals, conflict may be so uncomfortable, or the prospects of achieving goals so remote, that the goal is to remove oneself from conflict situations as quickly as possible. A high-assertiveness and low-cooperativeness orientation is characterized as a competing or contending conflict style. For these individuals, conflict is often seen as a contest to be won, even at the expense of damage to relationships. Accommodators take the opposite approach. Their strategy of

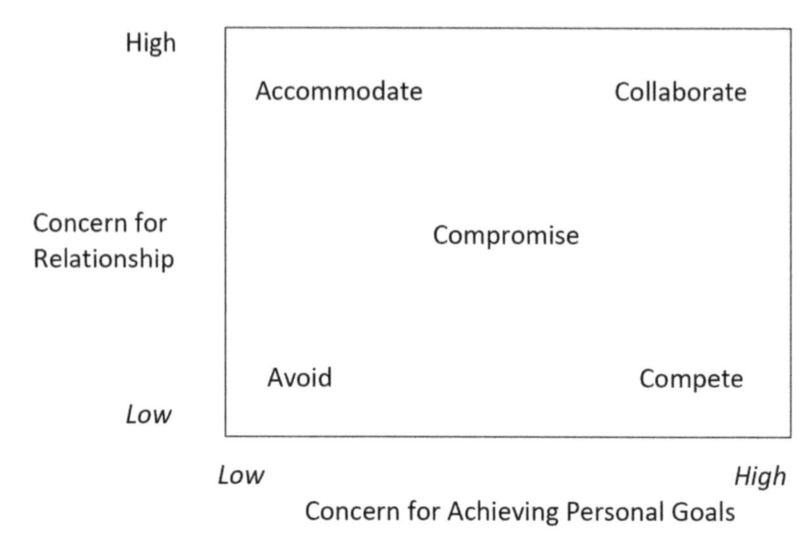

Figure 5.1. Conflict Style

high cooperativeness and low assertiveness serves to maintain harmony and stability, although at the expense of personal interests. Finally, compromisers and collaborators tend to place high value in both good relationships and achieving self-interest. In the case of compromisers, a need for expediency may lead to a "split the difference" approach to conflict management, where both sides are partially satisfied and partially dissatisfied with the outcome. Collaborators adopt what is known as a problem-solving mode, where creative or win-win solutions are sought and mutual problem-solving dominates. This last style is the focus of various theories of mediation and negotiation and mediation, which will be covered in chapters 8 and 9.

Two caveats are useful to consider when examining Figure 5.1. The first is that the context we are embedded in may change the conflict style we use. Someone may be accommodative in a work situation when they interact with their superior, but competitive when they interact with a close sibling. Thus the conflict style that a person adopts is likely to vary depending on the combination of personality traits and the situational environment. Second, it is tempting to believe that collaborative styles of conflict management are always superior to purely avoidant, competitive, or accommodative approaches. And indeed, constructive conflict management generally holds that collaborative approaches to conflict management are more sustainable, less damaging, and more satisfying. However, as illustrated in Table 5.1, under different conditions, all styles may be useful tools for conflict management. The goal is to match one's style to the situation rather than to blindly use the same style for every situation faced. So, for instance, in crisis situations where

Table 5.1. Conflict Styles and Conflict Situations: A Match Approach

Style Type	*Usefulness*
Collaborating	To learn from and merge insights for a better outcome. To gain commitment from others. To work through feelings and strengthen relationships.
Accommodating	Issues are more important to others. To build social credits. Harmony and stability are important. Concerns are too important for compromise.
Avoiding	People need to "cool down" before resuming their conflict. A better outcome requires time spend gathering additional information. The issue is trivial and time consuming.
Competing	Decision is vital and time is short. Critical moments of strategic change requiring leadership.
Compromising	A temporary settlement to complex issues is required. Important goals, but not worth disruption of competition. Stakeholders have equal power and mutually exclusive goals.

immediate action to stem a threat is required, a more controlling style may be useful. In situations where issues are more important to you than others, an accommodative approach that builds social credits may be most constructive.

Using conflict style as a predictor of strategic choice is useful when it comes to day-to-day interpersonal disputes where single individuals alone navigate the conflict environment. However, the individual lens of analysis is far less useful when it comes to deciphering why a group, community, or nation chooses the conflict strategy it does. Individuals can be said to have a personality and dominant style of conflict management, but collectives rarely do. For such conflicts, several other variables, reviewed in the following, may prove far more helpful.

PARTISAN GOALS

The strategies that members of one side choose to wage a conflict reflect the goals that they seek. If a group's goal is to unequivocally defeat an enemy, for example, that group will likely choose highly coercive means to achieve their ends. When goals are less extreme, and when adversaries are in an ongoing relationship from which they both benefit, less coercive strategies will be adopted. Conflict means, in other words, tend to match the ends being sought.

However, choosing a conflict strategy is not a simple unidirectional matter; some goals may be eschewed if the means to attain them seem to be morally unacceptable, too costly, or too time-consuming. For instance, a more powerful actor has the capacity to defeat an enemy it may nevertheless reject that option and pursue its interests noncoercively if it wished to achieve a "stable peace." Moreover, different members of the contending group may disagree about which strategy is best for the goal that is being sought. Different views on the protests that erupted across numerous American cities after the George Floyd murder at the hands of a Minneapolis police officer in 2020 are illustrative. A Pew Research Center survey of 9,654 U.S. adults in June 2020 showed that 55 percent of those surveyed saw protests and rallies as very or somewhat effective for the fight for equality for Black people, while 19 percent saw such tactics as "very effective." Survey respondents viewed other less coercive tools more effective including working directly on challenges facing Black people in local communities (82 percent), dialogue among different races about race (74 percent), and working to get more Black people elected to office (68 percent).[2]

In conflicts that are largely dissensual rather than consensual, strategies with significant components of persuasive inducements, such as appeals to reason, ethics, morality, or fairness, are often used. After all, in highly dissensual conflicts an alteration in the values or beliefs of the adversary is what is often sought, and in that case, some degree of conversion of the opponent is needed. In the debate over abortion rights, for instance, anti-abortion groups frequently use highly emotional images of developing fetuses to sway public support toward their cause. However, when the dissensual conflicts involve adversaries who view each other as an existential threat, persuasive inducements may be regarded by some as fruitless, and more extreme conflict strategies are adopted. In such cases, coercively overcoming the feared other may be viewed as the only reasonable strategy to adopt. Hence, in addition to changing "hearts," anti-abortion groups have also mounted sophisticated legal challenges to shut down access to safe abortion in a number of U.S. states.

In consensual conflicts, the possibilities of trade-offs between issues in contention with differing priorities makes negotiation feasible and often attractive, particularly when common interests and values are recognized. However, when the perceived incompatibility of the goals in a consensual conflict is great and seen in zero-sum terms, the preferred strategies tend to incorporate coercive and often violent components. For example, data from a study of the strategies used by U.S. social-movement organizations challenging the status quo from 1800 to 1945 indicate that the goal of displacing or destroying the target was moderately correlated (0.36) with accepting the belief that violence was legitimate or necessary under some circumstances.[3] Similarly, in the civil rights struggle in the 1960s, many members of the Congress of Racial Equality believed that their goals could be achieved with nonviolent action and its persuasive power because they believed that discrimination rested on isolated attitudes that were not deeply rooted and grounded in material interests.[4] Another example may be seen in a study of strikes and mutinies; those in which secession or seizure of power was sought were likely to use violence, imprisonment, or killing of superiors, while those in which improvement of interests was sought used work stoppage as their main weapon.[5]

Goals also vary in either desiring the adversary to initiate a new policy or in desiring the adversary to stop doing what it has undertaken. Strategies with positive sanctions rather than threats are likely to be regarded as appropriate for the former goals, while threats are likely to be seen as more suitable for the latter goals, since rewards might be seen as a form of bribery.

A conflict group may have goals that primarily benefit nonmembers (e.g., to end discrimination against another category of people) or that benefit members either as a collectivity (e.g., to establish cultural autonomy for an ethnic community) or as an aggregation (e.g., to provide for equality of individual opportunity). Goals for members as an entity are more likely to seem to require coercion than are goals for individual constituent members.

One or both adversaries may be seeking greater separation or greater integration between them. Thus, in communal struggles one ethnic group may be striving for greater autonomy or even secession from the polity controlled by another ethnic group, as have Kurds in Iraq and in Turkey. One group may even seek to expel or destroy another group by ethnic cleansing or genocide, as did the Islamic State during its campaign of killing and displacing the Yezidi population in Northern Iraq in the mid-2010s. Clearly, such extreme goals require brutal means to be attained.

At other times, ethnic communities may strive for closer integration with other groups within the larger society. In such cases persuasion is most often the preferred strategy. Following the 1994 genocide in Rwanda, for instance, the government of Paul Kagame sought to eliminate ethnic identity as a core organizing force in Rwandan life. The Rwanda Patriotic Front—which has governed Rwanda since 1994—argued that the ethnic divisions that had served as the impetus for the genocide were, in fact, an artifact of the German and Belgian colonial administrative state, which ethnically segmented Rwandan society to subdue the population.[6] Over the past twenty-five years, Rwanda claims to have successfully reengineered identity and created a new "Rwandanicity" that decolonizes social relations.[7]

To the degree that one or more sides believes its vital interest or survival is at stake in the conflict, there is a greater likelihood that they will resort to the most drastic strategies to feel secure. For instance, at the outset of the Arab Spring in 2011, some authoritarian regimes viewed the demands for reform as threatening their survival and used extreme violence to repress those seeking political reforms. Indeed, the early success of nonviolent movements in Tunisia and the subsequent disposition of leaders in Egypt, Libya, and Yemen served as a warning sign for leaders in Syria, resulting in the outbreak of an entrenched civil war.

PARTISAN CHARACTERISTICS

Conflict strategies are chosen partly based on a conflict group's internal predispositions, ideology, social structure, and resources, which we discuss in turn.

Predispositions

Much public and scholarly attention is given to the idea that members of conflict parties have specific cultural traditions, socialization experiences, and other characteristics that predispose them to prefer some conflict methods rather than others. In this section we consider this argument by comparing people of different socioeconomic statuses and different genders.

For the past half century, numerous scholars have focused on the possible relationship between low levels of income, education, and other indicators of socioeconomic rank and the greater likelihood of acting violently in family and other interpersonal disputes.[8] Evidence supports several explanations for such a correlation, including subcultural socialization, experience with interpersonal violence, degree of situational stress, embedded structural inequalities, and lack of access to institutionalized conflict-resolution methods or levers of political power. These patterns vary over time and regarding different types of conflicts. Thus, when it comes to waging a war, higher-ranking citizens are often more likely to be supportive than persons of lower ranks. One reason for this is that lower-ranking persons tend to have less confidence in the leadership of established institutions and are more skeptical of the policies they pursue.[9] For example, at the outset of U.S. military engagement in Vietnam, respondents with many years of education were much more likely than those with few years of education to support "taking a stronger stand." As the war went on, however, the consensus among the elites broke down and support for the war fell. The educational differences lessened, as the college-educated respondents' support for the war markedly dropped, in concert with dissenting political leaders.[10]

Following the attacks of September 11, 2001, the U.S. public overwhelmingly supported the initiation of U.S. military action in Afghanistan. Shortly after the U.S. air attacks began in early October 2001, respondents across the country were asked whether they favored or opposed the United States using ground troops in Afghanistan. Among persons with a college education, 84 percent supported the use of ground forces compared to 75 percent of those with a high school education.[11] Fourteen years later, as the Islamic State gained a territorial foothold in Syria and Iraq, this general pattern again appeared with 74 percent of individuals with postgraduate degrees approving of the U.S. military campaign against the Islamic State, 69 percent of college graduates favoring the U.S. military campaign, and 58 percent with only a high school education supporting U.S. military action.[12]

In the Israeli-Palestinian conflict, however, lower-status Israeli Jews have been relatively more militant in opposition to Palestinians than higher-ranking Jews. For example, in a survey conducted in January 1995, during a difficult period in Israeli–Palestine Liberation Organization negotiations, respondents were asked: "Should talks be stopped or continued if terrorism continues?" The respondents with fewer years of education were slightly more likely than those with more education to answer: "Stop the talks."[13] In this case, the less educated public tended to be more affiliated with the more hawkish political parties. On the other hand, among Palestinians in the occupied territories and in Gaza-Jericho, the more educated Palestinians were somewhat more likely to oppose continuing negotiations and more likely to support armed attacks against Israeli targets, compared with the less educated.[14] Probably the more educated persons were more attentive to the Palestinian political leadership at the time.

These varied findings indicate no consistent or strong tendency for persons of higher educational and class standing to support institutionalized rather than noninstitutionalized conflict strategies and of nonviolent rather than violent strategies, when engaged in large-scale external conflicts. Insofar as such relationships are found, they are not likely to be substantially due to subcultural differences in these regards. Rather, the differences are better explained by differences in trust of societal institutions and in the leaders of those institutions.

It turns out that ideological beliefs and political party affiliations affect preferences about different strategies for specific conflicts more significantly than educational or economic levels. For example, when asked about their support of sending United States ground troops to fight the Islamic State in Syria and Iraq in late 2015, a very strong party affiliation gap emerged with 67 percent of Republicans supportive and 31 percent opposed, whereas 32 percent of Democrats were supportive while 63 percent opposed.[15] In 2021 as the United States withdrew all ground troops from Afghanistan, a similar pattern of party affiliation emerged, with 59 percent of Democrats backing President Biden's withdrawal to 32 percent of Republicans.[16]

A second variable to consider is gender. Most of the work done on this topic treats gender as a binary, categorizing respondents into male and female categories only.[17] Of these studies, males are somewhat more likely than females to act aggressively in domestic relations and other interpersonal interactions.[18] Presumably, this derives from the socialization into gender roles between males and females. Feminists and other analysts of gender point out that in the United States and in many other societies, masculinity popularly stresses competitiveness, dominance, assertiveness, and readiness to inflict and accept pain and even death for honor, while femininity tends to emphasize relationships with others, nurturance, caretaking, and warmth.[19] Masculine and feminine, however, are more accurately regarded as overlapping socially constructed tendencies. Variations along many dimensions prevail rather than a set of qualities with little overlap between males and females. In most analyses of the relationship between gender and preferences regarding conflict methods, however, women and men are compared as separate categories, not as persons varying in degree of femininity and masculinity.

With these caveats in mind, public opinion surveys show that women are usually less likely to support the use of military means than are men. But the magnitude of the differences between men's and women's views varies with circumstances.[20] In general, analyses of numerous surveys reveal that women are more sensitive to the risk of casualties and tend to withhold support for military action more than do men, particularly as casualties mount. Thus, in a national survey conducted immediately following the attacks on September 11, 2001, support for military retaliation by the United States was extremely high: 90 percent among men and 88 percent among women.[21] As conditions are specified in the interviews, however, gaps between men and women appear. For example, support for military retaliation drops greatly to 76 percent among men and to only 55 percent among women if one thousand U.S. troops would be killed. When asked whether the United States should punish the groups involved in the attack or mount a long-term war on terrorism, 64 percent of the men chose the second alternative and only 42 percent of the women did.

In addition to sensitivity to casualties, men and women differ in their support for military action depending upon its stated purpose. Four purposes of U.S. military action were distinguished in analyzing 484 surveys conducted about the use of force by the United States from 1990 to 2003.[22] They are, in the order of their support, (1) humanitarian intervention, (2) coercion of a state or nonstate actor that threatens U.S. interests or allies, (3) change political order in another country, and (4) peacekeeping operations. The largest gender difference is for threatening or taking military action to advance U.S. interests that are threatened (men 68 percent and women 55 percent supportive) and the smallest gender difference is for humanitarian intervention (men 68 percent and women 63 percent supportive). The media reports of violence against women in some of the cases of humanitarian intervention probably contributed to relatively high support for intervention among women.

The effects of gender on the preferences about how to contend have also been examined in research about smaller-scale conflicts, in which the use of alternative conflict approaches is examined. Research includes observations, simulations, and self-reports regarding the alternatives used in various kinds of conflicts. The research includes studies of the choice of the conflict-handling styles identified in Figure 5.1: competing, collaborating, compromising, avoiding, and accommodating. Interestingly, very few differences between men and women are consistently found.[23] For example, research using self-reports finds only small differences, with women reporting competing less and compromising more than men.[24] The popular expectations of large gender differences in conflict-handling strategies well may lead people to incorrectly perceive and attribute differences in conduct to gender and so confirm their expectations.

Research indicates that societies with greater gender equality are less likely to engage in international violence. A quantitative analysis of international crises from 1945 to 1994 finds that as domestic gender equality increases, a state's use of violence significantly decreases.[25] Similarly, more recent large-scale quantitative analyses of women's empowerment, controlling for many other variables, find that societies in which women are more empowered and possess greater levels of gender equality are less likely to use force in international relations, and societies with less subordination of women are more likely to have lower levels of armed conflict.[26]

Finally, compelling research has shown that when women play an active role in peace negotiations both the quality of the agreement and the durability of the peace established improve. The reasons behind these correlations remain somewhat unclear; however, a likely explanation is that the diversity of perspectives created by including women at the table, as well as the strong connection of women to civil society groups, leads to agreements with more relevant content and higher implementation rates of negotiated provisions.[27]

Group Ideology

Broadly conceived, ideology refers to general ways of thinking, often implicit, that offer interpretations of the social world in which the group members function and by which their conduct is guided. Narrowly conceived, ideology provides an explicit analysis of a group and its place in a larger social context, and it prescribes conduct to advance the values and interests of the group and its members. The discussion here focuses on ideology, narrowly defined.

In general, all groups hold distinct ideological views that are articulated and institutionalized by group elites. In the extreme cases, ideologies are articulated by leaders of totalitarian political parties and used to control the societies they rule. In the cases of German Nazism and Soviet communism, an ideology extolled a particular race or class and provided reasons for its dominance; it set forth goals and the means to achieve the goals. It also provided the rationale for a leader and a political party to have the absolute right to interpret the ideology.

Ideologies, as understood here, also include religious as well as secular interpretations of the world and how to live in it. Religions usually provide a general vision of how individuals and communities should treat each other, including guidelines for engaging in conflicts.[28] The universalistic religions that are prevalent in the contemporary world all proclaim the equal and shared humanity of everyone. This principle provides the ethical basis for seeking solutions to conflicts that incorporate the partial truths known by the disputants in a more comprehensive shared truth. Some conflict transformation projects, for instance, bring together Christians, Jews, and Muslims by focusing on the shared religious values that are central to each faith.[29] It also may foster a problem-solving approach, whether as a partisan or as an intermediary. The belief in a common humanity also can provide an important basis for rejecting violence and killing. It is central in some religious denominations whose members adhere to pacifism, for example, within Christianity the historic peace churches include the Society of Friends (Quakers), Mennonites, and the Church of the Brethren.[30] Pacifist traditions are also found among a small proportion of followers of Catholicism, Judaism, Islam, Hinduism, Buddhism, and other major religions.

Other interpreters of the same holy writings, however, find support for the use of violence in the service of God's will. One recent study of thirty-four African nations found that individual religiosity generally decreases support for violence, but collective religiosity generally increases it.[31] Undoubtedly, many wars have been fought by followers of one religion against adherents of another, and by one religious sect against another. In many battles and struggles, members of each side expect their prayers for God's blessing to be answered, and the religious beliefs may be used to help demonize the enemy. Religious leaders often help legitimate, for their followers, the actions taken by political leaders. They may sometimes interpret religious beliefs to require engagement in a violent struggle and promise a place near God after martyrdom; bolstered by such beliefs, individuals may be recruited to commit terrorist actions.

For example, in Israel, members of the messianic Gush Emunim believed that the Israeli government, by signing the 1978 Camp David Accords with

Egypt, was committing an error that might stop a divine promise and process.[32] As disciples of Rabbi Zvi Jehuda Kook, they believed that the messianic age was at hand and formed an underground terrorist group within Gush Emunim to counter Palestinian attacks on Jewish settlers in the occupied territories. It planned and carried out several terrorist operations beginning in 1980 with attacks on Palestinian mayors. In 1984, the Israeli secret service discovered and disrupted plans to blow up five Arab buses full of passengers, and the group was put on trial and its members imprisoned.

Within Islam, too, some groups believe it is their religious obligation to wage a violent struggle to establish and defend a true and faithful Islamic society. For example, Osama bin Laden and his associates interpreted elements of the Islamic tradition and set goals and strategies to reach them, which had some appeal to Muslims. They were thus able to raise money and mobilize personnel to establish a transnational network organization that could conduct large-scale terrorist activities. The statement issued by bin Laden and his associates in February 1998, the "Jihad against Jews and Crusaders," condemns the wrongs committed by the United States against Muslims. They are:

> First, that for over seven years the United States has been occupying the lands of Islam in the holiest of places, the Arabian Peninsula, plundering its riches, . . . humiliating its people. . . . Second, . . . the great devastation inflicted on the Iraqi people by the crusader-Zionist alliance. . . . Third, if the Americans' aims behind these wars are religious and economic, the aim is also to serve the Jews' petty state and divert attention from its occupation of Jerusalem and murder of Muslims there. . . . On that basis, and in compliance with God's order, we issue the following fatwa to all Muslims: The ruling to kill the Americans and their allies—civilians and military—is an individual duty for every Muslim who can do it in any country in which it is possible to do it.[33]

The strategy al Qaeda used in attacking the United States was undertaken with the faith that it would damage American interests and provoke U.S. reactions that would strengthen al Qaeda, thereby forcing the United States to withdraw from Islamic regions.

Secular ideologies can also justify the use of violence or even extol it. Many ideologies focus on injustice and oppression as a legitimate ground for armed struggle. Frantz Fanon's writing, influential in the 1960s and 1970s, offers a powerful illustration.[34] He examines how the colonizer dehumanizes the natives, turning them into animals. To overcome this violence, the colonized people must also use violence, and through violent struggle the colonized free themselves and gain a new sense of power and self-respect. This process was considered essential in winning national liberation from colonialism anywhere. For example, in the Basque region of Spain during the 1960s the Basque Fatherland and Liberty evolved as an organization of Basque nationalism. Influenced by Fanon's analysis, it undertook a strategy of violent actions that continued into the twenty-first century. So too did Che Guevara, following his engagement in the Cuban revolution, pursue a violent revolutionary strategy as the way to reveal injustice, create a revolutionary situation, and win a revolution.

Social and Political Organization

Among the many aspects of a group's social structure affecting the choice of a conflict strategy is the relationship among those who represent one of the adversaries in a conflict and the constituent groups who support, challenge, or otherwise seek to influence them. This is what distinguishes intergroup conflicts from interpersonal ones. In intergroup conflicts, a leader, or a group of them, represent and commit their constituencies to the struggle, while in interpersonal conflicts the antagonists act largely independent of any constituency.

The relations among those who claim to speak for an adversary in a conflict vary greatly. Sometimes leaders are easily able to mobilize constituent support for the conflict strategies they choose. For instance, during crisis periods when group members collectively confront an external threat, leaders are often able to bring about broad group support for what might be considered extreme measures during "normal" times.[35] Other times, various coalitions of elite constituent groups work together to shape the external policy and determine the conflict strategies to be used. At still other times, rank-and-file constituents constrain the conflict strategies employed. The nature of these internal relationships matters because the various component groups tend to have different preferences and interests regarding strategic approaches. As the relationships among them change, shifts in the adversary's goals and strategies drive the conflict toward escalation or de-escalation. If intragroup fractionalization is strong enough, external opponents may be able to "split" the adversary group sufficiently that they are unable to coalesce around any cohesive strategy.

Group relationships, and the constraints that they place on strategic choices, are not just socially derived, but are politically derived as well. In any political entity there is a group of actors who, if they agree, have both the ability to commit the resources of the entity and the power to prevent other people from overtly reversing their position. The unit having this authority may (and frequently does) vary with the nature of the problem. For instance, in governments for issues of vital importance the highest political authorities often constitute the decision unit; there is a contraction of authority to those most accountable for the choices. For less dramatic, more technical issues, the decision unit generally varies depending on the type of problem the government is facing whether military, economic, diplomatic, scientific, and so on. In governments where policy normally involves multiple bureaucratic organizations, the problem may be passed among different units—within one agency, across agencies, or between interagency groups.[36]

The preferences of the many constituent groups within a conflict party also vary with the character of the struggle. For example, in highly regulated conflicts, with contentious matters managed routinely, leaders are more prone than their followers to prefer to use the established conflict management procedures, while followers or important segments of them tend to favor relatively antagonistic and coercive modes. On the other hand, when the conflicts are not highly regulated, particularly if the conflict party is becoming mobilized, the leaders tend to resort to relatively confrontational strategies. To illustrate, a study of union leaders in the United States finds that the highest leaders tend to be less militant than lower-ranking union officials.[37] Lower-ranking officials are more suspicious of management intentions, while the national leaders are more deeply involved in negotiations and other interactions with management, developing mutual dependence and understanding.

More generally, studies of elite groups' preferences regarding ways to conduct foreign policy reveal variations reflecting self-interests, general orientations, political ideology, network alliances, and other factors.[38] Their different positions and influence relative to the public and to elected national officials vary with the foreign policy issue and with the timeframe being considered. Thus, analyses of U.S. foreign policy indicate that the public is likely to be involved and have some autonomy in forming opinions over time about foreign policy issues where national security and economic security are important.[39]

Consider the large changes in the U.S. government's use of armed force and shifts in American public opinion. In the early 1970s, public opinion turned against increased military expenditures in reaction to the war in Vietnam. In the 1980s, support for military spending rose again, but U.S. military action carefully took the form of covert or very limited interventions. In the 1990s, the use of military force became more legitimate as it was used in multilateral engagements. In the beginning of the twenty-first century, highly militarized and unilateral U.S. military operations were undertaken.[40] This was followed by a popular backlash due to the perception that the U.S. government leaders had over-reached during the Iraqi and Afghan war, with disastrous consequences. In 2019, under President Trump, the United States withdrew ground forces from Syria and began withdrawing troops from Afghanistan after negotiations with the Taliban, a process completed by President Biden in 2021. In both cases, public opinion largely supported military disengagement, even as the United States was accused by critics of abandoning its local partners.

An important aspect of internal social organization is the leaders' need to sustain constituency support. Having an external enemy may appear to leaders to be an effective way of rallying support. For instance, after its annexation of the Crimea in 2014, Russia faced a significant international reaction that threatened to undermine President Putin's domestic standing. In response, Putin sought to maintain internal cohesion by characterizing the actions of Western powers as consistently hostile, in his December 2014 annual state of the union address: "The policy of containment was not invented yesterday. It has been applied to our country for many, many years . . . every time when anyone only thinks Russia has become strong, independent, such instruments are applied immediately."[41]

Furthermore, using certain conflict methods can help commit the constituencies to the course undertaken by the leaders. The leaders of a terrorist group, a state, or an ethnic separatist organization, by engaging their followers in violence against persons designated as enemies, make it difficult for the members to withdraw. They need to justify their bloody actions; they risk retribution from the enemy if they fail, and their compatriots in violence are bonded by their actions to continue the struggle. This pattern may be especially likely for ethnic groups that are culturally like the groups from which they seek to distinguish themselves, for example, the Kurds, Basques, and Croats.[42]

Finally, in large-scale conflicts adversaries are likely to have established units specialized to conduct extremely coercive actions and they tend to play important roles in the choice of strategies. These units include police departments, military organizations, and sometimes groups engaged in covert operations. They typically use coercive methods and often have standard operating procedures for applying them. Since they are expected to be prepared for action and have contingency plans when a fight erupts, officials and leaders are likely to turn to them for guidance and often delegate responsibility to respond to them. Frequently, this leads to a rapid escalation and sometimes a destructive conflict. Thus, following standardized procedures, police may try to control a crowd or a riot but act in ways that intensify the confrontation, as was observed in 2019 as racial justice advocates mobilized to protest the treatment of black and brown people across numerous cities in the United States. Procedures are designed to counter serious attacks, and when military personnel are asked to respond to a threat, they usually apply the method they have prepared to use. Police intervention to the protests in Ferguson, Missouri, in 2015, for example, was highly militarized in nature involving the use of armored vehicles, assault weapons, drones, and other military-grade equipment. These tactics rapidly escalated the conflict as protesters viewed the response of security personnel as heavy-handed and further evidence of a government that was against them.[43]

Cognizant of these risks, political leaders, members of specialized agencies, and other concerned persons have tried to develop responses that are less likely to result in destructive, counterproductive escalation. Much of the defund the police movement, for instance, seeks to reallocate or redirect funding from the police department to other agencies that have a capacity to respond to civil unrest or individual disturbances to public order in ways that do not risk escalation and violence. These range from decriminalizing minor offences, to creating unarmed mediation and intervention response teams capable of responding to community disturbance, to increasing funding for proactive mental health interventions for at risk individuals, to various deradicalization and violence prevention activities by public and nonprofit groups.[44]

Resources Available for Struggle

Adversary groups vary greatly in having the resources that are needed for conflict strategies. Hence, each group is careful to select from among the strategies it believes it has the capacity to employ. Consider the implications of the numerical size of the conflict group as a resource. Members of a small group, believing they lack the capability of openly challenging their adversary with other means, sometimes resort to terrorism.[45] They recognize that to wage even guerrilla warfare the group needs relatively large numbers of fighters and a supporting social environment. Similarly, nonviolent direct action requires many participants to be effective, and a goodly number is also needed for mutual support and protection. The costs of nonviolent action are likely to decrease and the gains to increase the greater the number of participants.[46] Violent uprising, too, requires many participants at a given locality, providing a sense of security and support. For example, research about racial uprisings in the United States between 1961 and 1968 found that the absolute number of nonwhites in a city was by far the single most important factor in accounting for widespread disorder.[47] When the grievances of Blacks were sufficiently widespread and protests were an accepted form of action, there were more incidents that might trigger violent unrest. Uprisings, depending in part on milling and contagion, require congeries of people: streets filled with people who are young enough to feel they can take risks may begin engaging in protest activity that draws in other participants and results in a mass act of unrest and protest.[48]

In general, a group's capabilities channel its selection of a conflict means. Groups with resources that can be conditionally awarded to an adversary, such as continued service or electoral votes, may choose to offer or withhold that resource. For example, a government representing the economically dominant class may offer concessions to members of the relatively deprived class to prevent or restrain challenging actions. Groups skilled in manipulating symbols are likely to try strategies with high degrees of persuasion, as is frequently done among environmental groups that seek to protect endangered species.

Finally, countries with powerful military capabilities are likely to depend on coercive conflict strategies. For example, since World War II, the U.S. Department of Defense has become a powerful and influential actor in U.S. foreign affairs. At the same time, and particularly in recent years, the Department of State's influence on foreign affairs has diminished. The vast capabilities of the military establishment make it an attractive tool to be used in a wide array of circumstances; consequently, U.S. foreign policy has become greatly militarized.[49] The global reach of American military forces is illustrated by the power and influence of regional commanders in chief.[50] The Department of Defense divides the world into geographical regions and a commander in chief commands all U.S. military forces in each region. The Department of State has only regional "desks" in Washington, DC.

Although each adversary has a repertoire of conflict techniques available, the repertoire tends to be limited to the methods previously used. Even using a method effectively once can make it a precedent for the future.[51] Many methods emerge from the members' routine conduct, for example, as a coercive inducement factory workers can stop working, withholding their labor. Of course, it is necessary to conceptualize first that such action might be a weapon.

An implication of these observations is that expanding the repertoire of conflict methods that adversaries possess increases the likelihood that a more constructive means of struggle will be adopted. This can include a wider array of novel means of violence. But it also means that adversaries with the resource of problem-solving conflict-resolution skills will be able to select a conflict mode that incorporates them. The growing use and success of these methods is a strong argument for increased training of social-movement organizations in nonviolent strategies, of schoolteachers and students in mediation skills, of police in nonprovocative methods of crowd control, and of military personnel in negotiation and collaborative decision-making skills for their peacekeeping, peace observation, and humanitarian-assistance duties. Trained persons charged to apply mediation and other problem-solving techniques in conflict situations increasingly staff special units within many kinds of organizations.

RELATIONS BETWEEN ADVERSARIES

Each adversary's choice of strategy greatly affects the other side's choice since their conflict is a relationship. The effects of three underlying aspects of the adversaries' relationship will be discussed: (1) the level of integration between the antagonists, (2) how they perceive and feel about each other, and (3) the degree of symmetry in the resources each control.

Integration

As discussed in chapter 2, among highly integrated adversaries, violent conflict modes tend to be avoided for several reasons. Crosscutting ties associated with integration reduce support for choosing means that presume animosity. The interdependence that is inherent in integration raises the costs of resorting to conflict methods that damage the relationship. And the greater likelihood of shared understandings and institutionalized rules for managing conflict among integrated adversaries increases the probability that they will use modes of conflict that are nonviolent and relatively low in coercion.

As evidence of these claims, a study of the rate of strikes in eleven industrial countries found the propensity to strike to be high in mining and the maritime industries; medium-high in lumber and textiles; medium in the chemical and printing industries; medium-low in clothing and services; and low in railroad, agriculture, and trade.[52] The authors conclude that one important determinant of the interindustry differences in the propensity to strike is the location of the workers in society. Workers who form "isolated masses" are particularly prone to strike, as has been the case for miners, sailors, and longshoremen, who tend to have separate communities, relatively homogenous work roles, and low mobility out of the occupation.

An example of another kind of crosscutting mechanism is provided by a study of cities in India that experience recurrent intercommunal riots, between Hindus and Muslims, and the many cities that do not have such riots.[53] Localities with organizations that bring people from the two communal groups together to work for a common cause, such as traders' cooperatives or community-development committees, tend not to have intercommunal riots.

Certain kinds of crosscutting ties inhibit or facilitate particular conflict modes. For example, since men are more often combatants in external conflicts, crosscutting bonds among the potential combatants are particularly relevant to the choice of war or other modes of violent conflict. This can be seen in cross-cultural research that found that societies with matrilocal residence patterns tend to have a sense of solidarity and lack intervillage warfare, while patrilocal residence societies are plagued by more dissension, fights, and feuds.[54] This occurs because among societies with the patrilocal residence pattern, the bride moves to the husband's village; in societies with a matrilocal residence pattern, the husband moves to the bride's village. Consequently, in patrilocal societies the men live in the same village with their brothers, while in a matrilocal society they live with their in-laws and face the possibility of fighting against their brothers if they engage in a fight with another village.

In interstate conflicts, too, integration increases the likelihood that problem-solving approaches will be tried and found effective. A variety of research findings support these expectations. For example, Karl W. Deutsch and his colleagues analyzed the emergence of "security communities," peoples within a territory who have a sense of community and have institutions that ensure, for a long time, that social problems will be resolved without recourse to large-scale physical force.[55] Examples of such security communities include "amalgamated" cases, such as the United States since 1877, England and Scotland since 1707, and Switzerland since 1848, and "pluralistic" cases, such as Norway and Sweden since 1907, and the United States and Canada since the 1870s. Three conditions seem essential for the success of both amalgamated and pluralistic security communities: the compatibility of major values relating to political decision making, the capacity of the participating units to respond to each other, and mutual predictability of behavior. Furthermore, in amalgamated security communities they find unbroken links of social communication both geographically between territories and socially between different strata, and there is a wide range of communication and transactions between the peoples.

Other research examines relations between trade and severe conflicts. For example, a study of wars between 1870 and 1975 found that countries that were more involved in foreign trade were less likely to be involved in wars.[56] Several other studies examine the relationship between trade and conflict among pairs of states, also finding that higher levels of trade lead to lower levels of conflicts. Finally, research has also show that extradyadic trade patterns are likewise associated with a reduced risk of interstate violence.[57]

Low levels of integration reduce many options that adversaries might otherwise employ, such as nonviolent coercive inducements exemplified by trade sanctions or severances of cooperative arrangements. This has been the case, for example, for the United States in trying to influence either North Korea or Iran. The low level of integration with those countries seems to leave few inducements available aside from violence or threats of violence. It is true that many noncoercive sanctions are conceivable, although politically awkward; however, starting at such low levels, even steps toward normalized relations could be a strong inducement for ongoing conflict transformation. More constructive forms of conflict management, for instance, seemed possible during and after the 2018 and 2019 summits between the United States and North Korea where recognition of Kim Jong-un's regime was granted by the Trump administration in exchange for active dialogue on North Korea's nuclear weapons program.

Although high integration between parties reduces the likelihood that they will use violence against each other, it does not preclude it. A shared culture may allow for certain kinds of violence, as is the case where family or clan feuds are traditional. And at the interpersonal level, relationship violence and domestic abuse illustrate that close integration. Furthermore, once a conflict erupts between integrated parties, the use of coercion may escalate into violence, even of a brutal kind, as the parties endure severe losses resulting from the special vulnerability arising from their mutual dependency and as the parties feel betrayed by those previously close. Such factors contributed to the extremely brutal fighting between some ethnicities during the breakup of the former Yugoslavia.

Views and Feelings Regarding Each Other

A critical feature of adversary relations influencing the choice of conflict strategies is the degree to which each party respects the other. If the opponents regard each other as legitimate and are responsive to each other, then problem-solving modes of conducting their emerging conflicts are likely. This is supported by one of the few well-documented empirical findings about the occurrence of war: democratic societies rarely if ever make war on each other.[58] The leaders and peoples of such societies tend to recognize important common values, shared norms, and common interests. In addition, acknowledgment of each other's concerns as having some legitimacy as they reflect popular legitimacy fosters efforts at mutual accommodation. Finally, they have shared experience and understandings about how conflicts can be managed cooperatively.

The content of the understandings and expectations that adversaries share affects which strategy each party will use. For example, traditional U.S. employer hostility to trade unions helps account for the violent and often bloody history of trade union organization in the United States.[59] Collective bargaining has been less institutionalized in the United States than in other industrialized, democratic societies. Consequently, in the past, U.S. union members have been involved in more strikes and for longer periods than union members in other pluralistic industrial societies.[60] This has also contributed to political policies that have weakened trade unions in recent decades.

Adversaries also bring experience to bear in deciding how to act toward one another. Thus, it might be expected that countries that have been wartime allies would subsequently be less likely to make war on each other. However, quantitative analysis of pairs of countries that have fought wars against each other does not indicate a strong tendency for countries to sustain former relations either as allies or as enemies.[61] On the whole, they often shift from being antagonists in one war to allies in another.

Some enmities do persist, but that requires additional circumstances. If people on one side feel they have been humiliated in a prior fight, they may later seek revenge.[62] Generations of young people may be taught about such humiliations and learn to demonize their enemy, opening the possibility of using dehumanizing conflict modes. Some ethnic conflicts have been plagued by such traditions, providing political leaders with sentiments that could be mobilized, as between the Hutus and Tutsi in Rwanda and the Serbs, Croats, and Bosnians in the former Yugoslavia. So too has humiliation been implicated in asymmetric conflicts involving terrorism, although the exact correlation between the two needs additional exploration.[63]

Sometimes, one conflict party holds views about an adversary that justifies its use of particularly harsh conflict modes. Those views may derive from political or religious ideologies or accounts of past atrocities.[64] Consequently, the adversary may be considered subhuman or evil and therefore its interests and concerns can be disregarded with self-defeating results. For example, during World War II, in accord with Nazi racist ideology, Germans treated even the anti-Soviet Russians and Ukrainians as racial inferiors, driving them to support the Soviet government.[65]

Resource Balance

The abundance of resources a conflict party has available as possible inducements, relative to its adversary, affects not only the emergence of a conflict, but also the choice of conflict strategies. Analyses of this matter tend to focus on the balance of capabilities to commit violence and the resort to physical force. Two contrasting views of coercive power differences as an explanation for resorting to violence have often been argued. According to one line of reasoning, a large power imbalance is expected to inhibit or deter the weaker party from coercively challenging the stronger one. By the same reasoning, the stronger party may be able to attain its goals merely by its dominance and the threat of coercion. Consequently, relationships in which one party has a clear preponderance of power are not likely to be marked by violent conflict. On the other hand, some analysts argue that it is a symmetrical balance of power that will inhibit either side from instigating a violent conflict, for unless one of the parties has considerable certainty that it will win a violent struggle, it will avoid initiating one.

The area in which these contrasting views have been most thoroughly examined pertains to the incidence of wars. Much of this work presumes a "realist" perspective, viewing each state as a unitary actor, rationally calculating the costs and benefits of waging war to maximize its power, and considering military force as the primary means to serve that end.[66] Each of the two lines of reasoning regarding power preponderance and power balance can be argued by using the realist approach. The research results, however, do not consistently support either argument.[67]

Reasons for not finding a consistent association between state power relations and initiating wars abound. Many of them flow from criticisms of the realist approach. For example, states are not truly unitary actors; rather, governments respond to diverse domestic pressures and themselves include persons and groups with varied interests and perspectives. Also, power cannot be measured only by the capability of doing violence and cannot be assessed without relationship to the goals toward which it is directed.

Even putting aside these problems of the realist approach, another reason for the failure in finding a consistent relationship between power differences and the onset of war is suggested by Bruce Bueno de Mesquita.[68] He explains the onset of war by utilizing two influential theoretical approaches. First, he postulates that a leader seeks to maximize his or her expected utility; in other words, the policymaker tries to maximize the net benefits expected from their policy choices. Bueno de Mesquita further argues that the decision to go to war is generally made by an individual, a strong leader. Second, he utilizes the theoretical approach emphasizing the importance of uncertainty in decision making and variations in preferences regarding risk taking. Uncertainty refers to the degree to which the probability of a course of action being successful is unknown. Individuals have their own preferences regarding risk and uncertainty. Persons who are risk averse require much more confidence of success than do those who are risk acceptant. Increased uncertainty enhances the differences between persons who tend to avoid risks and those who tend to accept risks. An implication of this reasoning is that individuals, even having the same expectations about the outcome of a war, may rationally make different choices about going to war. Therefore, even for rational actors, the immediate external conditions do not altogether determine the choices of conflict mode.

Despite the considerable research about wars, many disagreements about explaining the incidence of wars remain. One difficulty in achieving consensus is that wars are not homogenous; they vary greatly, and different explanations probably pertain to different kinds of wars.[69] Some are between rival states, or between complex alliances, or between a large expanding empire and a small neighboring people. They are fought for varying goals and by diverse means.

Although wars are often studied ostensibly to learn how to avoid them, relatively little research has been done about wars that have been averted.[70] In the present analysis, we consider how conflicts emerge and the alternative ways in which they are conducted. Shooting wars, in their manifold variety, are only one way among many to wage interstate struggles.

It is also useful to examine evidence from conflict domains other than interstate relations regarding the way resource differences affect the choice of conflict modes. Labor-management relations is another relatively well-studied domain. Based on reasoning about power differences, trade unions would be expected to strike when their chances of success are greatest. Indeed, strikes do tend to be more frequent during upturns in the economy, and therefore, when labor is in shorter supply.[71] This indicates that it is not increased grievances alone that account for the choice of institutionalized coercive means to wage a conflict, rather it is the greater likelihood of being successful if attempted.

The increased integration of the world economy in many ways reduces the strength of workers and of labor unions relative to corporate managers.[72] The increased ease of moving investments and the growth of the global market makes it easier for managers to drive a hard bargain with workers by threatening to close a plant and open a new one somewhere else in the country or the world. The threat does not have to be explicit to be understood and carry weight. The gradual decline in trade union strength and militancy, of course, is due to many other factors such as political ideologies and shifts in the composition of the labor force away from industrial jobs. Indeed, the transnational growth of corporate activities does not always strengthen the hand of management relative to the workers. The worldwide integration of a company with specialized components of the production located in different parts of the world makes the whole company vulnerable to a stoppage at one locality. For example, in June 1988, thirty-four hundred members of United Automobile Workers local 659 walked off their jobs at a General Motors metal-stamping plant in Flint, Michigan.[73] This quickly stopped production of parts essential for producing General Motors vehicles throughout North America.

This discussion of resource differences affecting selection of conflict strategies casts additional light on the findings that revolutions and uprisings often occur when previously improving conditions take a downturn. As discussed in chapter 3, this unrest is usually interpreted as expression of increased dissatisfaction resulting from an increased gap between attainments and expectations. But increased dissatisfaction alone does not lead to such actions. Some group must be held responsible, and action to change them must seem possible. It is when the ruling government is held responsible that noninstitutionalized coercive means tend to be undertaken. This is even more likely when the deterioration in conditions is attributable to the incompetence of the authorities. Such incompetence not only reduces their legitimacy, but also makes them appear weak and vulnerable, inviting rebellion. The deteriorated conditions and the authorities' reduced legitimacy also mean that they have fewer resources to be traded for continued obedience. Thus, the French, Russian, and Chinese revolutions broke out when the governments had been weakened by their international overextension.[74]

An authoritarian government that allows for greater freedom of communication among its citizens to win support by reducing the citizen's sense of oppression risks greater opposition and sometimes protest, demonstrations, and uprisings. This occurs in part because the government may be seen as showing its weakness and revealing the strength of opposition. The vastly speedier and more widespread interpersonal communication resulting from new social media technologies makes it possible for previously oppressed individuals to become aware of their shared discontent and take increasingly bold collective actions.[75]

Although coercive power differences affect the choice of coercive strategies, they do not do so strongly and consistently. The asymmetry of noncoercive dimensions of power also needs to be considered, since that affects the choice of strategies possessing significant components of persuasion and rewards. Thus partisans who believe they occupy the moral high ground tend to use moral claims to persuade not only allies to support them but also members of the adversary side who might come to agree with them. To illustrate, Palestinians won many resolutions in the UN General Assembly supporting their claims against Israel regarding the rights of Palestinians and then the Palestinian Authority gained greater recognition within UN organs.[76] Despite those successes on the world stage, the Palestinian leadership was less effective in its persuasive efforts toward Israelis because such efforts were for so long contradicted by violent attacks on Jewish noncombatants and ambiguities about acceptance of the State of Israel.

SOCIAL CONTEXT

Seven aspects of the adversaries' social context significantly affect their choice of strategy: (1) the institutions of the opponents' social system, (2) the norms and ways of thinking prevailing in their environment, (3) the roles of other parties, (4) resource inequalities, (5) changing technologies, (6) integration, and (7) response to stress.

Institutions

Adversary relations are embedded within larger social systems and play out through various societal institutions. For example, in some countries there are well-established judicial, legislative, and executive institutions that are regularly used to manage conflicts at all levels of society. Many non-Western countries have less institutionalized and formal entities that serve a similar function, such as the Jirga system in Afghanistan and Pakistan. Where conflict-management systems are regarded by its citizens as legitimate, even conflicts with the potential of breaking up the country may be successfully managed using these entities, with little or no violence. For example, this has been true in Canada, between largely French-speaking Quebec and the rest of Canada, and in Belgium, between its French- and Flemish-speaking citizens. However, where a less inclusive or legitimate government presides, ethnic, linguistic, religious, and other communal divisions have been the basis for unchecked violence in struggles for control of the state or for secession from the state.

When the state itself represents one of the contending communal groups or there is a single ruling elite, problem-solving modes are much less likely to be used. If opponents seriously challenge the government's authority and domination, the response can include resorting to violence by the state. This is illustrated by the very severe, long-lasting violence in Sri Lanka between the government, dominated by the Sinhalese, and the Liberation Tigers of Tamil Eelam, the secessionist organization of the Tamil population, violence which resulted in the military defeat and destruction of the Liberation Tigers of Tamil Eelam.[77] The Sudan provides another instance of great violence, between the government dominated by Muslims in the north and the non-Muslim peoples in the south, which resulted in division into two countries.[78]

Under extreme conditions of a government unable to govern, conditions of a failed state, violent conflicts among contending groups are likely to be persistent.[79] The resulting mass violence and great refugee flows often produce anguished cries for external intervention, which sometimes occur with dreadful consequences, as discussed in later chapters. At present, the world lacks global institutions with the authority to impose and enforce binding decisions regarding conflicts among states or between states and nongovernmental groups. At times transnational governmental and nongovernmental organizations contribute to problem-solving settlement modes.[80] More often, states resolve their conflicts by themselves, often with coercion and even through wars.

Norms and Prevailing Ways of Thinking

Members of a social system often share general understandings about the appropriate means to be used in pursuing and settling various conflicts. In the international domain, for example, ideas about national sovereignty and the right of governments to monopolize the legitimate use of violence internally are widely shared. Consequently, countries have long considered war a legitimate way to pursue foreign policy. Furthermore, governments have widely asserted the right to treat people in their territory as they deem correct, without other governments having any right to intervene. However, in recent decades ideas of sovereignty have been changed, as international norms limiting the rights of governments to harm their citizens or to act aggressively against other states have evolved. Consensus about human rights, for example, has been growing and with it a legitimate basis for intervention in the internal affairs of countries. This is exemplified by the United States and the North Atlantic Treaty Organization's intervention in the wars breaking up Yugoslavia and the subsequent trials of Slobodan Milosevic and others in the International Criminal Tribunal for the Former Yugoslavia, established by the UN Security Council in 1993. As discussed in later chapters, there is growing international discussion about the governments' responsibility to protect people.[81]

Certainly, within a society norms and understandings about how various groups should conduct themselves when in conflict are widely shared and often quite detailed. Those can constrain even a powerful adversary's choice of conflict modes, making some choices unlikely while increasing the likelihood of others. The context of such norms varies with the culture and social system of different populations.

New thinking about conflict resolution and public engagement can help avert destructive escalation. Also, conflict settlements may be better sustained, and destructive conflicts avoided by enhanced organizational transparency, accountability, and engagement. There is some evidence of this, but the effects are uneven across cases.

Other Parties

Protagonists in a fight are never isolated. Each has possible allies and additional enemies who may join the conflict. In addition, groups who are part of the constituency of one protagonist may defect or may shift their involvement in the struggle. Other groups may seek to intervene to pursue a mediating role. All these groups also help, wittingly and unwittingly, to shape the changing use of conflict modes.

An adversary's beliefs about these other parties and their possible actions profoundly shape the methods adopted in waging a conflict. Actions are often avoided in fear of alienating allies or of driving uninvolved parties to the opponent's side. Often, actions are chosen in hopes of getting the attention and sympathy of potential allies.

Thus, for the leaders of the U.S. Civil Rights Movement of the later 1950s and early 1960s, large demonstrations and nonviolent direct action appeared to be an effective means because these were persuasive to many citizens and government leaders who might support legislation and other actions to end discrimination and to foster integration and equal opportunity. Police attempts at repression in 1963 in Birmingham and elsewhere, as well as vigilante terrorism, vividly revealed the prevailing oppression.[82] Those violent responses to the nonviolent struggle of the Civil Rights Movement evoked widespread support for the 1964 civil rights legislation passed by the U.S. Congress.

On the other hand, separatist or other challenges by ethnic groups that have resorted to strategies with high components of violence, particularly involving noncombatants, receive little support or sympathy from external actors. Outside governments, international governmental organizations, and the attentive public may even condone harsh repressive actions against the challenging "terrorists."

External actors intervene in diverse ways that contribute to the course of most large-scale conflicts. They may intervene as supporters of one side or as advocates and supporters of some means of struggle and not others. They may also play a variety of intermediary roles. Intervention for one side may hasten an imposed settlement, but it may also help escalate and prolong a destructive conflict as other external actors join the fray on the opposing side. One of the destructive features of the East-West Cold War was that the Soviet Union and the United States supported and sometimes directly engaged in violence in many regions and counties, including Korea, Vietnam, Nicaragua, Southern Africa, Afghanistan, and the Middle East. More recently, the civil war in Yemen has become a proxy struggle between several regional and global players, including the Saudi Arabia, Iran, the United States, and Russia.

Finally, intermediary intervention, including mediation, advocacy, and other "third side" actions can greatly affect the trajectory of a conflict.[83] Domestically, intermediary intervention includes government agencies providing labor-management mediation and facilitation services and protection in civil rights cases. Intermediary interventions are also made by nongovernmental organizations, such as interreligious councils and conflict resolution and mediation centers. Internationally, this includes mediation by the UN secretary general's special representatives, national governments, and unofficial channels of diplomacy.

Resource Inequality

The earlier discussion of the preponderance or balance of power inhibiting the recourse to violence and war is applicable to the system level as well as to the relationship between two or more adversaries. The research about the incidence of wars in relationship to different power systems, whether unipolar, bipolar, or multipolar, however, has not yielded consistent results.[84] One reason for this may be that research focusing on polarity regards it as a discrete quality, either present or absent. That assumes a simple direct relationship between the incidence of war and either power preponderance or balance. But it may be that either extreme power concentration or extreme power diffusion reduces the likelihood of war, whereas a moderate degree of power dispersion increases the likelihood of war, the relationship being not monotonic but curvilinear. Some research, using an index of power concentration among the major states in the international system, treats concentration as a continuous variable. Evidence of a curvilinear relationship between concentration and the incidence of wars among major states was found, wars being less likely with either high or low levels of concentration. The evidence is less clear for other kinds of wars.

Clearly, the relationship between any one measure of systemic power inequality and all kinds of violence cannot be large. There are too many dimensions of power and kinds of violence for that. Moreover, many other dimensions of inequality, as well as the other aspects of the system as a whole, affect the choice of a conflict mode. The dynamics of power relations are important. For example, in international affairs, when a rising power is viewed as a challenger by a hegemonic power, it tends to set off hostile escalation and violent contention.[85]

Changing Technologies

Technological developments that are relevant for waging conflicts have received increasing amount of attention in recent years. For example, the tight coupling of information systems around the world has resulted in a new class of cyber weaponry, which can be used by both state actors and criminal actors to attack adversaries. Today it is possible for one government to shut down the critical infrastructure of another through cyber attacks alone. In 2021, for example, criminal actors associated with the Russian government were implicated by U.S. intelligence agencies in shutting a major U.S. pipeline network. Similar cyber attacks in recent years have shut down the power grid in the Ukraine, petrochemical facilities in Saudi Arabia, the computer system of the German Parliament, and Taiwan's state-owned energy company. Shortly after being elected president, Joe Biden warned that the most likely event that would lead to a shooting war between the United States and another major power would be a cyber attack on the United States. Cyber intrusions have also been used to undermine faith in electoral processes by, for instance, feeding false new stories into social media feeds. One example is a 2017 effort by Russian hackers to break into the social media accounts of government officials in several EU states with the goal of creating distrust of U.S. and North Atlantic Treaty Organization forces.[86]

Developments in weapons of mass destruction also represent a new front for conflict escalation. Readily available small but powerful weapons can be adopted by militia groups to undertake violent attacks, particularly against soft targets. Advanced delivery systems such as hypersonic missiles, drones, and smart bombs seem to enable powerful governments to undertake limited wars that inflict great destruction but avoid massive collateral damage and with little risk of deaths on their side. These and other war-making technological developments probably tend to make reliance on military force more attractive.

Many other new technological developments, however, can foster reliance on relatively constructive means of struggle. For example, as noted elsewhere in this book, increased global integration and shared information, based on new technologies, generate the interest and capability to effectively intervene to avoid or constrain destructive conflicts. Particular interest in recent years has focused on the new information technologies and social media and how they may facilitate mobilization of nongovernmental actors who might undertake nonviolent protests and other coordinated challenge to authoritarian rulers. That capacity may have somewhat increased, but dominant groups also have increased capabilities to limit and contain the effectiveness of reliance on social media.

In general, the broad use of many means of communication increases the importance of persuasive inducements in conflicts. Governments and nongovernmental actors increasingly rely on persuasive arguments to justify their actions and causes and gain support for them from broader audiences. The new information technologies and social media also increase the possible adoption of strategies involving for example co-engagement and co-optation. Admittedly, the new information and communication technologies can also enable the adoption of highly destructive conflict strategies. A small number of scattered persons can forge a unit to conduct terrorist acts and persuade susceptible persons to join them. Possible policies to counter such developments are discussed in the chapter on de-escalation.

Integration

The general level of integration in the system may affect adversaries' choices of conflict modes, even aside from the degree of integration between them. Higher overall levels of integration increase the interest and capability of other actors to affect the adversaries' choice of mode. In general, we expect that high levels of integration generate an effective interest in members of the system to constrain adversaries from choosing disruptive conflict modes such as wars or other organized violent actions.

Research relevant to these arguments has been conducted regarding the incidence of international wars. One set of studies examines the possible effects of the general level of international integration, measured by the growth of international governmental and of international nongovernmental organizations. The results have not consistently supported the expectation that a higher level of integration inhibits wars.[87] It is likely the level of integration at the international level, indicated by the network of international organizations, is simply not great enough to markedly impact on the likelihood of wars in the system.

Many thinkers have argued that the growth of world trade would inhibit recourse to international wars. States would avoid wars when they are especially likely to be disruptive of trade benefits. Indeed, there is evidence that the level of international trade is inversely related to the incidence of wars among major states and among smaller states.[88] That relationship is quantitatively large and statistically significant.

Responses to Stress

Social systems are sometimes subjected to great stress from large-scale changes that impact contending parties. These may be demographic changes that result from epidemics or changes in birth rates that affect the overall capacity of the system to materially and politically sustain itself. Societal institutions may be overwhelmed, and the management of conflicts may break down. Natural disasters such as earthquakes or hurricanes may be followed by looting, riots, and intensified contentions between different ethnicities or social classes. More resilient social systems may cope well with such crises and a resulting sense of solidarity can override previous antagonisms.

Finally, there is growing concern that global climate change will exacerbate emerging conflicts. For example, the brutal fighting in the Darfur region of the Sudan is attributable in part to the increasing desertification in that region that has pitted farming people against nomadic people, peoples who also tended to differ in ethnicity and religion.[89] Periods of severe drought in recent decades forced nomads, many of Arab ethnicity, to migrate southwards, resulting in conflicts with sedentary tribes, including the Fur and the Masalit. The Sudanese government's engagement in a civil war with rebel movements further contributed to the violent escalation of the conflicts in Darfur. Such conflicts are likely to expand in the coming years. In 2019 the *New York Times Magazine* published a special report titled "The Great Climate Migration" noting that even modest efforts to reduce climate change would still result in the migration of billions of people out of future uninhabitable hot zones by 2070.[90]

SUMMARY AND DISCUSSION QUESTIONS

This chapter examined six factors that jointly determine the choice of a conflict strategy: the conflict style adopted, goal sought, the characteristics of the adversary, the relations between the adversaries, their social environment, and the features of the system in which they operate. Readers are encouraged to deepen their thinking about these issues by considering the following discussion questions.

1. Complete a self-assessment of your own conflict style, such as the one found here: https://www.usip.org/public-education/students/conflict-styles-assessment. Think about your dominant conflict style, when it works and when it does not, and which style you would like to get better at practicing. What opportunities in your life offer a chance to do so?
2. Identify a conflict in your own community. Specify who the stakeholders are, whether the conflict is consensual or dissensual, and develop a timeline of strategies used by different stakeholders across the conflict. Then consider why stakeholders adopted the strategies they did. To what extent did their tactics result from their style of conflict management, their goals, their groups involved in a fight, their relationship, and the social context in which they are operating? What other variables not covered in this chapter help to explain strategies adopted?

Part III

CONFLICT ESCALATION AND DE-ESCALATION

Chapter Six

Escalation

Large-scale conflicts often go through periods of escalation during which partisans adopt increasingly destructive tactics to induce an adversary to change.[1] These may include committing more resources to a fight, mobilizing more people or new allies to participate in it, using increasingly threatening language, or carrying out threatened action. In such situations, conflicts may become highly destructive, especially when both sides adopt more severe tactics in reaction to each other, thereby creating a "spiral of escalation." The partisans themselves may feel dismay that the conflict has deteriorated so badly, even as they continue to engage in rhetoric or take actions that exacerbate it. In this chapter we consider how such escalations occur, why they sometimes develop a "life of their own," and what factors limit the spiral of escalation.

PROCESSES OF ESCALATION

Escalation may occur inadvertently, step by step, without the opponents having carefully considered the implications of their actions, or they may be part of a calculated strategy to raise the pressure against an opponent, either gradually or abruptly. In both cases the parties to a conflict often become locked into a spiral of action and counteraction, which is difficult to escape. For example, in 2017 and 2018 the United States and the Democratic People's Republic of Korea (DPRK) engaged in a series of escalatory actions that brough the two nations to the brink of a fighting war. In July 2017, the DPRK test-fired an intercontinental ballistic missile believed to be capable of reaching Alaska. Later, in September, the DPRK tested a 250-kiloton nuclear bomb. Paralleling these events, a war of words broke out between

President Trump and North Korean Supreme Leader Kim Jong-un, with Trump calling Kim "rocket man" and threatening to "totally destroy" North Korea. Kim, in turn, referred to Trump as "mentally deranged," stating that Trump's comments "have convinced me, rather than frightening or stopping me, that the path I chose is correct and that it is the one I have to follow to the last." Additional threats, missile tests by the DPRK, and economic sanctions championed by the United States followed. Each nation also repositioned its military forces to signal a readiness to fight. In early 2018 South Korea proposed negotiations, which lead to a period of de-escalation that coincided with the 2018 Winter Olympics in Pyeongchang, thus avoiding a direct violent confrontation.

Several analysts suggest that conflict escalations such as this one occur in stages, with each prior stage making the next one more likely. Friedrich Glasl's conflict escalation model, for instance, posits that escalation occurs across nine stages: hardening, debates and polemics, actions not words, images and coalitions, loss of face, strategies and threats, limited destructive blows, fragmentation of the enemy, and together into the abyss.[2] Similarly, Pruitt and Rubin suggest that conflict escalation involves five sequential processes: movement from relatively benign to more destructive tactics, an expansion of issues in contention, the development of hostile images of the enemy, the expansion of the number of parties involved, and a transformation in goals from winning to hurting the other side.[3]

Certainly, most conflict escalations are sequential with prior actions facilitating the adoption of more severe tactics. The metaphor of a ladder is therefore apt. Higher rungs of a ladder are only reached by first stepping on a lower rung. But how steeply an escalation occurs and what stages it moves through is situational; that is, a product of numerous variables that combine at distinct moments in time. We review the most significant of these variables in the following as well as discuss how they combine to either facilitate or thwart the escalatory process.

Issues in Contention

The type of issues in contention dramatically influences processes of escalation. Matters that are regarded as of vital interest by one or more of the adversaries naturally have great potential for severe escalation. The party defending what it believes to be essential to its existence will use whatever means it has to counter an adversary. For example, Ethiopia, Sudan, and Egypt are currently engaged in a contentious dispute over Ethiopia's construction of the Grand Ethiopian Renaissance dam on the Blue Nile River that flows north through Sudan and into Egypt. That project will affect water levels downstream, and Sudan and Egypt have warned that water level drops or sudden floods could have devastating impacts on their agricultural, industrial, and hydroelectric industries. In early 2021, President Abdel Fattah el-Sissi of Egypt warned Ethiopian leaders that Egypt's allocation of Nile waters was "untouchable" and if Ethiopia filled the reservoir without first completing a legally binding deal to protect downstream users the region would experience "instability that no one can imagine." Later in 2021 Sudan and Egypt completed joint war games in a show of force widely perceived to be directed at Ethiopia. Negotiations continue but given that a loss of water resources is viewed by Egypt as an existential threat, the possibility of rapid and steep escalation remains.[4]

In general, dissensual conflicts—those involving ideological and abstract values or moral issues—have a higher escalating potential than conflicts that are consensual—those involving divisible things. Dissensual conflicts tend to attract more parties, trigger emotional responses, and are viewed by the partisans as non-negotiable. Such conflicts foster escalation because the opponent is often viewed as wrong in principle and not merely on the wrong side of an issue. Therefore, constraints on conduct may be reduced, particularly if the other side is considered immoral.

Consensual conflicts are less prone to steep escalation for two reasons. First, the matters in contention generally do not threaten identity or core beliefs and thus have lower emotional resonance. Second, consensual conflicts are often transactional and thus amenable to compromise and trade-offs. They are, in other words, largely negotiable. Two caveats to this logic are important to note. If a consensual conflict involves a scarce and necessary resource, as in the case of water in the Nile River basin discussed earlier, the possibility of steep escalation is high. People will aggressively mobilize and fight to secure what is necessary for survival if a negotiated settlement is not possible. Thus, a conflict over the purchase price of a house is very different than a conflict over how to allocate freshwater resources in a region crippled by drought. The former involves a one-off transaction and alternative houses, and buyers are plentiful. The latter involves an ongoing interaction, few if any alternatives are available, and an argument about an essential resource. Second, many conflicts are neither purely consensual nor dissensual; they contain elements of both. Indeed, the most difficult conflicts have intersecting drivers; some of these drivers are related to a divisible resource, but others relate to alternative worldviews and identities, ingrained systemic inequalities, and the emotional responses animated by each of these. These intersections were discussed in chapter 2.

Social Psychological Response

Many theories and research findings in social psychology provide insights, helping to explain conflict escalation. Cognitive dissonance theory, for example, suggests that individuals seek consistency between what they do and what they think they should do.[5] Consequently, once having committed an action they seek to justify it in their own mind. For example, after one has suffered an ordeal to join a fraternity or a military unit, the value of being a member of that group must be regarded as great so as to maintain self-respect for having put up with the ordeal. It follows that as persons expend resources to hurt other humans, they tend to regard the cause for which those actions were taken as very important. As the cause becomes more valued, ever more harmful acts are justified. Partisans may even dehumanize their adversary to make extreme actions more palatable. After all, it is far easier to harm those that you see as being outside of your moral community, subhuman, or evil than it is to harm those you see as equals.[6] This dynamic was clearly on display at the outbreak of the 2022 Russian attack on Ukraine. To make the Russian invasion more palatable to his people, Vladimir Putin announced in a February 24, 2022, speech that the goal of the Russian attack on Ukraine (which he publicly framed as a special military operation) was the "demilitarization and denazification" of the Ukrainian government. By falsely associating Ukrainian leaders with Nazis, a group that had inflicted untold suffering on the Russian people during World War II, Putin was seeking to dehumanize his Ukrainian opponents, making acts of violence against them more palatable to his military and citizens.

Entrapment also contributes to conflict escalation. It refers to "a decision making process whereby individuals escalate their commitment to a previously chosen, though failing, course of action in order to justify or 'make good on' prior investments."[7] We can experience entrapment when telephoning if we are put on hold; the longer we wait the more we want to hang up but the more reluctant we are to do so, having already invested so much time. Having sunk resources into a fight, investing more resources seems called for to justify what has already been expended in money, honor, or blood. This ever-increasing commitment and allocation of resources may go beyond the original value of the goal, but the combatants on both sides may feel trapped into continuing and even escalating the struggle.[8]

Selective perception also contributes to conflict escalation. People tend to notice phenomena that fit their preconceived expectations. Once a struggle has entered a serious stage of mutual recrimination and contentiousness, even conciliatory conduct by the adversary is likely not to be noticed or, if noticed, to be discounted and considered deceptive. In this way conflict escalation often becomes a self-fulfilling prophecy, defined by Jussim as occurring when an originally false belief leads people to act in ways that objectively confirm that belief.[9] In other words, believing an opponent will never yield, cannot be trusted, and has bad intent leads one to search for evidence of that belief. The result is an escalation of one's own commitment to the cause, which in turn stimulates the other side to do the same.

The stress brought on by threatening and urgent situations is also implicated in conflict escalations. Thinking is often impaired when people feel they are threatened and must respond with to a situation quickly. Policymakers embroiled in what they regard as a crisis experience such pressures.[10] Under those circumstances, fewer alternatives are considered, and, curiously, previous conduct, even if ineffective, tends to be repeated.

Within groups, conflict situations often trigger a dynamic, known as "group think." In these cases, members of the group quickly coalesce around one course of action without considering alternative courses of action.[11] When group think is occurring, a group tends to disregard the views of those members who are critical of what is emerging as agreement; often then the would-be dissenters quickly go along in order to "get along." For example, group think within the White House and U.S. intelligence agencies appears to have played an important role in the decision to go to war against Iraq in 2003, which was made under an erroneous assumption the Saddam Hussein was developing weapons of mass destruction. In that case, key actors resisted views and information that did not fit into the already formed understandings, and alternative perspectives were not adequately voiced.[12]

Emotions play significant roles in the development of struggles that are protracted and destructive. Escalated conflicts may trigger feelings of collective solidarity, excitement, pride in one's bravery, pleasure in making history, securing one's place in the afterlife, and satisfaction in proving oneself are all exhilarating. For some people, being involved in a war is wonderfully exciting, giving meaning to life.[13] Such feelings enable participants to endure great discomfort and pain, and to risk death. Although such emotions cannot be sustained for long, they leave feelings of loyalty, obligation, and commitment, which help the group sustain terrible losses.

Fear, anxiety, and anger are also implicated in conflict escalations, contributing to impulsive action and defensive aggression.[14] Finally, emotions such as shame and humiliation may stimulate a desire for revenge that fuels many struggles.[15] These may be culturally elaborated and channeled, as in the institutions of duels, blood feuds, and wars. Unacknowledged, these feelings may hamper making decisions that can help wage a struggle constructively. Worse, they can lead to what Olga Botcharova—a Russian psychologist who studied trauma in the aftermath of the Bosnian civil war—has postulated as the seven steps toward revenge.[16] That sequence begins with shock and denial, flows through periods of panic, denial, and anger, and culminates in a narrative that justifies the use of aggression by the traumatized individual. Revenge, then, takes on a life of its own as an aggrieved party does to its opponent what the opponent originally did to them.

Cycles of revenge are possible to disrupt, and escalation thwarted, when actors in a conflict, often with the help for third parties, take steps to reframe and rehumanize their adversary. For example, through cathartic events that involve mourning a loss, by acknowledging wrongdoing, through truth telling and memorialization, and through restitution. We examine some of these strategies in more detail in the next chapter.

Calculation of Gains and Loses

The classic game of Prisoner's Dilemma shows that it often seems rational for adversaries to escalate a conflict, even when that escalation may cause greater injury to the self. The hypothetical story for this game is that two people have been arrested on suspicion of committing a serious crime. Although they are guilty, there is insufficient evidence for conviction of the serious offense but enough for a lesser one. Held in jail, they are not allowed to talk with each other. They have the following possibilities: If they both confess, they will be convicted of the serious offense, but their sentence will be reduced slightly for their cooperation. If one confesses and incriminates his accomplice, he gets off without punishment and his confederate gets the maximum sentence of twelve years. If they both hold out and do not confess, they can only be convicted for the lesser offense and be sentenced for one year.

This payoff choice poses a dilemma for the prisoners. Each would be better off if both held out and did not confess. Yet, if each considers what the other might do, there is compelling reason to confess. Thus, if B confesses, A is better off confessing. If B does not confess, A is again better off if he confesses. In other words, if each assumes the other prisoner cannot be trusted, and acts in his individual self-interest, they both will lose. The dilemma can be resolved only if the prisoners could trust each other not to confess.

Many actual conflict escalation situations appear to unfold according to the Prisoner's Dilemma logic. Consider two countries in an arms race with each other and suppose each has good reason to fear the other. If one government increases its arms expenditures while the other side does not, the escalating side can believe it will triumph. According to the payoff matrix presented in Figure 6.1 the escalating side would gain twelve and the other lose twelve. The side that does not increase its arms expenditures when the other side does thus becomes more vulnerable. If both sides continue to increase their arms expenditures both suffer some loss since they cannot employ the resources

		Nation A	
		Escalates	De-escalates
Nation B	Escalates	-9 (-9)	-12 (12)
	De-escalates	12 (-12)	15 (15)

Figure 6.1. Arms Race Payoff Matrix

used for arms for other purposes, each side losing nine. Finally, if both sides do not increase arms spending, they would both be better off at fifteen; each has additional security and funds previously used for arms could be repurposed. This last option is difficult to achieve, however, since the fear of not escalating when an opponent does escalate is the worst possible outcome, thereby making escalation the only rational move. All numbers used here are, of course, hypothetical. Actual values depend on the specifics of what is gained and lost in each scenario.

Of course, actual conflicts do not have such simple payoffs, and the payoffs are not stable or known. But the logic of these simple games is intriguing. Escalation can be overcome only if each side can find ways to signal a readiness to cooperate and there is enough trust between them. We will explore ways to achieve this end in the next chapter.

Changes in Relations

Once a conflict erupts, the relations between the adversaries often change in ways that escalate the fight. Three such changes are fundamental: (1) contentious interaction; (2) the expansion of the issues; (3) the polarization of relations.

Contentious Interaction

Even initially moderately contentious actions, when responded to harshly, can ignite an extraordinary escalation if the underlying conditions are already heated. For example, U.S. student strikes erupted in May 1970 in reaction to the U.S. military invasion of Cambodia and the subsequent killing of student protestors at Kent State University and at Jackson State University.[17] Quickly, across the country, about 1.5 million students left classes, campuses were barricaded, and sit-ins were conducted, forcing many colleges to close and some to end the school year.[18]

As adversaries exchange punitive behavior, each reasonably expects that the other will increase its pressure unless it is prevented or deterred by even greater coercion. In these contentious interactions, the expectations become self-fulfilling prophecies. Acting on the premise that the other side is guided only by a drive for power and can be influenced only by coercion tends to produce confirming results.[19] This appears particularly evident when issues of social identity are central to the conflict. In these cases, greater coercive efforts by one side often reinforces the social cohesion—and willingness to fight—of the other side.[20] That hostility is then reciprocated, after which the parties may come to feel that revenge has become a goal. Runaway escalation then ensues.

Furthermore, as one side imposes negative sanctions on the other, those sanctions themselves become issues. For example, when U.S. women were struggling for suffrage, they picketed the White House in 1917. Police harassed them, and many were arrested. When maltreated in prison, they went on hunger strikes that resulted in forced feeding.[21] For members of the women's movement, such behavior by the opposition created new issues of contention and grievances that broadened the movement. Many passive observers became supporters of the women's cause and public opinion on suffrage shifted.

Escalations may also occur when one party misperceives how its opponent will respond to a particular act. For example, a threat may be made with the expectation that the threat alone will suffice to change the behavior of the adversary. Then, if the opponent is not intimidated, the threatening party may appear to have been bluffing and has an additional reason to carry out the threat or lose credibility and face. Both sides have taken a step up the escalation ladder that was not intended, and the conflict has risen to a higher coercive level than either believed appropriate for the original subject of their quarrel.

If one of the parties commits extreme coercive acts, the other is likely to perceive the perpetrator as brutish and subhuman, and perhaps as evil. Such views then allow or even justify harsh countermeasures. The brutish enemy presumably can only understand brutish acts. Soon, each side is treating the other inhumanely, but feels it is acting out of necessity. The identities attributed to the other side become characteristic of their own identities.

Finally, once a struggle has begun to deteriorate destructively, even efforts to dampen the conflict may feed the flames of escalation. If one of the parties makes a conciliatory gesture or responds less aggressively than anticipated, the other may interpret that as a sign of weakness. The weakness then serves as an invitation to escalate demands and pressure. As a result, to restore credibility and demonstrate resolve, the previously conciliatory party may stiffen its posture and raise its own demands. And so the conflict escalates again, as the stakes are raised.

Expansion of Issues

Once a struggle has begun about one issue, additional issues that had been denied or hidden frequently emerge. There is less need to deny them, and the overt struggle may seem a good time to "settle accounts."[22] And so the goals expand. Issue expansion is particularly likely when there are underlying cleavages of fundamental values or interests among members of a community, organization, or other social system. For example, a community controversy over the inclusion of particular books in the school library may become generalized into a fight about educational, moral, or political philosophies.

Relatively minor issues in dispute may also take on great symbolic significance once a struggle has gotten under way. What might be a trivial matter between friends has great significance between enemies. For example, during the COVID-19 health pandemic most public health experts recommended that people wear masks when in enclosed public spaces. In many countries, such a Germany, Hong Kong, the Philippines, and South Korea, compliance with mask mandates or recommendations was generally high and, when coupled with lockdown measures, resulted in significant decreased rates of COVID-19 community transmission.[23] In other countries, however, masking mandates became a contentious political issue that took on broader symbolic meaning. In the United States, in particular, the dispute over wearing face masks became emblematic of a deeper conflict over individual rights and personal liberty versus collective responsibility and government mandates. In several states, Republican governors prohibited mask mandates. Nine states went so far as to ban public school districts from setting universal mask mandates to protect against community transmission.[24] Thus what started out as a relatively benign and noncontroversial public health recommendation became an escalatory proxy battle between conservatives and liberals.

Polarization of Relations

As a conflict emerges and develops, the adversaries tend to disparage each other, viewing themselves as moral and the opponents as immoral and unreasonable.[25] In extreme cases such views are used to justify moral exclusion, a denial of rights, and other forms of oppression.

When extreme polarization occurs within political systems the result is *political sectarianism*, a state of politics where three characteristics dominate relations among political groups: othering (seeing opponents as essentially different from the in group), aversion (high levels of distrust and dislike of the other party), and moralization (the tendency to see members of other political groups as sinful, wicked, or evil).[26] Under these conditions partisans devote more of their energies to harming the other side than they do solving shared problems. For example, studying political sectarianism in the United States, Eli Finkel and his colleagues have found that "out party hate" today exceeds in party warmth when it comes to interparty relations. The authors note:

> Democrats and Republicans—the 85% of U.S. citizens who do not identify as pure independents—have grown more contemptuous of opposing partisans for decades, and at similar rates. Only recently, however, has this aversion exceeded their affection for copartisans. On a "feeling thermometer" scale ranging from cold (0°) to neutral (50°) to warm (100°), affect toward co partisans has consistently hovered in the 70° to 75° range. By contrast, affect toward opposing partisans has plummeted from 48° in the 1970s to 20° today. And cold feelings toward the out-party now exceed warm feelings toward the in-party. Out-party hate has also become more powerful than in-party love as a predictor of voting behavior, and by some metrics, it exceeds long-standing antipathies around race and religion.[27]

As conflicts develop and sectarianism grows, adversaries tend to become increasingly isolated from each other. For example, before war erupts, governments often withdraw from joint membership in international organizations.[28] Similarly, as a prelude to avert conflict, groups may end economic cooperation and trade, cultural exchanges, or even the possibility of travel across borders.

A good example is found with current U.S.-China relations. As China opened to foreign investment and exchange starting in the 1970s and 1980s, significant economic and cross-cultural linkages formed between it and the United States. Among them were extensive education and cultural programs that brought students, academics, government officials, and others into direct contact with each other through various exchange programs. Such exchanges were viewed as an important vehicle for improving understanding and building peace. These are currently being revaluated and reduced by both the U.S. and Chinese governments. For its part, the United States has accused China of weaponizing education and cultural exchanges to steal intellectual property and technology. China, in turn, has accused the United States of using cultural diplomacy programs to destabilize its domestic politics.[29] As a result, support of and funding for such programs, often referred to under the umbrella term "cultural diplomacy," is being reevaluated and reduced by both sides. As conflict parties reduce the number of nonconflicting relations, they are less constrained by cross-pressures and crosscutting ties and are freer to indulge in more severe conflict strategies. This lack of contact also reinforces and may even institutionalize negative attitudes held by each group toward the other.[30]

Polarization is also aggravated by the tendency of partisans to try winning bystanders to their side. Insofar as a party feels morally superior and confident that the people not yet engaged in the struggle will be their allies if they must choose sides, it will urge them to do so. If it believes it can, it may even insist that other parties join with it. For example, the German Nazis asserted, "If you are not for us, you are against us." The striking coal miners in Harlan County, Kentucky, sang in the 1930s, "You either are a union man or a thug for J. H. Blair. Which side are you on, man, which side are you on?" Eldridge Cleaver said during the civil rights struggle, "If you're not part of the solution, you are part of the problem." In reaction to the September 11, 2001, terrorist attacks, President George W. Bush declared, "Either you are with us, or you are with the terrorists." Such formulations deny legitimacy to any neutrals or possible intermediaries who might play a role in containing or moderating the conflict. Reframing the conflict away from a simple binary narrative is key to disrupting the escalation cycle.

Involvement of Other Parties

Once an overt struggle has begun, parties not initially engaged may envision significant benefits by joining the fray.[31] The struggle may provide an opportunity to inflict harm and weaken an old foe, or it may be an opportunity to win a portion of the spoils that a victory might yield. Sometimes a party will intervene out of obligation to support its friends or allies who are in the fight.

External interveners can contribute to conflict escalation by providing weapons, funds, or other implements of struggle, which enable the combatants to raise the magnitude of the means being used and to sustain the struggle. Thus, a study of civil strife in 114 countries found that external support for dissidents correlated 0.37 with the length of the civil strife and 0.22 with its pervasiveness.[32] As such, a hostile neighboring state has become one important predictor of civil strife as well as the durability of peace agreements.[33]

Often intrastate conflicts erupt because of broader interstate struggles between global or regional powers. During the Cold War, many local conflicts in Africa, Central America, Asia, and the Middle East were exacerbated and perpetuated by the superimposition of the conflict between the Soviet Union and the United States. Each superpower lent support to the enemy of the government supported by the other. Today, various intrastate conflicts in the

Middle East and North Africa, such as those in Libya, Syria, Yemen, Sudan, and Afghanistan, can only be understood in reference to broader tensions between Turkey, Iran, Israel, and Saudi Arabia as well as between global players such as Russia and the United States. Each of these actors seek governing arrangements which will benefit them, with many funneling money, arms, and political support to chosen proxies.

Other parties also tend to become engaged in a struggle because as the partisans pursue their goals, they sometimes infringe on the interests of parties not engaged. For example, in World War I, Germany used submarines to attack shipping to Great Britain and began sinking U.S. vessels prior to American entry in the war.[34] Furthermore, the German government secretly telegrammed the Mexican government proposing an alliance such that if the United States entered the war, Mexico would reconquer its lost territories. The secret telegram was discovered in March 1917 and, together with the submarine warfare, created such outrage in the United States that on April 2, the U.S. Congress declared war against Germany.

Outside parties not only can act to escalate or prolong a conflict by joining the struggle on one side, but they may also pursue policies to contain the conflict, barring support to all sides in the struggle. In addition, they may provide intermediary services to facilitate a de-escalation of a destructive struggle or assist in a shift to a constructive escalation. Some specialized units can provide alternatives to violent escalation and channel escalation to be constructive. For example, within the United States agencies such as the National Labor Relations Board oversee union recognition and other collective bargaining conflicts. The work of the Community Relations Service of the U.S. Department of Justice is also illustrative, using mediation and other forms of conciliation to help adversaries ease or settle their conflicts, minimizing a destructive escalation.

Some interventions can help prepare for relatively constructive escalations of conflicts. Thus, nongovernmental organizations may help provide training or resources that develop the capacity for challengers in countries dominated by repressive regimes to conduct well-considered nonviolent struggles that are less likely to escalate to the point of civil war. For example, over many years, the Fellowship of Reconciliation and the Servicio Paz y Justicia en America Latina have been conducting training in nonviolence in Latin America.[35]

The U.S. Department of State provides support to civil society organizations in many countries with authoritarian governments, which includes aiding nongovernmental organizations pushing for social and political reforms. For example, the Middle East Partnership Initiative's mission is to create partnerships that help build pluralistic, participatory, and prosperous societies in the Middle East and North Africa. Founded in 2002, the Middle East Partnership Initiative brings young academics and young activists from the region to the United States where they can learn possible ways to foster the changes they are seeking to make in their respective countries.

Available Conflict Management Entities

The availability of conflict management entities able to help parties interact and jointly solve shared problems has important implication for escalation. Where such arrangements are robust, conflicts are typically managed through established rules and norms that make it unlikely that partisans will adopt more destructive tactics. For example, conflicts regarding the use and management of the Great Lakes, which border Canada and the United States, are managed in part by two organizational entities. Within the United States the Great Lakes Commission consists of the governments of eight Great Lakes states and "promotes the orderly, integrated, and comprehensive development, use and conservation of the water and related natural resources of the Great Lakes basin and St. Lawrence River."[36] Since its founding in 1955, the Great Lakes Commission has adopted hundreds of policy resolutions to harmonize interstate policy on issues related to transportation, environmental protection, energy production, water withdrawals, and other matters. Recent efforts have focused on, for instance, controlling invasive species, building climate change resilience, and facilitating a clean water infrastructure.[37] At the international level the International Joint Commission serves a similar function, helping to coordinate bilateral agreements about the Great Lakes between Canada and the United States. The International Joint Commission's mission is to prevent and resolve disputes between the United States of America and Canada concerning Great Lakes management, to pursue the common good of both countries, and to serve as an independent and objective advisor to the two governments.[38] In both cases jointly negotiated decision making and dispute management arrangements have limited escalatory actions when disagreements arise.

In cases where conflicting parties do not have access to conflict mitigation arrangements, or where such arrangements are weak, biased, or not trusted, escalation is more apt to occur. Partisans manage their conflicts in an ad hoc basis and social-psychological challenges, such as the Prisoner's Dilemma problem reviewed earlier, tend to push them to adopt more extreme tactics in fear that the other side is doing the same. International politics—a space where there are weak governing structures but no global government—is a case in point. Absent an authoritative body capable of setting and enforcing global rules, members struggle to reduce escalations when tensions emerge.

In the South China Sea, for instance, disputed territorial waters have embroiled China, Taiwan, the Philippines, the United States, and other regional actors in a series of military moves and countermoves that have significantly escalated tensions, becoming a potential flashpoint for military action.

Where conflict management entities dispense justice unevenly, radicalization—the process of adopting more extreme views and tactics—can occur. The aggrieved party "takes matters into their own hands" to achieve a justice denied. Hence the saying, there can be no peace without justice. A 2020 study, for instance, found that the perception that a system is unfair is a significant driver of both right- and left-wing radicalization and serves as a prelude to legitimize revolutionary thought.[39]

Organizational Dynamics

As a conflict persists and particularly as coercive inducements are used, the internal organization of the adversaries often changes in ways that tend to escalate the struggle destructively. Three interrelated developments are particularly noteworthy: leadership developments, mobilization of partisans, and raised expectations.

Leadership Developments

Since leaders generally represent their constituents in conflicts with outsiders, they are predisposed to become identified with the group's already established goals and the means being used to pursue them. They are prone to entrapment because the costs are particularly high for them to admit that their policies are failing. Usually, they have publicly claimed the course of prevailing action to be correct; to admit they were mistaken might subject the leaders to charges of weakness and submission to the enemy. Thus, the leader may double-down on the losing strategy to save face.

Competition and rivalry among alternative leaders may also foster conflict escalation. For example, a study of civil rights leaders in fifteen U.S. cities in the 1960s found that militancy was lower among leaders in cities with minimal competition and higher in cities with competition.[40] Demonstrations, although short lived, were also more frequent where there was rivalry. However, when relatively moderate leaders challenge the established leaders, they may reduce their militancy. This is more likely to occur in later stages of a struggle, in particularly heterogeneous conflict units, with adversaries who are consistently conciliatory, and in relatively regulated conflicts.

A growth in the influence of leaders who are "hardline" and who advocate coercive inducements also contributes to conflict escalation. As a fight persists and increasing reliance is placed on coercive means the advocates and managers of those means tend to gain influence. For example, once the armed forces become engaged in an interstate conflict, military leaders assume greater dominance.[41] Usually, as the fight goes on those who are reluctant or who are critical of the means being used are silenced, are forced out of the leadership circle, or withdraw. The remaining leaders can then escalate the struggle, with less and less challenge. Authoritarian systems are particularly susceptible to this type of escalation. Such systems typically lack institutional impediments to blunting hardline policies, such as a division of power between branches of government, legitimate elections of leaders, or a free press. Absent these checks on power, authoritarian leaders increasingly amass more authority over decision making. Such power allows them to eliminate internal adversaries and critical voices with greater ease. Russia under Putin is one of many examples of this dynamic.

Even within less highly organized adversaries, as a conflict intensifies, shifts in the leadership can occur that enhance the influence of more intransigent persons. The new members of the leadership circle may be less likely than the established leaders to have nonconflicting relations with the adversary, and they are less likely to have a stake in the status quo. In community conflicts if the new leaders are not former community leaders, they may lack the constraints of maintaining previous community relations and be less subject to the cross-pressures ordinarily felt by members of community organizations.[42]

Escalation by leaders is often supported by subordinates to curry favor. For example, when President Trump decided to contest the outcome of the 2020 presidential election, even those who had doubts about that characterization yielded to the president. Individuals previously committed to "law and order" nonetheless embraced conspiracy and repeating unproven and dubious claims about electoral malfeasance, even when those claims failed to be substantiated by facts or upheld in numerous courts cases.[43] Many of Trump's supporters still accept such claims, although several high-profile resignations occurred in the aftermath of the Capitol insurrection.

Mobilization of Partisans

At the early stages of a conflict, as members begin to share their experiences, their information about deprivations and their sense of grievance tend to increase. For example, the Black Lives Matter movement was initially created as a hashtag social media campaign in response to anti-Black racism in the U.S. justice system, namely the acquittal of a white man in Florida in the shooting death of an unarmed Black teenager in 2012. Nurtured by other instances of race-bias across the United States, the movement quickly grew from a hashtag campaign to an entity with dozens of chapters across the United States sponsoring hundreds of events a year. This loose collection of organizations and chapters has been critical in helping multiple Americans tell their stories, hear the stories of others, and learn that some difficulties that had seemed personal and singular were in actuality part of a general societal pattern requiring structural remedies, not simply personal accommodations.

As a fight goes on, and as participation widens, persons who are predisposed to use more intense means join the struggle. One reason this happens is particularly pertinent for members of oppressed groups. The most deprived members of such groups generally do not become involved in a struggle until possible gains have become credible. But their feeling of grievance, once aroused, is likely to be greater than among persons who had the resources to initiate the struggle. The newly aroused also tend to be more radical because they are less constrained by mutual understandings reached earlier with the adversary and are less likely to have experienced compromises with opponents. Evidence for elements of this argument can be seen in recent surveys of Generation Z adults (those born after 1996), which show that younger generations are more likely than older generations to favor policies that would drastically move energy reliance away from fossil fuels or even eliminate such fuels entirely.[44]

When geographically distant persons join a struggle, they are likely to be highly motivated fighters, due to political ideology or religious faith. Such motivation tends to give them tenacity and a commitment to support conflict escalation. Prior to his death, the ability of Osama bin Laden and his associates to build the transnational al Qaeda network illustrates the coercive potentialities of such recruitment. That network has been built through the social affiliations of like-minded persons, and their militancy was intensified within closely linked groups.[45] The emergence of the Islamic State has similarly benefited from the recruitment of a global network of fighters. One study put the number of foreign fighters for ISIS in Syria during the height of that conflict at twelve thousand to fifteen thousand or approximately one-half of the total ISIS fighting force. These fighters hailed from over a dozen countries across the Middle East, Europe, and North America, with the majority coming from Egypt, Tunisia, Saudi Arabia, Morocco, and Jordan, followed by France, Britain, and Germany.[46]

Commitment to the Cause

The third organizational development that contributes to conflict escalation is the heightened commitment to the cause and a growing conviction that it is attainable. This can bolster reliance on constructive strategies as well as destructive ones. Increasing commitment is likely to occur at an early stage of a struggle as a conflict party rallies its forces but has not yet experienced the other side's punishing sanctions. Before difficult tests of strength occur, a group's conviction of victory is likely to grow as its forces mobilize. Within the insularity of the partisan group, mutual reassurances go unchecked, reinforcing a sense of power. If there are also some initial gains, the support for escalation is likely to grow rapidly. Such swellings of feelings may be short lived, but they can escalate swiftly in the form of mass mobilization, riots, strikes, and nonviolent protests. The heightened commitment dynamic was clearly at play throughout Egypt, Tunisia, Libya, and Yemen during the Arab Spring in early 2011. In each of these countries the sense that revolutionary transformation was at hand appears to have escalated the commitment of the protestors to the cause, leading to the rapid mobilization of additional groups of protestors.

Leaders of a gang, a guerilla army, or a country sometimes commit followers to the struggle by requiring them to participate in acting violently against enemies. In accord with cognitive dissonance theory, noted previously, those recruits will tend to justify their actions and come to believe in their positive value. At the very least, they are likely to feel compromised and unable to return to their former position.

Finally, adversaries who are part of armed wings of a movement or government, such as armies or police, may escalate coercive behavior quickly once those units begin operations. These entities, following their standard operating procedures, sometimes pursue policies that are inappropriate for the circumstances in which they are undertaken, resulting in unforeseen self-defeating escalation.[47] Once military forces engage in operations the level of coercion is often much greater than had been anticipated. This has been true in civil wars and in military replacement of civilian governments, as well as in waging interstate wars.[48] The outbreak of World War I is a frequently cited example of how plans for mobilization and military actions, once triggered, seemed to generate uncontrolled escalation, hence, the image of unconstrained wildness when "the dogs of war are unleashed."[49]

Social Dynamics

Two social dynamics have important impacts on escalation: (1) group homogeneity and (2) group differentiation.

Homogeneity

Adversaries with little internal diversity tend to better sustain increases in the severity of a conflict. In such cases, members are likely to respond similarly to events and to drown out dissident voices. Common myths and rituals aid the management of dissonance help to heal in-group ruptures when they occur, thereby allowing members to better coalesce around an external threat. For example, religious homogeneity provides members of a community with a common set of precepts, behavioral expectations, and moral code, each of which helps to mitigate internal division while also facilitating expressions of in-group favoritism and out-group bias (see chapter 2). Homogeneous groups also tend to share common channels of communication through which mobilization and messaging can be streamlined, events understood, stories told, and meaning provided.

Group leaders are therefore likely to amplify internal homogeneity when they engage in a conflict with an external adversary. They may institute policies to build support for the goals of the struggle and portray the enemy as a grave threat to vital interests and identities. Insofar as they are effective in these policies and alternative voices are absent, their constituency is less open to divisive efforts, and to conciliatory overtures, by the opposing side.[50] Thus, challenging revolutionary and other political movements often set broad goals and try to mobilize diverse constituencies in a common cause against a narrow-isolated opponent. For example, the popular 2011 Egyptian movement against the Hosni Mubarak regime rallied Copts and Muslims, traditional Islamists and relatively secular Egyptians, women and men, old and young, and members of business, professional, and other occupational strata. Of course, once the movement succeeded, divisions among the victors again emerged. This is often the case in postrevolutionary societies as a winning faction imposes its preferences on many of its former allies, as happened after the Russian, Cuban, and Iranian revolutions.

Conversely, internal heterogeneity can provide a basis for limiting escalation since various segments of a heterogeneous party tend to have different priorities relating to the struggle.[51] Furthermore, the costs of waging the struggle in heterogeneous groups are likely to be unevenly experienced and such differences can provide the grounds for opposing conflict escalation and prolongation.

Differentiation

Opponents with specialized agencies to wage struggles are more capable of increasing the severity of a conflict without widespread constituency support. This is an advantage professional armies have over conscript armies for waging wars that lack popular appeal. More generally, training, discipline, threat of punishment, a sense of honor, and loyalty to comrades in arms combine to keep combatants risking their lives, even when the odds of avoiding death or injury are poor.

In some circumstances, it is the very lack of coordination and control that can result in escalating events, since the persons in direct confrontation are not under effective control by their superiors, which often results in conflict escalation. Wartime atrocities such as massacres, looting, and rape sometimes are carried out by individual soldiers or militia or by small groups acting without orders, but atrocities are much more extensive when higher authorities condone such behavior as a way of intimidating and punishing the enemy. Indeed, in the former Yugoslavia rape was an instrument of a genocidal policy by Serb officials against Bosnians and Croats.[52] The recourse to gross human rights abuses, whether due to official orders, overzealousness, or lack of supervision, thus often has grievous escalatory consequences.

Other Conflicts

Another important variable related to conflict escalation is the partisans' engagement in other struggles. When an additional conflict becomes superimposed on a given struggle, both tend to escalate and be prolonged. For example, the 1936–1939 Spanish Civil War was long and bloody, in part because both internal adversaries thought they could persist and triumph with external support.[53] The fascist rebels led by General Francisco Franco sought to overthrow the elected Spanish government and were aided by the fascist states of Germany and Italy. The Loyalists for their part were aided by antifascist organizations from many countries in the world.

How conflicts are linked depends in part on the ideological and other ties among the partisans in specific fights and the analyses made by partisans about those ties. Dr. Ayman al-Zawahiri, an Egyptian surgeon and a leader of Egyptian Islamic Jihad, which had de facto merged with al Qaeda in 1998, became al Qaeda's theorist and planner.[54] His initial goal had been to overthrow the secular and oppressive Egyptian government, headed by Hosni Mubarak, and bring about a revival of Islam there. He came to believe that the West upheld the Mubarak government, thereby corrupting and humiliating Islamic society. Therefore, to succeed in overthrowing the oppressive non-Islamic governments in Muslim-populated countries, the West's and particularly American support of those governments had to be ended.

Sometimes, too, a minor conflict within one of the major adversaries escalates rather than being subordinated in the general struggle against the common enemy. One or both sides in the subordinate conflict may regard the larger struggle as an opportunity to escalate its own fight. In the shadow of that larger struggle, brutal suppression or genocidal policies may be undertaken, as happened in the Ottoman Empire during World War I to the Armenians, and in many civil wars around the world since then.

Interaction

How adversaries respond to each other's contentious conduct makes a significant and immediate impact on a conflict's escalation. These range from no responsiveness, to overreacting and overreaching, to overaccommodating.

Nonresponsiveness

When a group that is satisfied with the current situation substantively ignores an adversary's contentious behavior, the result sometimes is little or no change in the status quo and no escalation. The quiet rebuff may be followed by the adversary's quiescent acceptance of the situation, for a time. Conversely, nonresponsive conduct can also result in escalating a conflict, as the adversary resorts to more extreme actions to get a response from the opposing party that is ignoring its claims. Sometimes, a contending party believes the other side is stalling and not treating its issues seriously, even if negotiations have begun. Furthermore, nonresponsiveness is often experienced as a denial of significance and is therefore humiliating and seems to demand increased pressure. How an adversary responds to nonresponsive conduct is often a matter of power. If the nonresponsive party has a high capacity to control events, then the less-powerful group may believe it can only acquiesce.

Overreacting and Overreaching

Strong coercive countermeasures sometimes are effective in terminating a violent struggle. They may suppress the other side, destroying its ability to continue the struggle, or they may induce members of the other side to turn to nonviolent and less coercive means.[55] Channeling the other side to use nonviolent or legitimate institutionalized procedures is likely to be effective when punitive actions are narrowly focused and limited, and particularly if legitimate channels for protest and attaining desired changes are available. For example, consider the evolution of the Puerto Rican national independence movement. Shortly after World War II, the U.S. Congress, President Harry S Truman, and the Puerto Rican Legislative Assembly took steps to establish commonwealth status for Puerto Rico.[56] Some Puerto Ricans, however, favored independence, and formed a political party, the Partido Independentista Puertorriqueño (PIP). But in 1950 and 1954 a group of nationalists, unsatisfied with the electoral strategy of the PIP, carried out armed attacks in Puerto Rico and in Washington, DC. Although the PIP dissociated itself from those nationalist tactics, it garnered few votes in subsequent elections. Instead, support for statehood as an alternative to commonwealth status increased. Social and economic developments in Puerto Rico, suppression of violent attacks, avoidance of general repression, and the openness of the electoral political process have therefore limited the appeals of Puerto Rican independence and channeled the struggle within the existing political system.

Very often, however, once adversaries are engaged in a conflict, their contentious interaction tends to escalate in severity, as one side or both seeks to impose a settlement by increasing coercive pressure. Escalation is particularly likely if the step up in severity exceeds the normative expectations of the other side. The reaction may be of such outrage that the acts are rendered counterproductive—they fail to intimidate and instead provoke intensified and broader opposition. This tends to be the case for terrorist attacks against civilians when conducted by marginal social groups and for wide-ranging arrests and killings by authorities with a narrow base of support. Within the context of U.S. civil society, severe reactions against social protest can result in the protest's escalation.[57] For example, a study of colleges that had demonstrations against Vietnam War–related campus recruitment in 1967 found that the more severe the control measures used against civil disobedience, the more likely was the protest to expand. More famously, the violent police actions to suppress the civil rights demonstrations of 1963 in Birmingham, Alabama, resulted in expanding protests and intervention by the federal government.

Repression of violent protest can be effective under certain conditions, at least for a time. This is consistent with resource-mobilization, political-process, and rational-choice approaches to the study of social movements, which stress the opportunities and capabilities to engage in protest actions. These approaches suggest that there is a curvilinear relationship between the repressiveness of governments and domestic political violence. Domestic political violence tends to be greatest in societies with intermediate levels of repression. In countries with relatively high levels of consistent repression, dissent and opposition tends to be suppressed. In societies with relatively little repression, opposition could be expressed more easily and nonviolently.[58] The quiet order of a society with a repressive regime is considered here to be a relatively destructive condition, referred to by Johan Galtung as a "negative peace." Struggles resulting in overturning a repressive regime could therefore contribute to a more constructive relationship.

Regarding interstate conflicts, a great deal of discussion has occurred about the effectiveness of military strength as a way of deterring escalation. On the one hand, the argument of traditional "realists" is that having the military strength to deter attack prevents wars. On the other hand, critics of that approach argue that as each side arms itself to deter the other, the resulting arms race generates mutual fear and hostility and often escalates disputes into wars. The evidence indicates that arms races increase the likelihood that serious interstate disputes do escalate to warfare.[59] This is the case when the dispute is between states that are rivals and contiguous. The evidence does not indicate that an arms race by itself results in a war, but that it contributes to the tendency to resort to war in the context of an ongoing crisis or militarized dispute. Furthermore, bullying strategies in militarized situations tend to escalate disputes into war.[60]

One form of overreaction is a result of failing to adequately recognize differences within the enemy side. In those circumstances, employment of violence may be indiscriminate or threats to use violence threaten to harm persons who are not directly engaged in the struggle. Those impacted by the broadness of the attack are made parties to the fight, thus increasing the scope and probably the severity of the struggle. Efforts at countering terrorist attacks from within or outside a country are susceptible to overreaction.

Another danger is that of overreaching. As a conflict party's leaders believe they are winning, they often raise their demands. However, that may well intensify resistance, resulting in a protracted destructive conflict. For instance, the decision of President Bush and his close associates to invade Iraq and remove the Saddam Hussein regime was eased by the quick U.S.-led attack that overthrew the Taliban regime in Afghanistan in October 2001.[61] This victory was accomplished by a small number of American personnel with few casualties, which gave the decision makers greater confidence that they would be successful in Iraq as well. The Afghan triumph also made public willingness to attack Iraq more likely. Moreover, public support for a war against al Qaeda's Afghan haven could be transferred to supporting the war on Iraq if it were presented as part of the war on terrorism. The government leadership so portrayed the war despite the lack of sound evidence, and the media gave little attention to dissenting views.

Overaccommodating

At times of a crisis, accommodative reactions to demands and threats can end the crisis and prevent a conflict from escalating. Over longer time periods, conciliatory responses even to significant demands can result in new, mutually acceptable relationships, without having escalated to highly destructive encounters. Thus, during the depression of the 1930s in the United States, large-scale movements and demonstrations arose, demanding assistance in the face of loss of income. The administration of President Franklin D. Roosevelt and the U.S. Congress introduced many welfare measures to satisfy the needs underlying the protests.[62] These assuaging measures averted greater demonstrations and radicalization of the demonstrators.

However, sometimes concessions or too mild responses can result in conflict escalation, since the party making the demands insists on even more, sensing weakness on the other side. Those making the concessions then fear even greater demands and increase their resistance; what is then demanded is seen as intolerably excessive and a highly intense fight may ensue. The 1938 meeting in Munich where the British and French governments yielded to Nazi Germany's demands regarding its incorporation of the Sudetenland region of Czechoslovakia is the most notorious example of the escalating consequences of appeasement.

In a variety of circumstances, acting in a conciliatory fashion in the face of demands and threats can be followed by raised demands by the adversaries and weakening resistance. Thus, when the East European governments led by Communist parties faced waves of demonstrations in 1989, concessions did not stem growing demands for fundamental change. For example, the president of the German Democratic Republic (GDR) made the concession of resigning on October 18, 1989. His successor, another Communist Party leader, Egon Krenz, yielded too many popular demands, but the moves were too late and insufficient. The end came quickly with the rupture of the Berlin Wall, which resulted from the conjuncture of bumbling mistakes, misunderstandings, and the actions of East Berlin crowds. The Krenz government drafted new travel laws for GDR citizens wishing to travel outside East Germany. Krenz gave an outline of the new laws to Günter Schabowski who was about to hold a press conference, on November 9, 1989, to announce the composition of the new Politburo. Asked about the travel laws, Schabowsk, being unfamiliar with the material given him, said that GDR citizens could travel abroad at the border crossings, without passports, starting immediately. News of this spread quickly and East Germans rushed to crossings at the Berlin Wall. West Berliners hurried to the wall to greet them. As people rushed to the crossing points, they called out that the gates be opened. The East German border guards had no orders, and they opened the gates. There was no violence. East and West Berliners danced, sang, and drank together.[63] Krenz resigned on December 3, 1989, and the East German Communist system soon collapsed.

SUMMARY AND DISCUSSION QUESTIONS

Multiple variables interact in every conflict to shape its escalatory trajectory and relative destructiveness. No single factor wholly determines the course of a struggle, and therein lie many possibilities for averting or transforming a prolonged and destructive struggle. Sometimes the mix of ingredients constituting a conflict is conducive to limiting destructive escalations. Adversaries may have at their disposal joint problem-solving institutions, be able to communicate and interact with each other with ease, share a superordinate identity, and have the skills needed to reframe a conflict from an existential threat to a negotiable and shared problem. Other times underlying forces converge to escalate a conflict rapidly and destructively. Leaders may emerge who issue stark ultimatums to their opponents, opponents' sense of in-group solidarity increases as they are threatened, polarization of relations expands, external parties join the quarrel, and new partisans who are unhindered by previous agreements and norms employ more coercive tactics to achieve their ends. For the conflict analyst this vast array of variables can be daunting. Yet the complexity of variables that contribute to the escalation of a fight also offers multiple targets upon which to build a constructive conflict intervention. Escalations can and are frequently interrupted. But to do so one must first understand their constituent parts.

To consider the issues raised in this chapter more deeply, readers are encouraged to consider the following questions, either individually or within a group setting.

1. Think about a conflict that you or your community recently experienced. How would you describe escalation that occurred during the conflict? Was it rapid and sharp, slow but sustained, or short-lived? What accounted for this trajectory; specifically, which variables shared in this chapter best help you understand the escalation phase?
2. Part of this chapter focused on how polarization of intergroup relations can lead to destructive phases of escalation. Where have you seen such polarization occurring? What dynamics appeared to feed the polarization process? How might such polarizations be contained or reversed?
3. Where have you seen the "spiral of escalation" occurring? Where have you seen that spiral interrupted? What lessons learned does the example you thought of offer to the field of constructive conflicts?
4. Both leaders and followers contribute to conflict escalations. Pick a case and examine how both groups contributed to the escalatory process.

Chapter Seven

De-Escalation

Just as conflicts escalate, so too they de-escalate. During these periods adversaries may moderate their language, pause their attacks, adopt less destructive conflict tactics, open new channels of communication, or engage with each other in a search for a mutual accommodation to the problem at hand. In very intense conflicts de-escalations often slowly and unevenly; periods of reduced intensity may be interrupted by periods of renewed escalation. A faction opposed to an improving relation with an enemy, for instance, may temporarily "spoil" peacemaking efforts by more moderate factions.[1] Other times de-escalations are relatively fast and steady as trust among opponents builds and pressure for improved conditions mounts. Thus the "ladder of escalation," introduced in the previous chapter, becomes a ladder of de-escalation, with every step down the ladder making the next step possible.

De-escalations occur for many reasons. It may be that those engaged in the conflict reach a precipice where they believe that continued belligerence risks mutual destruction. Or perhaps a de-escalation stage is reached because of new leadership, changing demographics, or the emergence of other conflicts that are more pressing, thus rendering the current one obsolete. Often a combination of factors needs to converge for de-escalation to occur and be sustained. We present several of the most significant variables that contribute to conflict de-escalation in Table 7.1. They include those related to social-psychological dynamics, organizational dynamics, relational dynamics, and systemic-structural dynamics.

Table 7.1. Pathways to De-Escalation

Social-Psychological Dynamics	*Organizational and Tactical Dynamics*	*Systemic and Structural Dynamics*
A hurting stalemate is reached. Belief that a "better option" exists becomes broadly accepted. Development of sympathy and empathy for the other. Cathartic events/rituals reduce the emotional saliency of the issue.	Constituencies for de-escalation mobilize. Conflict issues are contained. Conflict management skills are acquired and internalized. Ties between disputants are established.	Changing structural and systemic conditions. Windows of opportunity open. Intervention by external parties. Changing contexts.

SOCIAL-PSYCHOLOGICAL DYNAMICS

Three social-psychological dynamics are implicated in conflict de-escalation: (1) perceiving a hurting stalemate, (2) developing sympathy and empathy for an opponent, and (3) catharsis and emotional relief.

Hurting Stalemates, Ripeness, and a Better Option

Conflicts generally remain escalated as long as adversaries believe they can achieve their goals through coercive unilateral action. Both sides calculate that if they apply just a little more pressure their adversary will surely yield. As we saw in the previous chapter, such thinking is the basis for both entrapment and the Prisoner's Dilemma (PD), a situation where partisans jointly adopt increasingly severe tactics out of fear that if they de-escalate while an opponent escalates the consequences will be disastrous.

Sometimes, however, participants in a conflict reach a point called by Zartman a hurting stalemate: a belief that neither side is capable of prevailing over the other, that a better option is available, and that working with the adversary to contain the conflict is more likely to achieve desired ends than the unilateral imposition of will.[2] The perception of a hurting stalemate can transform a frozen conflict into dynamic one, opening new possibilities for climbing down the ladder of escalation. If all sides reach a hurting stalemate at the same time a conflict is said to arrive at a "ripe moment," a window of opportunity where new ideas and proposals can be more successfully introduced.

Hurting stalemates and the ripe moments they engender come about for a variety of reasons. An impending or recently avoided catastrophe sometimes facilitates de-escalatory steps as adversaries recognize the dangers of continued escalation.[3] During the 1962 Cuban Missile Crisis, for instance, the United States and the Soviet Union came horrifically close to nuclear war. In its aftermath, President Kennedy and Premier Khrushchev agreed on several steps to improve communication and provide an early warning for impending future crises, such as the "hot phone," which would allow instant communication between Washington and Moscow.

Ripe moments also occur once all sides perceive that the gains of compromising outweigh the costs of inaction. For example, scientific consensus and recent extreme weather events have convinced a growing number of countries that drastic actions to reduce greenhouse gases are becoming imperative. In 2021 a U.S. Department of Defense report concluded that "increasing temperatures; changing precipitation patterns; and more frequent, intense, and unpredictable extreme weather conditions caused by climate change are exacerbating existing risks" and argued that climate change should be elevated as a primary national security risk.[4] Thus the era of climate diplomacy is, perhaps, beginning to ripen as some nations reassess the costs and benefits of climate mitigation and adaptation policies. At the conclusion of the November 2021 COP26 Climate Summit in Glasgow, Scotland, participating diplomats committed to revisit and strengthen their current emissions targets to limit global warming limit of 1.5 degrees by 2030 and make additional commitments toward a one hundred billion dollar global Adaptation Fund for developing countries. Participants also finalized the "Paris rulebook," which outlines provisions related to governance, mitigation, transparency, finance, and other climate agreement matters.[5] Whether new climate commitments will mitigate the worst effects of climate change remains to be seen.

In asymmetrical conflicts, where one side enjoys superior power to another, ripe moments can be created by empowering the less powerful actor, thereby raising the cost to previously more powerful side for its intransience. These strategies can be thought of as "peace-pushing" in reference to the use of coercive but nonviolent strategies to induce an adversary to change its behavior or come to the negotiation table. For instance, a group of workers may organize a work stoppage or threaten to unionize their workplace to gain concessions from management related to working conditions and compensation. Or a social movement may take to the street to protest environmentally harmful practices of a corporation, perhaps disrupting production and drawing attention to their cause. So too alliances of less powerful actors may assemble to "push" more powerful players to compromise on their agenda. In 1955, for instance, a collection of nations including Indonesia, Egypt, India, and Yugoslavia formed the Non-Aligned Movement, an alliance of less-developed countries seeking to bypass the politics of an increasingly bipolar world and pursue their own agenda under the

"Bandung Principles" of Afro-Asian solidarity.[6] Of course, characterizing which peace-pushing activities are constructive and which are destructive is a matter of interpretation and positionality. Different observers looking at the same escalatory action may disagree as to whether that action taken is likely to result in a constructive or a destructive outcome.

Finally, ripe moments require the availability of "a way out"; that is, a viable pathway to a new situation that is better than the one currently being experienced. As one example, in the fall of 2020 the United Arab Emirates and Israel reached a breakthrough agreement to establish formal relations. Shortly thereafter Bahrain, Sudan, and Morocco also joined what has become known as the Abraham Accords, which were brokered by President Trump and his son-in-law Jared Kushner.[7] Key to its signing was convincing each stakeholder that the economic dividends and security provisions made possible through normalization offered a better alternative than continued hostilities. And indeed, new trade agreements rapidly followed diplomatic recognition with business exchanges between Israel and the United Arab Emirates alone reaching five hundred million dollars by August 2021.[8] The Trump administration further incentivized the deal by providing military hardware to some Arab signatories. Some now speculate that Saudi Arabia and Israel will normalize relations based on a similar model soon. Breakthroughs such as this often benefit by the existence of a mutual enemy, in this case Iran. Thus, the benefits of a rapprochement between two previous opponents needs to be balanced against the costs that such accommodations may have on future conflicts with other actors.

Sympathy, Empathy, and Transforming Otherness

Sympathizing with others significantly contributes to conflict de-escalation. A person sympathizing with another person feels what that other person feels and is emotionally moved by the other's feelings.[9] Being sympathetic to members of another group tends to inhibit harming them; indeed, it would evoke actions to help them. Certain policies and experiences can trigger and sustain these processes, even between enemies. For example, many conflict transformation practitioners use workshops, dialogues, and other means of intergroup contact to undermine the effects of earlier personal negative experiences between antagonistic individuals or groups (see chapter 8). Such interaction, under the right circumstances, has been shown to break down negative stereotypes, counteract dehumanization, build trust, and nurture the development of new shared identities.[10] Through interaction enemies may find they share common experiences, concerns, and passions that bridge the "otherness" that has grown between them.

The capacity of empathy, compared with sympathy, stresses taking the role of the other without losing one's identity.[11] Research confirms that empathy—or, as it is sometimes called, perspective-taking—is associated with a decrease in discriminatory attitudes and an increased willingness to engage in intergroup interaction.[12] Empathy is also associated with prosocial behavior in interpersonal relations as well as with a willingness to engage in reconciliation in the aftermath of conflict.[13] Among the several components often noted as constituting empathy, four are particularly relevant for ameliorating destructive conflict escalation. First, empathy includes accurately perceiving the other persons' feelings and thoughts relating to the conflict. Second, empathetic persons experience those feelings and thoughts as if they were their own. Third, persons distinguish their own thoughts and feelings from those of the persons with whom they empathize. Finally, empathy includes communicating that experience to the others. This may be most fully realized in a therapeutic or intimate interpersonal relationship, but some degree of these various components can also occur in larger social conflicts.

Catharsis and Memorialization

As discussed in chapter 1, intense conflicts are fueled not just by incompatible goals, but also by strong emotions such as rage, fear, humiliation, and hatred. Strong emotional responses, particularly in the wake of trauma, may fuel antisocial behavior and support in-group solidarity, out-group bias, and the cycle of revenge.[14] Moreover, the collective repression of emotions has been implicated in the initiation and sustaining of large-scale violent conflicts.[15] Finding ways to deal with intense and collective emotions is thus central to de-escalation.

In clinical settings cathartic techniques have been used to help patients manage unresolved grief. Re-grief therapy, for instance, is based on the principle that after a grief event people need to complete the mourning process to restore psychological equilibrium.[16] More generally, the notion of catharsis is used by psychologists in reference to prosocial activity that helps people discharge negative emotions, relieve anxiety and fear, and reduce stress (e.g., using art to represent a traumatic event, retelling the story of a traumatic event multiple times to overcome its emotional saliency, and "primal therapy" where pain, anger, and fear are released spontaneously and directed toward an imaginary source). The idea behind such interventions is that individuals generally face difficulties moving forward in their lives, or engage in living with or mending broken relationships, until they have a chance to fully express and process the emotional impacts that traumatic events have had on their lives.

In cases of collective trauma, public rituals can be used to help de-escalate the emotional resonance of a painful conflict episode, thus creating new pathways to the more constructive management of that conflict. Truth and reconciliation commissions, for example, have been used in the aftermath of civil wars and other forms of collective violence to provide a vehicle for public storytelling about traumatic events. Evidence suggests that such processes help some, but not all, individuals overcome a sense of disempowerment and marginalization associated with victimization.[17] Public memorialization and commemoration—the process through which societies impacted by violence reflect on and preserve memories of their past—has also been associated with emotional recovery and even reconciliation. Public apologies and annual commemoration events are also associated with emotional healing.[18]

ORGANIZATIONAL AND TACTICAL DYNAMICS

Among the organizational and tactical dynamics that appear to facilitate de-escalations are constituencies for de-escalation, reciprocity in interaction, issue containment, adopting of new conflict management skills, and ties between adversaries. Each is discussed in the following.

Constituencies for De-Escalation

The emergence of a constituency for accommodation within a contending group is an important condition for de-escalation. Constituencies for de-escalation arise from many sources. The costs of continuing a fight grow as the struggle goes on, raising doubts about the benefit of the goals sought. Moreover, the burdens of a long, escalating struggle often become increasingly unequal. Those suffering the inequities may dissent and withdraw support; in a war, this may take the form of draft riots, desertion, and flight. For example, in World War I, the Russian people's increasing losses yielded growing opposition to the war against Germany and generated support to the Communist party, which was able to seize power and take Russia out of the war.

Dissent and opposition to official hard-liner policies can be mobilized readily insofar as groups of people favoring accommodation with an adversary are already present and are linked by existing communication networks. Thus, American opponents to the U.S. intervention in Vietnam and to the invasion of Iraq were able to mobilize demonstrations and other acts of resistance by their ties to previous peace movement organizations, to traditional peace churches, to student organizations, and to civil rights organizations both at home and abroad.[19]

Even the increased severity of the means used by an individual or faction within a conflict organization, as a struggle escalates, can become a turning point toward de-escalation. If the actions cross the boundary of what most people regard as acceptable conduct, then the perpetrators and their cause suffer. In these cases, even other members of the organization to which the perpetrators belong may be so outraged as to withdraw support. This happened in the struggle for Quebec independence from Canada.[20] In the 1960s, the Quebec separatist movement grew rapidly, and the Front de Libération du Québec (Quebec Liberation Front), a tiny Maoist organization, carried out bombings and conducted robberies for funds. These actions culminated in October 1970 with the kidnapping of two officials, one of whom was killed. Prime Minister Pierre Trudeau invoked the War Measures Act, and the Front de Libération du Québec was made illegal. Since that time the separatist movement has used electoral and negotiation methods, while violence as a means of winning independence has been widely repudiated.

Once de-escalation has gotten under way, several organizational processes can come into play that advance the process of de-escalation and make turning back difficult. Particularly if a major agreement has been reached, the signers have a stake in pursuing the path they began. For example, the Good Friday agreement signed in April 1998 helped resolve the protracted conflict in Northern Ireland, even though implementing the agreement has been an arduous process. Although in a referendum 70 percent voted yes (with just over 50 percent among the unionists), resistance among many opponents remained strong. Then, in August 1998, twenty-eight persons were killed in an explosion in Omagh; the Real Irish Republican Army, a splinter group of the Provisional IRA, claimed responsibility. Nevertheless, despite such acts, and despite delays in implementation, and even threats of withdrawal from the agreed-on process, the supporters persevered, the institutions foreseen in the agreement were established, and the provisions of the agreement slowly fulfilled.[21]

Reciprocity in Interaction

In certain circumstances, a severe counteraction may force the other side to lower its resistance or to discontinue the struggle. Yet at the same time under-reaction may also bring about the de-escalation or even the termination of a struggle. One side, for example, may make such concessions to its adversary that the adversary's goals are sufficiently satisfied, the struggle then de-escalates. Some de-escalating strategies incorporate both processes (e.g., attacking the opponent's leadership harshly while offering concessions and positive inducements to the rank-and-file members of the opposing side).

Three related processes of adversary interaction help to aid de-escalation: (1) reacting equivalently, (2) learning about the struggle and the adversary, and (3) developing shared norms. In the first process, reacting equivalently, each side reacts in a measured and equivalent level to the other. In this scenario, one or both sides avoid acting in ways they think may be provocative or may invite an aggrandizing move by the other side. The response selected by President Kennedy to the Soviet emplacement of missiles in Cuba in 1962, noted previously, was "quarantine." It was not a dismissal of the matter as of little consequence or simply a protest at the United Nations, nor was it a provocative air strike or an invasion of Cuba. President Kennedy had recently read Barbara Tuchman's book *The Guns of August*, which analyzed the swift escalation to World War I, and he was determined to allow time for discovering acceptable ways out of the crisis, thereby avoiding a runaway escalation of words and deeds.[22] Having drawn that lesson from history, he took what he regarded as a measured response, which would not provoke an escalating interaction. He also communicated directly with Soviet Premier Nikita Khrushchev and closely monitored the operations of the U.S. quarantine.[23] Each side's actions during the crisis were roughly equivalent.[24]

The second interaction process that can have de-escalating effects is acquiring information and insight from research and from experience with the adversary.[25] As each side learns more about the other, about differences within it, and their views of themselves and their situation, each makes better estimates of how the other side will react to its initiatives, which reduces the likelihood of unintentional and ineffective escalation. For instance, engaging in backchannel communication to avert a crisis depends on the capacity of one side to accurately interpret the signals of the other.[26] Similarly, the theory of nonprovocative defense as an antidote to escalation is based on each side having a capacity to signal to the other that its military policies are based on defensive rather than offensive military thinking, China's "no first use" policy on nuclear weapons being one example.[27] In both cases, having an accurate understanding of an adversary's concerns and motivations can make the difference between conflict escalation and de-escalation.

Finally, adversaries sometimes develop shared norms guiding conduct in the arenas in which they are contending. The rules themselves may be matters of dispute for a time, but once agreed upon, they provide guidance for waging a conflict that constrains the antagonists from escalating very far. Thus collective bargaining between management and union representatives is carried out concerning certain matters, but not all matters about which workers and managers may disagree. In international affairs, normative regimes sometimes develop that help stabilize and manage areas of recurrent disputes.[28]

Issue Containment

Taking steps to make sure that a struggle is contained to a specific goal also facilitates de-escalation. In 1963, Martin Luther King Jr. and the Southern Christian Leadership Conference led the Blacks of Birmingham, Alabama, in an economic boycott, in demonstrations, in sit-ins, and into jail.[29] Although the local civil rights leaders did expand their goals to include national concerns, the local goals remained paramount. King's group kept focused on what they sought from Birmingham's economic elite: desegregation of public facilities in downtown department stores, fair hiring procedures in retail stores and city departments, and appointing a biracial commission to set a timetable for the desegregation of the public schools. A variety of tactics were used, but the focus on specific goals was sustained.

As a struggle persists, issues can even begin to contract. One of the adversaries, failing to attain its grand goals, may find settling for what it can get to be its best option. A conflict party that believes it is unable to impose its preferences will come to recognize that it must deal more realistically with its adversary. In such cases, the great matters in contention between them tend to be broken down into more manageable subissues. When adversaries fractionate the conflict into specific issues, some may appear easily settled and trade-offs among several issues become possible.[30] We discuss this further in the section on negotiation in the following chapter.

Finally, inflammatory issues may be contained by the development of superordinate goals, shared goals that are given primacy over the contentious ones.[31] One kind of superordinate goal that sometimes emerges, when antagonists believe they are mired in a situation that is increasingly destructive, is to find an acceptable mutual escape. Adversaries often decide to de-escalate their conflict and even agree upon a settlement when both believe that the continued destructive encounter risks a worst outcome. Superordinate goals also may arise because of the rising salience of a perceived common enemy or of a shared identity. Thus, tension between Catholics and Protestants in Northern Ireland was reduced in the wake of the 9/11 terrorist attacks. After that attack, financial backers of Sinn Féin and Irish paramilitary groups reconsidered support for violent tactics and a superordinate Christian identity temporarily emerged between Protestants and Catholics, which reduced sectarianism.[32]

Development of New Skills

Unfortunately, entities embroiled in a fight often become trapped in a conflict because they are not aware of, or do not know how to apply, proven tools and conflict management techniques. These tools include learning about and communicating across cultural difference, developing a capacity to reflectively listen to others, mapping the underlying drivers of conflict, negotiating and problem-solving based on shared interests, and developing a capacity to monitor and verifying agreements reached.

Conflict-management skills training appears to be somewhat effective in reducing instances of destructive conflict and facilitating de-escalation across multiple settings. In health care settings, for instance, interpersonal communications skills training was shown to reduce role conflict, decrease bullying, increase feelings of safety, and reduce absenteeism.[33] In school settings, peer mediation training has led to a decrease in the intensity of student-to-student conflicts as measured by the number of conflict referrals to teachers and administrators.[34] Other studies, however, show that violence reduction trainings among school children had less significant impacts, possibly due to the duration of the training and the limits of such training in settings impacted by daily violence.[35]

Assessing the impact of conflict-management skills training in complex settings, such as civil wars, is often difficult to do. In these cases, it is complicated to isolate the impact of a training program from other social, economic, and political developments that are occurring at the same time. In general, conflict-management trainings are more likely to be effective prior to a conflict emerging or escalating or during periods of de-escalation and settlement. During these periods of time the emotional intensity of a conflict is lower and opportunities for interaction across conflicting groups more feasible. Adversaries are unlikely to desire or use less destructive techniques in highly escalated disputes.

Building Ties between Adversaries

As a struggle persists and escalates destructively, some members of the opposing sides sometimes communicate with each other to facilitate a de-escalation of the conflict. They serve as quasi mediators, conveying information and suggestions between the antagonistic parties.[36] They may also develop bonds with each other and thus form an interest group within their own camps for de-escalation. Often, the leaders of one or more sides try to isolate the leaders of the other camp, making overtures to the subordinates and to supporters, as well as to dissenters within the other camp. This strategy may entail formulating objectives that are attractive to important groups within the opposing camps.

If the conflict persists with recurrent confrontations, the representatives of the opposing sides can develop shared expectations about how the next confrontation will be handled, and if previous confrontations were contained and settled in a mutually acceptable fashion, the next one tends to be guided by the positive previous experience. This is particularly likely in a setting with an ongoing personal relationship between the adversaries (e.g., within a given business organization, members often have problems in common).[37]

Finally, where official representatives of opposing sides are unwilling or unable to resolve their differences, unofficial representatives can step in to explore areas of agreement that could be possible. This was the case with the Geneva Accords, an unofficial roadmap for peace between Israelis and Palestinians, which was negotiated by former Palestinian and Israeli government officials and then presented to the public for consideration in 2003.[38] Difficult environmental conflicts have also benefited from informal and off-the-record exchanges between stakeholders from various sectors. In the 1990s, for instance, the Center for Policy Negotiation hosted a series of off-the-record interactions between representatives of business, labor, environmental, and state and federal government representatives. The goal was to determine if a common ground approach to addressing climate change might be possible outside of the glare of the public spotlight where posturing tended to occur. Such processes have varyingly been called track-two diplomacy, backchannel diplomacy, and policy dialogues. They are nearly always facilitated by a neutral third-party facilitator. We explore the ideas behind them in more detail in the next chapter.

SYSTEMIC AND STRUCTURAL DYNAMICS

De-escalations are not solely driven by how adversaries think, feel, and behave, nor by the way organizations are structured or the tactics they adopt. De-escalation may also be driven because of contextual changes in the external environment. We discuss four of these forces here.

Changing Structural and Systemic Conditions

The degree of economic and political inequality in a society is generally—though not always—predictive of social instability and violence.[39] Horizontal inequalities between identity groups and states have, for instance, been shown to significantly contribute to violent ethnonationalist conflict.[40] As reviewed elsewhere in this book the reasons for this correlation are complex. Inequality has corrosive impacts on social relations. Government failure to satisfy basic human needs can leads to social unrest, burgeoning social movements, rioting, terrorism, and war, particularly where disadvantaged populations perceive their relative depravation.[41] Societies with a high level of inequality are more likely to be comprised of individuals tolerant of group-based hierarchy.[42] High inequality combined with poor economic performance and weak political institutions tends to result in persistent political volatility.[43]

If such inequalities are reduced, however, de-escalations may occur. For example, between the late 1800s and the 1920s areas of the United States were convulsed by labor wars brought on by the industrialization of the American economy. As industrialization accelerated, industrialists such as Andrew Carnegie pursued a policy of vertical integration whereby all stages of production were owned by a single company and profits accumulated in the hands of a small group of shareholders. By the mid-1920s income inequality reached historic highs with the top 1 percent of families receiving nearly 0.25 percent of all pretax income. Throughout those decades workers in several industries, including coal and steel, began to organize to improve wages and safety, reduce time on the job, and guarantee speech. Violence often followed. For over two decades, Industrialists reacted by unionization efforts by hiring guards to disrupt organizational efforts and maintain surveillance. Active unionists were blacklisted, and striking workers replaced. Hundreds were killed in clashes. With the outbreak of World War I, government policy began to change as demand for coal spiked. Starting in the early 1930s the federal government passed a series of legislative initiatives aimed at protecting the right to unionize, such as the Norris-LaGuardia Act in 1932, the National Industrial Recovery Act in 1933, and the National Labor Relations Act of 1935. Other government provisions that were part of President Franklin Roosevelt's New Deal included banking reform, emergency relief programs, back-to-work programs, agricultural policy reforms, the Social Security Act, and aid for tenant farmers and migrant workers. Collectively the impact of these programs was to reduce inequality while also protecting the right of workers to organize. The decade of the 1930s did not bring an end to labor-management conflict, but it did usher in a stage of significant de-escalation facilitated by significant structural and systemic adjustments.[44]

Windows of Opportunity

Sometimes significant events outside of the domain of the conflict can open a window of opportunity for de-escalation. For example, as noted at the beginning of chapter 6, South Korea's hosting of the 2018 Winter Olympics in Pyeongchang provided an opportunity to propose dialogue between the United States and the Democratic People's Republic of Korea, which had erupted after North Korean nuclear and intercontinental strategic missile tests a year earlier. Moreover, the Pyeongchang Olympics provided South Korean President Moon Jae-in with cover to improve relations with his counterparts in the North. Notably, Kim Jong-un's younger sister, Kim Yo-jong, who attended the Olympics, became first member of the North's ruling family to visit the South since the Korean War, opening a period of renewed peacebuilding between the North and South.

Other examples of windows of opportunity that pave the way for de-escalation include Pope Francis's highly symbolic visit to Iraq in 2021, the funeral of the venerated public servant Senator John McCain, which temporarily thawed tensions between Republican and Democrat leaders in the United States, and the 2004 Indian Ocean earthquake and tsunami where the scale of the humanitarian disaster lead to a pause in hostility within the interstate conflict in the Aceh region of Indonesia and precipitated the Memorandum of Understanding between the Government of Indonesia and Gerakan Aceh Merdeka.[45] In each of these cases an external event triggered an opportunity for adversaries to interact in more constructive ways, to change the way they frame the conflict, and to build a new narrative of interaction not dominated by hostility and coercion.

Interventions by External Parties

Adversaries contend with each other within a social context involving many other parties, and those other parties often foster de-escalation. First, they sometimes provide models of the way de-escalation may occur, or at least provide the vision that de-escalation is feasible. Thus, to bring about the transformation of colonial Rhodesia into independent Zimbabwe and end internal warfare, a system of transition was negotiated in 1979, mediated by Lord Carrington. This helped provide a model for arrangements in Namibia and other countries, as well as to establish a system of transition for implementing ceasefires and providing procedures to legitimate new governments, for example, through monitored elections.[46]

Second, outside parties often set limits to the escalation of a conflict and intervene to enforce those limits. A prominent example is UN Peacekeeping operations, which in 2021 had deployments in twelve different countries involving over 74,655 troops from 121 countries.[47] Peacekeeping not only impedes direct confrontation between adversaries, but it also helps to establish a "cool-down" period where active confrontations cease, the emotional resonance of being in an active fight settles, and the cycle of revenge and counter-revenge is broken.

External interventions may at times impose a cessation of the use of particularly destructive means to ensure that one of the adversaries is not too badly damaged. For example, the United States and Russia collaborated in a major diplomatic effort to monitor and reduce chemical weapon stockpiles in Syria beginning in 2013; following Russian military escalation, they negotiated a ceasefire agreement in Syria in 2016.

Finally, other parties may assist the antagonists to de-escalate their struggle, for example, by providing a face-saving way out of the fight. This includes offering a peace proposal that an adversary would reject if made by its enemy but accepts when suggested by a mediator. The intermediaries may also forcefully intervene and help impose a settlement of the conflict, but such intervention sometimes only freezes the conflict at its status.

Changes in Context

Shifts in the salience of other conflicts with which a pair of adversaries are associated can profoundly contribute to the de-escalation of their struggle. For example, the shift to U.S.–Soviet détente in the early 1970s was fostered by changes in the prominence of other conflicts.[48] Thus, the Soviet–Chinese antagonism had intensified, demonstrated by bloody border skirmishes in 1969. That provided an incentive for each of those powers to be less intransigent toward the United States. Concurrently, the U.S. engagement in the Vietnam War was an overwhelming concern when Nixon was elected president in 1969. He and his advisors reasoned that an acceptable way out of Vietnam might be found by being more accommodating to the Soviet Union and the People's Republic of China, playing one against the other and isolating North Vietnam. Furthermore, the newly elected Social Democratic government of West Germany undertook a policy of accommodation with the Soviet Union, East Germany, and other countries of Eastern Europe, which eased and indeed fostered U.S.–Soviet accommodation.

The end of the Cold War, marked by the fall of the Berlin Wall in 1989, and then the dissolution of the Soviet Union in 1991, also impacted many conflicts throughout the world, including the struggles in South Africa and the Middle East. Many of these conflicts had been linked to the Cold War, with Soviet and American support going to the opponents waging bloody wars. The end of the Cold War required the local combatants to change their ways, hastening the end of their wars.

Many other contextual developments affect the possible de-escalation of conflicts, including changes in the protagonists' economies. Economic expansion, which is a goal shared by most adversaries, encourages cooperation and its increased attainment facilitates finding win-win outcomes. For example, the growth of the economy in the United States in the 1960s facilitated the integration of women, Blacks, and other minorities into the economy and, hence, into the general society. Demographic shifts as well can hasten conflict de-escalation. Memories fade as new generations are born and older generations gradually die. "Youth bulges," which put stress on social systems and are often considered a driver of instability, likewise eventually pass.[49]

DE-ESCALATION STRATEGIES

To this point we have discussed numerous variables that can advance de-escalation. For each engaged party, however, de-escalation is aided by choosing an appropriate and concrete strategy for de-escalation. Effective de-escalation strategies vary, depending on the level of escalation that a conflict has already attained, on who is to implement the policy, and on the timespan considered for the de-escalation goal sought.[50] After considering these conflict parameters, we discuss illustrative de-escalation strategies for conflicts at different levels of escalation, for different actors, and over different time spans.

Analytic Parameters

Seemingly intractable destructive conflicts do not begin that way but become so over time because of the actions committed and of actions not taken—by adversaries and by possible intermediaries.[51] This discussion differentiates among three starting levels: little escalation, sharp escalation (or crisis), and protracted stalemate. These levels tend to be mixed in actual struggles (e.g., a crisis may erupt in the context of a low-level of struggle or in the context of a protracted stalemate). Furthermore, various segments of a large-scale conflict may be in different stages simultaneously. For example, while at the societal level a struggle may be relatively stalemated, in one community one side may be sharply escalating the fight.

At their outset, conflicts generally exhibit expressions of dissatisfaction, assertions of demands, and probing behavior. That often leads to mutual exploration of the issues in contention and possible settlements. Sometimes, however, the conflict escalates with increasing threats and applications of coercive sanctions. As a conflict begins to become destructive and intractable, the adversaries, with or without the assistance of intermediaries, may implement policies that effectively prevent further deterioration. This can transform the conflict constructively, as happened in Latvia, Romania, and elsewhere in Eastern Europe in the 1990s.[52] Clearly, averting destructive escalation at this early stage is generally less costly and more likely to be enduring than after the conflict has become protracted.

More strenuous efforts at de-escalation are necessary when a conflict has markedly escalated. Among the many forms of sharp escalation, one form is much examined in international relations—the crisis. In general scholars agree that all crises are marked by three problematic elements.[53] First, crises threaten core values, that is, the intrinsic principles or qualities that leaders of an organization or society see as necessary for it to thrive. These might include, for instance, secure national borders, public confidence, or the health and welfare of people. Second, crisis situations are urgent, with a short and finite time available for decision makers to respond to the situation, or a "window of opportunity" in which to act. Third, and finally, crises contain a high degree of uncertainty. In crisis situations, decision makers often have an incomplete understanding of the origin and risks of the problem being confronted, and an uncertain understanding of the impact that their actions will have on alleviating or worsening it. Combined, high threat, short time to act, and high uncertainty tend to exacerbate social conflicts because these three traits mobilize stakeholder groups, increase public anxiety, magnify stress among decision makers, and create space for multiple interpretations of "what's going on."[54]

In addition to crises, escalation surges occur when one of the parties greatly intensifies its means of struggle. In community and societal conflicts, this may take the form of disorderly outbursts such as riots and widespread demonstrations. Within organizations, it may occur when subordinates refuse to follow orders, such as in a military mutiny or when buildings are seized by protesting persons and groups (e.g., when prisoners take control of parts of a prison or students occupy and hold college buildings).

The third starting level is that of a seemingly intractable struggle, a stage receiving increasing attention by scholars and policymakers.[55] In these long-standing struggles, discussed at the start of the book, neither side can impose a settlement on the other, nor is either side willing to accept the terms insisted on by the other. As a result, the parties are locked in a seemingly endless cycle of conflict characterized by stereotyping, dehumanization, and even an escalating spiral of recriminations.

Finally, some conflicts are at a stage where one side is increasingly dominating the other and can impose its preferred settlement. We give relatively little attention to how one side defeats or destroys the other because analysts and activists alike overemphasize that outcome, to the neglect of other courses of development. In large-scale conflicts, even if one side defeats the other, the adversary can and often does renew the fight later. The relationship, in any case, generally persists in some form, and one or another kind of mutual accommodation ensues. Admittedly, in the short run for many conflicts and particularly for interpersonal and small-scale conflicts, a total defeat of one side or an end of the relationship may occur.

De-escalation policies can be examined in terms of short- and long-term goals. Short-terms goals tend to focus on stopping ongoing violence and preventing imminent escalation. Long-term goals tend to emphasize changing the underlying conflict conditions, developing constructive alternative methods of struggle, building and institutionalizing conflict-management norms, and reaching stable mutual accommodations. Table 7.2 identifies a variety of de-escalation policies that may be used by different actors for short- and long-term goals, in conflicts at varying levels of escalation.

Table 7.2. Policies for Constructive De-Escalation

	Short-Term Goals		*Long-Term Goals*	
Starting Situation	*By Partisans*	*By Intermediaries*	*By Partisans*	*By Intermediaries*
Low-level Escalation	Delink issues; nonviolent action; measured reciprocity	Provide mediation; isolate conflict	Reduce inequalities; foster shared identities	Develop supportive norms, institutions; introduce more stakeholders
Sharp Escalation	Allow time; face-saving	Mediation; face-saving; suggest formula; sanctions	Reframe conflict; avoid provocation; confidence-building measures	Mediation; develop cross-cutting ties
Protracted Struggles	Conciliatory signals; track II; accept responsibility; reassure adversary	Mediation; isolate conflict; observers	Graduated reciprocation in tension-reduction; tit-for-tat; training in conflict resolution; confidence-building measures; introduce more stakeholders	Develop super-ordinate goals; foster communication

De-Escalation from Low Level of Escalation

It is easier to stop a conflict from escalating destructively if the struggle has not persisted for a long time and not escalated greatly. This underlies the high interest among conflict resolution practitioners in early warning and preventive diplomacy. Sadly, the problem is not so much ignorance that a conflict is likely to escalate badly, but that the political will to act is low when the salience of a conflict is low.[56] First, this is because intervention even at an early stage generally calls for the use of scarce or highly valued resources which potential interveners may wish to use elsewhere. Second, potential interveners tend to believe there is a good chance that intervention will not be necessary. Often this is because of the well-studied information fallacy known as "wishful thinking" whereby when an individual desperately wants something to be true they find evidence or reasoning to that effect.[57] Third, what action will be effective is uncertain, a good reason for caution. Fourth, ineffectively interfering will be regarded as a failure. Finally, little credit is likely to be won by preventing a conflict from deteriorating, since most people will hardly have noticed or believed that a disaster was averted. Many of these considerations, of course, also affect the leaders of each adversary group, reducing the chances that they pursue de-escalatory policies.

Short Term

Conflict partisans and intermediaries can pursue a variety of policies that tend to stop conflicts from escalating destructively and thus turn them toward constructive de-escalation. Earlier discussions have shown that how a challenging group pursues its goals and how the other side responds will greatly affect the likelihood that a struggle will de-escalate constructively. For example, conflicts in which challenging groups use relatively nonprovocative methods, such as conventional protest or nonviolent resistance, are less likely to escalate destructively than those in which challenging groups resort early on to violence, especially terrorist actions. Similarly, conflicts in which the challenged parties respond in an equivalent way rather than by overreacting tend not to escalate destructively.

Early de-escalation is likely to be fostered insofar as the partisans keep the issues in contention narrowly focused and isolated from other issues about which they might also fight. In addition, destructive escalation tends to be limited if participation by other parties does not spread, for instance through inflammatory rumors of outrages. Therefore, in periods of rioting, urban organizations may provide centers where citizens can seek verification about stories they had heard.

In the case of international conflicts or communal conflicts with transnational links, outside parties may strive to prevent the conflict from spreading into neighboring countries or try to stop or limit the sale of weapons in the country where the struggle is under way. Policies aimed at stopping a conflict spreading are illustrated by the conduct of the United Nations and other international organizations and governments in limiting the scope of the wars in the former Yugoslavia. Thus, at the request of the president of the Yugoslav Republic of Macedonia, in December 1992 the UN Security Council authorized the deployment of troops under command of the UN Protection Force along the Macedonian border with Albania and the successor Yugoslavia (Serbia and Montenegro). The troops not only acted as a deterrent to the spread of war, but also mediated border encounters and succeeded in achieving a withdrawal of soldiers on both sides.[58] Unfortunately, external intervention was not so effective and sometimes even counterproductive in preventing or quickly stopping many bloody wars as Yugoslavia broke apart.[59]

Within many social systems, agencies frequently exist that provide mediation, information- gathering, facilitation, and consultative services to defuse nascent conflicts, exemplified in the United States by the Community Relations Service of the U.S. Department of Justice, the National Labor Relations Board, and community human rights commissions. For example, in police-community relations that are prone to escalating confrontations, some cities establish civilian police review boards to investigate complaints and propose remedies to recurrent problems. In addition, political and religious leaders, acting informally, may also intervene to help settle community disputes. They often have bonds crossing religious and ethnic lines and can use such connections to bring together leaders from disputing communal groups.

Long Term

Long-term de-escalation policies include the promotion of crosscutting ties; institutionalized procedures for resolving conflicts; improvement of the social, economic, and cultural way of life of the disadvantaged within the social system; greater access to political participation by marginalized groups; and the creation of shared identities and vested interests in advancing those shared identities.

Within a society, policies fostering those conditions include establishing an electoral system that is conducive to participation by broad political parties, which are not based on a single ethnic, religious, or other exclusive identity. They also include educational systems and curricular material that emphasize shared identities, without denigrating minority ones. They further include the development of legitimate procedures for protecting fundamental rights of all members of the society and for enhancing public engagement in governance (e.g., constitutions that uphold equal protections under law for all citizens and guarantees of fundamental human rights for all citizens).

De-Escalation from Sharp Escalation

Policymakers, analysts, and the public at large generally exhibit great interest in the outbreak of crises and other sharp conflict escalations. They pose great risks. Considerable research about policies and procedures that enable adversaries to avoid abrupt destructive escalations during crises has been done, at least in some arenas.[60]

Short Term

One of the essential qualities of a crisis is the sense of urgency engendered among the partisans. That urgency often hampers taking actions that would avoid a disastrous escalation. One way to increase the likelihood of crisis de-escalation is for one or more adversaries to allow time for the other side to reflect on its course of action and not be pushed into a corner and face humiliation if it backs down. This is exemplified in some degree by the U.S. government's responses in the Cuban Missile Crisis of 1962.[61] In that crisis, sufficient time was allotted to find a formula for a way out of the crisis. The final formula included the withdrawal of the Soviet missiles from Cuba, the promise that the U.S. government would not try to overthrow the Cuban government, and the covert understanding that the United States would close its missile base in Turkey.

In domestic crises, hostages are often a crucial component, since they provide leverage for a small, relatively powerless group to counter the overwhelming power of state forces. The common understanding among police officers and other officials in responding to hostage situations is to be patient and to negotiate with those holding hostages, but not to accede to their demands. For persons not part of a larger group who have seized a hostage in desperation, this strategy generally results in a nonviolent resolution. With persons who are acting as part of larger organizations and identities, the negotiations are more difficult, since government officials are concerned about precedents and sometimes use the negotiations as ruses in preparation for storming the location where the hostages are held. Crises may also erupt while de-escalating conflicts if rejectionists try to disrupt the movement. During the transformation ending apartheid in South Africa such a threat arose. In April 1993, Chris Hani, a popular African National Congress leader, was assassinated by an immigrant from Poland, a member of the right-wing Afrikaner Weerstandsbeweging. The assassin was captured after an Afrikaner woman telephoned the police, providing his license plate number. Nelson Mandela and Frederik Willem de Klerk quickly acted together to isolate the event and move the transformation forward. Mandela spoke that evening on national television to prevent the negotiations under way from being derailed, saying,

> Tonight I am reaching out to every single South African, black and white, from the very depths of my being. A white man, full of prejudice and hate, came to our country and committed a deed so foul that our whole nation now teeters on the brink of disaster. A white woman, of Afrikaner origin, risked her life so that we may know, and bring to justice this assassin. . . . Now is the time for all South Africans to stand together against those who, from whatever quarter, wish to destroy what Chris Hani gave his life for—the freedom of all of us.[62]

The African National Congress organized protest demonstrations to allow for nonviolent expressions of anger and resentment; the government, for its part, arrested a member of the Conservative Party in connection with the murder.

Long Term

Among the many ways to foster de-escalation from sharp escalations is to develop institutions and procedures that constrain escalation. This may take the form of improving communication between the adversaries, making it swifter and better understood. For example, in 2004 India and Pakistan created a hot line that provides a direct and immediate connection between the foreign ministries of each country to reduce the threat of a nuclear confrontation.

Another long-term strategy is to develop groups, networks, or organizations that include persons from opposing sides, often engaging primary representatives or their advisors. Their getting to know each other reduces the likelihood of misunderstandings that may exacerbate emerging conflicts. Such crosscutting networks also provide channels for quickly considering alternative paths out of a sharp escalation when it occurs and to work together to identify and transform the underlying drivers that perpetuate intergroup conflicts. For example, many communities have established race dialogue groups in the wake of a string of racial bias incidences in U.S. cities that began in 2012 with the Trayvon Martin case in Florida. Prominent examples include Richmond, Virginia's, Hope in the Cities initiative, the National Voices Project, and Initiatives of Change USA. Dialogues related to race, racial bias, and diversity have been particularly extensive at hundreds of college campuses throughout the United States.

In international affairs, efforts to reduce changes of sharp escalations through confidence-building measures were developed in East-West relations in Europe during the Cold War. These measures included each side notifying the other in advance of large-scale military maneuvers and each side allowing representatives of the other to observe the maneuvers. Such measures provided reassurance, avoided misunderstandings, and thus contributed to the end of the Cold War. These methods have been discussed and to some extent implemented between other sets of international and domestic adversaries.[63]

Finally, of course, a basic policy for the prevention of conflicts from escalating destructively is to prevent provocative acts from happening. General agreements, even among unfriendly parties, can implement methods to reduce or even stop provocative actions. Thus, ideas and practices of nonprovocative defense, introduced earlier, contributed to the de-escalation of the Cold War.[64] Nonprovocative defense refers to the configuration of defensive military structures that will be readily perceived as designed purely for defense and not offensive fighting. Aspects of recent naval relations between China and the United States illustrate elements of such practices, which include high-level exchange visits and transparency of operations.

De-Escalation from Protracted Struggle

Many large-scale conflicts persist generation after generation, appearing to be intractable; they persist in self-perpetuating ways with varying degrees of destructiveness. We will discuss some of the many strategies that enable adversaries to move out of such conflicts and into more constructive ways of conducting or of resolving their fights.[65]

Short Term

Even profound and long-term conflict transformations have small beginnings, so tactical policies are crucial in initiating and sustaining them. One fundamental issue in protracted struggles is that at least one side feels that its basic interests, worldview, or way of life are threatened, and it must fight to sustain them. A crucial step in turning away from such fears is for at least one side to undertake actions that counter those feelings. When such actions are made on a reciprocal basis, appear credible, and seem irreversible, then the seemingly intractable conflict is in transition.

Policies that build support for de-escalation among members of the adversary parties also are necessary for transforming large-scale intractable conflicts, particularly communal ones, which are especially dependent on the sentiments of the rank-and-file members of the opposing sides. Leaders of major institutions as well as members of grassroots organizations often do undertake such policies. The mobilization effort may be part of a long-term policy or a short-term effort to rally support for a particular action. Mobilization may be attempted, for example, by social movement organizations arranging a demonstration or a campaign against officials reluctant to change. Ceremonies and celebrations provide other ways to mobilize and sustain support for the transformation process. Such mobilization has been a particular characteristic of the gay rights movement in the United States. In the year following the brutal 1968 police raid against homosexuals at the Stonewall Inn bar in New York City, gay rights organizations held the nation's first Gay Pride parades in New York, Chicago, and Los Angeles. The gay rights movement continued and expanded in subsequent years, relying almost exclusively on education, demonstrations, celebrations, court cases, and other constructive conflict avenues. Gradually cultural mores against homosexual rights and behavior began to fall, businesses and other organizations recognized domestic partnerships, and states began to recognize gay marriage. In 2015, in a dramatic ruling, the Supreme Court recognized the right of gay and lesbian couples to marry as a fundamental right under the U.S. Constitution.[66]

Of course, significant internal opposition to ending a protracted conflict, on terms not unilaterally imposed, is very likely. Once the transition toward a joint solution has begun, opposition often intensifies, and how leaders handle that opposition to continue with de-escalating moves is crucial. They may attempt to suppress it, placate it, or co-opt it, with varying degrees of success.[67] Yet, having entered this path, the leaders of both sides have a mutual interest in helping their negotiating partners stay in power and maintain support from their constituents. This poses a fundamental dilemma. The leaders must reassure their own followers that the course taken will yield what they want and convince their opponents that they will not lose what is critical for them. Particularly in seemingly intractable struggles, when the adversaries are frozen in mistrust, mediators and other intermediaries often play critical roles in facilitating de-escalating negotiation. We discuss this in detail in the following chapter.

Long Term

Moving out of large-scale, protracted struggles, barring one side's collapse, generally takes a long time. Many small steps usually must be taken before more significant ones can be made. The effectiveness of each action is likely to be enhanced if actions are considered as a series of steps along a path toward a shared objective. In addition, to be effective in large-scale struggles many de-escalating actions often must be taken by many elements of the opposing sides and by intermediaries in mutually supportive ways and in an appropriate sequence.

Two different strategies partisans may adopt to change from a confrontational relationship to a more cooperative one warrant discussion. One is graduated reciprocation in tension-reduction (GRIT), as set forth by Charles E. Osgood, and the other is a tit-for-tat (TFT) strategy, as discussed in the work of Anatol Rapoport and of Robert Axelrod.[68] Using the GRIT strategy, one of the parties in conflict unilaterally initiates a series of cooperative moves; these are announced and reciprocity is invited, but the conciliatory moves continue for an extended period, whether or not there is immediate reciprocity. GRIT was first prescribed in the early 1960s as a strategy for the United States to induce reciprocation from the Soviet Union.

While GRIT strategy was inferred from social psychological theory and research, the TFT strategy was derived from game theory, particularly work on the PD game. The strategy reasons that in a series of PD games, the payoffs are cumulative, and the player's strategy can be based on the other player's prior behavior. Experimental research and computer simulations of iterated games of PD indicate that cooperative relations often emerge and the most successful strategy for developing cooperative relations and yielding the highest overall payoff is for one player to initiate the series of games by acting cooperatively and afterward simply reciprocating the other player's actions, whether a cooperative or a noncooperative action.

Analysts have assessed these strategies by examining actual de-escalating interactions, particularly in the protracted U.S.–Soviet conflict. For example, Amitai Etzioni interprets the de-escalation in U.S.–Soviet antagonism in 1963 as an illustration of the GRIT strategy.[69] He views it beginning with President Kennedy's June 10 speech at American University announcing a unilateral halt to the atmospheric testing of nuclear weapons; the Soviets reciprocated and other cooperative moves soon followed, including the signing of the Limited Nuclear Test Ban in August 1963. These initial moves, however, were to some extent orchestrated by indirect communication between President Kennedy and Premier Khrushchev.[70] The GRIT and TFT explanations were compared in an analysis of reciprocity in relations between the United States and the Soviet Union, between the United States and the People's Republic of China, and between the Soviet Union and the People's Republic of China for the period 1948 to 1989.[71] It is ironic that GRIT was proposed by an American academic as a strategy to be undertaken by the U.S. government to break out of the Cold War, but it was a Soviet leader who undertook its most spectacular enactment. Gorbachev announced a change in policy toward the United States and Western Europe and made many conciliatory moves. It resulted in transforming relations with the United States, although initially, when the Soviets offered concessions, U.S. demands were raised. But Gorbachev's policy of saying "yes,

yes" until the U.S. government could no longer say "no, no" successfully resulted in cooperative moves by the U.S. government. The Soviet's GRIT strategy also led to normalized relations with China.

Policies pursued by nongovernmental persons and organizations are also important in long-term de-escalating strategies. As discussed elsewhere, nongovernmental organizations (NGOs) often orchestrate dialogue between parties who lack a capacity to communicate on their own. NGOs also provide peacebuilding support to areas impacted by conflict; often contract with governments, philanthropic organizations, and other sponsors to organize civil society; provide basic services to populations in need; deliver educational programs; facilitate disarmament and demobilization of former combatants; and foster economic development programming. Sometimes well-respected international figures can find ways to break an impasse when other cannot. The Elders, for instance, is an NGO founded by Nelson Mandela in 2007. Its members include a group of independent former leaders dedicated to help to "resolve conflict and address its root causes, to challenge injustice, and to promote ethical leadership and good governance."[72] Previously and currently they include or have included the likes of Kofi Anan, former secretary general of the United Nations; Desmond Tutu, Archbishop Emeritus of Cape Town; and Juan Manuel Santos, Nobel Peace Laureate and former president of Columbia.

Sometimes even the dominant faction in an adversary party can be the source of long-term policies to bring about fundamental changes in relations with its opponent. Dramatically, this was the case in the Soviet Union starting in 1985 with the ascension to power of Gorbachev. He and his associates believed that reform of the Soviet system was necessary to sustain itself as a superpower. The changes they instigated were not widely popular and indeed were not radical, but they did create the opportunity for those who desired reform to generate pressure for more change. Clearly, the forces for change soon gained enough strength to transform the Soviet Union, and they could not be stopped.

Finally, it should be noted that the failure to control and coordinate action sometimes undermines de-escalation once it has been undertaken. Insofar as the struggle has generated hostility and mistrust between the antagonists, de-escalating efforts must be clear and consistent to be effective. Internal opponents of a de-escalation policy, however, may attack the policy and its advocates in extreme ways and even attempt to sabotage it, making consistency more difficult. Policy opponents may violently attack the adversary and so provoke responses that will escalate the conflict again. Leaders in the de-escalation effort may try to placate the internal opposition to retain credibility with their constituents but doing that then undermines their credibility with members of the other side.

SUMMARY AND DISCUSSION QUESTIONS

This chapter reviewed the processes, conditions, and strategies that affect the de-escalation of conflicts. We noted that there are many variables that contribute to de-escalation, each of which can be classified into one of three overarching categories: social-psychological dynamics, organizational and tactical dynamics, and systemic and structural dynamics. How these variables manifest and what strategy is effective for de-escalation depends on the level of escalation that a conflict has already attained, on who is to implement the strategy, and on the timespan considered for the de-escalation goal sought.

Within each of the possible de-escalatory pathways numerous developments can scuttle de-escalatory advances. Phases of de-escalation are often fragile and subject to reversal as conditions change. Conciliatory probes and gestures may be unrecognized or go unanswered. Externally mediated or imposed processes often fail, and coercive, conciliatory, or externally driven de-escalatory processes often result in agreements that are not sustainable.

In the end the choice of de-escalating policies should be contingent upon the goals sought and the existing circumstances if they are to be effective. It is easier and certainly less costly to the antagonists to avoid destructive escalation in the first place than to attempt de-escalation after the conflict has been raging for a long time. But there may also be costs to taking actions before a conflict has visibly deteriorated. For potential intermediaries, de-escalating interventions may seem unnecessary, or at least difficult to mobilize support for. Furthermore, the preventive action may fail and those undertaking it are likely to bear the blame for further deterioration. For representatives of one of the adversaries, the risks and costs of premature de-escalation are even greater. They are likely to appear weak and be accused of losing what they might have won if only the struggle had been continued and even intensified. A better understanding of ways to escalate and de-escalate a fight constructively can contribute to reducing those risks and costs.

To consider the ideas presented in this chapter further, readers are encouraged to think about and discuss the following questions.

1. Think about a time in your life that you were part of a group that was in a struggle with another group that, for a time at least, de-escalated. What variables presented in the first part of this chapter help you to explain that escalation? Did variables not outlined in this chapter contribute to de-escalation as well?
2. Think about a conflict you are currently involved in that you would like to de-escalate. Using this chapter as a guide, identify five actions you could take today to start climbing down the ladder of de-escalation.

3. Consider the discussion of "ripeness" and a "hurting stalemate" reviewed in this chapter. Identify a destructive current conflict occurring in your community, your country, or the world. Are the parties to the conflict close to perceiving a hurting stalemate? Is there anything that internal or external parties to that conflict do to further ripen it?
4. The last section of this chapter suggested that de-escalation strategies differ according to whether the conflict is at a low level of escalation, is highly escalated, or is protracted. Think about examples of conflicts that fit in each of these categories. How might the de-escalation process differ due to the degree of escalation experienced by adversaries?

Part IV

MEDIATION, NEGOTIATION, AND POSTCONFLICT OUTCOMES

Chapter Eight

Mediation

In the previous chapter we noted that mediation is a powerful tool for de-escalating conflict. In this chapter we examine mediation in detail: what it entails, what different forms mediation work takes, and its uses and limitations. Having a separate chapter on mediation reflects the central role it plays in contemporary conflict management and its prominent role in facilitating constructive conflict transformation. Today mediation is used across all conflict domains from labor-management relations to community disputes, to interethnic relations, to divorce proceedings, to fights among students.[1]

DEFINITIONS, APPLICATIONS, AND BENEFITS

Mediation is a conflict-management process whereby a person or group, typically an outsider, intervenes in a conflict to help the adversaries negotiate an agreement themselves or take other joint de-escalating measures. Mediators do not decide what should be done about a conflict or make a ruling; rather, they help adversaries identify and commit to de-escalatory steps on their own. As such, mediation differs from arbitration, where the intermediary formulates the terms of a conflict's settlement and where the disputants agree in advance that they will abide by the arbitrator's decision.

Advocates of mediation argue that it has many advantages over traditional power and rights-based approaches to conflict management.[2] It contributes to speeding an escape from a destructive struggle, is more efficient and less costly than litigation, helps the parties reach an agreement that reflects a broader range of interests than would otherwise be apparent, and increases the likelihood that an agreement between the adversaries is fair and enduring.[3] During times of international crisis, mediation appears to increase the likelihood of achieving agreement, reduces the length of the crisis, and increases the partisan's satisfaction with the outcome.[4]

Services

Mediators perform a wide range of activities to help parties transform a conflict. However, what services mediators provide vary considerably with the conflict stage and degree of its intensity. As the conflict emerges, mediators may transmit information between the adversaries about the risks of escalation and possible options for preventing destructive escalation. They may also work as go-betweens, keeping lines of communication open among adversary groups as a check against conflict intensification. Once a conflict escalates mediators may be called in to provide an informal and unofficial venue for communication between partisans that might not be possible at the official level. As conflicts de-escalate mediation can lend legitimacy to an adversary party that is excluded from negotiations to reach a settlement. When the adversaries in a struggle move to settle their fight, they may be open to a wide variety of mediating activities. These include convening meetings, facilitating communication, suggesting options, and mobilizing support for the agreement to be reached. In the postsettlement stage, mediators may be enlisted to provide various kinds of guarantees that make it more likely that agreements will be sustainable in the long term.

There are three general types of services that mediators offer: resource providers, process managers, and process advocates. Not all mediators provide all, or often even most, of these services; rather, the services rendered change determine on the context of the conflict. Table 8.1 provides an overview of these services and is followed by a detailed description of them.

Table 8.1. Three Types of Mediation Services

Provision of Resources	*Managing Process*	*Advocacy for Process*
1. Provide a safe space in which stakeholders can gather	6. Convene interaction between stakeholders that would otherwise not communicate	12. Equalize power relations by providing less-powerful actors with skills and/or opportunity to interact with more powerful actors
2. Provide background documentation on the issue under discussion	7. Set ground rules that govern stakeholder interaction	13. Serve as a moral authority for fair, just, and enduring outcomes
3. Provide specific data needed to broker an agreement	8. Identify core issues and concerns	14. Identify pathways for mutual gain and integrative agreements
4. Educate stakeholders about dispute management processes	9. Reframe stakeholder statements	15. Rally support for agreements beyond immediate participants
5. Provide assistance or guarantees for implementation	10. Manage time and referee interaction	16. Block deterioration
	11. Document agreements	

Provide Opportunities for Communication

An important, and minimally intrusive, mediating service is to provide a safe place for adversaries or their representatives to meet. Sometimes adversaries want to meet to explore possible de-escalating moves but do not want this known until they work out an understanding about the move. This was the case in the year leading up to the 2015 nuclear deal between Iran and the United States when members of the U.S. State Department and their Iranian counterparts had a series of secret meetings mediated by Oman's Sultan Qaboos in the Omani capital of Muscat.

Mediators may discretely transmit messages between adversaries as well. A mediator may provide a channel for indirect communication, for example, by traveling between the enemy camps without public attention. Other times, however, one side of a conflict may wish to use a mediator in a very public way to gain attention, recognition, or status.

Provide Information

As a struggle escalates, the antagonists are increasingly likely to misinterpret each other's actions and words, exaggerating the other's hostility and intransigence. It is difficult to cross those barriers, so transmitting information from one side to another with relatively little distortion can contribute significantly to constructive de-escalation. Mediators may provide information to each side about how the struggle is viewed by the other. The information conveyed may be about the other side's readiness to de-escalate, the terms of a possible settlement, or the risks of escalating the struggle. Providing such information so that representatives of each side can hear it from and about the other requires that the transmitter have the confidence of both sides. It may require considerable skill on the part of the mediator (e.g., making the transmission more acceptable by omitting particularly provocative elements of the message or by explaining the context from the other side's point of view).

Information gathered by an intermediary may be presented as facts or rules that can be used to help settle disputes. Such fact-finding services may be sought, and the findings accepted by disputants.[5] For example, in a labor-management conflict, information presented by one side about prevailing wages and working conditions may be contested, while independently presented information is more likely to be accepted.

Help Adversaries to Enter Negotiations

Where conflicting parties have little or no interaction or trust, mediation can be used as a conduit to "soften up" hardened positions and enable subsequent formal negotiations.[6] In these cases one or both parties may explicitly ask for mediation assistance as they struggle to find viable avenues for peacemaking, or even indirect communication. The Basque separatist group ETA, for instance, followed up their September 2010 truce with the Spanish government with a request for international mediation to permanently end the conflict in the Basque region. In the years since then various members of the international community, including the Centre for Humanitarian Dialogue, have played a significant part in establishing regular back-channel communication between the Spanish government and ETA. Such communications have been credited with maintaining a fragile ceasefire in Spain for many years and contributed to the self-dissolution of ETA in 2018.[7]

Various mediating activities can also help adversaries undertake negotiations by making success seem more likely and by reducing the costs of failure. Mediators can explore with representatives of the antagonists what set of negotiating partners, agenda, and context would make negotiation seem worth trying. The formula for negotiations, presented by the mediator, is likely to have more appeal and legitimacy than if proposed by one of the partisans alone. This is illustrated by the effectiveness of Secretary of State James Baker in arranging the comprehensive 1991 Middle East peace conference held in Madrid.

Mediation can reduce the risks for adversaries entering negotiations with each other in several ways. The adversaries generally indicate to the mediator that they are serious in their effort to find a mutually acceptable settlement, and that becomes a kind of commitment to the mediator, aside from any commitment they may make to each other.

In addition, mediators may help determine who the negotiating partners will be. The choice of parties to be engaged in any de-escalating effort involves three competing principles. One is to exclude the intransigents so a deal can be made. The second is to include all those who have the capability to disrupt an agreement if one is reached. The third is to maximize participation by all those with a stake in the outcome. Difficult choices often must be made about the relative weight given to each principle, but the choice can change after the initial negotiations are undertaken.

Some external actors have the authority to simply convene a meeting of the adversaries or invite themselves to talk to each party and transmit information. Thus, the secretary-general of the United Nations can interject into a conflict even when one or more sides would prefer no such intervention. The president of the United States may convene a meeting that one or more parties regard as untimely. This was the case when President Clinton called Israel and the Palestinian Authority to come to Camp David in July 2000, although Yassir Arafat had told him he was not ready for such a meeting.[8]

Domestically, national and local governmental officials often have the authority to intervene and bring opponents together to settle their dispute. This is particularly true when vital interests are at stake. Such was the case in 2014 and

2015 when nine months of conflict between labor and management concerning west coast ports required intervention by the Obama administration. With billions of dollars of cargo unable to be off-loaded from container ships up and down the west coast, the president dispatched his labor secretary, Tom Perez, to assist in mediating a final agreement. That agreement eventually came in February 2015 when the Pacific Maritime Association and the International Longshore and Warehouse Union overcame months of stalemate. The capacity of the executive branch to intervene in this and other cases is enhanced by the discretionary power that the oval office has to impose the Taft-Hartley Act, passed by Congress in 1947, which limits the ability of unions to strike when the nation's health or safety is deemed to be threatened by such actions.

Help Penetrate Social-Emotional Barriers

Mediators and other intermediaries may act in many ways that help lessen the hostile feelings and antagonizing interactions that hamper members of one side accurately perceiving the other side or believing that its leaders are trustworthy. A mediator sometimes meets with each side privately, sympathetically listening to expressions of anger, hate, or fear. Members of an adversary party, having vented such emotions out of the enemy's hearing, are then better able to carry on without showing such feelings and provoking the other side.

Mediation also includes making suggestions that help build mutual appreciation between the adversary representatives. Thus a mediator may suggest to one side that it make a unilateral gesture or symbolic gift that would be difficult for the other side to misinterpret. Gestures as simple as acknowledging the bravery of persons in the adversary camp or recognizing their sacrifices may be moving and effective in de-escalating a conflict. Such gestures can win the adversary's attention and prompt a fresh look at the other side.

Mediators may introduce methods that help penetrate social-emotional barriers.[9] They can set ground rules for interaction that enable disputants to discuss differences yet minimize adversarial argument. They may suggest that representatives from each side take turns listening to each other and summarizing what the other side's representative said. The exercise improves hearing what the other side says and enhances the other side's feeling that it has been heard. Another, less formal technique is to work together on some collective task (preparing a meal or sharing an excursion) and having teams with members from different sides performing various aspects of the undertaking.

Help Stop Deterioration

If a conflict persists in escalation, it generally rises in destructiveness. Mediation services can help halt further conflict deterioration by assisting adversaries to envisage a possible settlement option that is better than continuing the ongoing level of fighting. More coercive interventions also can sometimes help stop the deterioration, perhaps freezing the conflict until a more opportune time develops to move toward a substantive de-escalation. Interveners may impose sanctions that raise the costs of escalating violence or may intercede to help implement a ceasefire agreed upon by the antagonists. The numerous UN peacekeeping missions exemplify this kind of service. In some domestic arenas, such as labor-management disputes, institutionalized arrangements may provide for cooling-off periods in which escalations such as lockouts or strikes are not allowed for a fixed period.

Save Face

Once in a fight, each side finds it difficult to appear to accept the ideas of the enemy. If a mediator voices an idea, it can be accepted without seeming to yield to the adversary. Furthermore, the idea may be accepted out of respect for the mediators or in deference to the relationship with them. Recognizing these considerations, an adversary, rather than offer an idea on its own, sometimes suggests that the mediator make it.[10]

Similarly, a commitment can be made to a mediator without appearing to bow meekly to an opponent's demands.[11] To illustrate, in the 1973 negotiations between the Israeli and Egyptian governments mediated by Henry Kissinger, the Israelis wanted a commitment from Egypt to reopen the Suez Canal and allow Israeli shipping companies to use the canal. President Anwar al-Sadat, not willing to appear to be limiting Egyptian sovereignty, refused. The commitment to allow passage was made to the U.S. government, which conveyed this commitment to the Israeli government.[12] Another way for adversaries to save face is to have the mediator take the blame for a mistake. If something goes wrong in the negotiation arrangements, the relationship between the adversaries is less likely to be damaged if the mediator accepts responsibility than if one of the adversaries is accused of a blunder or a deception.

Change Procedures

Negotiators sometimes become frozen in unproductive procedures, and suggesting new procedures may break the impasse. Bringing in high-ranking representatives of the opposing sides, who have more authority to take new positions than lower-level negotiators can, is an example of a significant procedure change. Alternatively, difficult issues may be delegated to specialists on the issues in contention to discuss options in small working groups.

Establishing small discussion groups to work on a subset of issues is a way to fractionate a conflict, resolving pieces of the total conflict one at a time.

Mediators may also use symbolism to facilitate de-escalation. Altering seating arrangements can be done to help empower marginalized voices. Where people sit and who they have access to may affect social interaction patterns, perhaps making them more informal. Altering the way proceedings unfold can also change the style of discussions (e.g., appointing a facilitator to lead the conversation). The facilitator moderates the discussion of proposals, at first allowing only clarifying questions. The facilitator then summarizes what has and has not been agreed to, setting the stage for new proposals to deal with the matters not yet in agreement.

Help Invent New Options

Once a conflict has persisted or has become severe, the adversaries tend to become locked into the positions they have previously staked out. Each side sees the other's preferred outcome as unacceptable and thus sees continuing or escalating the struggle as better than accepting those terms. Mediators often can help reframe the struggle and suggest ways to construct new options for consideration.

Mediators can sometimes be more inventive than the opposing sides because they recognize more clearly the underlying interests that the negotiators for all sides are trying to advance. Furthermore, they are not likely to be committed to the previous terms of settlement offered by the adversaries themselves and therefore are freer to think of new alternatives. Mediation often helps adversaries themselves to think more creatively. One way this is done is to bring together a few members of the opposing sides to informally discuss their relationship and identify a variety of possible solutions to the problem they face. This may occur in the context of problem-solving workshops, discussed later in this chapter. It may also be promoted by setting aside time for brainstorming. Members of the negotiating sides are encouraged to suggest possible solutions, putting aside likely difficulties in implementing them. The rule is to be imaginative and uncritical of one's own or of each other's suggestions. Only after many options have been mentioned can the necessary critical discussion begin.[13] Once it does, the mediator may help participants identify the criteria that they feel are necessary to adequately evaluate alternative options. Often, these criteria revolve around the "ABC" principle: achievable, believable, and cost-effective.[14]

Finally, mediators may encourage a different style of discussion.[15] For example, when a person says "no, no, no" to a proposal from another party, the mediator may ask, "What if the other person had said such and such, would that be better?" Then, if the person says, "That's better, but it's not enough," the mediator may ask, "What would you add to improve it?" The idea is to show participants how to get beyond rejecting a proposal to thinking about how to make it acceptable.

Represent Persons not Represented in the Negotiations

Conflicts generally affect many more parties than those represented in any set of negotiations, and those parties have a stake in the outcome. Mediators may be able to represent the more diffuse interests of others by upholding general norms of fairness or of human rights.[16] This function can help make discussions more inclusive of groups who may be omitted from discussions. Mediators can also push for broadened participation of underrepresented voices. For instance, women are frequently underrepresented in many peacemaking efforts as are the poor and ethnic minorities. Including them can make the difference between the failure and success of any agreements since their perspective on what the agreement requires to work is essential.[17] Mediators may also be expected to represent the interests of absent others (e.g., the public, consumers, taxpayers, or future generations).

Construct Deals

Often, mediation entails shuttling between opposing sides, learning what each side wants, what each will give up, and what each will not abandon. On that basis, a mediator may develop a possible settlement and propose it to the opposing sides. This may become the basis for further negotiations as the mediator modifies the proposed plan, considering the criticisms of each side. The mediator repeatedly modifies the plan and presents all negotiating parties this single negotiating text, which each side is asked to accept.[18] The mediator may be active in formulating the proposals, varying from combining elements of the positions of both sides to creatively constructing a deal. For instance, in 2020 the Federal Mediation and Conciliation Service (FMCS)—an independent agency of the U.S. government established in 1947 whose mission is to preserve and promote labor-management peace and cooperation—successfully helped Bath Iron Works and the International Association of Machinists Local S6 negotiate an agreement to end the shipyard worker strike in Bath, Maine. That strike had involved a complex set of issues including safety concerns related to the COVID-19 virus, pay and benefits, lay-offs, divisions between unionized and nonunionized workers, and Bath Iron Works fulfillment of high-profile U.S. Navy contracts. FMCS's involvement came a month after the strike occurred and was credited with closing the gap between the positions of management and labor, leading to a deal several weeks after mediated discussions began.[19]

Add Resources

Since expanding the size of the pie makes it easier to divide, mediators sometimes help the adversaries find additional resources that they can use. To illustrate, community groups contending about access to limited community facilities may be encouraged to go together to city hall requesting increased facilities that they would share. Sometimes, the mediator can assist in those efforts.

Some mediators themselves contribute resources that sweeten the settlement deal, resources that none of the adversaries will or can credibly contribute to the settlement. Thus, in 1979 when an Israeli-Egyptian peace treaty was finally negotiated with the Egyptian government, the assistance to each side and the monitoring services promised and provided by the U.S. government were crucial in reaching and sustaining the agreement. The explicit or implicit promise of assistance by external organizations, such as the United Nations or the European Union, to recover from the devastation of internal strife can encourage former adversaries to end their fight and reap benefits for doing so. Benefits may be targeted to gain the acquiescence of persons and groups who might be threatened by the conflict's outcome. Thus, external actors may promise them safety, and even funds they previously hid in other countries, as part of the agreement to end a civil conflict.[20] They may also facilitate postconflict power-sharing agreements to further incentivize peacemaking. Each of these is referred to in the literature as "commitment-enhancing provisions" and are often found to make a difference in the durability of peace agreements.[21]

Finally, in domestic conflicts about environmental issues such as building a waste disposal facility, siting a wind farm, or drilling for natural gas, reaching an agreement may entail external assistance to reimburse persons who would have to move their homes. Sometimes in these cases a pool of funding is set aside because of the mediation process to protect citizens in the event of a future environmental claim. Other times resources are added by having developers agree to pay additional taxes to support public works, schools, or community projects as an "off-set" to potential environmental damage down the road.[22]

Generate Pressures for an Agreement

Mediators sometimes pressure one or more of the adversaries to reach an agreement. One mild source of pressure is the obligation felt by the adversaries toward the mediators with whom the parties have a friendly relationship. Aware of the investment of time and the risk taken by the mediator by trying to help bring about a settlement, the adversaries frequently hesitate to abandon the negotiations, as this may seem disrespectful of the mediator's efforts. Mediator pressure is sometimes much more direct. Time constraints may be imposed, as when President Carter set a deadline for his mediation of the negotiations between President Sadat and Prime Minister Menachem Begin at Camp David.

The mediation pressure may be applied to one side more than another. One way this is done is to threaten public accusations that the failure to reach agreement is due to the intransigence of one party. In addition, a powerful mediator may directly threaten to impose negative sanctions on the recalcitrant party or parties.[23] U.S. diplomat Richard Holbrooke used such tactics during the mediation leading up to the Dayton Peace Agreement, which concerned the political status of Bosnia and Herzegovina. Holbrook was particularly concerned with Serbian President Milošević's willingness to come to the negotiation table with his Croatian and Bosnian counterparts unless coerced into doing so through U.S. diplomatic and military pressure. An agreement was eventually reached in 1992 at Wright-Patterson Air Force Base near Dayton, Ohio, which famously featured American military aircraft as a backdrop to the negotiations.[24]

Rally Support for an Agreement

Mediation often provides support for an agreement, which helps give it legitimacy for the negotiators' constituencies. A mediator may even testify how well the negotiators for each side strove to protect the interests of their respective constituencies, thereby protecting them from criticism that they were "too soft."

Mediators, insofar as they represent a broader community, frequently are seen as validating the fairness of the agreement. Furthermore, the negotiating sides are likely to regard the mediator's engagement in the negotiations as helping to guarantee that the agreement reached will be honored, since the mediator has an interest in ensuring that its efforts appear successful.

In short, many mediating services can enhance the de-escalating process. These activities may speed initiating and concluding settlements and may contribute to the fairness of a resulting agreement and help ensure its implementation. Some activities, however, are difficult for the same person or group to perform simultaneously. Other activities are readily combined by the same person and tend to be carried out by incumbents of particular social roles.

SOCIAL ROLES

The mediation services reviewed earlier are, in fact, carried out by a wide variety of individuals and organizations with different resources, backgrounds, skills, degrees of neutrality, and levels of authority. Some mediators, for instance, represent states, others international organizations, other nongovernmental organizations, and still others are simply private citizens. Some mediators bring with them formal powers to commit resources, while others are private individuals with few resources to bring to the table. In this section numerous mediator and other intermediary roles are discussed, including roles that some analysts and practitioners do not regard as embodying true or good mediation. We begin with a discussion of the conditions and contexts that impact mediator neutrality. We then discuss the variety of mediator roles and the kinds of services they tend to provide. Next, we discuss the factors that help shape the roles. The chapter concludes with a discussion of ways to assess the impacts that mediators have on social conflicts.

Mediator Neutrality

Mediator neutrality is often a matter of contention.[25] Many mediators and analysts of mediation stress that mediators should be neutral while playing mediator roles. Others argue that neutrality is not possible, and in any case is not necessary. Being trustworthy and honest with the disputants is sufficient to play the role effectively. To clarify this debate, we should recognize that neutrality in this context has a variety of meanings.

Neutrality of the mediator may refer to feelings and intentions, to conduct as perceived by the disputants or observers, or to effects on the disputants and the course of the conflict. Some mediators may be genuinely disinterested in the conflict or the disputants; this is more likely among mediators who play their role largely as facilitators. But even they may have strong interests in the use of processes and/or in reaching an agreement. Such concerns are likely to mean that whatever their neutrality about the dispute, their actions will have implications for the kind of settlement reached.

More often, the mediators are likely to have feelings and interests that are the bases for sympathy toward one party compared with another. How they act on such convictions, however, is another matter. Some may strive to act evenhandedly or to be an advocate for both sides, while others act to assist one side more than another or to advance their own interests. In addition, how the disputants perceive the mediators' intentions and actions influences the mediators' effectiveness. Some mediators, with past histories of relations with one or more of the parties in a conflict, may be regarded as too biased or untrustworthy to serve as a mediator. In many circumstances, particularly for potential mediators with great resources, disputants do not expect or want disinterested neutrality. One or more sides may prefer a mediator who can enlarge the pie to be divided, who can leverage the other side, or who can ensure the compliance with any agreement reached. This is one reason that antagonists in the Middle East and in other regions may accept U.S. official mediation, although it is viewed as aligned with one party.

Whatever the intentions or perceived conduct of mediators, the consequences of their efforts are not likely to be neutral. By their very act of mediation, they give some legitimacy to all the parties among whom they are mediating. Of course, that is a reason for a party that does not recognize the legitimacy of an opposing side to refuse mediation. This is particularly the case for official mediation. By according legitimacy, the mediators tend to provide a measure of equality, at least in rights, to the adversaries.

Finally, mediators may enhance adherence to societal and international norms about human rights and other principles of proper human relations.[26] Doing so can provide guidelines that help construct an acceptable agreement and improve the quality and the durability of any agreement reached. Thus, the Organization for Security and Cooperation in Europe has a High Commissioner on National Minorities (HCNM) with the authority to intervene at the earliest possible stage in response to a crisis related to national minority issues that threaten international peace. Max van der Stoel, during his tenure as the first HCNM, 1993 to 2001, helped avert escalating conflicts and resolve them consistent with international norms. For example, this was accomplished by his quiet mediation regarding the language and education rights of the Hungarian minority in Romania and the citizenship rights of ethnic Russians in the newly independent Estonia.

Types of Mediator Roles

Mediators play many different roles, at different times, and with varying degrees of intrusiveness. Nine diverse roles are reviewed here.

Quasi Mediator

At one pole of the wide range of mediator roles are actual members of one of the adversary parties who carry out some go-between activities. They usually are not recognized as mediators and are referred to here as quasi mediators.[27] Nevertheless, they frequently convey information from the adversary back to their own side. In international relations, ambassadors are expected to inform their home government about the thinking of the government to which they are assigned. Considering their insights, they may even suggest new options to their home government.

During negotiations, one or more members of the negotiating team may explore the possibility of the other side accepting a particular option and then seek their own side's acceptance of the idea. They may help breach the barriers of mistrust within their side by testifying to the sincerity and trustworthiness of members of the opposing side.

Ad Hoc Informal Go-Betweens

In all kinds of large-scale conflicts, persons acting as individuals or as representatives of religious, political, or other organizations often convey messages between adversaries whose hostility makes direct communication difficult. To be accepted as go-betweens, they may severely limit the range of activities they will perform. This has been the case for the work of a few Quakers in the protracted and severe struggle between the Sinhalese-dominated government of Sri Lanka and the now defeated separatist organization of the minority Tamils.[28] Conditions of their mediation included that the adversaries respect the confidentiality of the intervention and that each could veto continuing the mediation. This helped ensure that the mediators had no agenda of their own beyond helping the adversaries negotiate with each other.

Often, conflict resolution centers serve as a channel of communication between adversaries For example, when Hendrik W. van der Merwe, an Afrikaner, became director of a new center on intergroup relations at the University of Cape Town in 1968, he did research and organized intergroup workshops, but also actively opposed apartheid.[29] With his background and experience, he initiated and facilitated meetings between Afrikaner and African National Congress leaders and between leaders of the Inkatha Freedom Party and the United Democratic Front, rival Black organizations.

Consultant and/or Trainer

Increasingly, persons and organizations provide training and consultation services in conflict resolution methods. They are based in academic, governmental, business, religious, and philanthropic settings. The training includes developing skills in negotiation, active listening, mediation, strategic planning, nonviolent action, and other aspects of conducting a constructive struggle. The consultation often includes such training and helps in developing conflict-management systems, including democratic organizational and societal systems. Such intermediary activity is often carried out with one of the sides engaged in a struggle, but sometimes is provided to more than one side. The training and consultation may foster mediation and other ways to manage conflicts among the groups making up one side in a larger conflict.

Such efforts are often undertaken before intense struggles erupt, but they may be introduced even when a struggle has become protracted, and increasingly are used after a settlement has been reached to help transform adversarial relations and avert renewed violence. For example, in 1990 the FMCS, noted earlier, was authorized to expand its conflict resolution services in the United States and in other countries.[30] It now accepts invitations to provide training, facilitation, and consultation relating to a wide range of community and societal conflicts, as well as to labor-management disputes. Training in conflict resolution and alternatives to violence are increasingly offered in schools at all levels, in prisons, in governmental and business organizations, and in churches and other voluntary associations. The training may be part of managing adaptations to changes in the composition of the membership (e.g., as women and minorities become more significant participants in the organizations.

Facilitator in Problem-Solving Workshops

An important form of conflict resolution utilizes a workshop structure. Typically, a convener brings together a few members of the opposing sides and guides their discussions about aspects of the conflict in which they are engaged. Some workshops are designed to improve mutual understanding of each side's views and feelings, while others are designed to tackle issues in contention and generate possible mutually acceptable solutions to the contention. The participants' experiences and/or the possible solutions they construct may be directly or indirectly transmitted to the official representatives of the opposing side, to other elite groups, or to the attentive public. For instance, beginning in 2013 the Consensus Building Institute, a U.S.-based nongovernmental organization specializing in collaborative problem-solving, together with the Union of Concerned Scientists, held a series of stakeholder dialogues in California with various constituencies concerned with the historic drought taking place in the state. Participants included groundwater managers, environmental organizations, municipalities, academics, interest groups, and government agencies. By 2015 these conversations resulted in the drafting of a comprehensive set of recommendations about groundwater-use best practices that were shared with state officials.[31] In cases such as these, the recommendations developed are not binding in any sense. However, since they are developed through a mediated consensus-building process, they are often viewed as a legitimate representation of what should be done by public officials.

Participants in problem-solving workshops are often persons with ties to the leadership of their respective parties or have the potentiality to become members of the leadership in the future. The workshops usually go on for several days, moving through a few stages of discussion. At the international level, such workshops have evolved through the experience of John Burton, Leonard Doob, Herbert C. Kelman, Edward Azar, Harold H. Saunders, Ronald J. Fisher, and others.[32] In these cases, workshops often have been held in connection with protracted international and intranational struggles, such as those in Northern Ireland, in Cyprus, in the United States, and between Jewish Israelis and Arab Palestinians.

Former members of workshops sometimes act as quasi mediators on returning to the adversary group to which they belong. Furthermore, some later become participants in official negotiations, as has been the case with former members of some of Kelman's workshops who subsequently participated in the early negotiations between the Palestine Liberation Organization and the Israeli government.[33]

Problem-solving, interactive workshops are one kind of what is often referred to as "track-two diplomacy" in international relations.[34] Track one is the official mediation, negotiation, and other exchanges conducted by governmental representatives. Track-two channels include much more than problem-solving workshops and are best viewed as multitrack.[35] Among the many nonofficial channels are transnational organizations within which members of adversarial parties meet and discuss matters pertaining to the work of their organizations.[36]

Facilitators

A few members of adversary groups sometimes conduct an ongoing series of meetings at which they discuss aspects of the struggle in which their groups are engaged.[37] Such nonofficial, regular meetings between well-connected persons from adversary parties can provide a channel of communication and discuss possible solutions to contentious issues. Members act as unofficial mediators, but their actions are done consciously and are known to the leaders and others in the groups to which they belong.

Dialogue Groups

Some organizers have extended their problem-solving workshops into a series of meetings, becoming a dialogue group between representatives of opposing sides or those separated by identity differences. The goal of a dialogue is not to solve a problem; rather, it is to help individuals gain greater insight about self and other. As such, dialogues are sometimes thought of as a "prenegotiation" phase of conflict management, building trust, understanding, and new perspectives upon which eventual agreements might be built.

The practice of dialogue involves two primary skills.[38] First, participants need to be able to assert their opinions, feelings, and desires, as well as to explore the assumptions upon which those assertions rest. In a dialogue on gender, for instance, a facilitator might ask participants to talk about the first time in their life that they became aware of the concept of "gender" in their lives, what meaning it had, and how such a meaning constrained their behavior. Second, participants must have a capacity to hear what the other side has to say. This is frequently accomplished through reflective listening skills where listeners are asked to *reflect* the thoughts and feelings conveyed by a speaker in their own words. Throughout, the role of the dialogue mediator is to enforce rules of interaction that are designed to keep dialogue from degenerating into argumentative forms of exchange, to ask catalytic questions that help participants interact in thoughtful ways, and to model good interpersonal communication skills.

Dialogue groups can be found in many domestic conflict arenas, including industrial relations and community interreligious and interethnic relations. In the United States, dialogues related to racial differences and inequalities have been particularly prominent in multiple settings.[39] Ongoing dialogues have also been developed to deal with critical international issues and concerns. In 1957, nuclear physicists and others involved in the development of nuclear weapons and strategies about their possible use, working in the United States, Great Britain, and the Soviet Union, began to meet and exchange ideas about ways to reduce the chances of nuclear warfare. The first meetings were held in Pugwash, in Nova Scotia, Canada, and evolved into the Pugwash Conferences on Science and World Affairs.[40] In the 1950s, 1960s, and 1970s, discussions at these meetings contributed to the later signing of the Partial Test-Ban Treaty, the Nonproliferation Treaty, the Biological Weapons Convention, and the Antiballistic Missile Treaty. Later meetings helped build consensus for the Strategic Arms Reduction Treaties I and II, the Intermediate Nuclear Force Treaty, and the Chemical Weapons Convention. In 1995, the Pugwash conferences and Joseph Rotblat, its executive director, won the Nobel Peace Prize for their work. It continues to be transnationally active in organizing conferences and to issue reports relating to regional global security threats, most recently regarding global climate change.

Institutionalized Mediator

In many large-scale social systems mediators operate within the context of a legal system, with specified obligations for the mediator and the disputants.

In many countries, institutionalized mediation is most developed in the realm of labor-management relations. Even in such contexts, there are important variations in the social roles and how they are played. For example, Deborah M. Kolb compared official labor mediators in two organizations: the FMCS and a state board of conciliation.[41] She finds that the mediators of the FMCS thought of themselves and acted as orchestrators, assisting the union and management to reach an agreement. The mediators in the state board regarded themselves and acted as deal makers, actively constructing a package acceptable to both sides and using persuasion and even manipulation to win acceptance.

In recent years, alternative dispute resolution has greatly expanded in many conflict arenas. Thus, throughout the United States alternative dispute resolution is conducted in neighborhood conflict-resolution centers. In some judicial districts, mediation is mandated as part of the judicial process, as in child custody disputes between divorcing parents.

When the mediator functions within a highly institutionalized setting, the failure to reach a negotiated agreement tends to be followed by conflict-settlement procedures that are even less under the control of the parties to the dispute. Recourse to judicial proceedings is likely to follow or an executive branch agency imposes a settlement. Sometimes, however, the conflict escalates to a struggle in which each adversary resorts to coercion attempting to unilaterally impose its desired outcome.

Ad Hoc Mediator

On occasion, when conflicts erupt or their escalation is anticipated, a well-regarded person or organization is requested, by the disputants or by a governmental body with the requisite jurisdiction, to serve as a mediator. The nature of the social role of these mediators and the services they provide is quite variable. In many urban conflicts, a mayor or governor may request that someone serve as a mediator to help manage or resolve the conflict. Usually, there is little preexisting consensus about the kind of mediator role the designated person will assume. Sometimes, in a difficult conflict a series of mediators may be needed to help settle the dispute.[42]

Some religious organizations are highly engaged in humanitarian work in various parts of the world, and some of their members provide informal, facilitative mediation. For example, various members of the Society of Friends have served in this way in several conflicts around the world. This was true in the deadly 1967–1971 Nigerian civil war, when the eastern region struggled unsuccessfully for independence as the Republic of Biafra.[43]

Former U.S. Senator George Mitchell provided mediating services that contributed greatly to reaching the Good Friday Agreement of April 1998, regarding the status of Northern Ireland.[44] In 1995, he chaired an international committee to make recommendations on the issue of decommissioning (disarming) underground organizations. In September 1997, peace negotiations began in Belfast with an extraordinarily wide range of groups represented and Mitchell as chair. Besides chairing the sessions, he acted as a go-between for parties that would not talk to each other directly, and he helped provide norms for the discussion, creating a safe space for negotiations. He also helped establish rules to reach decisions by significant consensus; in addition, he had access to President Clinton who at times spoke directly to the parties.

Ad Hoc Deal Maker

In many communities or societal settings, an influential personage is called on to help settle a dispute, with more authority to act than as facilitating mediator. The intermediary may have the authority to act as an arbitrator but more often acts as deal-making mediator. The deal maker may have resources with which to offer benefits or threaten losses, but often relies largely on persuasion and manipulation.[45]

In international relations, often the deal-maker mediator has many resources that can be used to help reach an agreement. These are mediators with muscle, or clout. President Carter was such a mediator at the 1978 Camp David negotiations between the Israeli and Egyptian governments, which resulted in the peace treaty between Israel and Egypt. The president could provide political cover for the concessions that each side felt would otherwise be fearful to make, could provide Israel with alternative sources of oil and military security if needed, and could provide Egypt with the prospects of badly needed economic assistance.

Richard Holbrooke at meetings in Dayton, Ohio, in 1995 provides an extreme example of mediator as deal maker.[46] As U.S. assistant secretary of state for Europe, Holbrooke practically imposed a settlement for Bosnia, which had been largely divided by Serbia and Croatia in terrible fighting. The meeting followed North Atlantic Treaty Organization bombing and U.S. assisted military advances against Serbian forces. Holbrooke cajoled, threatened, and promised assistance in brokering a deal among the leaders of Serbia, Croatia, and Bosnia.

Summary

Mediator roles vary greatly in their degree of intrusiveness.[47] At one extreme, some mediation roles involve only facilitative activities, and at the other extreme, they include deal making or even near-imposition of settlements.

Activities at different ends of this continuum generally do not mix well within a single mediator role. This is one reason that different kinds of mediation are often carried out by different mediators in sequence or in parallel.

Many advocates of mediation in the context of the recent growth of conflict resolution practice stress that mediators should only facilitate the disputants reaching an agreement themselves. The power to make an agreement should lie in the disputants' own hands. This is counterpoised to a legal system in which judges and jurors determine the outcome of the dispute. But many other kinds of mediation also occur and are advocated. For example, some analysts stress the transformative potential of mediation that works for empowerment and recognition of the disputants.

Although the parties to a dispute are the ones who ultimately select the mediator role and sometimes the person(s) who occupy the role, they frequently face some degree of pressure to accept mediation and to reach an agreement. In large part, this depends on the institutional setting. In certain areas of labor-management relations, laws require a governmental effort at mediation. Once parties enter a mediation process, the degree of external pressure and influence varies greatly.

SHAPERS OF MEDIATOR ROLES

In the previous sections of this chapter, we examined the wide variety of roles that mediators adopt in conflict situations. What, then, determines which roles are played in each situation? Four major kinds of determinants of mediator roles warrant examination: the cultural setting, the institutional context, the characteristics of the conflict, and the characteristics of the mediator.

Cultural Setting

Every social system, whether a society or an organization, has a culture with rules about how conflicts should be managed, including rules about mediation.[48] In traditional societies, mediators tend to be political or religious leaders of their communities, and they use the resources of their positions to help resolve conflicts. In many small traditional societies, the goal is to heal the rupture that a conflict may have caused and to ensure that cooperative relationships within the community are sustained. For example, in traditional Hawaiian culture interpersonal conflicts are regarded as entanglements, which are unfortunate, as when fishing lines or nets become entangled.[49] Conflict resolution, therefore, is called *ho'oponopono*, or "disentanglement." In this process, still in practice, the disputants are gathered by a high-status community member who knows them. Prayers are offered, a statement of the problems is made, and for each problem, the leader asks questions, and a discussion follows, channeled through the leader. After a period of silence, confessions are made to the gods (or God) and to each disputant, and then restitution is arranged. Each problem is dealt with in this fashion, and then the disputants forgive each other, releasing each other from guilt. After a closing prayer, the participants share something to eat.

In highly differentiated societies, especially in Western societies, the judicial system tends to focus on the disputants and strives to determine who is right and who is wrong. Yet even in such societies, mediation is often used to discover or construct a mutually acceptable agreement between the disputants. Nevertheless, the mediation process is different in large societies from small, traditional societies. Within larger societies, disputes usually are treated in relative isolation, the mediator roles tend to be professionalized, and the value of mediator neutrality is emphasized. The previous discussion of the various mediator roles should demonstrate, however, the great variability among kinds of mediation in every society.

Institutional Context

Mediator roles range greatly, also due to their diverse institutional settings. Some mediator roles are part of the same hierarchical structure as the disputing parties. The mediators in those roles operate with considerable authority deriving from their position. A conflict unresolved by mediation is likely to be decided by other processes, such as litigation or administrative authority. Even looser overarching institutional structures can foster reliance on mediators to ease conflicts among members, for example, among members of the United Nations or of the North Atlantic Treaty Organization.

Many mediator roles, even in highly differentiated societies, are quite informal and without institutional support, so that the resources such mediators have at their disposal are generally small. Sometimes they consist of little more than personal ties with each side, the knowledge brought from previous mediating experience, and the information attained in the very process of the mediation. Thus, in interpersonal conflicts, even in large, bureaucratized societies, a local priest, a bartender, or coworker may mediate informally and represent the concerns of the local set of social relations.

In many settings, the institutions are relatively sparse or weak for managing certain conflicts among adversaries. Thus, in some societies institutionalized procedures are not well developed for family disputes, since these are considered private. Furthermore, communal conflicts are relatively inchoate and therefore often lack institutionalized ways to be managed. This is a precursor condition for destructive ethnic and religious conflicts in the Middle East and South Asia.

Characteristics of the Conflict

The scale and stage of a conflict and the nature of the adversaries and their relationship all affect the kind of mediation that is used. In large-scale conflicts, many kinds of persons are likely to be engaged in the mediation, sometimes at the same time. In small-scale conflicts, more often a single person serves as the mediator, whether in a facilitative or deal-making role.

Increasing attention is being given by analysts to specifying the kind of intermediary intervention that is appropriate for various stages of a conflict.[50] For example, unofficial mediation that is largely facilitative is most common and effective at early stages of a conflict. The adversaries and the relationship between them also strongly affect the kind of mediation practiced and the impact of the mediation. One important dimension of the relationship between adversaries in a conflict is the symmetry in resources between them. If adversaries differ greatly in resources and power, the party with more tends to refuse mediation that seems to place the adversaries on an equal level. Official mediation tends to make visible that recognition. Consequently, an informal and relatively facilitative kind of mediation is more likely to occur under those circumstances.

Adversaries with an ongoing relationship and with high levels of integration tend to utilize mediation or even arbitration in seeking to settle their disputes. Mediation or arbitration is expected to help reach a settlement quickly and prevent the escalation of antagonism, and so preserve the social relationship.

Characteristics of the Mediator

Each kind of person or group can play only a particular variety of mediator roles. For example, mediators with considerable material resources are likely to find it difficult to restrict themselves to facilitator roles; the adversaries tend to anticipate that such mediators will use their resources to help fashion a deal. Similarly, mediators who come to the table with strong moral authority are often relied upon to sanction any eventual agreement. In these cases, the moral authority of the mediator can ease the acceptance of the agreement among constituency groups. For example, former UN Secretary-General Kofi Annan used his high moral standing to successfully bring a close to the 2007–2008 electoral crisis in Kenya. The high standing Annan enjoyed helped to facilitate a sense among most stakeholder groups that the innovative power-sharing agreement that was crafted was fair and legitimate.[51]

The proliferation of mediation channels, including various official and unofficial mediator roles, raises the importance of understanding which types of mediators are most appropriate for different conflicts at various stages.[52] Mediators obviously differ in style, because of past mediating training, experience, and personality. Such individual differences make some kinds of mediation especially congenial to persons and provide a strong reason that no single way of filling a role will prove to be effective for every incumbent. Effective training for mediation takes that variability into account.

ASSESSING MEDIATOR CONTRIBUTIONS

Having noted many of the services that mediators and related intermediaries may provide to foster constructive conflict de-escalation, we must consider how effective their actual contributions are. For many analysts, the ambiguities of the terms "effectiveness" and "success" have led them to categorize simply reaching a settlement with the participation of a mediator to be a successful mediation.[53] If the overt struggle continues, the mediation is regarded as failed. Other analysts use several criteria of effectiveness, including durability of the agreement, fairness of the agreement, stakeholder satisfaction, and speed of reaching an agreement. The assessment of each of these dimensions varies in difficulty. Measuring durability may seem relatively straightforward, but even that can be uncertain when we consider the disputes that often arise about adherence to an agreement. Determining justness and efficiency are even more problematic, yet very important.[54]

A general problem in assessing the contributions of mediation efforts is that the agreement, when it does come, depends on many factors in addition to whatever an intermediary has done. It is extraordinarily difficult to separate out the value added by an intermediary's actions. For some purposes, the testimony of the adversaries is an important indicator. Research findings indicate high rates of user satisfaction with mediation, typically 75 percent or higher.[55] But to make an independent assessment of the contributions mediation makes, an analyst must use various kinds of comparative evidence of other mediating efforts in the same conflict at other times, of mediating conflicts in other similar conflicts, and of the consequences of similar conflicts lacking mediation.

Success is never complete for any single mediation effort to settle, resolve, or transform a large-scale conflict. Even if an agreement is reached, some people on each side are likely to reject it and some will become dissatisfied as the agreement is carried out; indeed, the agreement may fail to be implemented and be followed by renewed and even more intense struggle.

Furthermore, agreements are rarely reached without prior efforts, and earlier mediation efforts may have contributed to changes that ultimately resulted in reaching a mutually satisfactory agreement. Therefore, it is advisable to consider the specific consequences of various mediating actions for different people on the opposing sides.

In trying to assess what kinds of mediation affect a conflict's movement toward greater constructiveness, another question should be posed: Compared to what? In the realm of many interpersonal, family, or public disputes, mediation is generally compared to adjudication. Within hierarchical organizations, the comparison may be to arbitration by higher authority, and in international relations the comparison may be to coercive diplomacy or to coercive imposition. All these matters have not yet been systematically examined in a comprehensive fashion to assess what effects different kinds of mediation have in various circumstances. Pieces of relevant theory and research are noted here to indicate important empirically grounded generalizations and patterns. The discussion focuses on five issues: (1) gaining mediator entry, (2) helping reach an agreement, (3) enhancing the quality of the agreement, (4) contributing to the implementation and durability of the agreement, and (5) coordinating mediation efforts. This discussion is about persons enacting mediator roles that are so recognized by the adversaries. Too little research is available to make a comparable examination of informal mediation and of quasi mediation.

Gaining Entry

The intervention of mediators is anticipated and generally realized in many spheres of societal life, so that mediation entry is not problematic. For example, in countries with institutionalized labor-management collective bargaining, mediation is generally available and frequently used. In the rapidly growing arena of disputes mediated through community dispute-resolution centers, between one-third and two-thirds of the disputants to whom mediation is offered refuse it.[56] In some matters where mediation is required, interestingly, the likelihood of agreement and of user satisfaction is about the same for mandated and elective mediation.

Even in international conflicts, mediation by international organizations or by governments not engaged in the conflict frequently occurs. Thus, an analysis of 310 international disputes between 1945 and 1974 found that a mediator was involved in 82 percent of the cases.[57] A study of the seventy-two more severe international conflicts between 1945 and 1984 with at least one hundred deaths found that 61 percent were mediated.[58] Highly serious conflict episodes, in the context of protracted conflicts, are even less frequently mediated. Thus, in a study of international conflicts between 1945 and 1995, eighteen cases of intractable conflicts were identified; they lasted more than fifteen years, had recurrent violent episodes, and resisted conflict management efforts.[59] Among those eighteen cases, seventy-five serious militarized conflicts occurred, and only 44 percent were mediated. However, some of the conflicts received numerous mediation efforts and others only a few. Thus, there were eighty-seven mediation efforts in the four militarized conflicts in the Greece-Turkey relationship and only four such efforts in the five militarized conflict eruptions between the Soviet Union and the United States. The two superpowers were able to keep formal mediators from intervening and did so.

Contributing to the Attainment of Agreements

Settlement rates for mediated disputes vary greatly across domains, ranging between 20 and 80 percent.[60] Analyses of international conflicts indicate that the involvement of intermediaries is associated with reduced likelihood that the conflict will escalate and result in violence. Thus, an analysis of seventy-two major international conflicts between 1920 and 1965 found that only 28 percent of those that were handled through procedures involving intermediaries had outcomes determined by violence, compared with 76 percent for those conflicts in which the adversaries did not use intermediaries.[61]

Taking mediation events as the unit of analysis reveals that they attain agreements in 70 to 80 percent of community conflict mediations.[62] However, mediations frequently fail to produce an agreement in international conflicts. In an analysis of the ninety-seven international disputes between 1945 and 1990, with more than one hundred fatalities, 346 separate mediation attempts were made.[63] Only 6 percent of the mediation attempts yielded a full settlement, 12 percent a partial settlement, and 10 percent a ceasefire, while 72 percent were deemed unsuccessful. Clearly, the nature of the conflict at the time of the mediation limits the possibility of success. This analysis found that mediation was much more likely to be successful in conflicts with low complexity and few fatalities, and that had only recently begun.

An analysis of mediation in internationalized ethnic conflicts found that mediation was less likely to be successful if it dragged on for many months and the same mediator remained engaged.[64] Mediators tend to speed reaching an agreement, which occurs for several reasons. In social experiments when a mediator intervened to make suggestions, the subjects made larger and more frequent concessions.[65] Apparently the interventions enabled the adversaries to make concessions without considering themselves weak for doing so. Observations and analyses of industrial disputes indicate that mediators are able to make suggestions and generate pressures that tend to result in concessions that hasten reaching an agreement.[66] A study of negotiations involving municipal governments and police and firefighter unions found that mediators using a relatively aggressive strategy of making suggestions were associated with narrowing the differences between the bargainers, particularly about nonsalary issues.[67]

Although mediators often contribute to the reaching of an agreement, they certainly do not ensure it. Even powerful mediators can fail to produce an agreement at a particular mediation endeavor, as illustrated by the failure of Israeli and Palestinian leaders to reach an agreement at Camp David meetings in July 2000 mediated by President Clinton.[68] This failure is partly attributable to the attempt to reach a final status agreement within severe time constraints regarding issues about which the two sides held significantly different positions. Prime Minister Barak was facing elections, and President Clinton was soon to leave office. Major issues had not been subjected to official negotiations by the most senior leaders of the two sides, including those pertaining to the disposition of Jerusalem and of Palestinian refugees.[69]

Contributing to the Quality of Agreements

Reaching a settlement is not the only standard of success. The settlement should be regarded as a good one by the disputants and by other stakeholders it affects. A variety of evidence indicates that mediators often help produce agreements that are regarded as fair by analysts as well as those with a stake in the conflict. Experimental evidence, for example, indicates that third-party observers or mediators making even small interventions increase the pressures toward adhering to norms of fairness and equity.[70] Furthermore, experimental research indicates that mediators who are perceived to have high ability are especially likely to help produce settlements that yield high gains for the negotiators, perhaps because their suggestions can be readily accepted without losing face.[71]

There is evidence that mediated disputes result in agreements involving more equal sharing of resources and more compromise than adjudicated agreements. For example, divorce mediation resulted in more joint (rather than sole) custody agreements, and small claims disputes resulted in "awards going entirely to the plaintiff in almost 50 percent of the adjudicated cases, but in only 17 percent of the mediated ones."[72]

Observations and interviews with negotiators indicate several ways that mediators may help to produce relatively fair agreements and outcomes. One reason for this is that the presence of a trusted mediator who is considered skillful in mediation facilitates a fuller discussion of contentious issues.[73]

Contributing to the Implementation and Durability of Agreements

Compliance to mediated agreements appears to be relatively high. Thus, agreements reached in neighborhood justice centers have compliance rates of 67 to 87 percent; in the small claims area, full compliance was reported for the mediated cases, compared with 48 percent through adjudication.[74]

Several reasons for the relatively high compliance and durability of mediated agreements can be suggested. First, insofar as the disputing sides have participated in reaching an agreement, they are likely to feel that the agreement is fair and represents their interests, hence worthy of implementation and maintenance. The disputants' relations to the mediator are also important bases for honoring an agreement; disputants may have obligations to the mediator or wish to sustain their reputation with the mediator and therefore believe they should honor the agreement made with the assistance of that mediator. Particularly for mediators who have actively supported an agreement and have great resources, such considerations are important.

Mediating and other intermediary actions are increasingly geared to the postsettlement period and to sustaining the agreements reached. This increased activity follows from the recognition that agreements in large-scale conflicts frequently break down, in part due to inadequate external engagement in supporting the implementation and enabling further conflict transformation. Despite the many workshops, dialogue groups, and track-two negotiations that had attempted to de-escalate the Israeli-Palestinian conflict, not enough was done to transform the parties in the conflict and to fully implement the agreements previously made.[75] This contributed greatly to the failure of U.S. mediation of the Israeli-Palestinian negotiations in 2000, and the subsequent outbreak of the second intifada, years of violence, and greater mistrust.

When the mediation is limited, the adversaries' leaders grapple to improve their position, spoilers act to undermine the agreement, and external actors support rejectionist groups, an agreement is likely to fail. This happened disastrously in the case of the mediated 1993 Arusha Peace Agreement for Rwanda. The United Nations, the Organization of African Unity, and Tanzania were to aid in the implementation but were unable to prevent the genocide that killed eight hundred thousand Tutsis and moderate Hutus.[76]

Coordinating Intermediary Peacemaking Efforts

Whether consciously intended or not by the several intermediaries in large-scale conflicts, their activities often support each other, making them more effective jointly than each would have been alone.[77] However, different activities performed by various intermediaries sometimes unfortunately interfere with each other, impairing their effectiveness.

Two major types of coordination should be distinguished: sequential and simultaneous, and the many varieties of each. Intermediary activity may be coordinated over time in several ways. Thus, many times one intermediary prepares the ground or even initiates de-escalating negotiations and then the negotiations are taken up by a different set of intermediaries. Many instances of effective sequential complementarity can be cited, usually involving nonofficial or track-two methods preceding more traditional diplomacy.[78] Track-two operations may prepare the way for official negotiations, as noted earlier regarding the African National Congress and Afrikaner meetings about apartheid in South Africa. Thus, too, workshops involving Israeli Jews and Palestinian Arabs contributed to the later direct official negotiations between the Israeli government and the Palestine Liberation Organization.[79] For example, the understandings about each other's points of views and concerns, and possible ways to reconcile them, provided the basis for officials on each side to believe a mutually acceptable formula could be found. Some of the members of the Israeli and Palestinian negotiation teams had participated in such workshops.

In addition, negotiations may be initiated in a nonofficial track and then handed off to an official negotiating channel. Sometimes the traditional diplomatic channel has reached an impasse and a new track is opened informally. When progress is made, the negotiations are returned to the official channel. This is illustrated in the 1993 negotiations between Israelis and the Palestine Liberation Organization, conducted in Oslo, Norway.[80]

Simultaneous as well as sequential coordination may result from unofficial meetings and official back-channel conversations that complement relatively traditional diplomatic activities.[81] One way this occurs is when unofficial tracks parallel official negotiating tracks. For example, this was the case for the Pugwash and Dartmouth meetings during the years of U.S.–Soviet negotiations regarding arms control measures.

In large-scale conflicts, various intermediaries and approaches generally need to be blended to be effective. If they are well coordinated, their effectiveness enhances the efforts of each approach, as illustrated in the 1989–1992 peace process ending Mozambique's war.[82] Coordination may occur through regular gatherings of representatives from intermediary groups, at which they exchange information about what each is doing. Some organizations are acknowledged by others to be the "lead" organization, and some have the capacity and interest to give direction to many other organizations. This is increasingly the case as the U.S. government and other governments, as well as international governmental organizations, contract out much of the work in peacemaking. However, when a national government has a very strong interest in the political developments in another country, it may pursue those interests, hampering efforts by the United Nations or other governments in mediation efforts that are responsive to the concerns of a wide range of people in that country.

The destructive and protracted character of many communal conflicts, despite multiple efforts to intervene and resolve them, indicates that the interventions are often ineffective. We must consider why they fail. To what extent is failure due to the nature of the conflict and the existing conditions, and to what extent is it due to inappropriate intermediary actions? Was the time not ripe for the kind of interventions that were tried?[83] Does the multiplicity of intermediary efforts hamper effective de-escalation and reaching enduring mutually acceptable agreements? Does this occur because poorly coordinated efforts undermine each other as they convey inconsistent messages to the adversaries about what needs to be done? Were the wrong kinds of intermediaries used for the kinds of adversaries in the conflict? Under what circumstances do adversaries use one intermediary against another? Do intermediaries compete for attention and strain the capability of the adversaries' representatives to make appropriate responses?

Previous experience, theorizing, and research suggest answers to some of these questions.[84] Thus, possible intermediaries vary in the likelihood of effectively intervening in different kinds of conflicts. For example, conflicts within a country, between the government and challengers to the government, tend to be resistant to peacemaking interventions by other states, and even by international governmental organizations. Therefore, unofficial, facilitating interveners are probably more likely to gain access.[85] The difficulty that governments and governmental organizations have in intervening in domestic conflicts has created a void that nongovernmental organizations increasingly fill (e.g., the center established by Jimmy Carter in Atlanta and International Alert, based in London).[86] Once negotiations have been initiated, however, intermediaries with resources are relatively more effective than are nonofficial intermediaries in bringing about an agreement and to help implement it.[87]

Various intermediary activities also differ in their likely effectiveness for different kinds of conflicts and at different phases of a conflict. Thus, consulting and conveying information between the adversaries is likely to be more effective than strong, deal-making activities at the prenegotiation stage of a conflict.[88]

SUMMARY AND DISCUSSION QUESTIONS

This chapter has indicated that mediation is more or less effective, depending on the nature and stage of the conflict, the disputants, and their relations with each other, as well as the skill and appropriateness of the mediation effort. Overall, the less antagonistic and the more integrated the relations between the adversaries, the better are the prospects for mediation.[89] The more intensely and destructively a conflict has been waged, the greater is the difficulty in undertaking mediation and doing so effectively. But if the antagonists believe they are unable to impose a victory and begin to search for a way out, mediation begins to appear attractive.

Conflicts in which one side is more powerful than the other are more difficult to mediate than are conflicts in which the adversaries are relatively equal. The ethical dilemmas of trying to mediate asymmetrical conflicts can be reduced by championing international norms, as illustrated in the work of Max van der Stoel as HCNM.[90] Furthermore, mediation is more difficult under conditions of resource scarcity, as noted in studies of labor mediation and in divorce mediation. Finally, mediation is more difficult the greater the disparity in goals and the greater the sense by any side that its vital interests are threatened.

Many other conditions relating to the mediation process, the mediators, and the adversaries' relations with possible mediators influence the effectiveness of mediating efforts. In certain cultural and institutional settings, mediation is likely to be seen as widely appropriate to help resolve conflicts. Furthermore, mediation is more likely to occur and be effective if mediators are available whom the adversaries regard as legitimate and with whom they have ongoing relations.

Certainly, mediation is not a panacea for all conflicts. It can make significant contributions, however, to preventing or controlling destructive conflicts. It can contribute to the transition from escalation or stalemate to de-escalation, to constructing a mutually acceptable outcome, and to improving the equity and stability of the outcome. The size of such contributions depends on many conditions of a conflict, the kind of mediation efforts undertaken, and most significantly the match between them.

To consider the ideas raised in this chapter further, readers are encouraged to reflect on the following questions:

1. Consider several conflicts that are occurring in your community. Which of these are most likely to benefit from mediation and why? Who would make ideal representatives to attend a mediation session? Where might it be held? Who would be a credible facilitator?
2. What is your own definition of mediator neutrality? Do you believe it is possible to be completely neutral as a mediator?
3. Identify a destructive international conflict occurring somewhere in the world. Which of the mediator roles identified in this chapter has the greatest chance of contributing to de-escalation in this case?

Chapter Nine

Non-Negotiated and Negotiated Settlements

Conflict settlements take many forms. Sometimes settlements are enshrined in written documents, treaties, or new laws. The 1920 adoption of the amendment to the U.S. Constitution providing for women's suffrage, for example, ended the struggle of right of U.S. women to vote in the United States. Other times adversaries simply declare victory and disengage with each other, even though no fundamental change in their relationship or the conditions that underly their incompatibility occurred; ceasefires between Israel and Hamas at the end of bloody confrontations in 2014 and 2021 serve as good examples. Such settlements are usually fragile and temporary. Finally, some conflicts are considered settled simply because they melt away, with the incompatibility between the parties becoming less salient to them over time.

In this chapter we consider different processes for settling conflicts and the impact that different settlement pathways have on the quality of the agreement reached. We begin by briefly reviewing non-negotiated pathways to conflict settlement. We then turn to a deeper discussion of two types of negotiated settlement processes: competitive negotiation and integrative negotiation. The chapter concludes with a discussion of the seven stages of negotiated settlements.

NON-NEGOTIATED SETTLEMENTS

There are several non-negotiated ways to end a fight. Four types are distinguished here: coercive victory by one side over the other, institutionalized settlements, conversation of an adversary, and withdrawal.

Coercive Victory

The unilateral use of power to impose a settlement on an adversary is common in some interpersonal, community, state, and international relations, especially where there is significant asymmetry of power among stakeholders. For example, during international conflicts a more powerful actor may may unilaterally force the other side to capitulate or seek to destroy it as an organized entity. Indeed, war usually results in the victory of one side over the other with the defeated side capitulating to terms of surrender set by the victor. Similarly, mutinies, uprisings, revolutions, and other disruptive challenges to authority are often simply suppressed. Opponents are killed, disappeared, or imprisoned by the more powerful actor—as was seen in the failed student democracy and economic reform movement in China in 1989, the failed Green Revolution in Iran 2009, the defeat of the reform movement in Syria starting in 2011, and the unsuccessful Belarusian uprising of 2020–2021. In each of these cases, the costs of continuing the fight became unbearable for the defeated side, leading to its capitulation, retreat, or outright defeat. The conflict becomes settled, though through destructive means.

Using coercive strategies to defeat an opponent has much appeal to some adversaries, particularly when they are in a position of strength. It requires no trade-offs or compromises, can be accomplished relatively quickly if sufficient recourses are on hand, and does not require introspection. The coercive approach has many disadvantages as well. Recall Figure 5.1 in chapter 5 on alternative conflict styles. The use of superior power to achieve one's goals may be successful, but it is done at the expense of the relationships among adversaries. Coercive use of power alienates others, damages social relations, and creates new grievances by the defeated side. The result is usually a situation of "negative" peace; overt hostility has ended but the drivers of conflict, such as lack of integration, inequality, and hostile intergroup narratives often remain.[1] Moreover, success lasts only if the pressure is maintained. Once the coercive measures are removed an active phase of the conflict begins again. These disadvantages are most apparent in settlements involving parties that are in an ongoing relationship where past actions become the prelude to a new phase of a conflict. In these cases, the settlement is destructive. Joint damage is done.

Institutionalized Settlement Processes

Settlements are often a product of institutionalized process involving third parties that makes judgments about the case before them. This includes, for example, arbitration, judicial proceedings, police intervention, or rulings by elders or other respected members of a community, such as the Gacaca system in Rwanda.[2] In each case, the authoritative third party—whether a judge, a respected elder, or an expert—renders judgments about a dispute consistent with established law, precedent, or community interests. Disputants are expected to abide by those judgments as a condition of community membership. Those not abiding by the judgment are subject to additional sanctions by the enforcement bodies the system.

Litigation serves as a familiar example of the institutionalized settlement process. Failing to resolve a dispute on their own, individuals in many countries have the right to file a lawsuit as a plaintiff, seeking a remedy for a perceived wrong in a judicial proceeding. For instance, in 1951 the Topeka, Kansas, school district refused to enroll third-grader Linda Carol Brown, who was Black, at the school closest to her home. Brown's family was told that she must ride a bus to a segregated elementary school further away. The Brown family, along with other plaintiffs, filed a lawsuit in federal court claiming that the Topeka School Board directive was unconstitutional. After a U.S. district court upheld Topeka's segregation policy, the Browns appealed to the U.S. Supreme Court. In 1954 the U.S. Supreme Court ruled in the now famous *Brown v. the Board of Education* case that states could no longer sanction separate public schools based on race, declaring that "separate schools are inherently unequal."[3]

Such endings tend to occur in systems with well-developed constitutions and judiciaries and where citizens generally live within the frameworks of behavior, norms, and expectations enshrined in written documents and enforced by the law. Institutionalized settlement processes are generally more constructive than power-based approaches because contention is nonviolent and is contained to the institutionalized setting. However, the constructiveness of institutionalized settlements processes depends on systems being fair and unbiased. This is often not the case. Many systems have judicial proceedings designed to maintain advantages and disadvantages for some groups, political parties, or leaders. In such cases the outcome may once again lead to a settlement, but on negative terms.

Conversion

Third, settlements may come about through the fundamental conversion of one or both sides. Important members of one side may become convinced that the views of the adversary have great merit, undermining faith in their previous ideology or religious beliefs. New social currents, the improvement of economic and social conditions, technological changes, contact between conflicting groups, and targeted and pervasive arguments made via the social media or one's social network can all profoundly contribute to new attitudes and a willingness to settle a previously intransient conflict.[4]

Converting an opposing side is relatively rare in large-scale conflicts, but it does happen. Many white South Africans who had believed in the propriety of apartheid became convinced during the struggle against apartheid that it was wrong and inconsistent with Christianity, social justice, economic well-being, or ultimate security. Similarly, in the 1980s many persons in the Soviet Union increasingly found fault with the workings of the Soviet system and viewed the Western democratic and free market system as attractive.[5] Finally, support for climate diplomacy as has increased among some because of new ways of framing that issue within the news media.[6]

Withdrawal

Finally, conflicts sometimes become settled because one or more parties simply withdraws from the fight, dropping their claims to pursue other matters. Meeting strong resistance, it may abandon the pursuit and the conflict becomes dormant. The challenge withdrawn, the overt struggle dwindles away. Or a diffuse conflict may erupt in a demonstration or other protest, in which demands are voiced, but no settlement of the ostensible issues is reached and yet the protests cease. The grievance may remain, but the other factors essential to sustain the struggle are lacking. For instance, contentious leaders are sidelined or co-opted, fractures occur that disrupt internal homogeneity and common purpose of the movement, or material support dwindles. Such factors are difficult to untangle, but they appear to be significant in conflict terminations. For example, Uppsala University's Conflict Data Program (UCDP) maintains a conflict termination data set that contains information on how armed conflicts of different type and intensity have been terminated.[7] The UCDP identifies six different kinds of conflict terminations: peace agreement; ceasefire with conflict regulation; ceasefire agreement; victory; low level, which indicates that conflict activities continued but did not reach the UCDP "threshold" number of fatalities per year; and other (termination did not fit any of the above criteria). For the period 1946–2009, the UCDP data indicate that across all conflict types 24 percent of the conflicts were terminated with a peace agreement, 21 percent of the conflicts were terminated due to the victory of one side over the other, 12 percent were terminated though ceasefire with conflict regulation, 3 percent were terminated through ceasefire alone, but the majority of terminations, 40 percent, occurred because deaths resulting from the conflict simply dropped below the UCDP threshold.

NEGOTIATED SETTLEMENTS

We now turn now to settling conflicts through negotiation. Michelle Maiese describes negotiation in the following way:

> Negotiation is a discussion between two or more disputants who are trying to work out a solution to their problem. . . . Negotiations typically take place because the parties wish to create something new that neither could do on his or her own. During negotiations, the parties acknowledge that there is some conflict of interest between them and believe that they can use some form of influence to get a better deal, rather than simply taking what the other side will voluntarily give them. Negotiators prefer to search for agreement rather than fight openly, give in, or break off contact.[8]

Three things stand out in this overview. First, negotiation is a direct form of exchange between disputants. Second, negotiation tends to take place when the parties reach a realization that they can achieve *more* for themselves by interacting with their adversary than by defeating or sidelining them. Third, negotiation implies a degree of interdependency between adversaries; negotiated settlements create something that the parties cannot generate on their own.

Negotiation occurs in every aspect of social life, between companies buying and selling materials needed in production, among family members deciding where to spend a vacation, between a supervisor and a worker settling how long it will take to finish a task, or between governments setting the conditions to end a war.[9] The negotiating parties, in all these cases, are trying to find the terms they will mutually accept to act jointly: either to transfer ownership of a house or to cease firing weapons at each other.

Negotiating to end a fight, however, tends to be unlike negotiating a sale of a commodity. In commodity negotiations the seller usually has alternative buyers, and the buyer typically can find alternative sellers. An agreement to end a fight, however, must be made between existing adversaries; the parties cannot go elsewhere to get their needs met. Negotiations to end a fight also usually occur after interactions with the adversary have aroused anger and mistrust, heightening the emotional elements of the conflict in ways not typically the case when purchasing a car or a house.

Negotiations to de-escalate or to end struggles, nevertheless, share some qualities with all kinds of negotiations. For example, the logic of the search for a mutually acceptable agreement is generally shared in all negotiations. Trade-offs may be made in which negotiating partners exchange concessions on matters of relatively low priority. Furthermore, negotiations generally move through various stages: including each party preparing its positions, the parties arranging who will negotiate and what the agenda will be, and the sides setting forth their positions, exploring possible options, exchanging concessions, reaching an agreement, and implementing the agreement.[10] In addition, the nature of negotiations varies considerably, unrelated to whether they are part of an effort to settle a conflict or to sell a commodity. For example, the negotiating partners may anticipate an ongoing relationship with recurrent negotiations, or they may anticipate that after the agreement is reached their interactions will largely cease. The negotiations may also vary in their scope, being about a narrow matter, part of a larger set of negotiations, or about a wide range of matters at the same time. In examining negotiations to settle a struggle, therefore, some lessons can be drawn from other kinds of negotiations, but that should be done thoughtfully, considering the peculiarities of negotiations in the context of a fight and the degree to which the conflict or exchange context differs.

Two approaches to negotiation tend to dominate. The first is competitive negotiation, and the second is integrative negotiation, which was popularized in the field of conflict management by Fisher and Ury in their pathbreaking book, *Getting to Yes*.[11] In the former case, negotiation is treated as a way of waging a contest, and the goal is to win for yourself and your side. In the latter case, negotiation is considered a way to reach mutually acceptable and even mutually beneficial agreements. Both approaches are reviewed in the following.

Competitive Negotiation

In conflicts, people often view negotiations as a means to continue their fight. Consequently, each side tries to gain as much as it can, expecting that the gains will be at the expense of the other side. Some theorists reason that this is inherent in negotiations and therefore each side must pursue this effort or risk being badly exploited.

Adherents of this conventional approach tend to take a hard line in negotiations, believing that by firmly staking out a desired position and holding to it, negotiators will maximize their benefits. Conversely, making concessions will be viewed as indicating weakness and will invite increased demands or rigidity by the other side. From this perspective, conflicts are essentially zero-sum in character: what one side gains the other loses. Negotiations thus involve a series of concessions moving toward convergence somewhere between the initially stated positions. The most skilled negotiator makes the fewest concessions, the least skilled makes the most. Figure 9.1 illustrates these ideas in simple terms.

As illustrated, an incompatibility exists between two parties, A and B. Party A's best possible outcome is on the far left and its worst possible—but still acceptable—outcome is the terminus of its triangle to the right. Conversely, party B's best outcome is at the far right and its worst possible—but still acceptable—outcome is at the end of its triangle on the left. In the middle is an overlapping "zone of possible agreement" between the two parties.

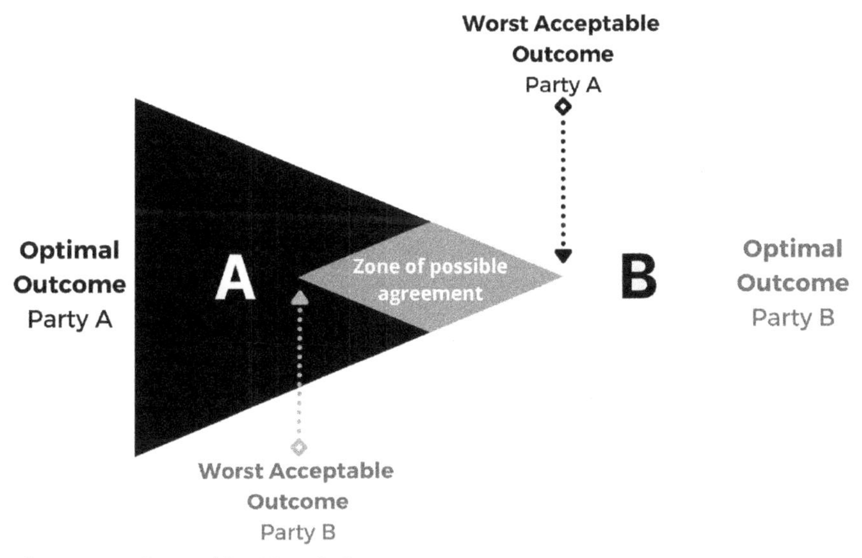

Figure 9.1. Competitive Negotiation

Both parties are pulling as hard as they can to achieve an agreement that is closest to their optimal outcome and farthest away from their worst possible outcome. The figure assumes that neither side is aware of what the other party will accept, and little trust exists between them.

Persons using this approach tend to stake out a relatively high opening position. They also tend to try convincing the other side that they cannot make significant concessions. Tactics that commit the negotiator to the position staked out and leave little room for maneuver are frequently made. For example, leaders may make their positions public, and even announce them prior to negotiations, so that they would suffer a loss of face if they later backed down. They may also say that they cannot change their positions because of constraints imposed by their constituency, who would not support any concession. Negotiators may also assert that they are under strict instructions and are not authorized to make any concessions.[12]

This conventional approach also tends to emphasize that one or more sides may use or threaten to use coercion to convince its adversary that rejecting agreement will be more costly than accepting the terms being offered. Indeed, in many cases negotiations are conducted while a mutually coercive struggle is being waged, as happens when collective bargaining is conducted while a strike is on, or peace negotiations are conducted while a war continues.

One side may even intensify the struggle to increase its bargaining power, whether by harming the adversary, increasing its coercive capacity, or strengthening support among coalition partners, as was the case with U.S.

President Ronald Reagan's aggressive pursuit of "star-wars" antimissile technologies even as U.S.–Soviet nuclear arms negotiations began in earnest. Such re-escalations of a conflict sometimes appear to succeed but other times may severely damage the process of reaching a negotiated settlement.

Duplicity is not so widely discussed in the scholarly literature, but its significance is noted by practitioners and feared by many members of each adversary party. One or more sides often provide deceptive or misleading information about their capabilities, alternatives, and preferences. The degree to which this is done, and is expected, varies by personality, social role, culture, and subculture.[13]

Collaborative Negotiation

An alternative to competitive bargaining is collaborative negotiation, which has become increasingly popular since first introduced in the early 1980s after being skillfully portrayed in the vastly influential book *Getting to Yes* by Roger Fisher and William Ury.[14] Fisher and Ury located their "principled," or interest-based approach between the hard line and soft line negotiation approaches. They argued that with such positional bargaining, negotiators play either a soft or a hard game, but that negotiators should change the game and negotiate on the merits. For example, the goal for those following a soft line is reaching agreement, and the goal for the hardliners is victory, but the goal for those negotiating on the merits is a *wise outcome* reached efficiently and amicably, focusing on the shared problem at hand rather than one's opponent.

Advocates of this approach contend that in traditional negotiation, bargaining positions are often set forth without adequate reflection about the underlying interests the positions are supposed to satisfy, so that gaining the positions becomes the goal, rather than satisfying the underlying interests. A party's position in this context is what they say they want. A party's interests are the underlying reason *why* they seek their position. Fisher and Ury observed that positions are often incompatible, zero-sum, and non-negotiable. Negotiators dig in on positions, defending them at all costs. Interests, however, can often be mutually satisfied, resulting in win-win outcomes.

Take the example of negotiations between Israel and Egypt in the aftermath of the 1967 Arab Israeli war when a victorious Israeli army seized and occupied all the Sinai. After that war Israel and Egypt entered a protracted period of hostility with Egyptians demanding a return of the Sinai and Israel rejecting that demand. The two countries remained entrenched in those positions until the 1979 peace conference between them, which was organized by U.S. President Jimmy Carter. At that conference Carter famously asked the Egyptians and Israelis what the interests underlying their positions were. For the Israelis the underlying interest was security. The Sinai was strategically located, making Israel vulnerable to future attacks if in the hands of a hostile neighbor. For Egypt the underlying interest was maintaining territorial sovereignty and the dignity of controlling its historic lands. Carter's solution was to engineer a trade-off which would satisfy the interest of both parties: Egypt regained sovereignty over all the Sinai, and Israel's security concerns were assuaged by the treaty provision severely limiting the presence of Egyptian military capability in the Sinai, creating a nonmilitarized zone observed by international peacekeepers.[15]

As this case illustrates, if both sides examine their interests and explore various options to meeting them, it is often possible to discover options that substantially meet the underlying interests of all the negotiating partners. The reason for this is that positions tend to be mutually exclusive, but interests are not. A simple way of illustrating this idea is found in Figure 9.2.

The figure imagines a conflict between two groups: one whose position is more gun ownership rights, the other whose position is more gun control. If the adversaries debate their positions the conflict will remain zero-sum; that is, more gun control means fewer gun ownership rights, and vice versa. Beneath the position of each group, however, is an underlying interest, which is

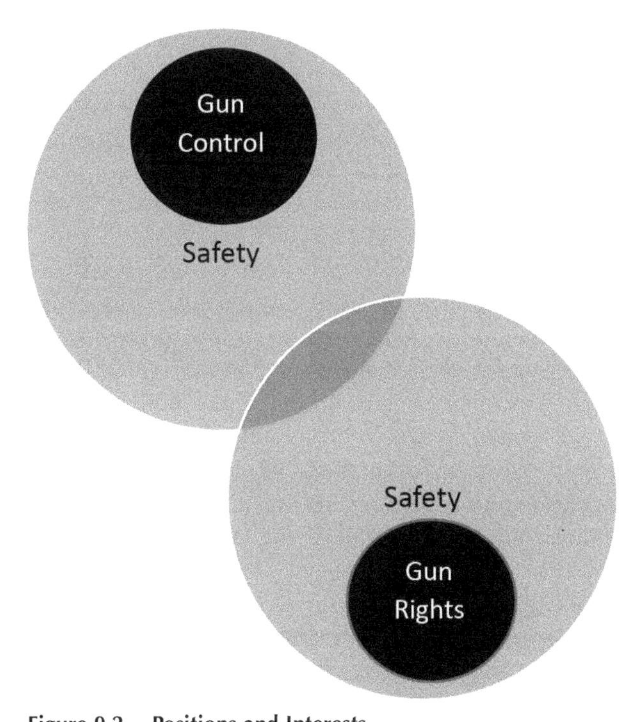

Figure 9.2. Positions and Interests

what motivates each side to adopt the position they have taken. In both cases, as is shown, that underlying motivation is to feel safer. If the conflict stays at the level of positions, there is little room for integrative bargaining. Each side views the other as the obstacle to achieving their goal. Once the parties recognize that they share an underlying interest, however, many creative ways to settle the dispute arise. Negotiators are no longer in opposition, instead they are free to engage with each other in a search for a solution to a *shared* problem; namely increasing a feeling of safety. Indeed, the conflict itself is not really about gun rights or gun control at all. Instead, it is about finding ways to make people feel more secure.

A variety of tactics can facilitate such a problem-solving strategy. For example, negotiators may ask questions, search to understand what the other side's interests are, and try to communicate their recognition of how the other side sees them. This only requires simple interpersonal communication skills such as reflective listening and productive assertion. Making such efforts contributes to converting a hostile negotiation session into a problem-solving discussion.

Another important technique is to generate many possible options to solve the problem. Special brainstorming periods may be used for this purpose, in which all participants are encouraged to suggest solutions; these ideas are not to be critiqued or discussed until very many options have been introduced. Only then are ideas that seem to be the basis for actual solutions selected, examined carefully, and modified in discussion. A related basic idea is that a conflict can be reconfigured, under certain conditions, so that a mutually beneficial or at least mutually acceptable agreement can be reached. Reframing the conflict and constructing a new formula to enter negotiations can help reach an agreement.[16]

To undertake constructive negotiations, each adversary must first believe three things: first, that a joint settlement of the contested issues is possible; second, that an integrative settlement will yield a better outcome than a unilaterally imposed settlement; and third, that the interests of the other side are legitimate and must be given some recognition. The diagnoses need not be totally shared, but they must be compatible for serious negotiations to be undertaken. As I. William Zartman and Maureen Berman state: "Negotiation is appropriate when the parties see that a problem can only be resolved jointly and when they have the will to end an existing situation, they consider unacceptable, while admitting the other party's or parties' claim to participate in that solution."[17]

Such diagnoses come about by reframing the conflict so that it is no longer viewed as purely zero-sum; rather, some common interests will be served by a joint solution. Along with the redefinition, possible formulas for settling the conflict emerge. The formulas may begin to be constructed in the prenegotiation stage of a conflict or in the early negotiation sessions. The formula may be the result of mutual concessions, as that which occurs in negotiations following a traditional bargaining model. But they also may be constructed by reference to a general conception or principle. A combination of a general framework with concessions and trade-offs is likely for complex, multidimensional problems.[18]

This new formula may be related to a redefinition of the primary parties involved in the conflict. Conflicts that appear non-negotiable for one set of parties may become negotiable for a subset of those parties or by including additional parties with a stake in the outcome.[19] One recurrent difference in the diagnoses of the conflict and of the possible formulas for resolution is whether the conflict is to be considered as a single, multifaceted conflict requiring a comprehensive settlement or a set of related conflicts best dealt with in a step-by-step fashion.

Formulas, in a similar way, may be based on one or two issues from the many in contention or by aggregating many issues to seek a more comprehensive settlement. Each strategy can be effective under different circumstances. By disaggregating or fractionating a conflict, particular issues may be selected that appear relatively easy to solve.[20] They may appear to be less contentious and less risky. Once successfully negotiated and implemented, they often become steppingstones to agreements regarding more fundamental issues. This reasoning was central to reaching a negotiated agreement in 2015, the Joint Comprehensive Plan of Action. The negotiations between Iran and the five permanent members of the UN Security Council (the United States, the United Kingdom, France, Russia, and China) and also by Germany (P5+1). The negotiations were narrowly focused on reversing the Iranian nuclear programs, which were close to producing nuclear weapons. The many other issues of contention between Iran and the P5+1 were left aside for future efforts, a criticism that was central to Donald Trump's foreign policy and used to justify the U.S. pullout from the agreement during his term in office.[21]

Aggregating several issues can also be the basis for a formula because linking issues facilitates trade-offs among them.[22] Although negotiating parties may have opposing interests on many issues, the priority they assign to each issue is likely to be different. By linking the issues, party A may give up to party B what is much more valuable to B than to A and in exchange, party B will give up what is more important to the other side than to itself.[23]

Finally, a formula may be based on a shared image of the future or an agreed-on conception of the conflict as a problem.[24] Particularly, in ethnic conflicts, having a shared vision of the future relationship between the contending communities is critical. The negotiators may anticipate an outcome in which their communities will become separate countries, establish a system of autonomous regions, or construct a political structure providing power sharing among the different communities. In the case of an international environmental dispute, a problem-solving process is aided if the negotiators agree that they are confronting a shared ecological problem. This likelihood is enhanced when the negotiators from different countries share common professional outlooks, have developed personal relationships, and are joined by nongovernmental representatives in the negotiations.[25]

What is critical in the integrative bargaining approach is working together to find solutions. Innovative thinking can often make conflicts that seem non-negotiable open to joint solutions, but such thinking must be convincingly communicated to significant segments of each side's members if the agreement is to be implemented and sustained.

Combining Competitive and Integrative Bargaining

In the minds of some advocates of the traditional one-sided maximizing approach and of some advocates of the integrative approach, the two perspectives are incompatible. Some traditionalists argue that ultimately one side wins and the other loses and negotiation simply reflects and ratifies that reality. They dismiss the adherents of the other approach as being naive and unrealistic. Moreover, some critics of the integrative approach argue that it often fails to deal with the existing asymmetries of power and enduring injustices.[26]

On the other hand, some advocates of the integrative problem-solving approach contend that every conflict can be converted into a set of negotiable interests and then reconfigured in a way that is mutually beneficial to those with a stake in the solution. They dismiss the adherents of the traditional approach as rigid and enamored with toughness such that each side seeks to advance its interests unilaterally, which fosters reliance on force and sustains injustice.

In actuality, the two approaches are often complementary, one being more appropriate and effective under some circumstances than others. Most analysts and practitioners believe that each of the two approaches can be carried too far and think that in practice negotiators tend to synthesize the approaches and their prescriptions derive from both. Some commonalities and complementarities deserve attention. Again, the U.S.-led negotiations with Iran during Obama's presidency are illustrative. Obama made it clear the United States respectfully recognized Iran's right to pursue peaceful nuclear programs, which opened the prospect of a possible agreement. That enabled the United States to marshal other major powers together and intensify punitive sanctions and combine carrots and sticks. Despite domestic opposition from hardliners in Iran and in the United States, the official representatives managed to focus on the technical problems in dismantling Iranian capacity to develop nuclear weapons and in ending the sanctions. Extended, intensive, and creative negotiations resulted in a signed and ratified agreement.[27] It is uncertain if a similar approach can be adopted by the Biden administration in the aftermath of the U.S. pull-out of the deal under President Trump. That withdrawal emboldened hardliners in Iran, and a return to the negotiation table on the terms agreed upon during the Obama administration are unlikely.

Analyzing any conflict that is to be settled by negotiations is an important first step to effective negotiation.[28] Such analyses also require attending to the alternatives each side has if a negotiated agreement is not reached. For rational calculation, the best non-negotiated alternative sets the minimum terms a party is willing to accept in negotiations. One or more side, however, may not fully estimate what its best alternative would be; its members may get caught up in the process of negotiation and consider not reaching an agreement to be necessarily a failure. A prescriptive admonition of many trainers and consultants of negotiation, therefore, is that a negotiating team must carefully considers what is its best alternative to a negotiated agreement (BATNA).[29]

Advocates of the one-sided maximizing and of the integrative bargaining approaches tend to differ in how to affect the other side's BATNA. Persons utilizing the traditional approach tend to believe that it is necessary to change the external reality, often by increasing the costs to the other side of failing to accept the terms offered or by enhancing its options to satisfy its interests in other ways. Problem solvers, however, tend to argue that changing the other side's BATNA may be affected by changing the frame within which the conflict is viewed. Such changes may be brought about by persuasive efforts and by insights gained from exploring the perspectives of the opposing sides.

Another matter of significance to analysts and practitioners of negotiations is the appropriate time for undertaking de-escalating efforts. There is widespread consensus that the effectiveness of de-escalating efforts, whether by partisans or by interveners, depends on the timing of such efforts. But there is much less consensus about what is the ripe moment for various strategies. Those taking a traditional approach tend to argue that until the adversaries have exhausted the coercive alternatives, de-escalating efforts are not likely to be effective. Ill-timed efforts to de-escalate a conflict will fail and can have undesired consequences.[30] On the other hand, integrative advocates tend to emphasize the value of de-escalating attempts in a wide variety of circumstances, arguing for finding an attractive possible outcome in the prevailing circumstances.[31] An emphasis on constructing an acceptable formula in combination with a hurting stalemate having been reached between the adversaries provides a synthesis of the two approaches.[32]

Some negotiating techniques fit within either approach. For example, one negotiating partner may offer a "side payment" to the other, which provides some compensation to the other side for a concession in the matter being negotiated.[33] This is feasible when there are significant asymmetries in the relationship between the negotiating sides. For example, a country that is located higher on a river running through another state has a geographic advantage over its downstream neighbor.[34] Although that situation is prone to conflict, it is the basis for many international treaties entailing significant cooperation. The Mekong River Commission, for example, has successfully coordinated international cooperation among the six countries that populate the Mekong Basin.[35] There are many issues relating to flood control, hydropower, and pollution that would be well served by upstream and downstream cooperation, whose achievement is attributable to compensation or side payments by one state to the other to balance off the costs and benefits of the cooperative arrangement.

Ethical issues confound the choice of either negotiating approach, as indicated by the moral critiques that can be made of each. Critics of the one-sided maximizing approach, for example, may argue that the failure to attend to possible mutually acceptable solutions tends to perpetuate struggles destructively and often results in imposed oppressive outcomes. On the other hand, critics of the integrative approach argue that in the rush to find an accommodation between adversaries, bad actors are rewarded, and injustices perpetuated.

Finally, we acknowledge that not all negotiations are serious attempts to resolve a conflict. Sometimes leaders of one party enter negotiations simply to demonstrate to their constituents, to a wider audience, or even to elements in the opposing side that they are devoted to peace, and they seek only to reveal the intransigence and unreasonableness of their opponents. They may formulate positions they expect to be rejected but that appear plausible to their own side. Some negotiations, even those pursued for years, then, may be fraudulent. Nevertheless, even these may be transformed and become serious. Changes within one of the parties or changes in the ongoing struggle may produce a shift that facilitates earnest negotiations. The preceding negotiation sessions then may turn out to have been useful, for example, by constraining the tendency toward escalation of familiarizing key people on each side of the conflict with each other.

This suggests that one side may be able to transform the course of negotiations, even when the other side entered them for duplicitous reasons. Treating a stated position, even one suspected of insincerity, as a serious offer and subject to modification may commit the side making the offer to become engaged in serious negotiations. Mediators sometimes are helpful in this regard, as was examined in chapter 8. They take a proposal submitted by party A, objected to by party B, and ask what changes would make it acceptable. They then take the modified proposal back to party A to discover what additional modifications the proposal requires to be acceptable.[36]

Cultural Considerations

One-sided maximization and integrative bargaining approaches share similar cultural limitations. They tend to focus on independent actors engaged in episodes of social interaction and that may reflect a particular cultural orientation. But other cultural views can be found. Thus, in some cultures, such as the traditional Chinese culture, conflict is viewed as a disruption of community relationships. Negotiation and accommodation are then seen as the right ways to restore relations within the community in which the antagonistic parties live.

More generally, the distinction is often made, in this context, between individualistic and collectivist world outlooks.[37] European and North American societies are regarded as generally having individualistic cultures, emphasizing personal freedom and achievement. Many non-Western societies, in contrast, tend to be collectivist, according high respect to authority and giving group welfare precedence over individual welfare. Conflicts within individualistic societies tend to be adjudicated within a legal framework based on individual rights, and that framework tends to characterize one side as right and the other as wrong. Conflicts in societies with collectivist cultures tend to be handled through conciliation to sustain group affiliation.

Regard should be given to such cultural orientations, but they should not be made into stereotypes. Within every society, individual differences exist as do subcultural variations by class, area of residence, gender, and many other factors. Moreover, all cultures include a broad range of conduct, and persons in each culture are familiar with a wide variety of ways of conducting themselves, differing in their tendencies to act in a particular way in specific circumstances. For example, U.S. negotiators are often reported to go directly to the issues to be negotiated and try to reach an agreement quickly, while negotiators from many non-Western cultures think it is important to build a relationship within which the negotiations can be conducted and therefore take time to build that potential relationship.[38] But obviously there are circumstances when Americans, too, recognize that building a relationship is important and takes time, for example, in courting a potential customer or romantic partner.

FORMS AND STAGES OF NEGOTIATION

Negotiations sometimes are completed in a single session, but generally, to settle large-scale conflicts a series of sessions are conducted over a period of months or even years.[39] The negotiations are conducted in a wide variety of forms and generally proceed through several stages. Before discussing the consequences of different negotiation approaches, these contexts need to be mapped out, because the likelihood and consequences of pursuing one or another strategy differ in those various settings.

Forms of Negotiation

Negotiations vary in their institutionalization, size, scope, isolation, privacy, and conflict setting. The variations reflect differences among struggles and their context, and they have significant implications for the results of the negotiations. The various characteristics of negotiations are varyingly intertwined, but they are discussed separately here.

Institutionalization of Negotiation Procedures

Every society has procedures for settling disputes, generally embodied in political institutions and judicial proceedings. Informal negotiations often are integral to the working of these formal procedures. This obviously is the case in the negotiations among legislators drafting a law. It occurs in adversarial legal proceedings when the lawyers, frequently with the encouragement of a judge, negotiate a settlement of the case before it goes to trial.[40] Afterward, the agreement frequently is made binding by the court.

Those formal legal and political procedures available to resolve disputes are the almost universal context for the relatively unofficial and informal methods, generally referred to as alternative dispute resolution.[41] The disputants often recognize that if the informal procedures they are using do not result in an agreement, they have recourse to legal proceedings or to political action. Alternative dispute resolution, then, serves as a complement to the formal and official procedures.

In the United States, and increasingly in many other societies, provisions are made for disputants to negotiate directly or with the support of mediators. The arenas in which such direct negotiations are conducted often function with legally enacted rules about procedures. In the case of collective bargaining, legislation and previous contracts define what is good faith bargaining and specify what is negotiable, but these are subject to change as power relations and ideological views regarding trade unions change. In recent decades, nevertheless, understandings about informal conflict resolution procedures have developed in public policy disputes concerning environmental issues and alleged discrimination by gender, age, or minority status.

The form of institutionalization, reflecting culture and institutional structures, influences which negotiation approach is used. For example, in the United States the adversarial style is deeply embedded in the political and legal culture. The founding document of the U.S. government, the Constitution, is based on a system of checks and balances, presuming that a struggle between different government units will preserve and protect liberty. A society in which individuals and groups seek their own advantage is thought best managed by having other individuals and groups contest them in an adversarial manner. This is evident in the way the U.S. electoral and judicial systems function.

Elements of collective solidarity, mutual support, and shared responsibilities, of course, are also to be found in U.S. society. In recent years, conscious efforts have been made to promote less adversarial methods to manage possibly disputatious relations and specific conflicts. This has been true within work organizations, among groups differing in religion or ethnicity, and between groups differing in policy positions.[42] The conflict resolution movement and the promotion of the problem-solving approach to negotiation in many ways have been part of those developments.[43]

Scale of Negotiations

Negotiations vary in scale by the number of parties engaged and by the number of persons representing each party. Although most theorizing about negotiations assumes two parties are engaged, actual negotiations increasingly include more than two parties. In international affairs, multilateral negotiations are becoming more frequent and are conducted in large conferences. For example, the UN Convention on the Law of the Sea was negotiated with more than 150 governments represented.[44]

The participation of many parties often enables some of them to provide intermediary services and so to foster a problem-solving approach. Some participating parties may not have interests at stake as vital as those of the primary adversaries in the conference, and hence they are subjected to appeals for support from the major antagonists. This also encourages persuasive efforts, couched in terms of shared principles and objective criteria, appeals consistent with a problem-solving approach. This was evident in the extended Conference on Security and Cooperation in Europe negotiations, culminating in the 1975 Helsinki Accords.[45]

In negotiations involving large entities, each delegation is often numerous, with representation of diverse constituencies. Hence, in interstate negotiations technical specialists, even military specialists, in each delegation may discover some commonalities in perspectives and experience not as well shared with other members of their own delegation. This can become the basis for alliances or at least increased channels of communication across delegation lines.

Scope of Negotiations

Everything about the relations between adversaries cannot be settled at the same time. A subset of issues can be jointly chosen for negotiation, although often the parties may not agree about which matters should be subject to bargaining. Negotiations vary greatly in the significance and number of issues that are considered. Negotiations covering many significant matters pose difficulties, particularly for traditional negotiations, but bring opportunities for newer integrative negotiations, since the multiplicity of issues on the table enhances the likelihood of finding advantageous trade-offs. Constructing a formula for a solution becomes increasingly important and hence more likely, since it will be more energetically sought.

Isolation of Negotiation Sessions

Negotiations vary in their degree of isolation in several senses. Some negotiations are brief, one-time sessions, while others are conducted in a series of sessions over many years. Some negotiations result in agreements in a relatively short time, and are regarded as unique agreements, some are viewed by the negotiating partners as part of a series of possible agreements, and some are one in a series of recurrent negotiations to renew expiring prior agreements. When agreements are viewed as the product of recurring negotiations, expectations about trade-offs over time may develop.

Some negotiations are conducted through one set of representatives in a single negotiating channel. For example, there may be only one official, highly visible channel and the negotiators take instructions and report back to the central authority of each negotiating party. But others are conducted through more than one channel. Thus, an official, but private "back channel" may be used in addition to the official and relatively public negotiation channel. Such a dual format was made famous (or infamous) when Henry Kissinger, while the official Strategic Arms Limitation Treaty (SALT I) negotiations were being conducted, met privately with the Soviet ambassador to the United States and shaped the terms of the SALT I agreement. He was criticized for keeping U.S. officials in the dark and not drawing on their expertise about the terms of the agreement. He later justified what he did by pointing out that he discussed SALT I in conjunction with several other matters in U.S.–Soviet relations, and explicit as well as implicit trade-offs were developed during those talks.[46] Such back channels have notable advantages in facilitating reaching agreements, but also severe disadvantages in getting the agreements enacted and implemented.[47]

In international relations, and other conflict arenas, various negotiation channels are used sequentially and concurrently with the official channel. Among the many nonofficial channels are transnational organizations within which members of adversarial parties meet and discuss matters pertaining to the work of their common organizations. Another kind of track includes occasional meetings or ongoing dialogue groups with members from the adversary parties discussing the issues in contention between their respective countries (or communities or organizations). Such meetings were held between whites and Blacks in Rhodesia beginning before official negotiating efforts were attempted for the transition to majority rule and the establishment of Zimbabwe.[48]

Privacy

Negotiations are conducted with varying degrees of confidentiality. Some are conducted in public; for example, community members may be important witnesses to a political or religious leader's mediation of a dispute between neighbors. Even negotiations between large-scale entities may be public, with news media providing coverage and the negotiators discussing their positions with the public. On the other hand, many negotiations are conducted in private, and they are considered confidential until they are concluded. Some negotiations are so confidential that only the participants and a few others are aware of them, and even the negotiators' constituents are not informed of them; the proceedings and sometimes even the agreements are considered secret.[49]

Several advantages can accrue with confidential negotiations. The negotiators can be more flexible in considering each other's ideas and suggesting possible options, thus encouraging a relatively problem-solving approach. They are also able to be more flexible in making concessions, thus facilitating traditional negotiation. These arguments are supported by social psychological experiments indicating that if negotiators are subject to attention and evaluation by their constituencies, they are more intransigent in their bargaining.[50]

In general, secrecy is particularly useful in the preliminary, prenegotiation stage. Explorations of possible agreements and steps to reach them can determine whether the time is ripe to undertake serious negotiations. Secret negotiations can also be useful when formal open negotiations become stalemated, and positions appear frozen. This was the case when the official Israeli-Palestinian negotiations became stalemated in 1992 and another channel was opened in Oslo for meetings that explored options and constructed a package agreement unbeknown to the official delegations. The resulting 1993 Declaration of Principles was a startling surprise to the people on both sides.[51]

Secret negotiations, however, also can have severe drawbacks. The negotiators may reach agreements acceptable to them that do not reflect the interest of their respective constituents or that may be neglectful of implications damaging to all sides. Furthermore, mobilizing the necessary support to ratify and implement an agreement tends to be hampered by secrecy. A full and open discussion of the agreement reached and a legitimate ratification process are ways to minimize those risks.

The Seven Stages of Negotiation

That negotiations move through several stages is generally recognized, even if there is no consensus about identifying them. Here, we discuss seven stages: prenegotiation, planning, initial presentations and analysis, search for options and formulas, drafting agreements, ratifying, and implementing. Different negotiation approaches and strategies are varyingly effective at each phase of negotiation.

Prenegotiation

In recent years, much attention has been devoted to the processes and conditions that bring adversaries to the negotiating table. In chapter 7, we considered the circumstances and policies that move adversaries toward de-escalation and ultimately toward settlement. Here, the proximate actions prior to direct negotiations are discussed, particularly after protracted struggle.

An early phase of this prenegotiation stage is the signaling by one of the adversaries to the other that it is interested in reaching a negotiated settlement.[52] This is not an easy matter. Adversaries often are mutually suspicious, and each side has been mobilized to sustain the positions staked out as its goals. Therefore, a leadership group thinking about making a conciliatory gesture as an overture to begin negotiations faces several risks. The other side may construe the overture as a sign of weakness and raise its demands; consequently, the leaders will appear foolish or weak to their followers. Another possibility is that the other side rejects the overture as a trick, aimed at appearing good to various audiences, but not serious; consequently, the overture may seem inept and be counterproductive.

Several policies can help minimize the risks associated with signaling a readiness to start negotiations. One is to use unofficial intermediaries to discover whether the basis for negotiations exists for the parties engaged in the struggle. Another tactic is to conduct secret meetings between high-ranking representatives of each side to probe for possible formulas for negotiations. Such communications help ensure that the overture will be appropriately reciprocated. For example, prior to President Sadat's dramatic visit to Jerusalem in November 1977, the Israeli foreign minister, Moshe Dayan, and the Egyptian deputy premier, Hassan Tuhami, discussed formulas for peace at a secret meeting hosted and facilitated by the king of Morocco in September 1977.[53]

Other policies involve taking a risk and by doing so making the overture particularly attractive and credible. The fundamental transformation of the Cold War between the blocs led by the United States and the Soviet Union was initiated in a series of statements and acts carried out by the government led by Premier Gorbachev. In many ways, the actions and their effects on President Reagan, his administration, the U.S. public, and the West generally were in accord with the idea of graduated reciprocation in tension-reduction, discussed in chapter 7. The Soviet actions, however, did entail substantial risks to the Soviet Union, much greater than those recommended by Charles E. Osgood, who directed his articulation of graduated reciprocation in tension-reduction at the United States. Gorbachev had reason to believe that the risks of the West taking unilateral advantage of the Soviets' military downsizing and restructuring were manageable, given the U.S. and Western opposition to the heightened militancy of the Reagan administration.[54] Gorbachev, however, underestimated the internal risks to the Soviet system.

The covert exploration and the grand public commitment can also be effectively combined. The adversary leaders can give each other some assurances, and then the apparently bold public gesture can win over mistrusting elements within the antagonistic side and rally constituents to the new course the gesture seems to initiate. The spectacle of the president of the largest Arab nation flying to Jerusalem in 1977 and addressing the Israeli Knesset was highly dramatic and constituted an irrevocable act. The prior secret direct and indirect communications ensured a warm response when President Sadat publicly expressed his readiness to go to Israel.

Some grand gestures can change the structure of the conflict and help transform it. This was true of the unconditional release of Nelson Mandela from prison by the Frederik Willem de Klerk government, in February 1990. It was a powerful transforming message for all people in South Africa that the struggle to end apartheid had entered a new phase. To a certain extent it is true as well for President Trump's dramatic meeting with Kim Jong-un in the Demilitarized Zone in 2019. President Trump became the first sitting U.S. president to step foot in North Korea after crossing the demarcation line, a powerful symbolic gesture that raised the possibility, briefly, of the possibility of a nuclear accord between the two nations.

Another prenegotiation aspect is the formulation of the structure for negotiations: this includes agreeing on the parameters of the negotiations, on the participants, and on the possible outcomes. Adversaries will avoid entering negotiations if they are convinced that the likely negotiated agreement will be worse than the status quo and deny them what they regard as minimally acceptable. Consequently, exploratory talks, through various intermediaries or directly between the adversaries' representatives at several levels, are often necessary before negotiations can begin.

Planning

Each negotiating party, before entering talks, generally reflects on what it seeks and how it proposes to reach its goals from the negotiations. In large-scale parties, difficult and complex negotiations are generally conducted among the various groups within each side that have a stake in the outcome. The goals of any large entity are always manifold, with varying priorities accorded different goals. The positions articulated for negotiation by each side reflect the relative influence of groups within that side.

It seems wise for each party entering negotiation to work out what it wants, what it will ask for, and what it will settle for prior to meeting with its negotiating counterparts. The negotiators will then enter discussions with detailed instructions about what they should try to get. But this fosters the traditional one-sided maximizing negotiation approach and makes integrative negotiation more difficult. The difficulties in combining the internal and external negotiations are severe. Roger Fisher suggests a strategy to reconcile them so as not to hamper a relatively problem-solving approach.[55] According to this strategy, the initial instructions should not include commitments, but directives, for example, to learn the other parties' views of their interests and concerns, to explain their own side's interests and concerns, and to generate a range of options that might satisfy both sides.

Initial Meetings and Analysis

What happens in the initial meetings varies with the negotiation approach being used. In the relatively traditional approach, representatives of each side argue their positions. When these sessions are public, the staking out of commitments may subsequently hamper reaching a mutually acceptable agreement. In confidentially held negotiations, and when the negotiations are anticipated to be lengthy, the initial sessions may involve a good measure of housekeeping matters, such as getting acquainted and agreeing on ground rules. The procedural understandings may pertain to confidentiality, ensuring space for informal socializing, and scheduling some shared activities.

In these initial meetings, attention may be given to discussing the issues in contention and the concerns underlying the stated positions to ensure that each side understands how the other views the matters being negotiated. A shared analysis of the conflict may then emerge that sets the stage for viewing the conflict as a common problem the negotiators will seek to solve, rather than a contest each will try to win. Obviously, this is particularly important for the integrative approach. Regardless of the approach used, initial sessions of negotiations that are anticipated to be conducted over many meetings are often devoted to establishing an agenda and common priorities.

Inventing Options and Constructing Formulas

At various times in extended negotiations, sessions may be devoted to thinking of new options and constructing possible formulas for an agreement. Such sessions may be held at junctures in the extended negotiation process when an impasse seems to have arisen. Changing the venue or composition of the negotiating teams, for example, by having subgroups of technical experts meet or by adding outsiders to discuss the issues or to help facilitate the sessions may enhance the effectiveness of such sessions. In addition, discussions of possible trade-offs and formulas may occur in informal conversations over drinks at the bar or in side-channel meetings.

Drafting an Agreement

The product of a negotiated agreement is nearly always a written document, and the processes of negotiation are directed at finding the words the negotiating parties can all accept. The more detailed and precise the terms of the agreement are, the more difficult the task of writing is, as provisions for likely but unwanted contingencies are considered and ways to counter them fashioned. An agreement that uses vague and ambiguous terms to paper over differences can be written much more easily. But of course, precisely written documents reduce the likelihood of later misunderstandings and alleged violations. Negotiators try to balance the urgencies of reaching an agreement with their concerns to forge an enduring agreement; as noted later, mechanisms can be instituted to minimize future disagreements arising from inevitable ambiguities in any document.

To reach complex agreements involving many items, another set of choices among approaches usually must be made. According to one strategy, a disposition is first reached on items, and these are treated as settled. They may be the relatively easy items but agreeing on them helps create a sense of confidence and trust. Another approach sets aside the items settled early on but allows them to be reintroduced later when they may be renegotiated in the context of a larger trade-off among several items. A quite different approach is to agree on general principles and then work out solutions to specific issues based on those principles. Finally, the agreement may be negotiated with changes made incrementally to a single negotiating text. The latter strategies fit better than the former with the integrative negotiation approach, but the best strategy may well vary from struggle to struggle and from its cultural, historical, and social context.

Finally, the style of discourse used in negotiations can affect the speed with which an agreement is reached and its equity. Undoubtedly, there are cultural variations in how positions are put forward, discussed, accepted, and rejected. The style in the United States is generally viewed as direct, matter of fact, even hasty.[56] But even in the United States, effective negotiators are not confrontational. There is evidence that effective negotiators tend to ask more questions of their counterparts than do less effective negotiators, and they do not preface their remarks with "I disagree."[57] Moreover, they avoid attributing feelings and motives to the other side but clearly identify their own thoughts and feelings.

Signing and Ratifying

The negotiation process is not over, even when the negotiators have finalized an agreement. Often, the heads of governments or organizations that the negotiators represented formally sign the agreement, frequently at a public event. This gives visibility to the agreement and further commits the signatories to honor the agreement; like a wedding ceremony, its public nature announces the new status of the relationship and serves to bind the parties who have jointly reached the agreement.

Frequently, in addition, the people represented by those signing the agreement must ratify it. For example, a treaty signed by the president of the United States must be ratified by two-thirds of the U.S. Senate for the treaty to be legally binding on the United States. A labor contract signed by a union president usually must be approved by a majority of the union's members for the agreement to commit the union.

Implementing

Finally, attention must be given to the degree to which an agreement is adhered to, and the signatory parties believe it is faithfully implemented. An agreement that is violated is a source of mistrust and renewed struggle. A sound agreement is one that is self-enforcing, giving both sides reason to comply with the agreement. In addition, committees and other mechanisms may be established to monitor compliance and to reconcile discrepant interpretations of the agreement. Implementation of agreements is increasingly recognized as a vital component in conflict resolution.

As we have seen, negotiations incorporate several interrelated stages. Furthermore, various forms of negotiation tend to be suitable at different negotiation stages. Being aware of these many possibilities helps those engaged in negotiations to conduct them more effectively. Experience and exchanging stories of past negotiations help expand negotiators' repertoires and so improve their skills. Of course, research and training can supplement and specify prior experience.

SUMMARY AND DISCUSSION QUESTIONS

In this chapter we reviewed both non-negotiated and negotiated processes for conflict settlement as well as the forms and stages through which negotiation takes place. We also took a deep dive on integrative negotiation, a practice considered to yield particularly constructive settlements. Through integrative negotiation, enemies can become persons with concerns that are appreciated, and the conflict becomes a problem to be solved by joint action. Readers are encouraged to reflect on the following questions and exercises to deepen their understanding of the concepts examined:

1. With a colleague, family member, or friend, choose a dispute that exists between you. Then practice the two types of negotiation discussed in the chapter, competitive and integrative, in two twenty-minute sessions each. In the first, focus on your position as well as on winning at the expense of your partner. In the second, identify the underlying interests behind both of your positions and seek a settlement that maximizes joint gains. Afterwards, debrief. What did you feel, see, and learn by conducting this exercise? What might you do differently in the future because of it?
2. Identify two or three large social conflicts that are widely deemed to be settled. Consider how the settlement was achieved. Was it though a negotiated or non-negotiated pathway? Who did what and how to bring about the settlement? Finally, do you consider the settlement to be constructive, destructive, or neutral? Upon what basis did you make that determination?
3. Select a major conflict occurring in the world today. Identify the positions taken by each stakeholder group. Then identify the underlying interests that is motivating them to take that position. Do the identified interests provide a possible pathway to conflict settlement? In what way?

Chapter Ten

Postsettlement Outcomes

A settled conflict may seem as if it has vanished. Partisans demobilize, the media moves attention to other matters, and public concern dissipates. However, conflicts are rarely resolved wholly and forever. In most cases, a conflict settlement simply transforms that conflict from one state to another. Sometimes that transformation is constructive: former enemies develop more equitable and stable relations, develop closer ties and less dehumanizing narratives about each other, or find ways to institutionalize their fight through less coercive means. Other times, however, postsettlement outcomes contain the seeds for new struggles and incompatibilities. The settlement achieved or imposed is viewed as unfair or humiliating. The losing side regroups and rises again, trying to regain what it lost in honor, land, freedom, or material wealth.

In this chapter we consider variations in conflict outcomes and their consequences. Of interest is helping conflict analysts to better understand and forecast what types of postsettlement outcomes lead to more constructive phase of contention and which are likely to result in the continuation of a destructive struggle later. The chapter begins by considering different kinds of postconflict sequences. We then examine variables that help to explain why one outcome occurs over others. Finally, we consider two powerful tools to help facilitate ongoing constructive outcomes: reconciliation and third-party intervention.

VARIATIONS IN POSTSETTLEMENT OUTCOMES

Figure 10.1 shows five variations in postsettlement outcomes that are common in the aftermath of conflict.

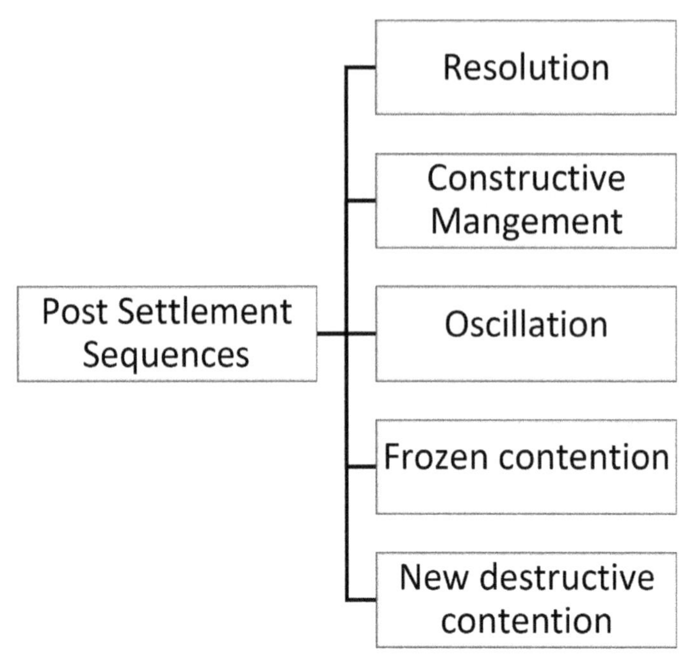

Figure 10.1. Five Post-Settlement Outcomes

In the first instance, resolution, the settlement leads to an end to the conflict. Core matters of contention are addressed, the solution satisfies all former adversaries, those actively contending demobilize, and relationships normalize or are strengthened. The conflict, in effect, ceases to exist. Though rare, such fundamental transformations do occur. They are more common in one-off situations where the parties are separated by a consensual matter, such as a commodity, piece of property, or a question of procedure. They are far less common in large-scale conflicts, involving disentail issues, and where ongoing interactions are unavoidable.

In the second instance, constructive management, the conflict is not resolved, but it is transformed to a situation where it can be constructively managed in an ongoing way. Opponents perhaps reach a settlement that serves as a stepping-stone toward increasingly comprehensive agreements and constructive relations at successive points in the future. Addressing relatively "low-hanging" issues builds a momentum to tackle successively more foundational conflict issues. Or perhaps, new institutionalized mechanisms are created as part of the settlement that allow the parties to continue contending, but in less destructive ways. For instance, postconflict reconstruction efforts often involve establishing civilian courts, which provides a way for adversaries to continue their struggle but through less violent means. So too, civil society organizations can establish ongoing dialogue sessions between conflicting parties, facilitating communication, understanding, and trust among former enemies.[1] Even social media has been harnessed to connect postconflict communities as they share, debate, and act on issues of peace and reconciliation.[2]

In the third instance, oscillation, a settlement only temporarily de-escalates a conflict, relieving some pressure but not transforming it in a foundational way. Only partially transformed, the conflict repeatedly escalates and de-escalates, oscillating in intensity, and moving back and forth from an escalated to a de-escalated state, but never disappearing. Race relations between Blacks and whites in the United States serve as a good example. The Civil Rights Movement resulted in major legislative victories that dismantled many structures of racism embedded within American systems. Those included the Civil Rights Act (1964), which prohibited segregation in schools, public spaces, and jobs; the 1965 Voting Rights Act that made it illegal to restrict voting based on race; the Fair Housing Act of 1968, which banned housing discrimination; and the 1972 Equal Opportunity Act, which sought to build Black representation in certain American industries. Those successes obviously did not, however, resolve the problem of race and racism in American. Post–civil rights–era racial discord has continued, most recently erupting in protests related to police brutality against members of the Black community. Foundational racial conflict remains, but it has vacillated between periods of calm and periods of intensity.

In the fourth instance, frozen contention, new outbursts of violence are avoided, but little progress made in reaching a mutually acceptable and permanent transformation. At the end of the Korean War, for instance, North Korea, South Korea, the United States, and the People's Republic of China agreed to an armistice which ended active fighting. Yet a formal peace treaty was never signed, and the terms of a postwar accommodation never reached. Today the Demilitarized Zone separating North and South Korea remains one of the most highly militarized areas of the world and a potential flashpoint for the eruption of a future war. Such frozen divisions in the aftermath of a war are not uncommon. Other instances include the Island of Cyprus, divided between Greek and Turkish communities in the aftermath of the 1974 war, and the Crimea, occupied and annexed from the Ukraine by Russia in the aftermath of its 2014 invasion. In each of these cases, settlement was built on a forceful separation of adversaries. Formal hostilities have largely ceased, but the conflict remains frozen and untransformed.

The fifth and last instance, new destructive contention, is hardly an ending at all. The adversaries reach a settlement, but the terms of that settlement are so damaging, painful, or humiliating that it triggers a coercive backlash. This was the case in the aftermath of World War I where the Treaty of Versailles, imposed on Germany by the Allied Nations of Britain, France, Italy, and Russia, became Adolf Hitler's rallying cry for the remilitarization of Germany and the rise of the Third Reich. Alternatively, the gains one side makes can be the impetus to strive for even further gains, igniting new struggles. A victorious side is so emboldened to engage in new destructive contention.

What explains why conflicts go down one of these roads and not the others? Why do some conflicts appear to be settled for good only to emerge again? To answer these questions, we must examine the consequences that the conflict outcome has on each party and on the broader sociopolitical context. Certain consequences appear to make it more likely that a conflict will re-emerge in new forms, while other consequences appear to dampen that likelihood. The following discussion focuses on internal and sociopolitical consequences in turn.

Internal Consequences

Every struggle of great magnitude has wide-ranging, long-term effects on the relations among the members within each party. These effects are a consequence of both the methods used in waging a struggle and the outcomes of that struggle. The way a conflict is waged helps set precedents, form preferences, and shape expectations about whether and how to engage in further struggles. We examine the effects particularly on internal equity and stability.

Consequences of Conflict Methods: Equality and Stability

Three developments affect the sense of equity among members of a collectivity who have engaged in a struggle: increased solidarity with each other, the development of new internal grievances, and the development of new policies that reduce the differential between group members who had benefited during the struggle and those who suffered losses.

The idea that external conflict fosters internal solidarity is one of the often-noted generalizations in conflict analysis. As Coser reformulated Georg Simmel, "Conflict with another group leads to the mobilization of the energies of group members and hence to increased cohesion of the group."[3] Another important proposition is "Conflict with other groups contributes to the establishment and reaffirmation of the identity of the group and maintains its boundaries against the surrounding social world."[4]

A strong sense of solidarity and common identity can mitigate the feelings of injustice at unequally shared costs, and they can foster compensations, to some degree, for the losses that some members of the group suffered. Compatriots, comrades, and survivors of persons who died fighting against an enemy are themselves celebrated and often awarded financial assistance. This may include benefits for the immediate family members of uniformed soldiers who were killed, suicide bombers who died, and victims of state repression. Honors and compensations are also often given to those who had participated in the past fight and may have suffered thereby. This is particularly evident in the various programs that provide benefits to war veterans.

Several processes can help overcome the internal dissension that external conflict might otherwise have exacerbated. Feelings of loyalty are aroused and called on by leaders, supported by group norms, and often fostered by interpersonal networks, all evident in the United States after the attacks on September 11, 2001. Furthermore, the increased prominence of an external conflict tends to reduce the salience of internal fights and tends to subordinate internal discord. For example, during the civil rights campaigns in the United States, aggressive crimes among Blacks decreased.[5] That decrease may have resulted from the civil rights struggle by absorbing energy and attention, by appearing to provide alternative ways of attaining what was sought, and by achieving improvements in rights and opportunities.

When the major basis for solidarity is a common enemy, increased hostility toward that foe will tend to strengthen solidarity. Thus, military alliances tend to have less internal dissension when confrontations with an adversary intensify. This was the case during the Cold War for changes in North Atlantic Treaty Organization solidarity.[6] However, internal solidarity may quickly dissolve once the external conflict loses salience or is terminated through agreement. This phenomenon can be seen in the tendency for previous allies to fight over power or the spoils after a victory has been won. Foreseeing this possibility should encourage preparing for cooperation after the fight ends.

Relatively constructive modes of conflict tend to produce a sense of group pride and solidarity and may be more enduring. For example, after the negotiations for a new constitution in Tunisia were completed in January 2014, and the transition to a new, freely elected government accomplished, many Tunisians were proud of what they had accomplished. This has helped the transition through very difficult challenges.

On the other hand, many persons who committed atrocities during a struggle, or are members of collectivities that do, later come to regard those actions as wrong and blame their leaders, assume responsibility, and feel guilty, while some deny what happened.[7] For example, in Bosnia and Herzegovina after the brutal fighting marked by "ethnic cleansing" was ended and the peace agreement forcefully mediated by the U.S. government began to be implemented, many former Bosnian Serb combatants expressed shame and bewilderment about what they had done. As one young man in a small rural town in what had become a Serb republic within Bosnia and Herzegovina said in January 1996, "I don't remember what we were trying to do with this war, and now I don't care. I got out alive, and now I want to leave the Serbian republic. I'll go almost anywhere else."[8]

An external conflict, then, may become a source of subsequent internal dissension and intense conflict. The externally induced internal cohesion tends to weaken as the conflict persists, as the burdens of waging the struggle rise, and particularly as those costs are unevenly borne. In addition, the insistence on loyalty sometimes is experienced as repression and a reason for increasing opposition to those pursuing the struggle against an external enemy.

The sense of equity is likely to be affected by the actual distribution of the costs of conducting a struggle and of its outcome. Given the internal differences in rank and power within any large-scale adversary group, it might seem reasonable to expect that the costs would be disproportionately borne by members of the low-ranking strata. There is abundant evidence supporting this generalization.

Where the fighting is intense and burdens great, often the relatively disadvantaged are further harmed. For example, during World War I, the health of the working class on the European continent suffered.[9] The effects of poor health are long lasting, particularly on children. Furthermore, many people, especially those who have few resources, become desperate refugees because of international wars, civil wars, and severe state repression.

Under certain circumstances, nevertheless, the waging of a struggle and its outcome do reduce the previous inequalities within an adversary party. Thus, in large-scale conflicts involving high levels of mobilization, the previously disadvantaged within an adversary party may improve their circumstances. In protracted international civil wars, minority groups, women, and other previously underutilized persons tend to become more valuable and gain new advantages. Thus, quantitative cross-national analyses indicate that countries with relatively high military participation ratios tend to have more income equality, holding other factors constant.[10] Erich Weede argues more generally that interstate conflict has tended to empower the middle and lower strata of the societies in Europe and contributed to the development of capitalism and freedom.[11] More particularly, research indicates that in the United States during World War II and in the Korean and Vietnam Wars wages increased relative to profits.[12] Other research finds that overall income inequality decreased in the United States during the Civil War and the two world wars, but not during the U.S. engagement in the Korean and Vietnam Wars.[13] The impact of war on societal inequality undoubtedly varies with the war's duration and the degree of mobilization associated with it. Furthermore, increased equality is not necessarily perceived as fair; the dominant groups may find this change wrong and threatening and then seek to restore their relatively higher rank.[14]

Advantaged groups, in some circumstances, suffer disproportionate costs of a fight. By taking the lead, they sometimes expose themselves to greater risks. In World War I, the British elite suffered casualties greater than the rest of the population.[15] The sons of the elite, graduates of Oxford and Cambridge, volunteered, and as military officers had very high mortality rates. This contributed to the subsequent antimilitarist and pacifist sentiments in Great Britain in the 1920s and 1930s.

Finally, how costs and benefits are distributed within an adversary party is not mechanically translated to varying feelings of equity. What appears to be fair depends on standards of judgment and on how the benefits and costs are presented. Thus, profiteering and corruption during wartime may arouse feelings of outrage. Public campaigns to control such behavior increase the sense of fairness among the members of a conflict party. On the other hand, if leaders and their families flaunt their personal gains, they risk repudiation and the discrediting of the cause they claim to lead, as illustrated by the opposition to some of the leaders after the wars in the former Yugoslavia.

Until recent decades, young men were particularly likely to bear the heaviest burdens in warfare, and that was often viewed as natural and inevitable. The decline of interstate wars waged on battlefields and the ferocity of civil wars has meant that casualties have become very high for civilian noncombatants, including children, women, and elderly men. Such casualties are widely regarded as horribly unjust and often produce a legacy of bitterness and hatred.

Class and ethnic differences associated with unequal sacrifices are traditional and often regarded as unfair. For example, during the U.S. Civil War a draft was instituted in the North, including the provision that a drafted man could hire a substitute or pay three hundred dollars and so escape service. Opposition was widespread and antidraft riots broke out in many cities.

In the U.S. engagement in the Vietnam War, Blacks suffered higher casualties than whites. While Blacks averaged about 9.3 percent of the total active duty personnel in 1965 to 1970, they suffered 12.6 percent of the deaths: "35.5 percent in excess of their percentage in the U.S. armed forces and 30 percent in excess of their percentage in Indochina."[16] This contributed to Blacks' sense of injustice within U.S. society even after the war was over. But the protests against the war, while it was being waged, were more evident among white college students when they were subject to the draft.

The destructiveness with which a conflict is waged and ended affects the chances that the antagonism and hostility relations among the members of each adversary party will be destructively renewed. Insofar as equity is increased, or at least not damaged, the chances of no hostile relations among the members of an adversary party are increased. Three other matters pertaining to stability warrant discussion: first, changes in social and material conditions within a conflict party; second, the previous use of conflict methods; and third, the degree of joint decision making in settling the conflict.

First, severe conflicts involving significant proportions of the members of the adversary parties generally disrupt routine life of many people within each adversary camp. When the disruptions are at a moderate level, they can produce new opportunities for many persons as they change roles and locations. The disruption may foster a spurt of growth, spurred by new ideas, combinations, and innovations arising from the experience of the struggle itself. The expansion may compensate for some of the losses of those who had suffered hardships. More generally, social systems confronting recurrent threats of conflict develop internal discipline and organizational efficiencies that tend to enhance their productivity in many arenas.

Large-scale violence in waging wars or revolutions, however, often imposes heavy burdens and significant declines in the well-being of populations in one or both sides of the conflict. The resulting disruptions are likely to create hardships for many persons, and if severe enough, produce social disorder resulting in widespread violence, famine, and flight. The decline can persist because the material and social bases for productive lives have been destroyed. This occurred in Somalia, Rwanda, Cambodia, and Lebanon. It may take years or even decades to overcome those losses. The costs are not only economic, but also social, such as fostering official secrecy, undermining social trust, reducing tolerance for dissent, and distracting attention from other social problems. These conditions threatened even the United States as people reacted to the 9/11 attacks.

Societal disruptions following large-scale, protracted violence sometimes are so great that government institutions fail to function adequately. Armed groups may engage in escalating interactions of revenge-seeking creating failed states. Corruption and criminal conduct may become rampant and institutionalized, and consequently extremely difficult to overcome.[17] A cross-sectional analysis of countries during the period 1960 to 1989 found that economic performance was negatively associated with engagement with interstate and with civil wars.[18] However, postwar economic performance was positively associated with wars, particularly civil wars. The wars' disruptions of entrenched coalitions and the engagement of many people in new experiences may be liberating and help account for this result. Such studies, however, do not compare wars with nonviolent revolutions or state breakups. It may be that the constructive consequences of war are due to the conflict in which the violent means are embedded, and if the conflict were waged with greater reliance on nonviolent means of struggle more beneficial consequences would result. Moreover, attention must be given to the policies followed after a war; if they are directed at recovery and reconciliation, as happened so significantly in Europe after World War II, but not after World War I, the consequences can be more constructive.

The second important factor affecting internal stability is the support developed for particular modes of conflict. Each adversary party, as a struggle goes on, becomes increasingly committed to its way of waging the fight. As it relies on armed attacks, covert actions, nonviolent protests, rent strikes, diplomacy, or persuasive appeals, it tends to devote more human and other resources to the chosen method. Even after the conflict is over, the resources devoted to the previously important mode tend to remain salient and be used again.

A variety of evidence demonstrates how these effects occur. For governments that have waged a war, the resources devoted to the military may decline afterward, but generally not to the prewar levels. There is frequently an upward ratchet effect, based on the vested interests created by past usage and on future expectations.

Despite what was written earlier about the energizing and equalizing effects of mobilizing resources to conduct a struggle, the effects are quite different if the mobilization is at a very high level, and it is sustained for an extremely long time. In civil and in international wars, if large proportions of the youth are preparing for and engaging in violent struggle, they fail to learn the skills and knowledge needed for economically and politically productive participation in civil life afterward. Even sustained mobilization to maintain readiness for armed struggle can drain and divert intellectual and material resources in ways that undermine the goals that the mobilization is supposed to serve. The collapse of the Soviet Union is illustrative. For decades, by Central Intelligence Agency estimates, the Soviet Union devoted 12 to 15 percent of its gross national product (GNP) to military expenditures; by Soviet and Russian sources after the Cold War ended, estimates are even higher, with percentages, in the 25–30 percent range. This allocation of resources greatly contributed to the failure of the Soviet system to satisfy the basic needs of the Soviet peoples. Even in the United States, a smaller percentage of a much larger GNP devoted to the military has contributed to a slower growth than many other advanced industrialized countries that devoted even smaller proportions of their GNP to military expenditures.[19]

The use of nonviolent and noncoercive means of struggle, on the other hand, often enhances internal stability.[20] For example, large-scale participation in nonviolent campaigns can be exhilarating and tends to build solidarity among the participants. Although difficult to sustain, it provides models and encourages approaches for settling internal disputes, which reduce the likelihood of destructive escalation of the conflict. Where nonviolent strategies are employed, popular engagement in political life is fostered. For example, the Zapatista movement in Chiapas, Mexico, fostered popular education and included a variety of local organizations engaging in civic and economic affairs, which are independent of the dominant political and economic structures; these endeavors provide the bases for effective political engagement.[21]

Third, negotiated endings of conflicts can have their own problematic consequences for internal stability. If leaders secretly agree to an ending, internal dissension may arise later, particularly if an internal opposition group exists and was excluded. Dissension tends to occur when the constituents have not participated in the transformative interactions among the persons engaging in the actual negotiations.[22] The way the Oslo meetings between the Palestine Liberation Organization and Israeli representatives were conducted, while effective in reaching an accord, provoked resistance among many Palestinians and Israeli Jews who were surprised by the 1993 Declaration of Principles agreement.[23] The problem can be reduced by enabling more segments of the constituents to be informed and participate in the process of change, or having parallel processes at various levels. At a minimum, if the negotiations are publicly concluded and ratified, the chances of the agreement receiving continued support are increased.

In short, the conflict mode used in a struggle often has lasting impacts on the equity and stability for relations within the party using them, including unintended consequences. The effects of the means used may undermine the goals they were intended to serve. Thus, struggles are often waged to improve the material conditions of the constituency in whose name the struggle is conducted or to gain more freedom and control for them. But even victory may bring about only a little of what was sought and, in some ways, may lower attainments for years. This is particularly the case when the means of struggle create high levels of disorder and resentment and high degrees of centralization and control within the organization conducting the struggle. Such consequences have often been noted in regard to revolutions. As Martin Oppenheimer observed in the late 1960s, when romanticism about armed struggle and guerrilla warfare was relatively widespread, "the types of personalities, as well as the forms of organization that usually emerge in a violent revolutionary struggle . . . are those which undercut the humanistic hopes of such endeavors."[24]

In short, the processes of waging and ending a conflict have diverse consequences for relations within each of the adversary parties, in some ways enhancing internal equity and stability, but in other ways reducing them.

Consequences of Conflict Outcomes: Equity and Stability

Conflict outcomes have long-term as well as immediate effects on the internal relations of the members of each side. The effects on equity and stability are likely to differ for the opposing adversaries since the outcomes of conflicts are usually not symmetrical. Thus, the side that believes it lost much of what it struggled for will experience quite different consequences than its adversary.

Members of the side suffering greater losses because of a conflict are likely to believe that they are suffering an injustice and feel disappointment, resentment, and anger. Those feelings may be directed not at the adversary, but at some people on their own side, especially the leadership. Trade union leaders who fail to win benefits desired by their constituency, for example, are likely to face factional disputes and challenges to their leadership.[25] Leaders of the winning party, foreseeing such consequences, may try to avoid framing the outcome as a defeat for the opponent to preserve the opponent's leadership and to preserve the outcome. They avoid public gloating and help their defeated foe save face.

Nevertheless, a faction within the losing side is likely to accuse another of being responsible for the loss. The accusations may be well grounded, but frequently they are self-serving, explaining away the accusers' own responsibility or justifying the accusers' rise to power. A classic example of this phenomenon was the claim by Adolf Hitler and many German former military leaders that Germany's defeat by the allies in World War I was due to internal enemies who had "stabbed Germany in the back."[26]

A defeat may also result in ongoing burdens. The hardships are the consequence of damaged assets, of reduced capacity to function effectively, and of increased demands arising from the inequities resulting from the different harms suffered by various segments of the population. These consequences may contribute to harsh economic or social conditions, pitting subgroups against each other, which can contribute to scapegoating, blaming a relatively vulnerable person, group, or people who had little capacity to affect the outcome. Policies, however, can be implemented that help limit the adverse consequences of severe losses. For example, after World War II the West German state took many measures to incorporate the German refugees from Eastern Europe.[27]

On the other hand, the members of the winning side more often feel content with each other. Insofar as the members share a common identity, the victory of their side is gratifying. Those who led in the struggle are likely to be honored and their cause in the struggle vindicated. But the gains of victory are rarely evenly distributed, and that can be the source of changes in the relative position of groups within the winning side and a source of internal dissension.

Thus, a collective bargaining agreement that gives all workers a fixed-sum increase will improve the relative position of the lower-paid workers, while an across-the-board percentage increase will be of greater benefit to the higher-paid workers. Either strategy, if pursued consistently for a long time, is likely to arouse opposition from the disadvantaged members.

Outcomes are rarely simply zero-sum; conflict outcomes generally have significant joint benefits and losses. The internal consequences of different combinations of benefits and losses vary greatly, depending on their characterization by the members of each side. Outcomes that have been regarded as failures for both sides are likely to produce high levels of cynicism and resentment among the rank-and-file members of each side. On the other hand, mutually beneficial outcomes, particularly if they seem to have averted anticipated disaster, tend to foster a sense of shared triumph and pleasure. This was the case for many of the people in South Africa as the transition to majority rule was made. Of course, many problems remain, and new ones have arisen, requiring new problem-solving negotiations.

External conflicts that result in one-sided defeats are often the basis for internal revolts against the leadership of the defeated party. As the discussion about the emergence of overt struggle in chapters 3 and 5 indicated, research on revolutions demonstrates the importance of severe and failed external conflicts in explaining revolutionary challenges and their success.

Victories, however, can also be the source of internal dissension. Expectations may be raised by triumphs; if the anticipated benefits are not forthcoming, the resulting disappointment may generate challenges against the leaders or the advantaged groups within the same side. This is particularly likely when the previously disadvantaged were mobilized to wage the struggle and therefore feel they have a special claim after victory. They may also have more capability than they had earlier to make their claims effectively. These factors contributed to the rise of the Civil Rights Movement in the United States after World War II.

Win or lose, the end of a fight allows people to turn their attention to previously submerged internal conflicts. The loss of an external enemy generally raises the salience of internal fights since the need for internal solidarity is reduced. For example, during World War II the U.S. federal government had induced the trade unions to make a no-strike pledge. Nevertheless, strikes increased each year of the war, except 1942, perhaps because the tight labor market increased the power of the workers relative to the managers, presenting an opportunity for them. Some labor disputes may have been held in abeyance, as indicated by the wave of labor strikes immediately after the war ended. The increase in strikes may also have been driven by workers seeking to counter the postwar inflation, and also by employers seeking to regain ground they lost when workers had greater bargaining power during the tight labor market of wartime.

After threats from a primary external enemy have disappeared, attention to new enemies often rises, in part from the tendency of some people to organize their lives around fighting against an enemy, so the loss of a major enemy produces a search for others. The new enemies may be internal as well as external. In the United States, after the end of the Cold War, some groups sought support for their struggle against domestic enemies, including the federal government itself or ethnic minorities.[28] As discussed in chapters 2 and 6, the dangers of a clash of civilizations, particularly between the Western and Islamic civilizations, became salient after the end of the Cold War.

Combined Effects of Methods and Outcomes

The way a conflict is waged and the way it comes out have many interacting effects for the equity and stability of each adversary party. They are discussed in the context of the relationship between external and internal conflicts. Although the proposition that external conflict strengthens internal cohesion is often cited, the evidence is not generally supportive of it. Rather, the nature of the relationship depends on many factors, such as the previous condition of solidarity, the kinds of internal conflict, and the severity and duration of the external conflict.

Consider the differing responses within the United States to waging World War II and the Korean and Vietnam Wars. Examinations of changing public attitudes, evasive draft behavior, and protests and repression indicate increasing disaffection and dissent during the Korean and Vietnam Wars, but not during World War II. Several factors help account for these differences. First, World War II was a relatively total war, which tends to be more equally depriving than a limited war. Thus, income inequality decreased during World War II, but not during the Korean War.[29] Second, the circumscribed goals of the limited wars were less likely to submerge internal differences than was the greater shared threat against which World War II was seen to be waged. Third, internal solidarity was already relatively low prior to the escalation of the Vietnam War, as the emerging civil rights struggle and university student uprisings indicated. In addition, the Vietnam War was waged for a relatively long time.

Finally, the results of the limited wars were not generally viewed as successful as were those of World War II. Failure is reason enough to punish leaders and withdraw support, as the Argentine military junta found after its

1982 attempt to unite the Malvina/Falkland Islands with Argentina by military force was defeated by Britain.[30] Moreover, leaders of failed endeavors are likely to be seen as less competent and therefore more readily challenged than are leaders of successful efforts. Whether dissatisfaction comes to be expressed in overt struggles with the government or among different groups within the society depends on additional factors.

The rationale for a war also matters. Immediately after September 11, 2001, American consensus was high to make war to overthrow the Taliban and destroy the al Qaeda leadership and organization. However, the reasons for going to war in Iraq were more dubious, and disagreement about the wisdom of the war quickly grew, as did protests against it. The obvious failure to discover weapons of mass destruction in Iraq and the failure to establish U.S.-friendly democracies in the Middle East made more evident that the policies pursued had been disastrously mistaken.[31]

A study of five major wars in which the United States was engaged between 1890 and 1970 indicates that the wars were associated with increases in domestic violence.[32] This was most evident following World War I, with violence by whites against Blacks in race riots, attacks by National Guard units against striking workers, and federal government raids during the "Red Scare" in 1919 and 1920. Not only were the differences within U.S. society exacerbated by the wars, but also resorting to violence appeared to be more acceptable. Several studies find a positive relationship between external conflict and internal conflict.[33]

Clearly, the oft-cited proposition that external conflict generates internal solidarity is not universally valid. It holds in some circumstances, depending on the way the external and internal conflicts are conducted and on the political character of the state.[34] External conflicts conducted for a short time and without recourse to violence tend to be associated with internal cohesion, at least in democratic countries. For example, considering increased approval for the president of a country as an indicator of internal cohesion, there is evidence that becoming engaged in a foreign conflict produces the "rally-round-the-flag" effect and a surge of support for the president.[35] However, engagement in peacemaking efforts also tends to have the same effect.[36]

Thus, moderate external challenges often foster internal equity and stability; on the other hand, destructive, protracted struggles result not only in heavy burdens at the time, but in internal changes perpetuating inequities and restrictions. Weede concludes from his analysis of the effect of interstate conflicts on revolutionary change and individual freedom that the "expansion of freedom seems best served by some modest amount of interstate conflict, by moderate threats to regime security rather than by extreme threats."[37]

Consequences for the Political and Social Context

The outcome of a conflict and the mode of reaching it affect not only internal dynamics within each party directly engaged in the struggle, but also the larger social systems of which they are a part. In addition, they often affect many other parties in the social environment who themselves were not participants in the previous struggle.

Consequence of Conflict Methods: Equity and Stability in Larger Context

A destructive conflict tends to create a variety of problems, because of the disruptions, dislocations, and traumas experienced not only by the combatants, but also by those associated with them. Thus, civil strife in one society may disrupt trade relations or generate mass movements of people, imposing severe burdens on members of nearby societies. For example, beginning in the late 1970s the number of refugees in the world has sharply increased. A time-series analysis of refugees between 1971 and 1990 indicates that generalized violence such as genocides/politicides, ethnic rebellion, and civil war with foreign military intervention are the best predictors of refugee flows.[38] Other factors such as human rights violations, ethnic conflict, and poverty or underdevelopment did not generate the large numbers of refugees that widespread violence did.

The conflict means used in past struggles affect how the former adversaries wage other conflicts. Thus, national independence movements in countries that became independent during the decolonization wave after World War II used varying amounts of violent and nonviolent actions preceding their independence. An analysis of those countries found a positive relationship between violence before independence and later external violent behavior.[39] In addition, the methods used in a conflict influence the choice of conflict methods by outside parties, adapting means that seemed effective. Thus, in the 1960s, nonelectoral methods of protest in the United States such as street demonstrations and nonviolent action spread among civil rights groups in different cities, to student groups on different campuses, to women's groups, and subsequently to many other identity and interest groups. Even people with quite different ideologies many years later have resorted to some of those nonelectoral tactics, for example Tea Party activists after the election of President Obama. Other social movements continue to surge using particular slogans and modes of protests such as "Occupy Wall Street," beginning in 2011, and "Black Lives Matter," beginning in 2013. Members of these movements are engaged in social conflicts that are interconnected over time and across issues.

Extremely severe means of struggle affect persons who are not directly engaged in the primary conflict and often create new injustices and long-lasting injuries. Violence in which people are driven from their homes, killed, tortured, and raped inflicts enduring emotional impairments on the surviving victims of such trauma and their family members. Consequently, they may act with desperation to find security and protect themselves, individually and collectively. In an extraordinary case, the largely successful Nazi effort to destroy European Jewry contributed immensely to the drive among the survivors to get to Palestine and to fight to establish a Jewish state there. That in turn resulted in a disaster for Palestinians, which reverberated throughout the Arab world.

A demonstration of an effective conflict strategy by partisans in one conflict can affect the sense of equity among parties that had not been engaged in that conflict. Thus, knowing about strategies that have been successful can help a group that previously did not act to redress its grievances, because its members believed they could not succeed, to strive for greater equity. In 2011, for instance, nonviolent democratization protests in Tunisia inspired similar movements in neighboring states, with a domino effect occurring as each movement adopted slogans and tactics used by others. Conditions that may have seemed inevitable and therefore tolerated may come to be seen as alterable and therefore regarded as intolerable. However, in some of those other Arab countries, such as Libya, the uprising lacked the preparation, planning, and adherence to a nonviolent strategy demonstrated in Tunisia.

This rise of claims for justice by groups who have endured discrimination and disadvantages may improve their condition, as happened in the 1960s and 1970s in the United States, and in the 1990s in Eastern Europe. But some groups may seek gains antagonistically, and the absence of problem-solving methods results in too little consideration of the adverse effects on the opponents. That may then contribute to still other groups feeling that satisfaction of those claims puts them at a new disadvantage, and they try to counter those gains by raising their own cries for justice. The backlash against affirmative action for minorities and women beginning in the 1980s in the United States is illustrative. To some degree the rise of the movement favoring traditional social values and practices and its growing strength in the United States into the first decade of the twenty-first century is a well-organized reaction to the many changes in social values and practices that had been contested and achieved in earlier decades.[40] Persons, who were offended by tolerance for abortions, gay rights, and multiculturalism, came to believe that their concerns about moral issues mattered more than other issues and allied themselves with Republicans who seemed to share their moral concerns.

The way a conflict is conducted tends to have enduring consequences for those who engaged in the struggle; usually, the mode tends to be perpetuated. For example, college students who had been activists in social struggles continue to be relatively active in advocating political and social change in their later years.[41] Under particular circumstances, such as great losses, the mode will be rejected in future struggles.

Major conflicts often have strong and enduring impacts on those reaching political maturity while the conflicts were fought. Through processes examined in the work on political generations by Karl Mannheim and others, certain identities and ways of thinking may be enduringly internalized.[42] For example, the Americans who became politically mature in the great economic depression of the 1930s became more class conscious than other American generations.[43] Similarly, certain issues and ways of managing them become salient as a result of a generation's experience. Thus, the age cohorts who became politically mature at the time of World War I or World War II (turning eighteen during either of the wars) tend to give higher salience to foreign policy matters and be more likely to favor recourse to war than are generations who became politically mature in the 1920s or 1930s.[44]

The Vietnam generation exhibits different consequences. Indeed, studies indicate that in 1973 and 1975, the Vietnam generation was disproportionately likely to say that the United States was spending too much on arms, while the World War II generation was likely to say that too little was being spent.[45] By 1978, however, the generational effects were no longer significant. The lack of consensus about the meaning of the Vietnam War probably reduced any enduring generational consequence of the experience.

If the struggle has brought severe and widespread destructive effects, attempts at developing a social-system solution to avoid its recurrence are likely to be made and generally be supported. For example, the devastating effects of World War II had many profound consequences for the global systems and for Europe, as well as for each of the countries of Europe. Thus, at the global level, the United Nations and many associated international governmental organizations were established to avert future wars. The presumed defects in the earlier structures, including the League of Nations, were to be avoided.

The devastating impact of World War II on the peoples in Europe followed many previous European wars and the failure of policies to prevent and control them. One consequence of these experiences, particularly on the continent, was the increased salience of a pan-European identity and support for binding the peoples of Europe together. These widespread sentiments nourished the European movement and the support given, for example, to the establishment in 1952 of the European Coal and Steel Community and then the later steps toward the European Union. The results were remarkably successful in ending the long-enduring enmity among countries in Western Europe, most notably between France and Germany.

Within European societies, too, political, religious, and intellectual personages strove to contain and reduce extreme ethnonationalism that might threaten the rights of minority groups or might result in threats against neighboring countries. This was especially the case in West Germany where de-Nazification policies were implemented, laws banning Nazi activities were passed, and policies toward German refugees from former German territories were undertaken to counter possible irredentist mobilizations. These historical developments affect the burgeoning conflicts among and within European countries in responding to the massive movement of refugees from the highly violent civil wars in Syria, Iraq, and Afghanistan.

The application of a problem-solving approach in a struggle contributes to the chances of sustaining stable relations in the larger system. For example, consider alternative ways of conducting struggles regarding discrimination against ethnic and other minorities and against women in the labor market. If framed and waged as a struggle in which increased opportunities for some are won at the expense of reduced opportunities for others, the struggle takes on zero-sum qualities. The matter in many circumstances, however, can be viewed differently, stressing common values and interests. Thus, it may be argued that cultural diversity within occupations will provide better service and production than hiring policies that sustain traditional homogeneity. The police force, for example, will better protect the citizens if its ethnic composition reflects the ethnic diversity of the citizenry. In addition, if the labor pool decreasingly consists of white males, a labor policy that does not prepare people of diverse identities to work together collaboratively reduces productivity and damages the collective standard of living. Discriminatory practice then is a problem that needs to be solved to satisfy the shared interest in improving productivity and the quality of service. Since the 1980s, this kind of reasoning has influenced much social policy and private practice.

Consequences of Conflict Outcomes: Equity and Stability in Larger Context

A struggle's outcome, as well as how it was waged, affects many other parties in the former adversaries' social environment and impacts the social system of which they are a part. The consequences affect the sense of equity and the stability of the adversaries' other relationships and of the social system as a whole.

Many conflicts are waged to increase equity in relations between the adversaries in the struggle. However, the outcome of a struggle often creates new injustices for people who had not been directly involved in the conflict itself. This is particularly likely for destructively waged and disastrously terminated conflicts. Often, persons whose lives are endangered by widespread violence and disorder resulting from civil strife or wars flee to other places and impose severe hardships for the host peoples. Precarious demographic, cultural, and economic balances may be upset, causing violent conflicts to erupt, as has happened in Lebanon and in several central African countries.

Leaders of groups waging conflicts generally claim they do so for their constituencies, but that wider constituency often does not share the intense convictions of those leaders and fighters. The peripherally engaged, even if the struggle is victorious, may find that the outcome burdens their lives. This is an important matter in assessing the consequences of major historic revolutions.[46]

Research indicates that long-lasting violent revolutionary turmoil generally produces significant and relatively long periods of reduced production. For example, France did not regain its prerevolutionary (1789) levels of foreign trade until well after 1815.[47] The relative gains and losses of different segments of the population, however, even more directly affect their sense of justice. A comparative analysis of social revolutions in Mexico, Bolivia, Cuba, and Peru finds that low-income groups made relative gains in each country during the new regime's consolidation of power, and land reform in each country generally improved the position of the rural groups.[48]

Nevertheless, in subsequent years the interests of the lower-income groups suffered relative to the middle- and upper-income groups. In these developing countries, the global economy seemed to limit labor's gains by fostering government policies primarily aimed at attracting foreign investment and financial assistance rather than policies that more directly targeted social inequities.

The long-term consequences of revolution for society members vary not only with the country's place in the world economy and outside engagement in building peace after civil wars, but also with the degree of destructiveness with which it is brought about and the character of the revolutionary change. Palace-guard revolutions, in which a ruling family or small faction is turned out and replaced by a similar small group, are not likely to have profound consequences. Such top-down revolutions may seem liberating at times, as when they are made in the name of national liberation, but their effects are likely to be disappointing and stultifying rather than economically and socially satisfying for the general population—perhaps partly because they were attained without popular involvement. For example, the countries that had been part of the Soviet Union or controlled by it became free of Soviet control with varying degrees of popular engagement. For most of the republics of the former Soviet Union, the union was dissolved by decisions made among a small group of officials. In a few countries, such as Lithuania, nonviolent demonstrations and other actions propelled the movement toward independence.

When a struggle is moderately constructive, it can be a catalyst for increased diffuse benefits, as indicated in the earlier analysis of external conflicts that are not very destructive. This is also indicated by studies of the effects of trade union struggles. Labor leaders and some economists provide evidence that if workers increase labor costs to the employer, workers will be used more efficiently and the employer will also have more incentive to replace workers by more efficient technologies. The general economy will be improved by pressures on management to be more efficient, to introduce technical improvements, and to increase capital investments.[49]

Theoretical approaches stressing the centrality of power or of ideology raise the expectation that victors in one conflict tend to initiate additional conflicts. The victors, with confidence in their ability to fight, will have heightened conviction in the justness of their cause and greater resources to use in a fight. For example, triumphant revolutionary regimes often try to spread the doctrines that provided the ideological basis for their coming to power, as illustrated by the French, Russian, Cuban, and Iranian Revolutions.

Attention should also be given to the consequences for the social environment of what one side regards as defeat. As discussed earlier, a humiliating destructive loss may lead to renewed struggle against the victor to recover what was lost or to gain revenge. But if that path is effectively blocked by superior force, more vulnerable targets may be sought out.

The consequences are likely to be different insofar as members of a defeated group interpret their failure as indicating that their goals and their means were unrealistic or ethically wrong. To the extent that they have become persuaded about the erroneous nature of their past struggle, a new course of action will be chosen that makes possible constructive struggle or even a fundamental reconciliation.

When conflicts end with negotiated outcomes or otherwise incorporate the concerns of many of the previously struggling parties, the former adversaries are more likely to see the need and the possibility for continuing work with each other. That will tend to absorb their attention and energy. This is one of the values of collaborative decision making and public participation making policy decisions.[50] When the conflicts end without significant inclusiveness, however, some groups are likely to regard themselves as losers and seek redress or withdraw to fight battles in other arenas.

Successful accommodative solutions can serve as models for members of other societies and organizations. In social systems challenged by divisions along ethnic lines, for example, many kinds of arrangements have averted or mitigated destructive struggles, such as provisions for cultural autonomy, structures of confederation, educational integration, and norms of tolerance. In societies torn by ethnic-related struggles, successes elsewhere have been held up as exemplary ways out of their troubles. The achievements of the civil rights struggle in the United States, the establishment of a system of regional autonomy in Spain, and the ending of apartheid in South Africa have been so used. In some circumstances, separation by mutual agreement may be the preferred solution by the engaged peoples, as in the separation of Norway from Sweden and the division of Czechoslovakia into Slovakia and the Czech Republic.[51]

Combined Effects of Methods and Outcomes on Larger Contexts

Conflicts may be expected to foster an ever-widening circle of additional conflicts, but they may also inhibit new conflicts. The research on the relationship between internal and external conflicts can help assess which is more likely. There are several reasons to expect that internal conflicts will generate external ones. Thus, it may be argued that domestic turmoil encourages leaders to engage in an external conflict as a distraction and a way to create solidarity. It may also be reasoned that when one domestic party triumphs over an internal enemy, it will believe itself able to defeat other groups who are holding the wrong ideas or exercising unjust domination. In addition, internal disorder may harm or endanger groups who have external ethnic, ideological, or economic ties with external groups who intervene to counter the threats. Finally, domestic conflict may weaken the party so much that it becomes an inviting target for aggressive action by external parties.

However, there are also reasons to expect that internal conflicts make external conflicts less likely. Thus, internal disorder can so weaken a party that it tries to avoid engagement in external conflicts, believing it will be defeated. Furthermore, posing little threat to external adversaries, the potential adversaries will not engage in threatening actions themselves and will pursue cooperative relations. Quantitative analyses from the 1960s support each line of argument, depending on specific conditions, such as the nature of the countries' regimes and the kind of conflict behavior. Thus, for countries with authoritarian regimes, internal warfare is somewhat negatively correlated to external war one and two years later.[52] Much recent research has focused on the efforts of external interveners to foster economic development and democracy as ways to regenerate peace after civil wars. These efforts are based on research on the relations between economic conditions and violent conflict and on the relations between democracy and war. There is systematic evidence that, overall, internal conflicts, external conflicts, and economic recessions are mutually reinforcing.[53] The findings suggest a self-perpetuating dynamic of violent conflicts breeding poverty and poverty breeding violent conflicts.

Since the end of the Cold War, there has been a great increase in multilateral interventions to stop civil wars and severe violent repressions and also to assist in building peaceful societies.[54] The results have been mixed.[55] Significant success was achieved in preventing a renewed outbreak of civil wars in Namibia and Mozambique, while renewed war quickly followed peace-building efforts in Angola and Rwanda. In some countries democratic institutions seem to have taken root and economic progress was made, but in other countries elections resulted in authoritarian rule and economic inequities increased.

The policies of external interveners affect the long-term consequences of how conflicts are conducted and ended. The degree of stability and equity that is achieved depends partly on the persistence of the external parties' engagement; overcoming the disasters of war takes time. Rushing to hold elections before the institutional base has been adequately developed and before demilitarization has sufficiently progressed does not yield dependably democratic societies. Insisting on moving quickly to a market economy characterized by privatizing state-owned enterprises, reducing government subsidies, liberalizing state regulations, and reducing government spending results in immediate economic hardships, whatever the long-term benefits may be. These hardships can undermine the nascent democracy. Recognition is increasing that policies need to be based on analyzing each society's particular problems and not be dominated by ideology or the immediate self-interests of the external interveners.[56]

CONSTRUCTIVE TRANSFORMATIONS

The previous discussion examined the variety of conflict outcomes that emerge after a fight seems to have ended, and the factors that push sequences in one direction or another. We now turn to two processes that appear effective in fostering sequences that are relatively constructive: reconciliation and intermediary work.

Reconciliation

The recurrence of brutal struggles often related to communal identities demonstrates the importance of reaching an enduring and just accommodation between enemies.[57] Conflict partisans and analysts alike increasingly stress reconciliation as an important ingredient in achieving such accommodations and ending recurring destructive conflicts. Normative changes have raised expectations that reconciliatory actions be taken to help resolve differences even long after the direct violence of the conflict has ended.

The developments that tend to perpetuate destructive conflicts, as discussed earlier, include dehumanizing opponents, blaming the others for the harms that have been experienced, and denying the validity of the other side's experience. Reconciliation is a multifaceted process, often occurring over an extended period, which contributes to reducing or overcoming these phenomena. Progress in that process requires many people to undertake a wide variety of actions. The various aspects of reconciliation need to be distinguished before examining their implications for the subsequent course of conflicts.

Aspects of Reconciliation

One important aspect of reconciliation pertains to the entities that are being reconciled with each other. The reconciling parties, for example, may be individuals from the antagonistic sides who interact with each other in ways that demonstrate mutual regard and trust. They may be persons or groups who represent the antagonistic sides and express contrition for past acts of injury by members of the collectivity they are representing. They may be writers, religious leaders, or others who address their own community and acknowledge that members of their community had injured people in another community. These persons or groups may be acting with little support from others in their community or they may be part of a mainstream consensus.

Reconciliation processes can occur in several domains, varying in scope and context. We focus this discussion on four important dimensions of reconciliation along which the process occurs.[58] The processes relate to truth, justice, regard, and security.

Truth is often noted as an important dimension of reconciliation since members of antagonistic sides are so prone to deny what the other side experiences and believes to be true. At a minimal level, persons on each side may openly recognize that they have different views of reality. They may even acknowledge the possible validity of part of what members of the other community believe. At a fuller level, members of the different communities may develop a shared and therefore more comprehensive truth. Official investigations, judicial proceedings, scholarly research, and mass media reporting are all ways to expose and acknowledge abuses that had been hidden or denied. In some societies, formal truth commissions may seem unhelpful "talk-talk" to locals more concerned with their immediate material needs.[59] Moreover, in some circumstances the recitation by perpetrators of their atrocities can be painful and have adverse consequences for the victims.

Recognizing the truth about past abuses ideally includes acknowledgment by those who belong to the collectivity that had inflicted the harm or benefited from it and acceptance of responsibility or complicity for what happened. Such acknowledgments may relate to individual perpetrators or to collective entities. The acknowledgment may incorporate offering apologies and expressing regrets and be part of discovering and facing the truth. This is difficult to achieve, particularly for members of the relatively victorious and dominant groups.

The second major dimension of reconciliation pertains to justice in its manifold meanings. Many persons who have suffered oppression and atrocities during an intense struggle seek redress for the injustices they endured. Redress may be in the form of tangible restitution or compensation for what was lost, it may take the form of punishment for those who committed injustices, or it may be exhibited in policies that offer protection against future discrimination or harm. Many actions of the Federal Republic of Germany illustrate these methods in relation to the Jewish people.[60] For example, compensation has included payments to Jewish survivors of the Holocaust and assistance to the State of Israel. Trials have been held of persons charged with crimes against Jews and other victims of Nazism, and laws were enacted against organizations advocating racism and to provide asylum for victims of political repression.

The third important dimension in reconciliation involves expressions of regard and respect between victims and perpetrators. It includes expressions by those who have suffered the harms acknowledging the humanity of those who committed the injuries. Most extremely, the acknowledgment may convey mercy and forgiveness, stressed by some advocates of reconciliation. Expressions of forgiveness may be a way for some people to shed the burdens of hate, while for others it may be contingent on expressions of guilt, remorse, and shame by members of the perpetrating community. The ability of humans to treat each other with respect is given support by widespread religious beliefs regarding the value of every human being before God.

Many instances of such conduct are reported at conferences held at Mountain House, established in 1946 in Caux, Switzerland.[61] It has served as a place where persons from countries and peoples who had warred against each other meet for unofficial dialogue and become open to reconciliation. In the first years of operation, many participants came from France and Germany and in many personal encounters and public statements reciprocated requests for forgiveness.

Frequently, recognition of the other side's humanity entails only recognizing that many members of the adversary community did not personally and directly carry out harmful actions and the next generation is not responsible for the acts of previous generations. Even less directly, persons from communities who had suffered injury may engage cooperatively in projects relating to past harms with members of the community that had inflicted the harm, but not express any apology or forgiveness.

The fourth dimension of reconciliation pertains to security. Members of each side have reason to believe they can look forward to living together without being threatened by the other. This may be in the context of high levels of integration or in the context of separation and little regular interaction. The nature of the anticipated peaceful relations varies, but the realization of the mutual preferences is what is critical.

Clearly, all these aspects of reconciliation are rarely fully realized and certainly not at the same time. Indeed, they are often contradictory at a given time. Thus, forgiveness and justice often cannot be satisfied at the same time, although they may occur sequentially. Nevertheless, if done by different members of the previously antagonistic sides they may be compatible even simultaneously. In some ways, furthermore, these various elements are interdependent. If members of one party acknowledge that their actions have imposed great harm on another community, forgiveness or at least acceptance of their humanity becomes easier to be felt and expressed.

Reconciliation generally is neither a one-sided matter nor symmetrical. Some members of one side may seek justice from another party that is viewed as responsible for the injustice, but members of the other side deny responsibility and there is no reconciliation movement. Expressions of regret may be recognized by members of the injured party and not deemed fully adequate by some of them. Often, both sides have suffered injuries at the hand of the other, although not in equal measure. Reconciliation actions may reflect such asymmetries, but usually do not.

Implications

This discussion thus far stresses that there are many kinds and degrees of reconciliation, with different mixes of elements over time. One implication of this complexity is that full reconciliation among all members of the former adversaries is improbable in large-scale conflicts. Some persons remain unreconciled and some claims that seemed impossible to achieve become feasible only at a much later time. The process of reconciliation, then, can go on for many generations, as standards of fairness change and the ability of various groups to make claims shift. Thus, indigenous peoples in Australia, Canada, and the United States toward the end of the twentieth century insisted that they had suffered injustices as Europeans settled what had been their land and the truth of what they suffered had been hidden in subsequent generations. Indeed, descendants of the European settlers in those countries have acknowledged some past abuses, such as placing children in boarding schools away from their families, and have provided monetary compensation for lands unlawfully taken from indigenous peoples.

Some people in Africa and in countries to which Black Africans were brought as slaves have also called for recognition of the losses they currently suffer as a legacy of past injustice and exploitation. Some of them argue that reparations should be made. In April 1993, the first pan-African conference on reparations was convened in Abuja, Nigeria, and declared that the international community owed a moral debt to the African peoples that had yet to be paid. In the United States, the issue of compensation for the losses suffered by African Americans because of slavery, of legally enforced discrimination, and of informally imposed restrictions has become the subject of growing debate. On January 5, 1993, John Conyers, a Black Democratic congressman from Detroit, introduced a bill in Congress "to establish a commission to examine the institution of slavery, subsequent de jure and de facto racial and economic discrimination against African Americans, and the impact of these forces on living African Americans, to make recommendations to the Congress on appropriate remedies, and for other purposes."[62] At the outset of the twenty-first century, Randall Robinson and others have undertaken a campaign to raise awareness of the debt owed to African Americans.

The failure to carry out any substantial measures of reconciliation endangers the stability in the relationship between former antagonists. For example, the atrocities committed during World War II in Yugoslavia, particularly by the Croat Ustasha forces against Serbs, were not explicitly and openly adjudicated or investigated by the Yugoslavian government headed by Josip Broz Tito. The government leaders, partly on ideological grounds and concerned about stirring up ethnic animosities, treated the internal struggles among Yugoslavs in terms of class and ideological differences. The unreconciled ethnic hostilities were available to be aroused later and contributed to the breakup of Yugoslavia in bloody wars a generation later.

Actions that foster reconciliation need not await the ending of a specific fight. Even when a conflict is being waged and escalated, attention to future coexistence and ultimate reconciliation can affect the way a struggle is conducted. For example, if the opposing ethnic group is not treated as a single unit and all its members are not dehumanized, reconciliation will be more readily attainable when the fighting ceases. This was done in good measure by the African National Congress in South Africa and contributed greatly to the constructive transformation of South African society.

Occasionally, efforts to attain certain aspects of reconciliation sometimes hamper ending a conflict and establishing a stable relationship. Thus, demands for justice by the aggrieved party may seem to pose unacceptable demands to the leaders of the dominant party. Requiring that they be charged with human rights violations or held accountable for economic corruption and put on trial is likely to be resisted by those leaders. Sometimes they are allowed an escape in order to avoid large-scale civil war. The earlier analyses of the course of struggles and their outcomes indicate that reconciliation is not an inevitable stage in every conflict. Mutual recriminations can persist, as they do in the relations between the United States and North Korea. Furthermore, the reconciliation that does occur is often fundamentally one sided, incorporating only a few elements of a full and mutual reconciliation. Other groups use that reality to justify their own brutalities.

Acts intended to advance the process of reconciliation do not necessarily do so. This is exemplified by developments relating to the ethnic Germans who were expelled from the Sudetenland area of Czechoslovakia at the end of World War II, because they had been instrumental in the Nazi dismemberment of Czechoslovakia.[63] After Vaclav Havel was elected president of Czechoslovakia in 1990, he denounced the expulsions as deeply immoral. The post-Communist Czech leaders made other reconciliatory gestures. But this reconciliation process broke down in an escalating exchange of charges and demands between the Sudeten Germans living in Germany and the Czechs. Public exchanges of recriminations endangered the emerging rapprochement between Germany and the Czech Republic. In secrecy, senior Czech and German officials tried to fashion a declaration that could be acceptable to both countries. On January 21, 1997, Czech Premier Vaclav Klaus and German Chancellor Helmut Kohl signed a joint declaration, which was approved by both countries' parliaments. Ultimately, the government policies helped attain a higher level of mutual accommodation and reconciliation than existed earlier.

The establishment and functioning of the Truth and Reconciliation Commission (TRC) in South Africa is rightfully well regarded throughout the world. Yet many South Africans have not agreed that it was so good, as may be seen in the findings of a national public opinion survey conducted in November 1998.[64] While overall 57 percent said they thought the TRC has been good for the country and 72 percent of the Black South Africans agreed, only 44 percent of the Colored, 40 percent of the Indians, and merely 25 percent of the whites responded favorably. Clearly, particularly for many whites, the revelations of the TRC were difficult to accept. The TRC hearings and findings received wide public attention, aroused much discussion, and helped promote reconciliation and the emergence of a common history. Consensus is high on the value of reconciliation in principle, but differences between whites and Blacks about what is needed for reconciliation remained.

Intervening Constructively

Conflicts in the contemporary world are seldom isolated. Many kinds of interventions by various actors are widespread, and they are often crucial in sustaining accommodations that have been achieved. Since the variety of intermediary activities that contribute to transforming conflicts was examined in previous chapters, this discussion of interventions is relatively brief. It focuses on peace-building interventions after an accommodation has been reached, not emphasized earlier.

Kinds of Interveners

The government is generally the pivotal actor in settling and managing grave domestic conflicts. States usually maintain the institutions by which innumerable conflicts are settled, including labor-management, intercommunal, and environmental fights. However, the state itself is often a party to such fights, as in the case of civil strife and civil wars. In such cases, external intervention is increasingly likely. Civil wars have usually ended by one side defeating the other, but after the Cold War, the United Nations, the United States, and other international actors more actively intervened to avert or stop genocidal killings or massive refugee flows. Such interventions contributed to more negotiated endings and consequently increased ongoing international engagement to preserve the peace.

The number of external actors who might help sustain a conflict settlement is now large and growing. They include the United States and many other countries so acting when their officials believe that their countries' national interests would otherwise suffer. They include numerous global and regional international governmental organizations, such as the United Nations, the World Bank, the Organization on Security and Cooperation in Europe, the Organization of American States, and the European Union. The growth in the role of transnational nongovernmental organizations is especially striking.[65] What is particularly relevant in the context of intervention efforts is the expansion of nongovernmental organizations working in the fields of humanitarian assistance, human rights, democratization, and other programs of advocacy, as well as conflict resolution.

Contributions of Intervention

Intermediaries often perform valuable services in reaching and sustaining an agreement between adversaries.[66] As mediators, they may help produce agreements that are relatively fair, and they may provide some representation for stakeholders who are not sitting at the table. This may include consideration of the rank-and-file constituents of the negotiators, for example, by incorporating provisions for elections in the settlement. To some extent, this can be seen in the mediating role that Oscar Arias, the Costa Rican president, provided in Central America and that U.S. Assistant Secretary of State Chester A. Crocker provided in linking the withdrawal of Cuban military forces from Angola with implementation of UN Resolution 435 in Namibia.[67]

Intervener organizations can provide a variety of resources that help stabilize an accommodation and contribute to a conflict's constructive transformation. They can provide material resources such as food, medical care, and funds for developing the infrastructure, and they can enhance skills to help rebuild social institutions. Intermediaries often play critical roles in implementing an agreement. They sometimes monitor agreements, and if violations occur, impose sanctions or provide compensation to the disadvantaged side. They may observe an election, prescribed in an agreement, to help ensure that it is fair and regarded as legitimate. Following protracted civil strife, demobilization of armed forces is generally needed, and intermediaries have assisted in this process, as in Namibia and El Salvador.

Often, factions on each side of the conflict continue to strive to better their position, which undermines an agreement. Mediators and other intermediaries are often needed to inhibit such undermining "spoiler" actions. However, interveners are likely to find that staying engaged after an accommodation is politically difficult. From the interveners' perspectives, support from the people who provide funds and personnel tend to decline after the conflict seems to have been settled. Furthermore, a variety of undesirable accidents and events are likely to occur over time as the interveners' engagement wanes. Yet over time relations and understandings also can be built that give everyone confidence that an enduring transformation is under way.

No single way of intervening is likely to be effective in transforming large-scale destructive conflicts. The probability of effectiveness is enhanced when interveners pursue many strategies and not only military ones, when interventions involve many agents at various levels, and when they involve a variety of activities such as peacekeeping, economic development, and fostering legitimate political institutions. Since the early 1990s, multilateral engagement in societies that had been rent by civil wars greatly increased; the policies generally pursued attempts to speedily bring about democratic procedures and free market economies. These efforts, however, are often too quickly and too ideologically implemented; consequently, even if civil wars are not soon renewed, considerable inequalities and acts of violence result.[68]

SUMMARY AND DISCUSSION QUESTIONS

Few agreements can forever end conflicts between large-scale adversaries. Some agreements, however, are part of the transformation of a conflict such that the adversaries can engage in largely cooperative relations. An agreement, however, is only a part of that process; internal developments within each adversary party and changes in their environments impact the course of each conflict once a settlement has occurred. Whether a settlement is effective in the long term depends on the difficulty that the conflict poses for settlement and how strong the interest of major external actors in preserving it is.

The nature of a struggle's consequences depends significantly on how the former adversaries and others interpret the way the conflict ended. Thus the consequences vary with the degree to which protagonists regard the outcome as fair and reached through a joint process. Conflicts waged and terminated destructively tend to perpetuate destructive relations. Such persisting cycles, however, can be broken. To interrupt and alter these tendencies requires wise transforming policies that are resolutely pursued. Intermediaries based outside of the primary adversaries can be crucial in undertaking and carrying out such policies. In addition, individuals and groups within one or more of the antagonistic sides can initiate and help implement such policies. Of course, conducting a struggle constructively in the first place makes the task easier and can contribute afterward to stronger cooperative relations between former adversaries.

Readers are encouraged to reflect on the following questions to gain additional insights on the ideas presented in this chapter.

1. Using Figure 10.1 as a guide, select two or three settled large-scale conflicts not reviewed in this chapter and decide about the kind of postsettlement outcomes that occurred.
2. Using the same cases, identify five to ten variables that you believe impacted to postsettlement outcome you observed.
3. Finally, sticking with the same cases, characterize the relative constructiveness of the outcome. How could the postsettlement sequence have been improved?
4. Personalize this chapter by considering an intense conflict that you have experienced in your life and that you regard as "over." What does "over" mean to you? What legacy has that conflict had on your life? What was not done that could have been done to improve the outcomes?

Chapter Eleven

Toward Constructive Conflict Transformation

Good conflict analysis is at the heart of successful conflict transformation. Done well, conflict analysis gives the investigator a comprehensive understanding of the "conflict landscape"—who is fighting about what, why, and how—upon which to design a conflict transformation intervention. A good analogy is that of a medical doctor examining and treating a patient. Prior to treatment, a competent doctor will always review the patient's medical history, conduct an examination presenting symptoms, and consider various explanations for why the patient is sick. Only then is a diagnosis given and a treatment prescribed. In the same way, we hope that the past ten chapters have given the reader a new set of diagnostic tools—a framework for analysis—to better understand the "why" of conflict emergence, escalation, and de-escalation as well as the "how" of constructive transformation.

We recognize the complexity of this task. The trajectory of large-scale conflicts is rarely driven by just one factor. Instead, numerous crosscutting factors intermingle, to determine the lifecycle of a conflict. These include, among others, social-psychological dynamics related to identity formation; emotional dynamics triggered by loss, fear, and trauma; structural conditions and inequalities that privilege some and disadvantage others; sociocultural norms and expectations that shape conflict behavior; the narratives about self and other internalized by adversaries; the availability of legitimate institutional mechanisms to manage a conflict; the degree of scarcity within a system; the previous actions of conflict stakeholders; the availability of well-intended third-party intermediaries; the communication and problem solving skills internalized by conflict actors; the characteristics of leaders and followers; and even underlying genetic and epigenetic forces that shape human behavior.

Determining which of these dynamics are most salient, how they interact, and which are ripe for transformation can be highly challenging. It requires not just a framework for analysis, but also a theory of change; that is, a clear sense about how specific change activities interact and lead to an ultimate outcome sought. Such analysis is time consuming and difficult. Moreover, it often reveals that no single action is capable of constructively transforming the most difficult conflicts facing us. Instead, multiple actors need to do multiple things at just the right time to change the trajectory of a conflict for the better. A good analogy would be to imagine a door with multiple locks which need to be turned in just the right sequence if the bolt is to slide inward and the door to open.

Fortunately, this book stands alongside a host of other excellent resources now available to those committed to doing this analytical work. For example, the U.S. Agency for International Development's *Conflict Assessment Framework* provides conflict management practitioners with a how-to guide for conducting assessments and generating practical recommendations to bolster social and institutional resilience in different conflict settings. Various nongovernmental organizations have published workbooks on conflict analysis designed to aid in decision making, including World Vision's *Making Sense of Turbulent Contexts*, Search for Common Ground's *Conflict Scan Methodology*, the Berghof Foundation's *Berghof Handbook for Conflict Transformation*, and Swisspeace's *Conducting Conflict Assessments* training guide. The U.S. Institute of Peace Academy offers a wide range of courses for peacebuilding practitioners looking to transform violent community conflicts. The website beyondintractability.org, created by Guy and Heidi Burgess at the University of Colorado's Conflict Information Consortium, provides a wealth of resources from hundreds of contributors on intractable conflict and conflict transformation. Each of these guides, reports, and trainings are free, available online, and used regularly by practitioners working on peacebuilding and conflict transformation around the world.

The need for these resources has never been greater. Human communities stand on a precipice as new global challenges threaten human security and new tribalism flares. In the early 2020s the percentage of people living in poverty globally increased for the first time in twenty years.[1] In 2021 the number of people fleeing conflict reached its highest level since World War II.[2] The number of civil wars in the world has reached a level not seen since the end of the Cold War and instances of conflict recurrence within five years of war termination have become pronounced.[3] Russia's recent attack on Ukraine reveals that the era of interstate war is not over. Add to these challenges other foundational threats to human security. Global health pandemics, such as COVID-19, SARS, and Ebola are likely to become regular features of the global community. Ecological disasters ranging from climate change to the loss of biodiversity, to deforestation, desertification, and water scarcity continue to mount. Politically, the commitment to plural democracy has faltered. Frightened by uncertainty and change, even citizens in consolidated democracies have turned to authoritarian leaders in a bid to feel more secure. Finally, conspiratorial thinking, antiscience sentiment, and a distrust of traditional institutions is confining adversaries to isolated spaces where truth is local and intergroup dialogue rare.

It is easy to become despondent in the face of these challenges. However, glimmers of hope endure. Despite Russia's war in Ukraine, international war is today a rarity, likely due to a combination of integrated economies, the unthinkable cost of all-out war in a nuclear age, the rise of consolidated democracies, and development of new international norms related to human rights and communal responsibility.[4] Intriguing evidence exists as well that there has been a dramatic decline in human violence when viewed across long time scales.[5] By some measures we are living in one of the most peaceful eras of modern human history.

Most importantly, the formula for constructive conflict management is known, can be taught and measured, and is increasingly discussed. Communities that deal with conflicts well tend to share a set of common features. Among them are the (1) institutionalization of conflict management practices that are deemed legitimate by all community members; (2) reduction of structural inequalities which drive grievance and undermine just outcomes; (3) training of young people, teachers, government officials, and others in interest-based problem-solving, intercommunal dialogue, stakeholder analysis, and conflict mapping; (4) wide use of third-party intermediaries to creatively intervene in protracted disputes; (5) promotion of regular and ongoing contact between identity groups to undermine the development of prejudice and dehumanization; (6) building of awareness among citizens about noncoercive forms of conflict management, such as persuasion and positive sanctions; (7) creation of common rituals and opportunities for emotional release and healing for those traumatized by conflicts and loss; and (8) establishment of functional interdependence between members of a community, such that destructive escalations are mutually disadvantageous.

The vast array of entry points to constructively intervene in a conflict means that everyone can get involved. Conflict transformation isn't just for diplomats or elites; it is something that can be practiced at home, in schools, in offices, among community members, and across transnational civil society organizations. Everyone can contribute something to the amelioration of struggles of any magnitude. The interconnectedness of many conflicts and the ever-growing interdependence of people throughout the world will only accelerate this trend. Furthermore, there is no such thing as a purely intractable conflict; rather, there is always something, someone, somewhere can do to transform a conflict, if only very modestly.

So let us end where we began: Conflicts are natural and inevitable aspects of political and social interaction. They alert us to the underlying tensions that exist in social relationships, give us a pathway to change the status quo, and can even improve when they are properly managed. Accordingly, the goal for conflict management is not to avoid conflicts, but rather to help people find ways to contend that harms fewer people and result in settlements that are fair, mutually satisfying, and enduring. Knowledge about how to achieve such constructive outcomes is growing, although much more work is needed. We hope this book facilitates new insights, research, and practice.

Appendix A

Selected Organizations in the Field of Constructive Conflicts

This list suggests the diversity of organizations contributing to the constructive waging of conflicts. It provides a sampling of centers, associations, and institutions engaging in relevant activities including:

- Education (EDU): degree-granting and certificate programs, outreach
- Intermediary services (INT): mediation, facilitation, and consultation
- Research and theory building (RTB): reporting, analyzing data
- Training (TRA): workshops in conflict resolution applications

ACCORD, African Centre for the Constructive Resolution of Disputes (EDU, INT, RTB, TRA)
Private Bag X018, Umhlanga Rocks, 43320, South Africa
Tel: 27 (31) 502-3908
https://www.accord.org.za/

American Arbitration Association (INT)
140 W. 51st Street
New York, NY 10020
Tel: 212-484-4000 Fax: 212-765-4874
www.adr.org

Association for Conflict Resolution (EDU)
1015 18th Street NW
Washington, DC 20036
Tel: 201-464-9700
https://acrnet.org/

Berghof Conflict Research (RTB, TRA)
Altensteinstraße 48a
D-14195 Berlin
Phone +49 (0)30 844154-0
http://www.berghof-conflictresearch.org/en/

The Carter Center of Emory University (INT, RTB)
One Copenhill
Atlanta, GA 30307
Tel: 404-420-5151 Fax: 404-420-5196
www.cartercenter.org

Centre for Conflict Resolution (EDU, RTB, TRA)
Department of Peace Studies, University of Bradford
Bradford, BD7 1DP, UK
Tel: +44 (0) 1274-23-5235
www.bradford.ac.uk/acad/confres/

CDR Associates (INT, TRA)
100 Arapahoe Avenue, Suite 12
Boulder, CO 80302
Tel: 303-442-7367
www.mediate.org

Beyond Intractability (EDU, RTB)
Conflict Research Consortium
University of Colorado, Campus Box 327
Boulder, CO 80309
Tel: 303-492-1635 Fax: 303-492-2154
http://beyondintractability.com/

CONTACT Peacebuilding Program (TRA, EDU)
School for International Training
SIT/World Learning, Inc.
1 Kipling Road
Brattleboro, VT 05302-0676
Tel: 802-257-7751
https://graduate.sit.edu/program/graduate-certificate-conflict-transformation
-across-cultures-contact-peacebuilding-workshop/

Department of Conflict Resolution (EDU, RTB, TRA)
Nova Southeastern University
3301 College Avenue, Ft. Lauderdale, FL 33314
https://hcas.nova.edu/departments/conflict-resolution-studies/index.html

Federal Mediation and Conciliation Services (INT)
250 E. Street SW
Washington, DC 20427
Tel: (202) 606-8100
https://www.fmcs.gov/

Fellowship of Reconciliation (TRA, INT)
Box 271
Nyack, NY 10960
Tel: 914-358-4601 Fax: 914-358-4924
https://forusa.org/

Global Partnership for the Prevention of Armed Conflict (GPPAC)
Laan van Meerdervoort 70–6th floor
2517 AN The Hague
The Netherlands
Telephone: +31 (0)70 311 0970
https://www.gppac.net/

Jimmy and Rosalynn Carter School for Peace and Conflict Resolution (EDU, INT, RTB, TRA)
George Mason University
4400 University Drive
Fairfax, VA 22030-4444
Tel: 703-993-1300 Fax: 703-993-1302
https://carterschool.gmu.edu/

Heidelberg Institute for International Conflict Research (RTB, TRA)
Bergheimer Str. 58
69115 Heidelberg
Germany
+49.6221.54.3198
https://hiik.de/?lang=en

Inclusive Peace and Transition Initiative (EDU, TRA)
Maison de la paix, Chemin Eugène-Rigot 2, 1202
Geneva, Switzerland
Tel: +41 22 908 62 66
https://www.inclusivepeace.org/

Joan B. Kroc Institute for Peace and Justice (EDU, TRA)
5998 Alcalá Park
San Diego, CA 92110
Tel: 619-260-7509
https://www.sandiego.edu/peace/institute-and-center/institute-for-peace
-justice/

Kroc Institute for International Peace Studies (EDU, RTB)
University of Notre Dame
P.O. Box 639
Notre Dame, IN 46556-0639
Tel: 219-631-6970
http://kroc.nd.edu/

Mennonite Conciliation Service (INT, TRA)
21 South 12th Street, P.O. Box 500
Akron, PA 17501-0500
Tel: 717-859-3889
https://mcc.org/centennial/100-stories/mennonite-conciliation-service

Program on Conflict Resolution (EDU, INT, RTB, TRA)
University of Hawaii at Manoa, 2424 Maile Way
Honolulu, HI 96822
Tel: 808-956-7792 Fax: 808-956-921
http://www.hawaii.edu/graduatestudies/fields/html/departments/cd/conflict
res/conflictres.htm

Program on Negotiation at Harvard Law School (EDU, INT, TRA, RTB)
500 Pound Hall
Cambridge, MA 02138
Tel: 617-495-1684 Fax: 617-495-7818
https://www.pon.harvard.edu/

The Program for the Advancement of Research on Conflict and Collaboration (PARCC) (EDU, INT, RTB, TRA)
Syracuse University
Syracuse, NY 13244
Tel: 315-443-2367 Fax: 315-443-3818
https://www.maxwell.syr.edu/parcc.aspx

Search for Common Ground (INT, TRA)
1601 Connecticut Ave NW
Washington, DC 20009
Tel: 202-265-4300 Fax: 202-232-6718
www.sfcg.org

SIPRI Stockholm International Peace Research Institute (RTB)
Signalistgatan 9, SE-169 70
Solna, Sweden
Tel: 46-8-655 97 00
www.sipri.org

TRANSCEND: A Peace and Development Network (EDU, INT, TRA)
Tel: 914-773-3400; email: transcend@transcend.org
http://www.transcend.org/

United States Institute of Peace (EDU, RTB, TRA)
1550 M Street NW
Washington, DC 20005-1708
Tel: 202-457-1700 Fax: 202-429-6063
www.usip.org

Uppsala Universitet
Department of Peace and Conflict Resolution (EDU, DTB, TRA)
SE 751 20
Uppsala, Sweden
Tel: 46 (0) 18 471 00 00
www.pcr.uu.se

World Learning
1015 15th Street NW, Suite 950
Washington, DC 20005
Tel: 202-408-5420
https://www.worldlearning.org/

Notes

CHAPTER 1. THE CONSTRUCTIVE CONFLICTS APPROACH

1. Coser, L. A. (1956). *The Functions of Social Conflict*. New York: Free Press, 8.
2. Ramsbotham, O., Tom Woodhouse, and Hugh Miall. (2005). *Contemporary Conflict Resolution*, third edition. Cambridge: Polity.
3. Pruitt, D. G., J. Rubin, and S. H. Kim. (1986). *Social Conflict: Escalation, Stalemate, and Settlement*. New York: Random House.
4. Rioux, R.-F., and V. N. Redekop. (2012). *Introduction to Conflict Studies: Empirical, Theoretical, and Ethical Dimensions.* Toronto: Oxford University Press.
5. Burton, J. (1990). *Conflict: Resolution and Provention*. New York: St. Martin's.
6. See, for example, Coser. (1956). *The Functions of Social Conflict*; Simmel, G. (1955). *Conflict and the Web of Intergroup Affiliations*. New York: Free Press.
7. The relationship between the United States and North Korea is illustrative as the two countries have vacillated between periods of belligerence including 2003 and 2017, to periods of communication and negotiation in 1994, 2005, and 2018.
8. All conflicts do not adhere to such a linear process of development. Some become stuck at one stage or another, and many will backslide.
9. See, for example, Palumbo, S., V. Mariotti, C. Iofrida, and S. Pellegrini. (2018). "Genes and Aggressive Behavior: Epigenetic Mechanisms Underlying Individual Susceptibility to Aversive Environments." *Front Behav Neurosci* 12: 117.
10. Zartman, I. W., and M. Berman. (1982). *The Practical Negotiator*. New Have, CT: Yale University Press.
11. Howard, L. M., and A. Stark. (2018). "How Civil Wars End: The International System, Norms, and the Role of External Actors." *International Security* 42 (3): 127–71.
12. Davis, W. H. (1942). "Aims and Policies of the National War Labor Board." *The Annals of the American Academy of Political and Social Science* 224: 141–46.
13. The significance of socially constructing reality was developed in the work of Berger and Luckman. Later it became a major approach in international relations

theory, in the form of constructivism. See, for instance, Berger, P. L., and T. Luckman. (1966). *The Social Construction of Reality*. New York: Doubleday.

14. Adwan, S., D. Bar-On, E. Naveh, and Peace Research Institute in the Middle East. (2012). *Side by Side: Parallel Histories of Israel/Palestine*. New York: The New Press.

15. For an interesting discussion of the role of framing in the construction of meaning, see Bruner, J. S. (1990). *Acts of Meaning*. Cambridge: Harvard University Press.

16. Bruner, J. (1990). *Acts of Meaning*. Cambridge: Harvard University Press, 30.

17. World Health Organization. (n.d.). "Infodemic. Health Topics." https://www.who.int/health-topics/infodemic#tab=tab_1.

18. State-sponsored disinformation campaigns are particularly notable in this regard. See Zhang, Y., J. Lukito, M.-H. Su, J. Suk, Y. Xia, S. J. Kim, L. Doroshenko, and C. Wells. (2021). "Assembling the Networks and Audiences of Disinformation: How Successful Russian IRA Twitter Accounts Built Their Followings, 2015–2017." *Journal of Communication* 71 (2): 305–31.

19. Kriesberg, L. (1980). "Interlocking Conflicts in the Middle East." *Research in Social Movements, Conflicts, and Change*. Edited by L. Kriesberg. Stamford, CT: JAI Press: 99–118.

20. See, for instance, Fridman, O. (2018). "Too Young to Remember Determined Not to Forget":Memory Activists Engaging With Returning ICTY Convicts." *International Criminal Justice Review* 28 (4): 423–37. See also Gutman, Y. (2017). *Memory Activism: Reimagining the Past for the Future in Israel-Palestine*. Nashville: Vanderbilt University Press.

21. Orjuela, C. (2017). "Divides and Dialogue in the Diaspora during Sri Lanka's Civil War." *South Asian Diaspora* 9 (1): 67–82.

22. See, for example, Karuna Center for Peacebuilding. (2018). "Hands Across the Hills: A Place for 'Red State-Blue State' Peacebuilding." https://www.karunacenter.org/2018/11/03/hath/.

23. For a review of collaborative governance in the United States, see O'Leary, R., and L. B. Amsler. (2009). *The Collaborative Public Manager: New Ideas for the Twenty-First Century*. Washington, DC: Georgetown University Press. For a review of nonprovocative defense, see Murret, R. (2017). "Non-Provocative Defense in the Asia Pacific." *Perspectives in Waging Conflicts Constructively: Cases, Concepts, and Practice*. Edited by B. W. Dayton and L. Kriesberg. Lanham, MD: Rowman & Littlefield Publishers.

24. Kelley, H. H. (1973). "The Process of Causal Attribution." *American Psychologist* 28 (2): 107–28.

25. Ndahiro, K. (2019). "In Rwanda, We All Know About Dehumanizing Language." *The Atlantic*. https://www.theatlantic.com/ideas/archive/2019/04/rwanda-shows-how-hateful-speech-leads-violence/587041/.

26. Hodson, G., and M. Hewstone. (2013). *Advances in Intergroup Contact*. Hove, UK: Psychology Press.

27. Bellamy, A. J., P. D. Williams, and S. Griffin. (2004). *Understanding Peacekeeping*. Cambridge: Polity Press.

28. Blake, P. R., D. G. Rand, D. Tingley, and F. Warneken. (2015). "The Shadow of the Future Promotes Cooperation in a Repeated Prisoner's Dilemma for Children." *Scientific Reports* 5 (1): 14559.

29. Russett, B., and J. R. Oneal. (2001). *Triangulating Peace: Democracy, Interdependence, and International Organization*. Princeton, NJ: Princeton University Press.

30. The benefits of functional interdependence vis-à-vis peace are explored in Long, D., and Ashworth, L.M. (1999). "Working for Peace: The Functional Approach, Functionalism and Beyond." *New Perspectives on International Functionalism*. Edited by L. M. Ashworth and D. Long. London: Palgrave Macmillan.

31. In addition to the power over others and the power *with* others to accomplish collective tasks, the power *from* others (autonomy) is an important kind of power. Coleman, P. T. (2014). "Power and Conflict." *The Handbook of Conflict Resolution: Theory and Practice*. Edited by P. T. Coleman, M. Deutsch, & E. C. Marcus. San Francisco: Jossey-Bass. Power *over* others presumes a zero-sum relationship. See Blalock Jr., H. M. (1989). *Power and Conflict: Toward a General Theory*. Thousand Oaks, CA: Sage. Power with others has been a meaning of power used by some structural functionalists. Parsons, T. (1969). *Politics and Social Structure*. New York: Free Press. For a feminist perspective, see Woerhle, L. M. (1992). "Social Constructions of Power and Empowerment: Thoughts from Feminist Approaches to Peace Research and Peace-Making." *Social Theory and Nonviolent Revolutions: Rethinking Domination and Rebellion*. Edited by N. Bell & L. R. Kurtz. Austin, TX: University of Texas at Austin Press; Woerhle. (1992). "Social Constructions of Power and Empowerment."

32. See Boulding, K. E. (1989). *Three Faces of Power*. Thousand Oaks, CA: Sage. See also Sharp, G. (1973). *The Politics of Nonviolent Action*. Boston: Porter Sargent.

33. Mitchell, C. R. (1995). "Asymmetry and Strategies of Regional Conflict Reduction." *Cooperative Security: Reducing Third World Wars*. Edited by I. W. Zartman and V. A. Kremenyuk. Syracuse, NY: Syracuse University Press: 25–57; Kriesberg, L. (2009). "Changing Conflict Asymmetries Constructively." *Dynamics of Asymmetric Conflict* 2 (1): 4–22.

34. Gramsci, A. (1971). *Selections from the Prison Notebooks*. New York: International Publishers.

35. Galtung, J. (1969). "Violence, Peace, and Peace Research." *Journal of Peace Research* 3 (3): 168.

36. Blau, P. M. (1964). *Exchange and Power in Social Life*. Hoboken, NJ: John Wiley.

37. See Article 2.7 of the Charter of the United Nations which states that "Nothing contained in the present Charter shall authorize the United Nations to intervene in matters which are essentially within the domestic jurisdiction of any state or shall require the Members to submit such matters to settlement under the present Charter; but this principle shall not prejudice the application of enforcement measures under Chapter VII."

38. Lebow, R. N., and J. G. Stein. (1994). *We all Lost the Cold War*. Princeton, NJ: Princeton University Press.

39. Center for Security Studies. (2008). *Human Security Brief 2007*. https://css.ethz.ch/en/services/digital-library/publications/publication.html/55856.

CHAPTER 2. PRECONDITIONS

1. Jang, K. L., W. J. Livesley, and P. A. Vernon. (1996). "Heritability of the Big Five Personality Dimensions and Their Facets: A Twin Study." *J Pers* 64 (3): 577–91.
2. Wilson, E. O. (2012). *The Social Conquest of Earth*. New York: Liveright Pub. Corp., 241.
3. Kvalevaag, A. L., P. G. Ramchandani, O. Hove, J. Assmus, M. Eberhard-Gran, and E. Biringer. (2013). "Paternal Mental Health and Socioemotional and Behavioral Development in Their Children." *Pediatrics* 131 (2): e463–69.
4. Morrone, M. C. (2010). "Brain Development: Critical Periods for Cross-Sensory Plasticity." *Current Biology* 20: 934–36.
5. Marusak, H. A., K. R. Martin, A. Etkin, and M. E. Thomason. (2015). "Childhood Trauma Exposure Disrupts the Automatic Regulation of Emotional Processing." *Neuropsychopharmacology* 40 (5): 1250–58.
6. For a fascinating review of three different works on the biological basis of conflict among primates, see Somit, A. (1990). "Humans, Chimps, and Bonobos. The Biological Bases of Aggression, War, and Peacemaking." *The Journal of Conflict Resolution* 34 (3): 553–82.
7. For example, see Ardrey, R. (1966). *The Territorial Imperative*. New York: Dell.
8. Mazur, A. (1973). "A Cross-Species Comparison of Status in Small Established Groups." *American Sociological Review* 38 (October 1973): 513–30.
9. Bowles, S., and H. Gintis. (2013). *A Cooperative Species: Human Reciprocity and Its Evolution*. Princeton, NJ: Princeton University Press.
10. For an overview, see Boag, S. (2014). "Ego, Drives, and the Dynamics of Internal Objects." *Frontiers in Psychology* 5 (666).
11. Rothbart, M., and S. Lewis. (1994). "Cognitive Processes and Intergroup Relations: A Historical Perspective." *Social Cognition: Impact on Social Psychology*. Edited by P. G. Devine, D. L. Hamilton and T. M. Ostrom. San Diego: Academic Press. The work that generated much subsequent research is Adorno, T. W., E. Frenkel-Brunswik, D. J. Levinson, and R. N. Sanford. (1950). *The Authoritarian Personality*. New York: Harper Brothers.
12. For a complete overview of this and other psychiatric diagnoses, see American Psychological Association. (2013). *Diagnostic and Statistical Manual of Mental Disorders*. Arlington, VA, American Psychological Association.
13. A recent study of the personality traits of political leaders and candidates shows that "populist leaders" score higher on extraversion, narcissism, and psychopathy than do nonpopulist leaders. See Nai, A., and F. Martínez i Coma. (2019). "The Personality of Populists: Provocateurs, Charismatic Leaders, or Drunken Dinner Guests?" *West European Politics* 42 (7): 1337–67.
14. Tay, L., and E. Diener. (2011). "Needs and Subjective Well-being Around the World." *J Pers Soc Psychol* 101 (2): 354–65.
15. Yang, K. S. (2003). "Beyond Maslow's Culture-Bound Linear Theory: A Preliminary Statement of the Double-Y Model of Basic Human Needs." *Nebr Symp Motiv* 49: 175–255.
16. Burton, J. (1990). *Conflict: Resolution and Prevention*. New York: St. Martin's.

17. Goldberg, L. R. (1990). "An Alternative Description of Pesrsonality: The Big Five Factor Structure." *Journal of Personality and Social Psychology* 59: 1216–29.

18. Bouchard, T. J., and L. C. Loehlin. (2001). "Genes, Evolution, and Personality." *Behavioral Genetics* 31: 243–73.

19. While the tendency to categorize others into in- and out-groups is seen as an inherent part of human nature, what categorizations are most salient is not fixed. Thus, categorizing according to skin color, language, or gender is not an inevitable outcome of social life, rather one of many possible social constructions.

20. For a discussion of in-group favoritism and out-group bias, see Rubin, M., and M. Hewstone. (2004). "Social Identity, System Justification, and Social Dominance: Commentary on Reicher, Jost, Sidanius et. al." *Political Psychology* 25 (6): 823–44.

21. Ghani, B., and L. Fiske (2020). "'Art is my Language': Afghan Cultural Production Challenging Islamophobic Stereotypes." *Journal of Sociology* 56 (1): 115–29.

22. Selecting for temperament among animal species for domestication has a long tradition across human communities. One of the most interesting research projects to study how quickly animals can be domesticated is the Silver Fox Domestication Project that began in Russia in 1959. Dugatkin summarizes findings of that experiment in this way: "Starting from what amounted to a population of wild foxes, within six generations (6 years in these foxes, as they reproduce annually), selection for tameness, and tameness alone, produced a subset of foxes that licked the hand of experimenters, could be picked up and petted, whined when humans departed, and wagged their tails when humans approached." See Dugatkin, L. A. (2018). "The Silver Fox Domestication Experiment." *Evolution: Education and Outreach* 11 (1): 16.

23. For a discussion of this debate, see Winegard, B., B. Winegard, and J. Anomaly. (2020). "Dodging Darwin: Race, Evolution, and the Hereditarian Hypothesis." *Personality and Individual Differences* 160: 109915.

24. Elias, R., and J. Turpin, Eds. (1994). *Re-Thinking Peace*. Boulder: Lynne Rienner.

25. Ross, M. H. (1993). *The Culture of Conflict*. New Haven: Yale University Press, 61–62; Montagu, A., Ed. (1978). *Learning Non-Aggression*. New York: Oxford University Press.

26. Biglan, A., B. R. Flay, D. D. Embry, and I. N. Sandler. (2012). "The Critical Role of Nurturing Environments for Promoting Human Well-being." *Am Psychol* 67 (4): 257–71.

27. Ross. (1993). *The Culture of Conflict*. Also see Volkan, V. (1988). *The Need to Have Enemies and Allies: From Clinical Practice to International Relationships*. New York: Jason Aronson.

28. See Ross. (1993). *The Culture of Conflict*; see also Whiting, B. B., and J. W. M. Whiting. (1975). *Children of Six Cultures: A Psycho-Cultural Analysis*. Cambridge, MA: Harvard University Press.

29. Inkeles, A., and D. Levinson. (1954). "National Character: The Study of Modal Personality and Sociocultural Systems." *Handbook of Social Psychology*. Edited by G. Lindzey. Reading, MA: Addison-Wesley: 977–1020.

30. Brett, J. M. (2000). "Culture and Negotiation." *International Journal of Psychology* 35 (2): 97–104.

31. Cohen, R. (1990). *Culture and Conflict in Egyptian-Israeli Relations: A Dialogue of the Deaf.* Bloomington: Indiana University Press.

32. Information on the GLOBE project and findings can be found at https://globeproject.com/.

33. Theodore Schwartz writes, "Culture consists of the derivatives of experience, more or less organized learned or created by the individuals of a population, including those images or encodements and their interpretations (meanings) transmitted from past generations, from contemporaries, or formed by individuals themselves." See Schwartz, T. (1992). "Anthropology and Psychology: An Unrequited Relationship." *New Directions in Psychological Anthropology*. Edited by T. Schwartz, G. White, and G. Lutz. Cambridge: Cambridge University Press: 324.

34. Berger, P. L., and T. Luckman. (1966). *The Social Construction of Reality*. New York: Doubleday; Goffman, E. (1974). *Frame Analysis*. New York: Harper Colphon; and Shapiro, M. J., and H. R. Alker, Eds. (1996). *Challenging Boundaries*. Minneapolis: University of Minnesota Press.

35. Northrup, T. A. (1989). "The Dynamic of Identity in Personal and Social Conflict." *Intractable Conflicts and Their Transformation*. Edited by L. Kriesberg, T. A. Northrup, and S. J. Thorson. Syracuse: Syracuse University Press: 55–82.

36. As quoted in Wehner, P. (2019). "The Deepening Crisis in Evangelical Christianity." *The Atlantic*.

37. Manheim, K. (1952). *Essays on the Sociology of Knowledge*. London: Routledge and Kegan Paul; Kriesberg, L., H. Murray, and R. A. Klein. (1982). "Elites and Increased Support for U.S. Military Spending." *Journal of Political and Military Sociology* 10 (Fall 1982): 275–97.

38. Bacevich, A. J. (2002). *American Empire: The Realities and Consequences of U.S. Diplomacy*. Cambridge, MA: Harvard University Press.

39. Dayton, B. W. (1999). *In Between Science & Decision: Policy Frames and the Global Climate Discourse*. Syracuse, NY: Syracuse University; Hunter, S. (1989). "The Roots of Environmental Conflict in the Tahoe Basin." *Intractable Conflicts and their Transformation*. Edited by L. Kriesberg, T. A. Northrup, and S. J. Thorson. Syracuse: Syracuse University Press; and Moyers, B. (2005). "Welcome to Doomsday." *New York Review of Books*: 8–10.

40. Gilligan, C. (1982). *In a Different Voice: Psychological Theory and Women's Development*. Cambridge, MA: Harvard University Press; Nye, A. (1988). *Feminist Theory and the Philosophies of Man*. New York: Croom Helm.

41. Hewstone, M., and K. Greenland. (2000). "Intergroup Conflict." *International Journal of Psychology* 35: 136–44.

42. President Eisenhower said, "In our councils of government we must guard against the acquisition of unwarranted influence, whether sought or unsought, by the military-industrial complex. The potential for the disastrous rise of misplaced power exists and will persist." Cited in Kegley, C. W., and E. R. Wittkopf. (1982). *American Foreign Policy Pattern and Process*. New York: St. Martin's Press: 255. Also see Mills, C. W. (1956). *The Power Elite*. New York: Oxford University Press; Rosen, S. J., Ed. (1973). *Testing the Theory of the Military-Industrial Complex*. Lexington, MA: Heath; and Herspring, D. R., and I. Volgyes, Eds. (1978). *Civil-Military Relations in Communist Systems*. Boulder, CO: Westview.

43. Bacevich, A. J. (2005). *The New American Militarism: How Americans Are Seduced by War*. New York: Oxford University Press.; Wheeler Leng, R. J., and H. Wheeler. (1979). "Influence Strategies, Success and War." *Journal of Conflict Resolution* 23 (December): 655–84.

44. Google Scholar searches demonstrate the rapid growth of publications pertaining to the military-industrial complex: 1955–1964: 45 results; 1965–1974: 1,200; 1975–1984: 1,600; 1985–1994: 3,060; 1995–2004: 8,600; and 2005–2014: 15,600. For recent examples, see Wheeler, W. T. (2004). *The Wastrels of Defense: How Congress Sabotges U.S. Security*. Annapolis, MD: Naval Institute Press; Stiglitz, J. E., and L. J. Bilmes. (2008). *The Three Million Dollar War: The True Cost of the Iraq Conflict*. New York: W. W. Norton.

45. Pew Research Center. (2019). "Attitudes on Same-Sex Marriage." https://www.pewresearch.org/religion/fact-sheet/changing-attitudes-on-gay-marriage/.

46. See, for instance, Gee, G. C., and C. L. Ford. (2011). "Structural Racism and Health Inequities: Old Issues, New Directions." *Du Bois Rev* 8 (1): 115–32.

47. The debate between relativism and universalism in the creation of good societies is extensive and contested. For example, secular Western values related to the treatment of women, or the promotion of human rights are often critiqued by non-Western voices as being paternalistic. From this point of view what constitutes a good life is subjective and socially constructed, not ordained by natural law. For a discussion, see Agyeman, N. K., and A. Momodu. (2019). "Universal Human Rights 'Versus' Cultural Relativism: the Mediating Role of Constitutional Rights." *African Journal of Legal Studies* 12 (1): 23–46.

48. Doyle, M. W. (2011). *Liberal Peace: Selected Essays*. New York: Routledge.

49. While consolidated democracies tend not to engage in armed struggle with each other, they do engage in armed struggle with non-consolidated democracies and authoritarian states. See Hegre, H. (2014). "Democracy and Armed Conflict." *Journal of Peace Research* 51 (2): 159–72.

50. See chapter 4 in Mearsheimer, J. J. (2018). *The Great Delusion: Liberal Dreams and International Realities*. New Haven, CT: Yale University Press.

51. Weiss, T. G., D. Forsythe, R. A. Coate, and K.-K. Pease. (2020). *The United Nations and Changing World Politics*. London: Routledge.

52. Avruch, K. (1998). *Culture and Conflict Resolution*. Washington, DC: U.S. Institute of Peace. Cultural similarities help account for the finding that democratic countries do not wage wars against each other.

53. Mitrany, D. (1948). "The Functional Approach to World Organization." *International Affairs* 24 (3): 350–63.

54. Coleman, J. S. (1957). *Community Conflict*. New York: Free Press. For theories about strain generating social movements, see Smelser, N. (1963). *The Theory of Collective Behavior*. New York: Free Press.

55. Johnson, C. (1966). *Revolutionary Change*. Boston: Little, Brown: 60.

56. Boretti, A., and L. Rosa. (2019). "Reassessing the Projections of the World Water Development Report." *npj Clean Water* 2 (1): 15.

57. Miklian, J., and P. Schouten. (2019). "Broadening 'Business,' Widening 'Peace': A New Research Agenda on Business and Peace-Building." *Conflict, Security & Development* 19 (1): 1–13.

58. Adekola, O. (2018). "Nigeria's Conflict is a Result of Environmental Devastation across West Africa." https://theconversation.com/nigerias-conflict-is-a-result-of-environmental-devastation-across-west-africa-91694.

CHAPTER 3. EMERGENCE

1. Initially, these components may become manifest within one party in the conflict, but once that party begins to take actions to achieve its goals, the target of the actions generally counters them, and the conflict emerges for it as well.

2. "Identity" is a contested term with multiple definitions. This one is offered by Terrel Northrup. See Northrup, T. A. (1989). "The Dynamic of Identity in Personal and Social Conflict." *Intractable Conflicts and Their Transformation*. Edited by L. Kriesberg, T. A. Northrup, and S. J. Thorson. Syracuse: Syracuse University Press: 55–82.

3. For an informative overview of how individuals gain identity and the role that identity plays in development, see Leary, M. R., and Tangney, J. P. (Eds.). (2012). *Handbook of Self and Identity*, second edition. Guilford, CT: The Guilford Press.

4. Snow, D., and C. Corrigall-Brown. (2015). "Collective Identity." *International Encyclopedia of the Social & Behavioral Sciences*. Amsterdam: Elsevier Ltd.

5. Social identities and the forces that trigger identity emergence were originally explored in depth by Henri Tajfel. See Tajfel, H. (1974). "Social Identity and Intergroup Behaviour." *Social Science Information* 13 (2): 65–93.

6. Two terms widely used not to interrogate the relationship between power, privilege, and identity across various contexts are "intersectionality" and "positionality." See, for example, Wilson, A. R. (2013). *Situating Intersectionality: The Politics of Intersectionality: Politics, Policy, and Power*. New York: Palgrave Macmillan. See also Gadling-Cole, C. (2021). *African American Women in Academia: Intersectionality of Race and Gender*. New York: Nova Science Publishers.

7. Ashmore, R. D., L. J. Jussim, and D. Wilder. (2001). *Social Identity, Intergroup Conflict, and Conflict Reduction*. Oxford: Oxford University Press; Coy, P. G., and L. M. Woehrle, Eds. (2000). *Social Conflicts and Collective Identities*. Lanham: Rowman & Littlefield; Northrup, T. A. (1989). "The Dynamic of Identity in Personal and Social Conflict." *Intractable Conflicts and Their Transformation*. Edited by L. Kriesberg, T. A. Northrup, and S. J. Thorson. Syracuse: Syracuse University Press: 55–82; Herb, G. H., and D. H. Kaplan, Eds. (1999). *Nested Identities: Nationalism, Territory, and Scale*. Lanham: Rowman & Littlefield.

8. Hardin, R. (1995). "Self Interest, Group Identity." *Perspectives on Nationalism and War*. Edited by J. L. Comaroff and P. C. Stern. Luxembourg: Gordon and Breach: 15–45.

9. Chassman, A. (2016). "Islamic State, Identity, and the Global Jihadist Movement: How is Islamic State Successful at Recruiting Ordinary People?" *Journal for Deradicalization*: 205–59.

10. For an interesting overview of identity vulnerability and its relationship to Islamic extremism, see Provines, C. G. (2017). "Understanding Radicalization Through the Lens of 'Identity Vulnerability.'" *Journal of International Affairs*.

11. See https://www.washingtonpost.com/opinions/2021/04/06/capitol-insurrection-arrests-cpost-analysis/.

12. Perlman, S. (1928). *A Theory of the Labor Movement*. New York: Augustus M. Kelley; Bok, D. C., and J. T. Dunlop. (1970). *Labor and the American Community*. New York: Simon & Schuster: 30.

13. Form, W. H. (1976). "Conflict within the Working Class: The Skilled as a Special-Interest Group." *The Uses of Controversy in Sociology*. Edited by O. N. Larsen. New York: Free Press: 51–73.

14. For evidence that the husband's class location is a major determinant of the wife's subjective class identity, see Baxter, J. (1994). "Is Husband's Class Enough? Class Location and Class Identity in the United States, Sweden, and Australia." *American Sociological Review* 59 (April): 220–35.

15. Skocpol, T. (1979). *States and Social Revolutions: A Comparative Analysis of France, Russia, and China*. Cambridge, England: Cambridge University Press: 92.

16. Areddy, J. T. (2015). "China Pushes to Rewrite Rules of Global Internet." http://www.wsj.com/articles/china-pushes-to-rewrite-rules-of-global-internet-1438112980.

17. Dual citizenship is increasingly common. See Aleinikoff, T. A., and D. Klusmeyer, Eds. (2001). *Citizenship Today: Global Perspectives and Practices*. Washington, DC: The Carnegie Endowment for International Peace; also see Delanty, G. (2000). *Citizenship in a Global Age*. Buckingham: Open University Press.

18. Clark, J. D., Ed. (2003). *Globalizing Civic Engagement: Civil Society and Transnational Action*. London: EarthScan.

19. Stanislawski, B. (Ed.). (2008). "Para-States, Quasi-States, and Black Spots: Perhaps Not States, But Not 'Ungoverned Territories,' Either." *International Studies Review* 10: 366–96.

20. Tilly, C. (1978). *From Mobilization to Revolution*. Reading, MA: Addison-Wesley; Tarrow, S. G. (1998). *Power in Movement: Social Movements and Contentious Politics*. Cambridge, England: Cambridge University Press; McAdam, D., J. D. McCarthy, and M. Zald, Eds. (1996). *Comparative Perspectives on Social Movements*. New York: Cambridge University Press.

21. Morris, A. D. (1984). *The Origins of the Civil Rights Movement*. New York: Free Press.

22. Fang, L. (2020). "Inside the Influential Evangelical Group Mobilizing to Re-elect Trump." *The Intercept*.

23. Smith, J., and H. Johnston, Eds. (2002). *Globalization and Resistance: Transnational Dimensions of Social Movements*. Lanham: Rowman & Littlefield. For websites with reports of Seattle and other locations of protests relating to globalization, see www.globalexchange.org/ and www.infoshop.org/no2wto.html.

24. See https://www.pewresearch.org/internet/fact-sheet/social-media/#find-out-more.

25. Tajfel, H. (1978). *Differentiation between Social Groups: Studies in the Social Psychology of Intergroup Relations*. London: Academic Press.

26. The most famous experiment illustrating the tendency of in-group favoritism among randomly assigned group members is the Robbers Cave Study conducted by Sherif in the mid-1950s. In it, twenty-two boys were sent to a remote summer camp

at Robbers Cave State Park. At the camp, they were randomly assigned to two different groups and spent several days participating in group-building activities. When the two groups were later brought together for a series of competition Sherif found that members of each group characterized their own groups in favorable terms while characterizing the opposing group in unfavorable terms. Only by later working together to overcome a common problem did Sheriff observe the reduction of intergroup prejudice and conflict. See Sherif, M. (1958). "Superordinate Goals in the Reduction of Intergroup Conflict." *American Journal of Sociology* 63 (4): 349–56.

27. Levine, R. A., and D. T. Campbell. (1972). *Ethnocentrism: Theories of Conflict, Ethnic Attitudes, and Group Behavior*. New York: John Wiley & Sons; Elliott, W. A. (1986). *Us and Them: A Study of Group Consciousness*. Aberdeen: Aberdeen University Press.

28. Druckman, D. (1995). "Social Psychological Aspects of Nationalism." *Perspectives on Nationalism and War*. Edited by J. L. Comaroff and P. C. Stern. Luxembourg: Gordon and Breach: 56–59.

29. Brewer, M. (2001). "Inter-group Identification and Inter-group Conflict." *Social Identity and Intergroup Conflict Reduction*. Edited by L. J. R. Ashmore and D. Wilder. Oxford: Oxford University Press; Korostelina, K. V. (2007). *Social Identity and Conflict: Structures, Dynamics and Implications*. New York: Palgrave Macmillan.

30. John Jost, M. B., and B. Nosek. (2004). "A Decade of System Justification Theory: Accumulated Evidence of Conscious and Unconscious Bolstering of the Status Quo." *Political Psychology* 25 (6): 881–919.

31. Johnson, C. A. (1962). *Peasant Nationalism and Communist Power*. Stanford, CA: Stanford University Press.

32. Race popularly refers to genetically determined differences among major groupings of humans. Biologically, however, the only meaning to "race" is too broad, overlapping genetic pools and lacking clear boundaries. On the basis of selecting some traits, people in many societies construct "social races." These are often bounded by social rules, allowing for the classification of individuals. See Nagle, J. (1994). "Constructing Ethnicity: Creating and Recreating Ethnic Identity and Culture." *Social Problems* 41 (1): 152–76.

33. This effect is emphasized by analysts of mass societies, where many people are isolated and alienated. Kornhauser, W. (1959). *The Politics of Mass Society*. New York: Free Press.

34. Klandermans, B. (1992). "The Social Construction of Protests and Multiorganizational Fields." *Frontiers in Social Movement Theory*. Edited by A. Morris and C. Mueller. New Haven, CT: Yale University Press.

35. Brinton, C. (1955). *The Anatomy of Revolution*. New York: Vintage; Davies, J. C. (1962). "Toward a Theory of Revolution." *American Sociological Review* 27 (February): 5–19.

36. Thomas, D., and J. M. Horowitz. (2020). "Support for Black Lives Matter has Decreased since June but Remains Strong among Black Americans." New York Pew Research Center.

37. Lerner, D., and L. W. Pevsner. (1958). *The Passing of Traditional Society: Modernizing the Middle East*. Glencoe, IL: Free Press.

38. Ellsworth, J. S. (1952). *Factory Folkways*. New Haven, CT: Yale University Press.

39. Schneider, S. M. (2019). "Why Income Inequality Is Dissatisfying—Perceptions of Social Status and the Inequality-Satisfaction Link in Europe." *European Sociological Review* 35 (3): 409–30.

40. Blauner, R. (1964). *Alienation and Freedom: The Factory Worker and His Industry*. Chicago: The University of Chicago Press.

41. Buchanan, W., and H. Cantril. (1953). *How Nations See Each Other*. Urbana, IL: University of Illinois Press.

42. The Brennan Center for Justice at New York University Law actively monitors and reports on voting restrictions. See https://www.brennancenter.org/.

43. In addition, the identification problem arises from the difficulty in distinguishing an additive effect from an interactive effect of two or more variables. See Blalock Jr., H. M. (1967). "Status Inconsistency and Interaction: Some Alternative Models." *American Journal of Sociology* 73 (November): 305–15.

44. Coser, L. A. (1956). *The Functions of Social Conflict*. New York: Free Press.

45. Ronfeldt, D., J. Arquilla, G. E. Fuller, and M. Fuller. (1998). *The Zapatista Social Netwar in Mexico*. Santa Monica, CA: RAND Arroyo Center. For internet material, see the links provided by the U.S. Institute of Peace Library, www.usip.org/library/regions/chiapas.html. Mueller, J. (1993). "American Public Opinion and the Gulf War." *The Political Psychology of the Gulf War*. Edited by S. A. Renshon. Pittsburgh: University of Pittsbrugh Press: 199–226.

46. Bell, I. P. (1968). *CORE and the Strategy of Non-Violence*. New York: Random House; National Advisory Commission on Civil Disorders. (1968). "Report of the National Commission on Civil Disorders (Kerner Commission)." New York: Bantam.

47. Azar, E., and N. Farah. (1981). "The Structure of Inequalities and Protracted Social Conflict: A Theoretical Framework." *International Interactions* 4: 317–35.

48. The earlier findings are in East, M. A. (1971). "Status Discrepancy and Violence in the International System: An Empirical Analysis." *The Analysis of International Politics*. Edited by J. N. Rosenau, V. Davis, and M. A. East. New York: Free Press. The later findings are in Volgy, T. J., and S. Mayhall (1995). "Status Inconsistency and International War: Exploring the Effects of Systemic Change." *International Studies Quarterly* 39 (March): 67–84.

49. The terms "left" and "right" are used with different meanings in different historical contexts. For example, in the initial post-Soviet period in Russia, "left" sometimes meant those favoring radical change and increased freedom and sometimes those favoring maintaining a great deal of socioeconomic equality and much of the old state apparatus. In the United States, at the end of the twentieth and beginning of the twenty-first century, left and right differences also pertained to issues of morality, with the right often advocating the use of state power to ensure adherence to what were claimed to be traditional values.

50. Tilly, C. (1978). *From Mobilization to Revolution*. Reading, MA: Addison-Wesley.

51. Demanding the abolition of private ownership of large agricultural estates is proclaiming a unitary goal, while demands for a 10 percent increase in wages is a

divisible goal. See Paige, J. M. (1975). *Agrarian Revolution: Social Movements and Export Agriculture in the Underdeveloped World*. New York: Free Press.

52. Hobsbawm, E. J. (1965). *Primitive Rebels*. New York: W. W. Norton.

53. Hughes, B. B. (1978). *The Democratic Context of American Foreign Policy*. San Francisco: W. W. Freeman: 38; see also Mueller, J. E. (1973). *War, Presidents and Public Opinion*. New York: John Wiley and Sons; and Mueller, J. (1993). "American Public Opinion and the Gulf War." *The Political Psychology of the Gulf War*. Edited by S. A. Renshon. Pittsburgh: University of Pittsbrugh Press: 199–226.

54. Hetherington, M. J., and M. Nelson. (2003). "Anatomy of a Rally Effect: George W. Bush and the War on Terrorism." *PS: Political Science and Politics* 36: 37–42; Woodward, B. (2004). *Plan of Attack*. New York: Simon & Schuster.

55. Hswen, Y., X. Xu, A. Hing, J. B. Hawkins, J. S. Brownstein, and G. C. Gee. (2021). "Association of "#covid19" versus "#chinesevirus" with Anti-Asian Sentiments on Twitter: March 9–23, 2020." *American Journal of Public Health* 111 (5): 956–64.

56. Hetherington and Nelson. (2003). "Anatomy of a Rally Effect: George W. Bush and the War on Terrorism."

57. Branch, T. (1988). *Parting the Waters: America in the King Years, 1954–63*. New York: Simon & Schuster.

58. Schmitt, D. R. (1965). "An Attitudinal Correlate of the Status Incongruency of Married Women." *Social Forces* 44 (December): 190–261; Broom, L. and F. L. Jones. (1970). "Status Consistency and Political Preference: The Australian Cae." *American Sociological Review* 35 (December): 989–1001.

59. For information about the activities of the American Jewish Committee, see www.ajc.org. For the American-Arab Anti-Discrimination Committee, see www.adc.org.

60. For analyses of the decline in take-home earnings from wages and the growing income inequality in the United States, see Berman, Y., E. Ben-Jacob, and Y. Shapira. (2016). "The Dynamics of Wealth Inequality and the Effect of Income Distribution." *PLOS One* 11 (4): e0154196; Braun, D. (1991). *The Rich Get Richer*. Chicago: Nelson-Hall; Blumberg, P. (1980). *Inequality in an Age of Decline*. New York: Oxford University Press; and Smeeding, T. (1996). "America's Income Inequality: Where Do We Stand?" *Challenge* (September–October): 45–53.

61. Gurr, T. R. (1970). *Why Men Rebel*. Princeton, NJ: Princeton University Press.

62. See Millet, K. (1970). *Sexual Politics*. New York: Doubleday: 125–27; and Collins, R. (1975). *Conflict Sociology*. New York: Academic Press: 225–85.

63. Many other economic and cultural factors contributed to the Iranian revolution and to the appeal of anti-Westernism. See Moshiri, F. (1991). "Iran: Islamic Revolution Against Westernization." *Revolutions of the Late Twentieth Century*. Edited by J. A. Goldstone, T. R. Gurr, and F. Moshiri. Boulder: Westview Press: 116–35; and Parsa, M. (1989). *Social Origins of the Iranian Revolution*. New Brunswick: Rutgers University Press.

64. Daalder, I. H., and J. M. Lindsay. (2003). *America Unbound: The Bush Revolution in Foreign Policy*. Washington, DC: Brookings Institution Press.

65. Wistrich, R. S. (1991). *Antisemitism: The Longest Hatred*. New York: Pantheon; Barkun, M. (1994). *Religion and the Racist Right: The Origins of the Christian Identity Movement*. Chapel Hill, NC: The University of North Carolina Press.

66. Gurr, T. R. (1970). *Why Men Rebel*. Princeton, NJ: Princeton University Press: 125–26.

67. Rosecrance, R. N. (1963). *Action and Reaction in World Politics*. Boston: Little, Brown.

68. Such considerations affect changes in goals as well. For example, the relatively radical Palestinian organization, the Popular Democratic Front for the Liberation of Palestine, published a circular in 1969 arguing that its goal of "throwing the Jews into the sea" had done "grave damage" to the Arab position and argued for creating a "democratic Palestinian state" in which Arabs and Jews would live in peace. Harkabi, Y. (1970). "Liberation or Genocide?" *Transaction* 7 (July/August): 63.

69. Mittleman, J. H. (2000). *The Globalization Syndrome: Transformation and Resistance*. Princeton, NJ: Princeton University Press.

70. Ayres, J. M. (1998). *Defying Conventional Wisdom: Political Movements and Popular Contention Against North American Free Trade*. Toronto: University of Toronto Press; Starr, A. (2000). *Naming the Enemy: Anti-Corporate Movements Confron Globalization*. New York: St. Martin's Press.

71. Smith, J., B. Gemici, S. Plummer, and M. Hughes. (2018). "Transnational Social Movement Organizations and Counter-Hegemonic Struggles Today." *Journal of World-Systems Research* 24: 372–403.

72. For accounts of Jewish–Palestinian relations, see Kimmerling, B., and J. S. Migdal. (1993). *Palestinians: The Making of a People*. New York: Free Press. Similarly, in Sri Lanka, Tamil nationalism grew in response to Buddhist revivalism. See Little, D. (1994). *Sri Lanka: The Invention of Enmity*. Washington, DC: U.S. Institute of Peace Press.

73. Paige, J. M. (1975). *Agrarian Revolution: Social Movements and Export Agriculture in the Underdeveloped World*. New York: Free Press; Aaker, J., and A. Smith. (2010). *The Dragonfly Effect: Quick, Effective and Powerful Ways to use Social Media to Drive Social Change*. San Francisco: Jossey Bass: 36.

74. Lodge, T. (2009). "Revolution Deferred: From Armed Struggle to Liberal Democracy." *Conflict Transformation and Peacebuilding: Moving From Violence to Sustainable Peace*. Edited by B. W. Dayton and L. Kriesberg. London: Routledge: 156–71.

75. Zald, M. N., and J. D. McCarthy. (1979). *The Dynamics of Social Movements*. Cambridge, MA: Winthrop; Tilly, C., and S. Tarrow. (2015). *Contentious Politics*, second edition. New York: Oxford University Press.

76. Lazarsfeld, P. F., B. Berelson, and H. Gaudet. (1944). *The People's Choice*. New York: Columbia University Press; Kriesberg, M. (1949). "Cross-Pressures and Attitudes." *Public Opinion Quarterly* 13 (Spring): 5–16.

77. Jackson, E. (1962). "Status Consistency and Symptoms of Stress." *American Sociological Review* 27 (August): 476.

78. Alinsky, S. (1946). *Reveille for Radicals*. New York: Vintage.

79. Mizrahi, T., and B. B. Rosenthal. (2001). "Complexities of Coalition Building: Leaders' Successes, Strategies, Struggles, and Solutions." *Social Work* 46 (1): 63–78.
80. Marx, K., and F. Engels. (1954). *The Communist Manifesto*. Chicago: H. Regnery.
81. Medrano, J. D. (1995). *Divided Nations: Class, Politics, and Nationalism in the Basque Country and Catalonia*. Ithaca: Cornell University Press.
82. Skocpol, T. (1979). *States and Social Revolutions: A Comparative Analysis of France, Russia, and China*. Cambridge, England: Cambridge University Press. Revolutions often follow wars for other reasons as well. Walter Laqueur writes that the "general dislocation caused by war, the material losses and human sacrifices, create a climate conducive to radical change. A large section of the population has been armed; human life seems considerably less valuable than in peacetime." See Laquer, W. (1968). "Revolution." *International Encyclopedia of the Social Sciences* 13: 501.
83. Ruppert, M. C. (2004). *Crossing the Rubicon: The Decline of the American Empire at the End of the Age of Oil*. Gabriola, BC: New Society Publishers; Bacevich, A. J. (2008). *The Limits of Power: The End of American Exceptionalism*. New York: Metropolitan Books.
84. Some conflict analysts combine particular components in order to distinguish different kinds of conflicts. For example, identity conflicts refer to struggles about dissensual issues such as the core values and values held by the contending parties, while interest conflicts are based on what is regarded here as consensual issues. See Rothman, J. (1997). *Resolving Identity-Based Conflict in Nations, Organizations, and Communities*. San Francisco: Jersey-Bass.

CHAPTER 4. ALTERNATIVE CONFLICT STRATEGIES

1. Psychologists and economists have called this dynamic the sunk cost fallacy. See Arkes, H., and C. Blumer. (1985). "The Psychology of Sunk Costs." *Organizational Behavior and Human Decision Processes* 35 (1): 124–40. The relationship of such entrapment to sustaining and escalating conflict is examined in Brockner, J., and J. Z. Rubin. (1985). *Entrapment in Escalating Conflicts: A Social Psychological Analysis*. New York: Springer Verlag.
2. Analysts of social conflicts use many different terms to make these or similar distinctions. "Influence," "threats," and "promises" are the terms used by Deutsch, M. (1973). *The Resolution of Conflict: Constructive and Destructive Processes*. New Haven, CT: Yale University Press. "Persuasion," "inducements," and "constraints" are used by Gamson, W. A. (1968). *Power and Discontent*. Homewood, IL: Dorsey Press. "Persuasion," "coercion," and "bargaining" are distinguished by Turner, R. H. (1970). "Determinants of Social Movement Strategies." *Human Nature and Collective Behavior: Papers in Honor of Herbert Blumer*. Edited by T. Shibutani. Englewood Cliffs, NJ: Prentice-Hall. "Coercive," "utilitarian," and "normative bases of compliance" are distinguished by Etzioni, A. (1961). *A Comparative Analysis of Complex Organization*. New York: Free Press. "Threat," "exchange," and "love forms of power" are distinguished by Boulding, K. E. (1989). *Three Faces of Power*.

Newbury Park: Sage. Other writers stress the differences between threats and promises or between negative and positive sanctions. See, respectively, Singer, D. (1963). "Inter-Nation Influence: A Formal Model." *American Political Sience Review* 57 (June): 420–30; and Baldwin, D. A. (1971). "The Power of Positive Sanctions." *World Politics* 24 (October): 19–38.

3. One example is the Obama administration's warning to the Syrian government during the Syrian civil war. See Pearlman, W. (2020). "Syrian Views on Obama's Red Line: The Ethical Case for Strikes against Assad." *Ethics & International Affairs* 34 (2): 189–200.

4. For a detailed discussion of nonviolent coercion, see Crespingny, A. D. (2006). "The Nature and Methods of Non-violent Coercion." *Political Studies* 12: 256–65.

5. Officially, assassination of foreign government officials is banned in the United States by executive order. In the post-2001 period, however, this ban was reinterpreted to allow targeted assassinations related to the War on Terror. For a fascinating review of the evolution of targeted killings by U.S. government agencies, see Banka, A. and A. Quinn (2018). "Killing Norms Softly: US Targeted Killing, Quasi-secrecy and the Assassination Ban." *Security Studies* 27 (4): 665–703.

6. Cortright, D., and G. A. Lopez, Eds. (1995). *Economic Sanctions: Panacea or Peacebuilding in a Post-Cold War World*. Boulder, CO: Westview.

7. For an overview of the evolution of deterrence during and since the Cold War, see Morgan, P. M. (2012). "The State of Deterrence in International Politics Today." *Contemporary Security Policy* 33 (1): 85–107.

8. Ross, M. H. (1993). *The Culture of Conflict*. New Haven: Yale University Press; Montagu, A., Ed. (1978). *Learning Non-Aggression*. New York: Oxford University Press.

9. Law, B. M. F., A. M. H. Siu, and D. T. L. Shek. (2012). "Recognition for Positive Behavior as a Critical Youth Development Construct: Conceptual Bases and Implications on Youth Service Development." *The Scientific World Journal*: 809578.

10. President Lyndon B. Johnson during the war against North Vietnam offered aid for reconstruction, linked to ending the war, but this was not wholly credible and in any case reflected a grave cultural and political misunderstanding. Kearns, D. (1977). *Lyndon Johnson and the American Dream*. New York: New American Library: 278–82.

11. Stedman, S. J. (2000). "Spoiler Problems in Peace Processes." *International Conflict Resolution After the Cold*. Edited by P. Stern and D. Druckman. Washington, DC: National Academies Press.

12. One definition that incorporates many shared ideas is that persuasion is "symbolic activity whose purpose is to effect the internationalization or voluntary acceptance of new cognitive states or patterns of overt behavior through the exchange of messages." See Smith, M. J. (1982). *Persuasion and Human Action*. Belmont, CA: Wadsworth: 7.

13. Lee, H.-Y., and D. C. Mutz. (2019). "Changing Attitudes Toward Same-Sex Marriage: A Three-Wave Panel Study." *Political Behavior* 41 (3): 701–22.

14. Kleiboer, M. (1998). *The Multiple Realities of International Mediation*. Boulder, CO: Lynne Rienner; Lederach, J. P. (1997). *Building Peace: Sustainable Reconciliation in Divided Societies*. Washington, DC: U.S. Institute of Peace Press.

15. Allard, S. (1970). *Russia and the Austrian State Treaty*. University Park, PA: University of Pennsylvania Press; Kriesberg, L. (1992). *International Conflict Resolution: The U.S.-USSR and Middle East Cases*. New Haven: Yale University Press.

16. You can learn about the work of the BlueGreen Alliance here: https://www.bluegreenalliance.org/.

17. Tedeschi, J. T. (1970). "Threats and Promises." *The Structure of Conflict*. Edited by P. Swingle. New York: Academic Press: 155–91.

18. Simpson, C. (1994). *Science of Coercion: Communication Research and Psychological Warfare*. New York: Oxford University Press.

19. Gulliver, P. H. (1979). *Disputes and Negotiations: A Cross-Cultural Perspective*. New York: Academic Press.

20. Nef, J. (1950). *War and Human Progress*. Cambridge, MA: Harvard University Press.

21. For the texts of the Geneva conventions regarding warfare, see the International Committee of the Red Cross website: www.icrc.org/eng.

22. Diamond, L. (1999). *Developing Democracy: Toward Consolidation*. Baltimore, MD: John Hopkins University Press.

23. Kiernan, B. (1996). *The Pol Pot Regime: Race, Power, and Genocide in Cambodia under the Khmer Rouge, 1975–1979*. New Haven, CT: Yale University Press.

24. We consider "legitimate" to mean generally accepted by the population being covered by such regulations as fair in both scope and application.

25. Axelrod, R. (1986). "An Evolutionary Approach to Norms." *American Political Science Review* 80 (December): 1095–111; Foucalt, M. (1980). *Power-Knowledge*. New York: Panteon.

26. Sumner, W. G. (1906). *Folkways*. Lexington, MA: Ginn.

27. For instance, on the frequency of political coups in Africa, see Assensoh, A. B., and Y. M. Alex-Assensoh. (2001). *African Military History & Politics: Coups and Idealogical Incursions, 1900–Present*. New York: Palgrave.

28. Sayles, L. R., and G. Strauss. (1953). *The Local Union: Its Place in the Industrial Plant*. New York: Harper & Brothers.

29. Galtung, J. (1969). "Violence, Peace, and Peace Research." *Journal of Peace Research* 3 (3): 168.

30. The observation is based on my interviews with Catalans in Barcelona conducted in 1994. Also, Medrano, J. D. (1995). *Divided Nations: Class, Politics, and Nationalism in the Basque Country and Catalonia*. Ithaca: Cornell University Press.

31. Avruch, K. (1998). *Culture and Conflict Resolution*. Washington, DC: U.S. Institute of Peace.

32. The International Court of Justice, which sits at The Hague, Netherlands, was established in 1945 under the Charter of the United Nations. Its predecessor was the Permanent Court of International Justice (1922–1946). See www.icj-cij.org/. The International Criminal Court was established in 2002 to prosecute individuals' crimes against humanity, genocide, and war crimes; however, the United States, China, and a few other countries have not joined the International Criminal Court.

33. Sageman, M. (2004). *Understanding Terror Networks*. Philadelphia: University of Pennsylvania Press; Palmer, M., and P. Palmer. (2004). *The Heart of Terror: Islam, Jihadist, and America's War on Terrorism*. Lanham: MD: Rowman & Littlefield.

34. Wehr, P., H. Burgess, and G. Burgess, Eds. (1994). *Justice Without Violence*. Boulder: Lynne Rienner; Powers, R. S., and W. B. Vogele, Eds. (1997). *Protest, Power, and Change: An Encyclopedia of Nonviolent Action from ACT-Up to Women's Suffrage*. New York: Garland Publishing Co.

35. Sharp, G. (1973). *The Politics of Nonviolent Action*. Boston: Porter Sargent; Sharp, G. (2005). *Waging Nonviolent Struggle: 20th Century Practice and 21st Century Potential*. Boston: Porter Sargent.

36. Telhami, S. (2020). "What do Americans Think of the BDS Movement, Aimed at Israel?" Brookings Institute, Washington, DC.

37. Gandhi, M. K. (1940). *An Autobiography of My Experiments with Truth*. Almedabad, India: Nvajivan; Bondurant, J. V. (1965). *Conquest of Violence: The Gandhian Philosophy of Violence*. Berkeley: University of California Press.

38. Chenoweth, E., and M. J. Stephan. (2011). *Why Civil Resistance Works: The Strategic Logic of Nonviolent Conflict*. New York: Columbia University Press.

39. Tilly, C., and D. Snyder. (1972). "Hardship and Collective Violence in France 1830–1960." *American Sociological Review* 37 (October): 520–32.

40. King Jr., M. L. (1963). *Why We Can't Wait*. New York: The New American Library.

41. Reitzes, D. C., and D. C. Reitzes. (1987). *The Alinsky Legacy: Alive and Kicking*. Greenwich, CT: JAI Press.

42. Cortright, D. G. L., with R. W. Conroy, J. Dashti-Gibson, and J. Wagler. (2000). *The Sanctions Decade: Assessing UN Strategies in the 1990s*. Boulder: Lynne Rienner; Cortright, D., and G. A. Lopez. (2002). *Sanctions and the Search for Security*. Boulder: Lynne Rienner.

43. Cassidy, J. (2015). "The Iran Deal is a Victory for Reason and Economic Sanctions." http://www.newyorker.com/news/john-cassidy/the-iran-deal-is-a-victory-for-reason-and-economic-sanctions.

44. Drezner, D. W. (2003). "How Smart are Smart Sanctions?" *International Studies Review* 5 (1): 107–10.

45. For a discussion of the challenges and possibilities of targeted sanctions, see Wallensteen, P., C. Staibano, and M. Eriksson. (2003). *Making Targeted Sanctions Effective: Guidelines for the Implementation of UN Policy Options*. Uppsala: Uppsala University Department of Peace and Conflict Research.

46. Stohl, M. (1990). "Demystifying the Mystery of International Terrorism." *International Terrorism: Characteristics, Causes, Controls*. Edited by C. W. Kegley Jr. New York: St. Martin's: 83. For a taxonomy of definitions, see Schmid, A. P. (2004 Summer). "Frameworks for Conceptualising Terrorism." *Terrorism and Political Violence* 16 (2): 197–221. For the U.S. Department of State's definition of terrorist activity, see www.state.gov/s/ct/.

47. Kennedy, S. (1995). *After Appomattox: How the South Won the War*. Gainesville, FL: University of Florida Press.

48. Marshall, M. G. (2002). "Global Terrorism: An Overview and Analysis." Report of the Integrated Network for Societal Conflict Research, University of Maryland Center for Systemic Peace.

49. In 1996, bin Laden issued a declaration of war, titled "Against the Americans Occupying the Land of the Two Holy Places (Expel the Infidels from the Arab Peninsula)." For the text, see www.lib.ecu.edu/govdoc/terrorism.html#binladen; see also, www.fas.org/irp/world/para/docs/980223-fatwa.htm.

50. Quoted from "The Truth About the New Crusade: A Ruling on the Killing of Women and Children of the Non-Believers," cited in Cullison, A. (2004). "Inside Al-Qaeda's Hard Drive." *The Atlantic Monthly* (September): 55–70.

51. In October 2005, the U.S. Department of State designated forty-two foreign terrorist organizations, including the Liberation Tigers of Tamil Eelam, the Basque Fatherland and Liberty, HAMAS, Real IRA, Kahane Chai, and the Kurdistan Workers' Party. www.state.gov/s/ct/rls/fs/37191.htm.

52. Clark, S. (2020). *How White Supremacy Returned to Mainstream Politics*. Washington, DC: Center for American Progress.

53. Among the numerous accounts, see Marchetti, V., and J. D. Marks. (1974). *The CIA and the Cult of Intelligence*. New York: Dell; Chavkin, S. (1961). *The Murder of Chile: Eyewitness Acounts of the Coup, the Terror, and the Resistance Today*. New York: Everest House; and Carmack, R. M., Ed. (1988). *Harvest of Violence: The Maya Indians and the Guatemalan Crisis*. Norman: University of Oklahoma Press.

54. Central Intelligence Agency definition at http://www.cia.gov/terrorism/faqs.html. The Department of Defense definition is: "The calculated use of unlawful violence or the threat of unlawful violence to inculcate fear; intended to coerce of intimidate governments or societies in the pursuit of goals that are generally political, religious or ideological." U.S. Army CDSINT Handbook No. 1 (Version3.0), "A Military Guide to Terrorism in the Twenty-First Century," August 15, 2001. See www.fas.org/irp/threat/terrorism/index.html.

55. For a discussion of the psychological motivations of suicidal terrorism, see Crenshaw, M. (2000). "The Psychology of Terrorism: An Agenda for the Twenty-First Century." *Political Psychology* 21 (2): 405–20.

56. Selznick, P. (1949). *TVA and the Grass Roots*. Berkeley: University of California Press.

57. Such approaches come under the rubric of "regulatory negotiation." See Susskind, L., and J. L. Cruikshank. (1987). *Breaking the Impasse: Consensual Approaches to Resolving Public Disputes*. New York: Basic Books.

58. Clark, K. B., and J. Hopkins. (1969). *A Relevant War Against Poverty*. New York: Harper & Row; Moynihan, D. P. (1970). *Maximum Feasible Misunderstanding*. New York: Free Press.

59. Kerner Commission. (1968). *Report of the National Commission on Civil Disorders*. New York: Bantam: 279.

60. Piven, F. F., and R. A. Cloward. (1979). *Poor People's Movements*. New York: Vintage Books; Coy, P. G., and T. Hedeen. (2005). "A Stage Model of Social Movement Co-Optation: Community Mediation in the United States." *The Sociological Quarterly* 46: 405–35.

61. Kerr, C. (1954). "The Trade Union Movement and the Redistribution of Power in Postwar Germany." *The Quarterly Journal of Economics* 68 (November): 535–64.

62. O'Leary, R., and N. Vij. (2012). "Collaborative Public Management: Where Have We Been and Where Are We Going?" *The American Review of Public Administration* 42 (5): 507–22.

63. Sisk, T. D. (2001). "Democratization and Peacebuilding: Perils and Promises." *Turbulent Peace: The Challenges of Managing International Conflict*. Edited by C. A. Crocker, F. Osler Hampson, and P. Aall. Washington, DC: U.S. Institute of Peace Press: 785–800.

64. Holland, J. (1999). *Hope Against History*. New York: Henry Holt.

65. Ross, M. H. (1998). "Democracy as Joint Problem Solving: Addressing Interests and Identities in Divided Societies." *Nationalism & Ethnic Politics* 4 (4): 19–46; Saunders, H. H. (1999). *A Public Peace Process: Sustained Dialogue to Transform Racial and Ethnic Conflicts*. New York: St. Martin's Press; Weiner, E., Ed. (1998). *The Handbook of Interethnic Coexistence*. New York: Continuum. For links to websites with basic information about conflict resolution, see www.crinfo.org/.

66. Saunders, H. H. (1999). *A Public Peace Process: Sustained Dialogue to Transform Racial and Ethnic Conflicts*. New York: St. Martin's Press.

67. Fisher, R. (1997). *Interactive Conflict Resolution*. Syracuse: Syracuse University Press; Rothman, J. (1992). *From Confrontation to Cooperation: Resolving Ethnic and Regional Conflict*. Thousand Oaks, CA: Sage.

68. Kelman, H. C. (1995). "Contributions of an Unoffical Conflict Resolution Effort to the Israeli-Palestinian Breakthrough." *Negotiation Journal* 11 (January): 19–27.

69. Kane-Berman, J. (1990). *South Africa's Silent Revolution*. Johannesburg: South African Institute of Race Relations; Sparks, A. (1995). *Tomorrow is Another Country*. New York: Hill and Wang; van der Merwe, H. (1989). *Pursuing Justice and Peace in South Africa*. London: Routledge.

70. Blake, R. R., H. A. Shephard, and J. S. Mouton. (1964). *Managing Intergroup Conflict in Industry*. Houston, TX: Gulf Publishing; Rahim, M. A. (1986). *Managing Conflict in Organizations*. Westport, CT: Praeger.

CHAPTER 5. ADOPTING CONFLICT STRATEGIES

1. This formulation was introduced in Blake, R. R., and J. S. Mouton. (1964). *The Managerial Grid*. Houston, TX: Gulf. Various diagnostic surveys are available online for those interested in assessing their own style. For example, the U.S. Institute of Peace survey found at https://www.usip.org/public-education/students/conflict-styles-assessment.

2. Paker, K., J. Horowitz, and M. Anderson. (2021). "Amid Protests, Majorities Across Racial and Ethnic Groups Express Support for the Black Lives Matter Movement." Pew Research Center.

3. The data are from Steedlly, H. R., and J. W. Foley. (1990). "The Success of Protest Groups: Multivariate Analyses." *The Strategy of Social Protest*. Edited by W. A. Gamson. Belmont, CA: Wadsworth: 188, table 1.

4. Bell, I. P. (1968). *CORE and the Strategy of Non-Violence*. New York: Random House: 59.

5. Lammers, C. J. (1969). "Strikes and Mutinies: A Comparative Study of Organizational Conflicts Between Rulers and Ruled." *Administrative Science Quarterly* 14 (December): 558–72.

6. Rafi, O. (2021). "The Post Genocide Reconciliation in Rwanda: Erasing Ethnicity and Building Citizenship." *International Journal of Peace and Development Studies* 12 (1): 23–29.

7. Significant debate on the success of this project remains. See Purdeková, A., and D. Mwambari. (2021). "Post-Genocide Identity Politics and Colonial Durabilities in Rwanda." *Critical African Studies*: 1–19.

8. Goldstein, A. P., and M. H. Segall. (1982). *Aggression in Global Perspective*. Elmsford, NY: Pergamon Press.

9. Lipset, S. M., and W. Schneider. (1983). *The Confidence Gap: Business, Labor and Government in the Public Mind*. New York: Free Press.

10. Mueller, J. E. (1973). *War, Presidents and Public Opinion*. New York: John Wiley and Sons: 122–36; Kriesberg, L., H. Murray, and R. A. Klein. (1982). "Elites and Increased Public Support for U.S. Military Spending." *Journal of Political and Military Sociology* 10 (Fall): 275–97.

11. The Gallup poll analysis of October 24, 2001: www.gallup.com/poll/releases/pr01024.asp.

12. "A Year Later, U.S. Campaign Against ISIS Garners Support, Raises Concerns." Washington, DC: Pew Research Center.

13. Arian, A. (1995). *The Peace Process and Terror: Conflicting Trends in Israeli Public Opinion in 1995*. Tel Aviv: Tel Aviv University, Jaffee Center for Strategic Studies.

14. Among respondents with fewer than nine years of education, 17 percent opposed continuing negotiations, compared with 31 percent among those with university degrees. Similarly, among the respondents with fewer than nine years of education, 27 percent supported armed attacks against Israeli targets, compared with 47 percent of those with university degrees. Data from public opinion poll no. 16, conducted and reported by the Center for Palestine Research and Studies, Nablus, West Bank.

15. "More Approve of U.S. Campaign Against Islamic Militants in Iraq and Syria . . . And Public Is Now Divided Over Possible Use of Ground Troops." (2015). http://www.people-press.org/2015/02/24/growing-support-for-campaign-against-isis-and-possible-use-of-u-s-ground-troops/2-24-2015_01/.

16. Yokley, E. (2021). "Voters Increasingly OK With Taliban Takeover as Consequence of Military Withdrawal From Afghanistan." Morning Consult, Washington, DC.

17. Transgender identity has only recently appeared as an independent variable in some large-scale public surveys. Meaningful correlations are therefore difficult to establish, as yet.

18. Goldstein, A. P., and M. H. Segall. (1982). *Aggression in Global Perspective*. Elmsford, NY: Pergamon Press.

19. Northrup, T. A. (1990). "Personal Security, Political Security: The Relationship between Conceptions of Gender, War, and Peace." *Research in Social Movements,*

Conflicts and Change. Edited by L. Kriesberg. Greenwich, CT: JAI Press: 267–99; Hartsock, N. C. M. (1989). "Masculinity, Heroism, and the Making of War." *Rocking the Ship of State*. Edited by A. Harris and Y. King. Boulder: Westview Press: 133–52.

20. Eichenberg, R. C. (2003). "Gender Differences in Public Attidues toward the Use of Force by the United States, 1990–2003." *International Security* 28 (1): 110–41.

21. CNN/USA Today/Gallup poll analysis by Jeffrey M. Jones, October 5, 2001; see www.gallup.com/poll/Releases/Pr011005.asp.

22. Eichenberg. (2003). "Gender Differences in Public Attidues toward the Use of Force by the United States, 1990–2003."

23. Keashly, L. (1994). "Gender and Conflict: What Does Psychological Research Tell Us?" *Conflict and Gender*. Edited by A. Taylor and J. B. Miller. Cresskill, NJ: Hampton Press: 167–90.

24. See Ruble, T. L., and J. A. Schneer. (1968). "Gender Differences in Conflict-Handling Styles: Less Than Meets the Eye?" *Conflict and Gender*. Edited by A. Taylor and J. B. Miller. Cresskill, NJ: Hampton Press: 155–66.

25. Caprioli, M., and M. A. Boyer. (2001). "Gender, Violence, and International Crisis." *The Journal of Conflict Resolution* 45 (4): 503–18.

26. Forsberg, E., and L. Olsson. (2020). "Examining Gender Inequality and Armed Conflict at the Subnational Level." *Journal of Global Security Studies* 6 (2).

27. Krause, J., W. Krause, and P. Bränfors. (2018). "Women's Participation in Peace Negotiations and the Durability of Peace." *International Interactions* 44 (6): 985–1016.

28. Gopin, M. (2000). *Between Eden and Armageddon: The Future of Religion, Violence and Peacemaking*. New York: Oxford University Press; Gopin, M. (2001). *Holy War, Holy Peace*. New York: Oxford University Press; Abu-Nimer, M. (2003). *Nonviolence and Peace Building in Islam: Theory and Practice*. Gainesville, FL: University Press of Florida.

29. For examples, see Little, D., Ed. (2007). *Peacemakers in Action: Profiles of Religion in Conflict Resolution*. Cambridge: Cambridge University Press.

30. Brock, P. (1968). *Pacifism in the United States: From the Colonial Era to the First World War*. Princeton, NJ: Princeton University Press; Holmes, R. L., Ed. (1990). *Nonviolence in Theory and Practice*. Belmont, CA: Wadsworth.

31. Adamczyk, A., and G. LaFree. (2019). "Religion and Support for Political Violence among Christians and Muslims in Africa." *Sociological Perspectives* 62 (6): 948–79.

32. Sprinzak, E. (1988). "Fundamentalism,Terrorism, and Democracy: The Case of Gush Emunim." *New Outlook* 31 (September/October): 8–41.

33. For full text, see www.lib.ecu.edu/govdoc/terrorism.html#binladen.

34. Conversi, D. (1993). "Domino Effect or Internal Developments? The Influences of International Events and Political Ideologies on Catalan and Basque Nationalism." *West European Politics* 16 (July): 245–70; see also Fanon, F. (1966). *The Wretched of the Earth*. New York: Grove Press; Rejai, M. (1977). *The Comparative Study of Revolutionary Strategy*. New York: David McKay; Castenero, J. (1997). *Companero: The Life and Death of Che Guevara*. New York: Knopf.

35. For an example of this principle as applied to the Woodrow Wilson's leadership style, see Schulzke, C. E. (2007). "Wilsonian Crisis Leadership, the Organic State, and the Modern Presidency." *Polity* 37 (2): 262–85.

36. Hermann, M. G. (2001). "How Decision Units Shape Foreign Policy: A Theoretical Framework." *International Studies Review* 3 (2): 47–82.

37. Mills, C. W. (1948). *The New Men of Power*. New York: Harcourt, Brace.

38. Mills, C. W. (1956). *The Power Elite*. New York: Oxford University Press; Rose, A. M. (1967). *The Power Structure*. New York: Oxford University Press.

39. Hughes, B. B. (1978). *The Democratic Context of American Foreign Policy*. San Francisco: W. W. Freeman.

40. Kriesberg, L., H. Murray, and R. A. Klein; (1982). "Elites and Increased Support for U.S. Military Spending." *Journal of Political and Military Sociology* 10 (Fall): 275–97; Hyland, W. (1999). *Clinton's World: Remaking American Foreign Policy*. Westport, CT: Praeger; Bacevich, A. J. (2005). *The New American Militarism: How Americans Are Seduced by War*. New York: Oxford University Press.

41. Address by President of the Russian Federation. (2014). Moscow, The Kremlin.

42. Conversi, D. (1994). "Violence as an Ethnic Border: The Consequences of a Lack of Distinctive Elements in Croatian, Kurdish and Basque Nationalism." *Nationalism in Europe: Past and Present*. Edited by X. Beramendi, R. Maiz, and X. M. Nunez. Santiago de Compostela: University of Santiago Press.

43. Chokshi, N., and S. L. Se. (2014). "Ferguson-style Militarization Goes on Trial in the Senate." *The Washington Post*.

44. For example, the Department of Homeland Security has recently launched a new program to address domestic radicalization and terrorism, the Targeted Violence and Terrorism Prevention Grant Program. The program provides funding to state, local, tribal, and territorial governments, nonprofits, and institutions of higher education to prevent targeted violence and terrorism through public education, early intervention, and other means.

45. In the case of state terrorism, government resources may be very great, and even if some terrorist acts may be conducted by factions of state police or security agencies, a policy of state terrorism requires the engagement of large numbers of people and authoritarian or totalitarian controls.

46. Oberschall, A. (1989). "The 1960 Sit-Ins: Protest Diffusion and Movement Take-Off." *Research in Social Movements, Conflict and Change*. Edited by L. Kriesberg. Greenwich, CT: JAI Press: 31–53.

47. Spilerman, S. (1970). "The Causes of Racial Disturbances: A Comparison of Alternative Explanations." *American Sociological Review* 35 (August): 627–49.

48. Youth tend to feel invulnerable, with fewer assets that are hostage to those with superior power, and therefore are disproportionately involved in violent disruptions. Coser, L. A. (1967). *Continuities in the Study of Social Conflict*. New York: Free Press; Kerner Commission. (1968). *Report of the National Commission on Civil Disorders*. New York: Bantam.

49. Bacevich, A. J. (2005). *The New American Militarism: How Americans Are Seduced by War*. New York: Oxford University Press.

50. Priest, D. (2003). *The Mission: Waging War and Keeping Peace with America's Military*. New York: W. W. Norton & Co.

51. Tilly, C. (1978). *From Mobilization to Revolution*. Reading, MA: Addison-Wesley: 156. In Labrador, Canada, one community of indigenous people, the Inuit, had a history of passively responding in conflicts. After cooperating with another community, the Innu, in carrying out civil disobedience by successfully blockading a work project on their land, were ready to threaten such actions again. Dunn, L. A. (2002). "Negotiating Cultural Identities: Conflict Transformation in Labrador." Unpublished PhD dissertation, Syracuse University.

52. Kerr, C., and A. Siegel. (1954). "The Interindustry Propensity to Strike: An International Comparison." *Industrial Conflict*. Edited by A. Kornhauser and A. M. Ross. New York: McGraw-Hill: 189–212. Other studies of interindustry strike propensity in France and in Italy did not find the same pattern. See Shorter, E., and C. Tilly. (1974). *Strikes in France, 1830–1968*. Cambridge, UK: Cambridge University Press; and Snyder, D., and W. R. Kelly. (1976). "Industrial Violence in Italy, 1878–1903." *American Journal of Sociology* 82 (July): 131–62.

53. Varshney, A. (2002). *Ethnic Conflict and Civic Life: Hindu and Muslims in India*. Princeton: Yale University Press.

54. Murdock, G. P. (1949). *Social Structure*. New York: Macmillan; LeVine, R. A. (1965). "Socialization, Social Structure, and Intersocietal Images." *International Behavior*. Edited by H. C. Kelman. New York: Holt, Rinehart & Winston: 45–69.

55. Deutsch, K. W., S. A. Burrell, R. A. Kann, M. Lee Jr., M. Lichterman, R. Lindgren, F. L. Loewenheim, and R. W. Van Wagenen. (1957). *Political Community and the North Atlantic Area*. Princeton, NJ: Princeton University Press; Kacowicz, A. M., Y. Bar-Siman Tov, O. Elgstrom, and M. Jerneck, Eds. (2000). *Stable Peace Among Nations*. Lanham: Rowman & Littlefield.

56. Domke, W. K. (1988). *War and the Changing Global System*. New Haven: Yale University Press. Also see Gasiorwski, M. (1986). "Economic Interdependence and International Conflict: Some Cross-National Evidence." *International Studies Quarterly* 30: 23–28; and Polachek, S. W. (1980). "Conflict and Trade." *Journal of Conflict Resolution* 24 (March): 55–78.

57. Kleinberg, K. B., G. Robinson, and S. L. French. (2012). "Trade Concentration and Interstate Conflict." *The Journal of Politics* 74 (2): 529–40.

58. Rummel, R. J. (1985). "Libertarian Propositions on Violence Within and Between Nations." *Journal of Conflict Resolution* 29 (September): 419–55; Russett, B. (1993). *Grasping the Democratic Peace: Principles for a Post-Cold War World*. Princeton, NJ: Princeton University Press; Gates, S., T. L. Knutsen, and J. W. Moses. (1996). "Democracy and Peace: A More Skeptical View." *Journal of Peace Research* 33 (1): 1–10; Russett, B. (2005). "Bushwacking the Democratic Peace." *International Studies Perspective* 6: 395–408.

59. Taft, P., and P. Ross. (1969). "American Labor Violence: Its Causes, Character, and Outcome." *Violence in America*. Edited by H. D. Graham and T. R. Gurr. New York: Bantam: 281–395; Haydu, J. (1989). "Managing 'The Labor Problem' in the United States ca. 1897–1911." *Intractable Conflicts and Their Transformation*.

Edited by L. Kriesberg, T. A. Northrup, and S. J. Thorson. Syracuse: Syracuse University Press: 93–106.

60. Ross, A. M., and D. Irwin. (1951). "Strike Experience in Five Countries, 1927–1947: An Interpretation." *Industrial and Labor Relations Review* 4 (April): 323–42.

61. Lewis F. Richardson found that of the 186 pairs of opposed belligerents in wars from 1820 to 1929, 48 percent had fought against each other in the past and only 29 percent had been wartime allies. J. David Singer and Melvin Small, using somewhat different indicators, found that of the 209 who had ever fought in opposition between 1816 and 1965, 19 percent had fought in opposition at least once before, but 21 percent had been partners in the past. See Richardson, L. F. (1960). *Statistics of Deadly Quarrels*. Pittsburgh, PA: The Boxwood Press: 345.

62. Scheff, T. J. (1994). *Bloody Revenge: Emotions, Nationalism, and War*. Boulder: Westview; Volkan, V. (1988). *The Need to Have Enemies and Allies: From Clinical Practice to International Relationships*. New York: Jason Aronson.

63. McCauley, C. (2017). "Toward a Psychology of Humiliation in Asymmetric Conflict." *American Psychologist* 72: 255–65.

64. See, for instance, Judah, T. (2000). *The Serbs: History, Myth and the Destruction of Yugoslavia*. New Haven, CT: Yale University Press.

65. Fischer, G. (1952). *Soviet Opposition to Stalin: A Case Study in World War II*. Cambridge, MA: Harvard University Press.

66. This topic is influentially developed in Morgenthau, H. J. (1950). *Politics among Nations*. New York: Alfred A. Knopf. Among recent discussions, see Vasquez, J. (1993). *The War Puzzle*. Cambridge, UK: Cambridge University Press.

67. J. David Singer, Stuart A. Bremer, and John Stuckey find that in the nineteenth century, wars among major states were less likely when power was dispersed, consistent with the balance of power argument, but in the twentieth century, wars were less likely when capability was concentrated, consistent with the preponderance argument. See Singer, J. D., S. A. Bremer, and J. Stuckey. (1979). "Capability Distribution, Uncertainty, and Major Power War, 1820–1965." *The Correlates of War I: Research Origins and Rationale*. Edited by J. D. Singer. New York: Free Press: 265–97.

68. de Mesquita, B. B. (1981). *The War Trap*. New Haven: Yale University Press.

69. Vasquez, J. (1993). *The War Puzzle*. Cambridge, UK: Cambridge University Press.

70. However, see Juhnke, J. C., and C. M. Hunter. (2004). *Missing Peace: The Search for Nonviolent Alternatives in U.S. History*, second edition. Kitchner, Canada: Pandora Press.

71. Business upturns also tend to be accompanied by price increases and a fall or slowing down of real income, but the relative power interpretation seems particularly compelling in that strikes to organize unorganized workers show the same pattern as do strikes to secure wage increases and other benefits. See Christman, L., W. R. Kelly, and O. R. Galle. (1981). "Comparative Perspectives on Industrial Conflict." *Research in Social Movements, Conflict and Change*. Edited by L. Kriesberg. Greenwich, CT: JAI Press: 4.

72. For information about the workers in the global economy project of Cornell University's School of Industrial Relations, see www.laborrights.org/projects/global

econ/. See also the Institute for Policy Studies Global Economy Project: http://www.ips-dc.org/projects/glabal—econ.

73. Herod, A. (2000). "Implications of Just-in-time Production for Union Strategy: Lessons from the 1998 General Motors—United Auto Workers' Dispute." *Annals of the Association of American Geographers* 90 (3): 521–47.

74. Skocpol, T. (1979). *States and Social Revolutions: A Comparative Analysis of France, Russia, and China*. Cambridge, England: Cambridge University Press.

75. Aaker, J., and A. Smith. (2010). *The Dragonfly Effect: Quick, Effective and Powerful Ways to use Social Media to Drive Social Change*. San Francisco: Jossey Bass; Shirky, C. (2011). "The Political Power of Social Media." *Foreign Affairs* 90 (1): 28–41; Keck, M. E., and K. Sikkink. (1998). *Activists beyond Borders: Advocacy Networks in International Politics*. Ithaca, NY: Cornell University Press.

76. Khouri, F. J. (1985). *The Arab-Israeli Dilemma*. Syracuse, NY: Syracuse University Press. With the expansion of UN membership by the admission of many newly independent countries, the economically developing countries were able to exercise their voting strength to pass resolutions they favored. African countries favored resolutions condemning South Africa's apartheid policy and the Middle Eastern countries favored strong resolutions condemning Israeli policies relating to Palestinians. By joining together, each voting group was able to win many resolutions that it sought.

77. The Sinhala, predominantly Buddhist, make up about 75 percent of the population of Sri Lanka and the Tamil, mainly Hindu, constitute about 18 percent of the population. In addition, about 7 percent of the population is Muslim, mostly Tamil speakers. Little, D. (1994). *Sri Lanka: The Invention of Enmity*. Washington, DC: U.S. Institute of Peace Press. In 2009, the Liberation Tigers of Tamil Eelam was militarily defeated by the government's armed forces.

78. In 2011, the results of an agreed-upon referendum in Southern Sudan signaled the independence of Southern Sudan.

79. Rotberg, R. I., Ed. (2003). *When States Fail: Causes and Consequences*. Princeton, NJ: Princeton University Press; Chomsky, N. (2006). *Failed States: The Abuse of Power and the Assault on Democracy*. New York: Metropolitan Books.

80. Goodhand, J. (2006). *Aiding Peace? The Role of NGOs in Armed Conflict*. Boulder: Lynne Rienner.

81. Mills, K., and C. O'Driscoll. (2010). "From Humanitarian Intervention to the Responsibility to Protect." *The International Studies Encyclopedia*. Edited by R. A. Denemark. Blackwell Reference Online. http://www.isacompendium.com/subscriber/tocnode?id=g9781444336597_chunk_g97814443365978_ss1-28.

82. Martin Luther King Jr. and his associates thought about the effects on national opinions of demonstrations and the local reactions against them while planning and conducting their nonviolent actions. King Jr., M. L. (1963). *Why We Can't Wait*. New York: The New American Library.

83. Ury, W. (2000). *The Third Side*. New York: Penguin.

84. Zinnes, D. A. (1980). "Empirical Evidence on the Outbreak of International Violence." *Handbook of Political Conflict: Theory and Research*. Edited by T. R. Gurr. New York: Free Press; Mansfield, E. D. (1994). *Power, Trade, and War*. Princeton, NJ:

Princeton University Press; Mearsheimer, J. J. (2014). *The Tragedy of Great Power Politics*. New York: W.W. Norton.

85. Mearsheimer, J. J. (2014). *The Tragedy of Great Power Politics*. New York: W.W. Norton.

86. The Center for Strategic and International Studies has collected records of cyber incidents around the world as part of its Strategic Technologies Program. See https://www.csis.org/programs/strategic-technologies-program/significant-cyber-incidents.

87. Smoker, P. (1967). "Nation State Escalation and International Integration." *Journal of Peace Research* 1: 60–74; Singer, J. D., and M. Wallace. (1970). "Intergovernmental Organization and the Preservation of Peace, 1816–1964: Some Bivariate Relationships." *International Organization* 24 (Summer): 520–47.

88. Mansfield, E. D. (1994). *Power, Trade, and War*. Princeton, NJ: Princeton University Press: 233.

89. O'Fahey, R. S. (2004). *Environmental Degradation as a Cause of Conflict in Darfur*. Conference Proceedings, Khartoum, University for Peace.

90. Lustgarten, A. (2019). "The Great Climate Migration Has Begun." *New York Times Magazine*.

CHAPTER 6. ESCALATION

1. Conflict escalation has long been a topic of scholarly analysis. See Coleman, J. S. (1957). *Community Conflict*. New York: Free Press; Northrup, T. A. (1989). "The Dynamic of Identity in Personal and Social Conflict." *Intractable Conflicts and Their Transformation*. Edited by L. Kriesberg, T. A. Northrup, and S. J. Thorson. Syracuse: Syracuse University Press: 55–82; Kennedy, R. F. (1971). *Thirteen Days: A Memoir of the Cuban Missile Crisis*. New York: W. W. Norton; Brockner, J., and J. Z. Rubin. (1985). *Entrapment in Escalating Conflicts: A Social Psychological Analysis*. New York: Springer Verlag; Pruitt, D. G., and S. H. Kim. (1986). *Social Conflict: Escalation, Stalemate, and Settlement*. New York: Random House.

2. Glasl's stages were originally published in Konfliktmanagement. Ein Handbuch für Führungskräfte, Beraterinnen und Berater. Those stages were later summarized in English in Jordan, T. (2000). "Glasl's Nine-Stage Model of Conflict Escalation." *International Journal of Conflict Management* 8 (2): 170–74.

3. Pruitt and Kim. (1986). *Social Conflict: Escalation, Stalemate, and Settlement*.

4. For an overview of the history of the conflict and recent negotiations, see Mbaku, J. M. (2020). "The Controversy over the Grand Ethiopian Renaissance Dam." Brookings. https://www.brookings.edu/blog/africa-in-focus/2020/08/05/the-controversy-over-the-grand-ethiopian-renaissance-dam/.

5. Festinger, L. (1957). *A Theory of Cognitive Dissonance*. Evanston, IL: Row, Peterson.

6. The meaning and history of dehumanization is comprehensively reviewed in Bain, P. G., J. Vaes, and J. P. Leyens, Eds. (2014). *Humanness and Dehumanization*. Hove, East Sussex: United Kingdom Psychology Press.

7. Brockner, J., and J. Z. Rubin. (1985). *Entrapment in Escalating Conflicts: A Social Psychological Analysis*. New York: Springer Verlag.

8. Frequently cited examples of this dynamic include the escalation of commitment on the part of the Lyndon Johnson and Richard Nixon administrations during the Vietnam War, and the escalation of commitment in Iraq by George W. Bush. See, for example, Hermann, C. F. (2007). "When Policy is Failing: Applying Theories of U.S. Decision Making in the Iraq War." International Studies Association Annual Convention, Chicago, Illinois

9. Jussim, L. (2001). "Self-fulfilling Prophecies." *International Encyclopedia of the Social & Behavioral Sciences*. Edited by N. J. Smelser and P. B. Baltes. Oxford: Pergamon: 13830–33.

10. Robinson, J. A., C. F. Hermann, and M. C. Hermann. (1969). "Search Under Crisis in Political Gaming and Simulation." *Theory and Research on the Causes of War*. Edited by D. G. Pruitt and R. C. Snyder. Englewood Cliffs, NJ: Prentice Hall; Cohen, R. (1979). *Threat Perception in International Crisis*. Madison, WI: Wisconsin University Press; McGowan, P. J., and C. W. Kegley Jr., Eds. (1980). *Threats, Weapons, and Foreign Policy*. Beverly Hills: Sage.

11. Janis, I. L. (1972). *Victims of Groupthink*. Boston: Houghton Mifflin.

12. Badie, D. (2010). "Groupthink, Iraq, and the War on Terror: Explaining US Policy Shift Toward Iraq." *Foreign Policy Analysis* 6: 277–96. For an example of how discourse analysis has been used to examine "coherence-seeking" in this same case, see Eder, F. (2017). "Making Concurrence-Seeking Visible: Groupthink, Discourse Networks, and the 2003 Iraq War." *Foreign Policy Analysis* 15 (1): 21–42.

13. Hedges, C. (2002). *War Is A Force That Gives Us Meaning*. New York: Public Affairs. For pride in nonviolent action, see Bell, I. P. (1968). *CORE and the Strategy of Non-Violence*. New York: Random House: 115.

14. Vaeroy, H., F. Schneider, and S. O. Fetissov. (2019). "Neurobiology of Aggressive Behavior-Role of Autoantibodies Reactive With Stress-Related Peptide Hormones." *Frontiers in Psychiatry* 10: 872.

15. Scheff, T. J. (1994). *Bloody Revenge: Emotions, Nationalism, and War*. Boulder: Westview; Fontan, V. (2008). *Voices from Post-Saddam Iraq: Living with Terrorism, Insurgency and New Forms of Tyranny*. Westport, CT: Praeger.

16. Botcharova, O. (1998). "Implementation of Track Two Diplomacy: Developing a Model of Forgivenes." *Forgiveness and Reconciliation*. Edited by S. J. Raymond, G. Helmick, and R. L. Petersen. Philadelphia: Templeton Foundation Press: 279–304.

17. The Ohio National Guard fired into a crowd of students at Kent State University, killing four persons and wounding nine others. Heinman, K. J. (1992). "Look Out Kid, You're Gonna Get Hit! Kent State and the Vietnam Anitwar Movement." *Give Peace a Chance: Exploring the Vietnam Anitwar Movement*. Edited by M. Small and W. D. Hoover. Syracuse: Syracuse University Press: 201–22.

18. DeBenedetti, C., and C. Chatfield. (1990). *An American Ordeal: The Antiwar Movement of the Vietnam Era*. Syracuse: Syracuse University Press.

19. Vasquez, J. (1993). *The War Puzzle*. Cambridge, UK: Cambridge University Press.

20. Cuhadar, E., and B. W. Dayton. (2011). "The Social Psychology of Identity and Intergroup Conflict: From Theory to Practice." *International Studies Perspective* 13 (1): 223–73.

21. Flexner, E. (1959). *Century of Struggle*. Cambridge, MA: Harvard University Press.

22. Ikle, F. C. (1971). *Every War Must End*. New York: Columbia University Press.

23. Stutt, R. O. J. H., R. Retkute, M. Bradley, C. A. Gilligan, and J. Colvin. (2020). "A Modelling Framework to Assess the Likely Effectiveness of Facemasks in Combination with 'Lock-down' in Managing the COVID-19 Pandemic." *Proceedings. Mathematical, Physical, and Engineering Sciences* 476 (2238): 20200376.

24. Decker, S. (2021) "Which States Ban Mask Mandates in Schools, and Which Require Masks?" *Education Week*.

25. Bar-Tal, D., and Y. Teichman. (2005). *Stereotypes and Prejudice in Conflict: Representations of Arabs in Israeli Jewish Society*. Cambridge: Cambridge University Press.

26. Finkel, E. J., C. A. Bail, M. Cikara, P. H. Ditto, S. Iyengar, S. Klar, L. Mason, M. C. McGrath, B. Nyhan, D. G. Rand, L. J. Skitka, J. A. Tucker, J. J. V. Bavel, C. S. Wang, and J. N. Druckman. (2020). "Political Sectarianism in America: A Poisonous Cocktail of Othering, Aversion, and Moralization Poses a Threat to Democracy." *Science* 370 (6516): 533–36.

27. Finkel, Bail, Cikara, Ditto, Iyengar, Klar, Mason, McGrath, Nyhan, Rand, Skitka, Tucker, Bavel, Wang, and Druckman. (2020). "Political Sectarianism in America: A Poisonous Cocktail of Othering, Aversion, and Moralization Poses a Threat to Democracy," 533.

28. Skjelsbaek, K., and J. D. Singer. (1971). *Shared IGO Memberships and Dyadic War, 1865–1964*. Conference on the United Nations, Center for International Studies.

29. Li, C., and R. M. Wednesday. (2020). "The Deception and Detriment of US-China Cultural and Educational Decoupling." Brookings. https://www.brookings.edu/blog/order-from-chaos/2020/10/14/the-deception-and-detriment-of-us-china-cultural-and-educational-decoupling/.

30. Hewstone, M., and K. Greenland. (2000). "Intergroup Conflict." *International Journal of Psychology* 35: 136–44.

31. Eckstein, H., Ed. (1966). *Internal War: Problems and Approaches*. New York: Free Press.

32. Gurr, T. R. (1970). *Why Men Rebel*. Princeton, NJ: Princeton University Press.

33. Bercovitch, J., V. Kremenyuk, and I. William Zartman, Eds. (2009). *Sage Handbook of Conflict Resolution*. London: Sage; Hartzell, C. A., and A. Yuen. (2014). *The Durability of Peace*. Oxford: Oxford University Press.

34. Tuchman, B. W. (1958). *The Zimmermann Telegram*. New York: The Viking Press.

35. Pagnucco, R., and J. D. McCarthy. (1992). "Advocating Nonviolent Direct Action in Latin America: The Antecedents and Emergence of SERPAJ." *Religion and Politics in Comparative Perspective*. Edited by B. Misztal and A. Shupe. Westport, CT: Praeger: 125–47. Also see www.aeinstein.org for information about the work of Gene Sharp, in providing information about nonviolence.

36. See the home page of the Great Lakes Commission at https://www.glc.org/.

37. Commission member states include Illinois, Indiana, Michigan, Minnesota, New York, Ohio, Pennsylvania, and Wisconsin. In 1999 the Commission granted Associate Member status to the governments of Quebec and Ontario.

38. See the International Joint Commission home page at https://ijc.org/en.

39. van den Bos, K. (2020). "Unfairness and Radicalization." *Annu Rev Psychol* 71: 563–88.

40. McWorter, G. A., and R. L. Crain. (1967). "Subcommunity Gladiatorial Competition: Civil Rights Leadership as a Competitive Process." *Social Forces* 46 (September): 8–21.

41. Ikle, F. C. (1971). *Every War Must End.* New York: Columbia University Press.

42. Coleman, J. S. (1957). *Community Conflict.* New York: Free Press.

43. Numerous insider accounts of activities by Trump and administrative insiders have been published since the 2020 election. Among them: Bender, M. C. (2021). *Frankly, We Did Win this Election: The Inside Story of How Trump Lost.* New York: Twelve; and Woodward, B., and R. Costa. (2021). *Peril.* New York: Simon & Schuster

44. Funk, C. (2021). "Key Findings: How Americans' Attitudes about Climate Change Differ by Generation, Party and Other Factors." Pew Research Center.

45. Sageman, M. (2004). *Understanding Terror Networks.* Philadelphia: University of Pennsylvania Press.

46. Leggiero, K. (2015). "Countering ISIS Recruitment in Western Nations." *The Journal of Political Risk* 3.

47. For example, when the Soviet rocket units built the bases in Cuba for the nuclear-tipped missiles, they did so following their standard procedures, laying out their insignia on the ground. That revealed the bases that were discovered by U.S. intelligence flights. See Allison, G. (1971). *The Essence of Decision.* Boston: Little, Brown.

48. Despite a long tradition of political civility in Chile, the democratically elected government led by Salvador Allende was subjected to destabilizing efforts, covertly assisted by the U.S. Central Intelligence Agency. A military junta led by General Augusto Pinochet Ugarte seized power on September 11, 1973, and unleashed a bloody repression. Chavkin, S. (1961). *The Murder of Chile: Eyewitness Acounts of the Coup, the Terror, and the Resistance Today.* New York: Everest House.

49. Thus, the German Kaiser believed that once mobilization had been ordered, he was unable to halt or even modify the next steps, and the war came. See Tuchman, B. W. (1962). *The Guns of August.* New York: Macmillan.

50. Quester, G. H. (1970). "Wars Prolonged by Misunderstood Signals." *The Annals of the American Academy of Political and Social Science* 392 (November): 30–39.

51. For an interesting discussion of the relationship between homogeneity and the escalation of violent conflict, see Laitin, D. D. (2007). *Nations, States, and Violence.* Oxford: Oxford University Press.

52. Allen, B. (1996). *Rape Warfare: The Hidden Genocide in Bosnia-Herzegovina and Croatia.* Minneapolis: University of Minnesota Press.

53. Thomas, H. (1977). *The Spanish Civil War.* New York: Harper & Row; Ellwood, S. M. (1991). *The Spanish Civil War.* Oxford, UK: Blackwell.

54. Cooley, J. K. (2002). *Unholy Wars: Afghanistan, America and International Terrorism*. London: Pluto Press: 117–26; Wright, L. (2002, September 16). "The Man Behind bin Laden." *The New Yorker*: 56–85; National Commission on Terrorist Attacks upon the United States., T. H. Kean, and L. Hamilton (2004). *The 9/11 Commission Report: Final Report of the National Commission on Terrorist Attacks upon the United States*. Washington, DC: National Commission on Terrorist Attacks upon the United States.

55. Schock, K. (1999). "People Power and Political Opportunities: Social Movement Mobilization and Outcomes in the Philippines and Burma." *Social Problems* 46 (3): 355–75.

56. Carrion, A. M. (1983). *Puerto Rico: A Political and Cultural History*. New York: W. W. Norton, 276ff.

57. Morgan, W. R. (1970). "Faculty Mediation of Student War Protests." *Protest! Student Activism in America*. Edited by J. Foster and D. Long. New York: Morrow: 365–82; Branch, T. (1988). *Parting the Waters: America in the King Years, 1954–63*. New York: Simon and Schuster: 756–802.

58. Weede, E. (1987). "Some New Evidence on Correlates of Political Violence: Income Inequality, Regime Repressiveness, and Economic Development." *European Sociological Review* 3 (September): 97–108; Muller, E. N. (1985). "Income Inequality, Regime Repressiveness, and Political Violence." *American Sociological Review* 50 (February): 47–61.

59. Vasquez, J. (1993). *The War Puzzle*. Cambridge, UK: Cambridge University Press: 177–84; Wallace, M. D. (1982). "Armaments and Escalation: Two Competing Hypotheses." *International Studies Quarterly* 26 (March): 37–51; Houweling, H. W., and J. G. Siccama. (1981). "The Arms Race—War Relationship: Why Serious Disputes Matter." *Arms Control* 2 (September): 157–97.

60. Leng, R. J., and H. Wheeler. (1979). "Influence Strategies, Success and War." *Journal of Conflict Resolution* 23 (December): 655–84.

61. Woodward, B. (2004). *Plan of Attack*. New York: Simon & Schuster: 66; Snyder, G. H., and P. Diesing. (1977). *Conflict Among Nations: Bargaining, Decision Making, and System Structure in International Crises*. Princeton, NJ: Princeton University Press: 205–07.

62. Piven, F. F., and R. A. Cloward. (1979). *Poor People's Movements*. New York: Vintage Books.

63. Stent, A. (1999). *Russia and Germany Reborn: Unification, the Soviet Collapse, and the New Europe*. Princeton, NJ: Princeton University Press.

CHAPTER 7. DE-ESCALATION

1. For a review of spoiling behavior during peace processes, see Greenhill, K. M. and S. Major. (2006/07). "The Perils of Profiling: Civil War Spoilers and the Collapse of Intrastate Peace Accords." *International Security* 31 (3): 7–40; Stedman, J. S. (1997). "Spoiler Problems in Peace Processes." *International Security* 22 (2): 5–53.

2. Conflict 'ripeness' is explored in Zartman, I. W. (2005). "Ripeness: The Hurting Stalemate and Beyond." *International Conflict Resolution After the Cold War*. Edited by N. R. Council. Washington, DC: National Academies Press: 225–50.

3. Zartman, I. W., and M. Berman. (1982). *The Practical Negotiator*. New Haven, CT: Yale University Press.

4. National Security Council. (2021). "Department of Defense Climate Risk Analysis." Department of Defense, Washington, DC.

5. Information about the COP26 conference and its outcomes can be found at https://ukcop26.org/.

6. Keethaponcalan, S. I. (2016). "Reshaping the Non-Aligned Movement: Challenges and Vision." *Bandung: Journal of the Global South* 3 (1): 4.

7. Text of the Abrahamic Accord can be found at https://www.state.gov/the-abraham-accords/.

8. AFP and TOI Staff. (2021). "A Year after Normalization, Israel-UAE Ties Continue to Bear Fruit." *The Times of Israel*.

9. Goldstein, A. P., and G. Y. Michaels. (1985). *Empathy: Development, Training, and Consequences*. Hillsdale, NJ: Lawrence Erlbaum Associates. To take the role of other persons is a basic human capability and essential for the development of a sense of self. Mead, G. H. (1934). *Mind, Self and Society*. Chicago, IL: University of Chicago Press.

10. Research supporting the beneficial impact of contact between enemy groups is extensive in the field of conflict transformation. For examples, see Bruneau, E., B. Hameiri, S. L. Moore-Berg, and N. Kteily. (2021). "Intergroup Contact Reduces Dehumanization and Meta-Dehumanization: Cross-Sectional, Longitudinal, and Quasi-Experimental Evidence From 16 Samples in Five Countries." *Personality and Social Psychology Bulletin* 47 (6): 906–20; Kelman, H. C. (1995). "Contributions of an Unoffical Conflict Resolution Effort to the Israeli-Palestinian Breakthrough." *Negotiation Journal* 11 (January): 19–27; Fisher, R., Ed. (2005). *Paving the Way: Contributions of Interactive Conflict Resolution to Peacemaking*. Lanham: Lexington Books; Premaratna, N., and R. Bleiker. (2010). "Art and Peacebuilding: How Theatere Transforms Conflict in Sri Lanka." *Palgrave Advances in Peacebuilding: Critical Developments and Approaches*. Edited by O. P. Richmond. London: Palgrave.

11. Goldstein, A. P., and G. Y. Michaels. (1985). *Empathy: Development, Training, and Consequences*. Hillsdale, NJ: Lawrence Erlbaum Associates: 4–7.

12. Broockman, D., and J. Kalla. (2016). "Durably Reducing Transphobia: A Field Experiment on Door-to-Door Canvassing." *Science* 352 (6282): 220–24.

13. Klimecki, O. M. (2019). "The Role of Empathy and Compassion in Conflict Resolution." *Emotion Review* 11 (4): 310–25.

14. Lopez, C. C. (2011). "The Struggle for Wholeness: Addressing Individual and Collective Trauma in Violence-Ridden Societies." *EXPLORE* 7 (5): 300–13.

15. Scheff, T. J. (1994). *Bloody Revenge: Emotions, Nationalism, and War*. Boulder: Westview.

16. Volkan, V. D., and L. Zintl. (1993). *Life After Loss: The Lessons of Grief*. London: Routledge.

17. The case for such impacts in Timor-Leste and Solomon Islands is found in Guthrey, H. L. (2015). *Victim Healing and Truth Commissions: Transforming Pain through Voice in Solomon Islands and Timor-Leste*. Berlin: Springer

18. Tunamsifu, S. P. (2018). "Memorialisation as an Often Neglected Aspect in the Consolidation of Transitional Justice: Case Study of the Democratic Republic of the Congo." *African Journal on Conflict Resolution* 18: 33–57.

19. DeBenedetti, C., and C. Chatfield. (1990). *An American Ordeal: The Antiwar Movement of the Vietnam Era*. Syracuse: Syracuse University Press; Marullo, S., and J. Lofland, Eds. (1990). *Peace Action in the Eighties*. New Brunswick: Rutgers University Press; Meyer, D. S. (1990). *A Winter of Discontent: The Nu lear Freeze and American Politics*. New York: Praeger.

20. McRoberts, K. (1988). *Quebec: Social Change and Political Crisis*. Toronto: McClelland and Stewart.

21. Holland, J. (1999). *Hope Against History*. New York: Henry Holt.; McCartney, C., Ed. (1999). *Striking a Balance: The Northern Ireland Peace Process*. London: Conciliation Resources; see also cain.ulst.ac.uk/.

22. Kennedy, R. F. (1971). *Thirteen Days: A Memoir of the Cuban Missile Crisis*. New York: W. W. Norton: 40.

23. Lebow, R. N., and J. G. Stein. (1994). *We All Lost the Cold War*. Princeton, NJ: Princeton University Press: 110–45.

24. Holsti, O. R., R. A. Brody, and R. C. North. (1964). "Measuring Affect and Action in International Reaction Models: Empirical Materials from the 1962 Cuban Crisis." *Journal of Peace Research* 3–4: 170–89.

25. Breslauer, G. W., and P. E. Tetlock, Eds. (1991). *Learning in U.S. and Soviet Foreign Policy*. Boulder, CO: Westview Press.

26. Pruitt, D. G. (2009). "Escalation and De-escalation in Asymmetric Conflict." *Dynamics of Asymmetric Conflict* 2 (1): 23–31.

27. Pan, Z. (2018). "A Study of China's No-First-Use Policy on Nuclear Weapons." *Journal for Peace and Nuclear Disarmament* 1 (1): 115–36.

28. Krasner, S. D. (1983). *International Regimes*. Ithaca, NY: Cornell University Press.

29. Morris, A. D. (1993). "Birmingham Confrontation Reconsidered: An Analysis of the Dynamics and Tactics of Mobilization." *American Sociological Review* 58 (October): 621–36.

30. Fisher, R. (1964). "Fractionating Conflict." *International Conflict and Behavioral Science*. Edited by R. Fisher. New York: Basic Books.

31. Sherif, M. (1966). *In Common Predicament*. Boston: Houghton Mifflin.

32. Sloat, A. (2020). "Horror at the 9/11 Attacks Contributed to Peace in Northern Ireland." Brookings Institute.

33. Leon-Perez, J. M., G. Notelaers, and J. M. Leon-Rubio. (2016). "Assessing the Effectiveness of Conflict Management Training in a Health Sector Organization: Evidence from Subjective and Objective Indicators." *European Journal of Work and Organizational Psychology* 25 (1): 1–12; Romain Dagenhardt, D., A. Heideman, V. Knoche, and T. Freiburger. (2021). "An Evaluation of a De-escalation Conflict

Management Training in a Behavioral Health Hospital Setting." *International Journal of Conflict Management* 33 (1).

34. Johnson, D. W., and R. T. Johnson. (1996). "Conflict Resolution and Peer Mediation Programs in Elementary and Secondary Schools: A Review of the Research." *Review of Educational Research* 66: 459–506.

35. Orpinas, P., G. S. Parcel, A. McAlister, and R. Frankowski. (1995). "Violence Prevention in Middle Schools: A Pilot Evaluation." *J Adolesc Health* 17 (6): 360–71.

36. Kriesberg, L. (1995). "Varieties of Mediating Activities and of Mediators." *Resolving International Conflicts*. Edited by J. Bercovitch. Boulder, CO: Lynne Rienner: 219–33.

37. Saunders, H. (2005). *Politics is about Relationship: A Blueprint for the Citizens' Century*. New York: Palgrave.

38. Schiff, A. (2010). "'Quasi Track-One' Diplomacy: An Analysis of the Geneva Process in the Israeli-Palestinian Conflict." *International Studies Perspectives* 11 (2): 93–111.

39. The reasons for this correlation are complex. See Wilkinson, R. (2004). "Why is Violence More Common Where Inequality Is Greater?" *Ann N Y Acad Sci* 1036: 1–12. See also Conceição, P. (2020). *Human Development Report 2020*. New York: UN Development Programme.

40. Cederman, L.-E., N. B. Weidmann, and K. S. Gleditsch. (2011). "Horizontal Inequalities and Ethnonationalist Civil War. A Global Comparison." *American Political Science Review* 105: 495.

41. Gurr, T. R. (1970). *Why Men Rebel*. Princeton, NJ: Princeton University Press.

42. Kunst, J. R., R. Fischer, J. Sidanius, and L. Thomsen. (2017). "Preferences for Group Dominance Track and Mediate the Effects of Macro-level Social Inequality and Violence across Societies." *Proceedings of the National Academy of Sciences of the United States of America* 114 (21): 5407–12.

43. Sánchez-Ancochea, D. (2020). *The Costs of Inequality in Latin America: Lessons and Warnings for the Rest of the World*. New York: Bloomsbury Publishing Inc.

44. There are many excellent books on the history of the labor movement in the United States. Among them is Dray, P. (2011). *There Is Power in a Union: The Epic Story of Labor in America*. New York: Anchor.

45. Kristian, S., T. Olle, and M. S. Gyda. (2009). "Conflict Resolution and Democratisation in the Aftermath of the 2004 Tsunami: A Comparative Study of Aceh and Sri Lanka." *PCD Journal*: 129–50.

46. Stedman, S. J., D. Rothchild, and E. M. Cousens, Eds. (2002). *Ending Civil Wars: The Implementation of Peace Agreements*. Boulder: Lynne Rienner; Wiseman, H., and A. M. Taylor. (1981). *From Rhodesia to Zimbabwe: The Politics of Transition*. New York: Pergamon.

47. See https://peacekeeping.un.org/sites/default/files/peacekeeping_missions_fact_sheet_july2021_en.pdf.

48. Kriesberg, L. (1992). *International Conflict Resolution: The U.S.-USSR and Middle East Cases*. New Haven, CT: Yale University Press.

49. Wagschal, U., and T. Metz. (2016). "A Demographic Peace? Youth Bulges and Other Population-Related Causes of Domestic Conflict." *Statistics, Politics and Policy* 7 (1–2): 55–97.

50. Keashly, L., and R. J. Fisher. (1996). "Complemenatity and Coordination of Conflict Interventions: Taking a Contigency Perspective." *Resolving International Conflicts*. Edited by J. Bercovitch. Boulder, CO: Lynne Rienner: 235–61.

51. Kriesberg, L. (2005). "Nature, Dynamics, and Phases of Intractability." *Grasping the Nettle : Analyzing Cases of Intractable Conflicts*. Edited by C. A. Crocker, F. O. Hampson, and P. Aall. Washington, DC: United States Institute of Peace: 65–97.

52. Lund, M. S. (1996). *Preventing Violent Conflicts*. Washington, DC: U.S. Institute of Peace Press; McMahon, P. C. (2007). *Taming Ethnic Hatred: Ethnic Cooperation and Transnational Networks in Eastern Europe*. Syracuse, NY: Syracuse University Press.

53. Dayton, B. W. (2010). "Crisis Management." *Oxford International Encyclopedia of Peace*. Oxford: Oxford University Press: 572–81.

54. Boin, A., P. t'Hart, E. Stern, and B. Sundelius. (2005). *The Politics of Crisis Management*. Cambridge: Cambridge University Press.

55. Azar, E. A., P. Jureidini, and M. Ronals. (1978). "Protracted Social Conflict: Theory and Practice in the Middle East." *Journal of Palestine Studies* 29 (Autumn): 41–60; Kriesberg, L., T. A. Northrup, and S. J. Thorson, Eds. (1989). *Intractable Conflicts and Their Transformation*. Syracuse: Syracuse University Press; Crocker, C. A., F. O. Hampson, and P. Aall, Ed. (2005). *Grasping the Nettle: Analyzing Cases of Intractable Conflicts*. Washington, DC: U.S. Institute of Peace Press.

56. Kriesberg, L. (1998). "The Phases of Destructive Conflicts: Communal Conflicts and Proactive Solutions." *Peace in the Midst of Wars: Preventing and Managing International Ethnic Conflicts*. Edited by D. Carment and P. James. Columbia, SC: University of South Carolina Press: 33–60.

57. See, for example, Walt, S. M. (1999). "Never Say Never: Wishful Thinking on Democracy and War." *Foreign Affairs* 78 (1): 146–51.

58. United Nations. (1995). "United Nations Peacekeeping, Update: December 1994," 31; United Nations. (1995). "The United Nations and the Situation in the Former Yugoslavia." United Nations Reproduction Service, New York; Ackermann, A. (2000). *Making Peace Prevail: Preventing Violent Conflict in Macedonia*. Syracuse, NY: Syracuse University Press.

59. Gibbs, D. N. (2009). *First Do No Harm : Humanitarian Intervention and the Destruction of Yugoslavia*. Nashville: Vanderbilt University Press.

60. See, for instance, McConnell, A., and L. Drennan. (2006). "Mission Impossible? Planning and Preparing for Crises." *Journal of Contingencies and Crisis Management* 14 (2): 59–70.

61. Brecher, M. (1993). *Crises in World Politics*. Oxford: Pergamon: 84–85, 250–53.

62. Kriesberg, L. (1972). "International Nongovernmental Organizations and Transnational Integration." *International Associations* 24 (11): 520–25; Pentz, M. J., and G. Slovo. (1981). "The Political Significance of Pugwash." *Knowledge and Power in a Global Society*. Edited by W. M. Evan. Beverly Hills: Sage: 175–203; Chufrin,

G. I., and H. H. Saunders. (1993). "A Public Peace Process." *Negotiation Journal* 9 (April): 155–77; Rotbalt, J. (1972). *Scientists in the Quest for Peace: A History of the Pugwash Conferences*. Cambridge, MA: MIT Press.

63. In December 1993, Kriesberg traveled with a group of the U.S. Interreligious Committee for Peace in the Middle East to Israel, Syria, Egypt, and Jordan. The group met with government officials, academics, and other persons, with varying opinions. Nearly everyone spoke of the irreversibility of what had happened.

64. Evangelista, M. (1999). *Unarmed Forces: The Transnational Movement to End the Cold War*. Ithaca: Cornell University Press; Wiseman, G. (2002). *Concepts of Non-provocative Defence: Ideas and Practices in International Security*. New York: Palgrave.

65. Dayton, B. W., and L. Kriesberg, Eds. (2009). *Conflict Transformation and Peacebuilding: Moving From Violence to Sustainable Peace*. Oxford, UK: Routledge.

66. For a timeline of the gay rights movement, see http://www.pbs.org/wgbh/americanexperience/features/timeline/stonewall/.

67. See "Report of the Truth and Reconciliation Commission," volume 2, chapter 7, at www.polity.org.za/govdocs/commissions/1998/trc/2chap7.htm. For an account of the National Peace Accord, see Gastrow, P. (1995). *Bargaining for Peace*. Washington, DC: U.S. Institute of Peace.

68. See Osgood, C. E. (1962). *An Alternative to War or Surrender*. Urbana: University of Illinois Press; Rapoport, A. (1967). "Escape from Paradox." *Scientific American* 217: 50–59; Axelrod, R. (1984). *The Evolution of Cooperation*. New York: Basic Books.

69. Etzioni, A. (1967). "The Kennedy Experiment." *The Western Political Quarterly* 20 (June): 361–80.

70. Based on Arthur Schlesinger Jr. interview by Kriesberg, New York, October 9, 1978; and Ted Sorenson, interview by Kriesberg, New York, March 20, 1979. See also Cousins, N. (1972). *The Impossible Triumverate*. New York: Norton; Kriesberg, L. (1981). "Noncoercive Inducements in U.S.-Soviet Conflicts: Ending the Occupation of Austria and Nuclear Weapons Tests." *Journal of Political and Military Sociology* 9 (Spring): 1–16.

71. Goldstein, J. S., and J. R. Freeman. (1990). *Three-Way Street: Strategic Reciprocity in World Politics*. Chicago: The University of Chicago Press.

72. For an overview of the work of the Elders, see https://theelders.org/.

CHAPTER 8. MEDIATION

1. See, for instance, McCorkle, S., and M. J. Reese. (2018). *Mediation Theory and Practice*. Thousand Oaks: Sage; Kolb, D. M. (1994). *When Talk Works: Profiles of Mediator*. San Francisco: Jossey-Bass; Moore, C. W. (1996). *The Mediation Process: Practical Strategies for Resolving Conflict*. San Francisco: Jossey-Bass; Laue, J. (1973). "Intervenor Roles: A Review." *Crisis and Change* III (Fall): 4–5; and Bush, R. A. B., and J. P. Folger. (2005). *The Promise of Mediation: The Transformative Approach to Conflict*. San Francisco: Jossey-Bass.

2. For a discussion of the difference between interest, rights, and power as processes by which conflict is resolved, see chapter 1 in Ury, W. (1988). *Getting Disputes Resolved: Designing Systems to Cut the Costs of Conflict*. San Francisco: Jossey-Bass.

3. Moore, C. W. (2003). *The Mediation Process: Practical Strategies for Resolving Conflict*. San Francisco: Jossey-Bass.

4. See Wilkenfeld, J., K. Yong, V. Asal, and D. Quinn. (2003). "Mediating International Crises." *Journal of Conflict Resolution* 47 (3): 279–301; Wallensteen, P., and I. Svensson. (2014). "Talking Peace: International Mediation in Armed Conflicts." *Journal of Peace Research* 51 (2): 315–27.

5. Laue, J. (1973). "Intervenor Roles: A Review." *Crisis and Change* III (Fall): 4–5.

6. See Greig, J. M., and P. F. Diehl. (2009). "Softening Up: Making Conflicts More Amendable to Negotiation." *International Mediation: New Approaches and Findings*. Edited by J. Bercovitch and S. S. Gartner. New York: Routledge.

7. Whitfield, T. (2015). *The Basque Conflict and ETA: The Difficulties of an Ending*. Washington DC: U.S. Institute of Peace.

8. Arafat told Clinton that he was not ready for Camp David II. Hanieh, A. (2000). "The Camp David Papers." Ramallah, Palestine, Al-Ayyam Newspaper: 1–98; Ross, D. (2004). *The Missing Peace": The Inside Story of the Fight for Middle East Peace*. New York: Farrar, Straus and Giroux; Malley, R. (2004, October 7). "Israel and the Arafat Question." *The New York Review of Books*: 19–23.

9. Garcia, A. (1991). "Dispute Resolution without Disputing: How the Interactional Organization of Mediation Hearings Minimizes Argument." *American Sociological Review* 56: 818–35. Wedge, B. (1971). "A Psychiatric Model for Intercession in Intergroup Conflict." *Journal of Applied Behavioral Science* 7 (6): 733–61.

10. Carter, J. (1982). *Keeping Faith*. New York: Bantam Books.

11. Rubin, J. Z., and B. R. Brown. (1975). *The Social Psychology of Bargaining and Negotiation*. New York: Academic Press.

12. Golan, M. (1976). *The Secret Conversations of Henry Kissinger: Step-by-Step Diplomacy in the Middle East*. New York: Bantam.

13. Brainstorming was used in developing the National Peace Accord in South Africa at the planning meeting on June 22, 1991.

14. Amsler, L. B., J. K. Martinez, and S. E. Smith. (2015). "Christina Merchant and the State of Dispute System Design." *Conflict Resolution Quarterly* 33 (S1): S7–S26.

15. Ways that one mediator does this are reported in Forester, J. (1994). "Lawrence Susskind: Activist Mediation." *When Talk Works: Profiles of Mediator*. Edited by D. M. Kolb. San Francisco: Jossey-Bass: 309–54.

16. Babbitt, E. F., and E. L. Lutz, Eds. (2009). *Human Rights and Conflict Resolution in Context*. Syracuse, NY: Syracuse University Press.

17. Adjei, M. (2019). "Women's Participation in Peace Processes: A Review of Literature." *Journal of Peace Education* 16 (2): 133–54.

18. This was done in the Israeli-Egyptian negotiations mediated by President Carter and his associates at Camp David. See Fisher, R. (1981). "Playing the Wrong

Game?" *Dynamics of Third Party Intervention: Kissinger in the Middle East*. Edited by J. Z. Rubin. New York: Praeger: 95–121; and Fisher, R., E. Kopelman, and A. K. Schneider. (1994). *Beyond Machiavelli: Tools for Coping with Conflict*. New York: Penguin: 126–32.

19. A statement by the FMCS can be found here: https://www.fmcs.gov/fmcs-statement-on-labor-agreement-between-bath-iron-works-and-international-association-of-machinists-local-s6/.

20. This happened as 1994 efforts to restore Bertrand Aristide to the presidency of Haiti were coming to a climax. Following a period of UN-imposed sanctions and failed negotiations, a U.S. invasion force was dispatched to force the transfer of power from the Haitian military rulers. Former President Carter, Senator Sam Nunn, and former Chairman of the Joint Chiefs of Staff Colin Powell were sent to Haiti and arranged a nonviolent transfer of power. The Haitian military leadership, General Raoul Cedras, General Philippe Biamby, and Chief of Police Lieutenant Colonel Michel Francois went into exile. Tata, R. J. 2001. "Haiti." Microsoft Encarta Online Encyclopedia.

21. Mattes, M., and B. Savun. (2009). "Fostering Peace After Civil War: Commitment Problems and Agreement Design." *International Studies Quarterly* 53: 737–59.

22. For example, in Pennsylvania and Upstate New York efforts to manage conflict over the extraction of natural gas from shale deep below the surface through a process known as fracking has focused on finding the appropriate compensation for landowners and communities where fracking is being proposed.

23. Carter, J. (1982). *Keeping Faith*. New York: Bantam Books: 392; see also Babbitt, E. F. (1994). "Jimmy Carter: The Power of Moral Suasion in International Mediation." *When Talk Works: Profiles of Mediator*. Edited by D. M. Kolb. San Francisco: Jossey-Bass.

24. Chollet, D. (2011). *The Unquiet American: Richard Holbrooke in the World*. Powder Springs, GA: Big River Books.

25. De Girolamo, D. (2019). "The Mediation Process: Challenges to Neutrality and the Delivery of Procedural Justice." *Oxford Journal of Legal Studies* 39 (4): 834–55; Carnevale, P. J., and S. Arad. (1996). "Bias and Impartiality in International Mediation." *Resolving International Conflicts: The Theory and Practice of Mediation*. Edited by J. Bercovitch. Boulder, CO: Lynne Rienner; De Girolamo, D. (2019). "The Mediation Process: Challenges to Neutrality and the Delivery of Procedural Justice." *Oxford Journal of Legal Studies* 39 (4): 834–55; Mayer, B. S. (2004). *Beyond Neutrality: Confronting the Crisis in Conflict Resolution*. San Francisco: Jossey-Bass.

26. Ratner, S. R. (2000). "Does International Law Matter in Preventing Ethnic Conflicts?" *New York University Journal of International Law and Politics* 32 (3): 591–698; Babbitt, E. F., and E. L. Lutz, Eds. (2009). *Human Rights and Conflict Resolution in Context*. Syracuse, NY: Syracuse University Press; Babbitt, E. F. (Forthcoming). *Principled Peace: Conflict Resolution and Human Rights in Intra-State Conflicts*. Ann Arbor, MI: University of Michigan Press; Kaufman, E., and I. Bisharat. (2002, March). "Introducing Human Rights into Conflict Resolution: The Relevance for the Israeli-Palestinian Peace Process." *Journal of Human Rights* 1 (1): 71–91.

27. Kriesberg, L. (1995). "Varieties of Mediating Activities and of Mediators." *Resolving International Conflicts*. Edited by J. Bercovitch. Boulder, CO: Lynne Rienner: 219–33.

Also see the discussion of an important kind of quasi mediator, the insider-partial mediator, in Wehr, P., and J. P. Lederach. (1991). "Mediating Conflict in Central America." *Journal of Peace Research* 28 (1): 85–98.

28. Princen, T. (1994). "Joseph Elder: Quiet Peacemaking." *When Talk Works: Profiles of Mediator*. Edited by D. M. Kolb. San Francisco: Jossey-Bass: 427–58; Yarrow, C. H. M. (1978). *Quaker Experiences in International Conciliation*. New Haven, CT: Yale University Press.

29. van der Merwe, H. W. (2000). *Peacemaking in South Africa: A Life in Conflict Resolution*. Cape Town: Tafelberg.

30. Strimling, A. (2002). "The Federal Mediation and Conciliation Service: A Partner in International Conflict Prevention." Unpublished report, February 27.

31. Christian-Smith, J., and K. Abhold. (2015). "Measuring what Matters: Setting Measurable Objectives to Achieve Sustainable Groundwater Management in California." Union of Concerned Scientists.

32. Fisher, R. (1997). *Interactive Conflict Resolution*. Syracuse: Syracuse University Press. See also Fisher, R. J. (2005). *Paving the Way: Contributions of Interactive Conflict Resolution to Peacemaking*. Lanham: Lexington Books.

33. Kelman, H. C. (1995). "Contributions of an Unoffical Conflict Resolution Effort to the Israeli-Palestinian Breakthrough." *Negotiation Journal* 11 (January): 19–27; Cuhadar-Gurkaynak, C. E. (2004). *Evaluating Track Two Diplomacy in Pre-negotiation: A Comparative Assessment of Track Two Initiatives on Water and Jerusalem in the Israeli-Palestinian Conflict*. Ph.D. dissertation, Syracuse University.

34. Montville, J. V. (1991). "Transnationalism and the Role of Track-Two Diplomacy." *Approaches to Peace: An Intellectual Map*. Edited by W. S. Thompson and K. M. Jensen. Washington, DC: U.S. Institute of Peace: 253–69.

35. See McDonald, J. W. (1991). "Further Explorations in Track Two Diplomacy." *Timing the De-Escalation of International Conflicts*. Edited by L. Kriesberg and S. J. Thorson. Syracuse: Syracuse University Press: 201–20; Davies, J. and E. Kaufman, Eds. (2002). *Second Track / Citizens' Diplomacy*. Lanham: Rowman & Littlefield; and Fisher, R. J. (2005). *Paving the Way: Contributions of Interactive Conflict Resolution to Peacemaking*. Lanham: Lexington Books.

36. Evan, W. M., Ed. (1981). *Knowledge and Power in a Global Society*. Beverly Hills: Sage; Kriesberg, L. (1972). "International Nongovernmental Organizations and Transnational Integration." *International Associations* 24 (11): 520–25.

37. Many such dialogue groups have been organized between Jews and Palestinians in Israel and elsewhere in the world, working with Jews and Palestinians in the Diaspora. For discussions about the theory and practice of such groups, see Fisher, R. (1997). *Interactive Conflict Resolution*. Syracuse: Syracuse University Press: 121–41.

38. Dayton, B. W. (2010). "Dialogue Processes." *Oxford Encyclopedia of Peace*. Edited by N. Yong. Oxford: Oxford University Press.

39. Cook, A. L., R. Troeger, A. Shah, P. Donahue, and M. Curley. (2020). "Re-envisioning Family-School-Community Partnerships: Reflecting on Five Years of

Dialogues on Race Programming within an Urban School Community." *The School Community Journal* 30 (2): 121–54.

40. Pentz, M. J., and G. Slovo. (1981). "The Political Significance of Pugwash." *Knowledge and Power in a Global Society*. Edited by W. M. Evan. Beverly Hills: Sage: 175–203; Rotblat, J. (1972). *Scientists in the Quest for Peace: A History of the Pugwash Conferences*. Cambridge, MA: MIT Press. For current activities, see http://www.Pugwash.org.

41. Kolb, D. M. (1983). *The Mediators*. Cambridge, MA: MIT Press.

42. Raskin, A. H. (1983). "The Newspaper Strike: A Step-by-Step Account." *The 50% Solution*. Edited by I. W. Zartman. New Haven, CT: Yale University Press: 4520480.

43. Yarrow, C. H. M. (1978). *Quaker Experiences in International Conciliation*. New Haven, CT: Yale University Press.

44. Holland, J. (1999). *Hope Against History*. New York: Henry Holt; Mitchell, G. J. (2000). *Making Peace*. Berkeley: University of California Press.

45. Carnevale, P. J. (2002). "Mediating from Strength." *Studies in International Mediation*. Edited by J. Bercovitch. New York: Palgrave Macmillan: 25–40.

46. Gibbs, D. N. (2009). *First Do No Harm : Humanitarian Intervention and the Destruction of Yugoslavia*. Nashville: Vanderbilt University Press; Cohen, R. (1995). "Taming the Bullies of Bosnia." *The New York Times Magazine* (December 17): 58–63, 76–78, 90, 95; Holbrooke, R. C. (1998). *To End a War*. New York: Random House.

47. Many analysts make similar distinctions; for example, Princen, in *Intermediaries in International Conflict*, distinguishes between neutral mediators and principal mediators. For a discussion of transformative mediation, see Bush, R. A. B., and J. P. Folger. (2005). *The Promise of Mediation: The Transformative Approach to Conflict*. San Francisco: Jossey-Bass.

48. Gulliver, P. H. (1979). *Disputes and Negotiations: A Cross-Cultural Perspective*. New York: Academic Press; Lederach, J. P. (1995). *Preparing for Peace: Conflict Transformation Across Cultures*. Syracuse: Syracuse University Press; Carnevale, P. J., Y. S. Cha, C. Wan, and S. Fraidin. (2003). "Culture and the Mediation of Disputes." *Culture and Negotiation: Integrative Approaches to Theory and Research*. Edited by M. Gelfand and J. Brett. Palo Alto: Stanford University Press; Carnevale, P. J., Y. S. Cha, C. Wan, and S. Fraidin. (2004). "Adaptive Third Parties in the Cultural Milieu." *Handbook of Negotiation and Culture*. Edited by M. Gelfand and J. Brett. Palo Alto: Stanford University Press: 280–94. For a general discussion of culture and conflict resolution, see Avruch, K. (1998). *Culture and Conflict Resolution*. Washington, DC: U.S. Institute of Peace.

49. Wall Jr., J. A., and R. R. Callister. (1995). "Ho'oponopono: Some Lessons From Hawaiian Mediation." *Negotiation Journal* 11 (January): 45–54; Shook, E. V., and L. K. Kwan. (1991). "Ho'oponopono: Straightening Family Relationships in Hawaii." *Conflict Resolution: Cross-Cultural Perspectives*. Edited by K. Avruch, P. Black, and J. Scimecca. New York: Greenwood Press. Also see Salem, P., Ed. (1997). *Conflict Resolution in the Arab World: Selected Essays*. Beirut: American University of Beirut.

50. Keashly, L., and R. J. Fisher. (1996). "Complemenatity and Coordination of Conflict Interventions: Taking a Contigency Perspective." *Resolving International*

Conflicts. Edited by J. Bercovitch. Boulder, CO: Lynne Rienner: 235–61; Mitchell, C. (1993). "The Process and Stages of Mediation." *Making War and Waging Peace: Foreign Intervention in Africa*. Edited by D. R. Smock. Washington, DC: U.S. Institute of Peace: 139–59; Kriesberg, L. (1992). *International Conflict Resolution: The U.S.-USSR and Middle East Cases*. New Haven, CT: Yale University Press; Carnevale, P. J., and D. Conlon. (1988). "Time Pressure and Strategic Choice in Mediation." *Organizational Behavior and Human Decision Processes* 42: 111–33.

51. Lindenmayer, E., and J. L. Kaye. (2009). *A Choice for Peace: The Story of Forty-One Days of Mediation in Kenya*. New York: International Peace Institute.

52. Kriesberg, L. (2001). "Mediation and the Transformation of the Israeli-Palestinian Conflict." *Journal of Peace Research* 38 (3): 373–92.

53. Ross, M. H. (2000). "Creating the Conditions for Peacemaking: Theories of Practice in Ethnic Conflict Resolution." *Ethnic and Racial Studies* 23 (6): 1002–34; Ross, M. H., and J. Rothman. (1999). *Theory and Practice in Ethnic Conflict and Management: Theorizing Success and Failure*. Basingstoke: Macmillan; d'Estree, T. P., L. A. Fast, J. N. Weiss, and M. S. Jakobsen. (2001). "Changing the Debate about 'Success' in Conflict Resolution." *Negotiation Journal* 17 (2): 101–13.

54. For a general discussion of the challenges of evaluating conflict resolution interventions, see Gurkaynak, E. C., B. Dayton, and T. Paffenholz. (2009). "Evaluation in Conflict Resolution and Peacebuilding." *Handbook of Conflict Analysis and Resolution*. Edited by D. J. D. Sandole, S. Byrne, I. Sandole-Staroste, and J. Senehi. London: Routledge.

55. Kressel, K., and D. G. Pruitt. (1989). "Conclusion: A Research Perspective on the Mediation of Social Conflict." *Mediation Research*. Edited by K. Kressel and D. G. Pruitt. San Francisco: Jossey-Bass: 394–435.

56. Kressel, K., and D. G. Pruitt. (1989). *Mediation Research*. San Francisco: Jossey-Bass; Hedeen, T., and P. G. Coy. (2000). "Community Mediation and the Court System: The Ties that Bind." *Mediation Quarterly* 17 (4).

57. Butterworth, R. (1976). *Managing Interstate Conflict 1945–1974*. Pittsburgh, PA: University of Pittsburgh Press.

58. Bercovitch, J. (1986). "International Mediation: A Study of the Incidence, Strategies and Conditions of Successful Outcomes." *Cooperation and Conflict* 21: 155–68.

59. Bercovitch, J. (2005). "Mediation in the Most Resistant Cases." *Grasping the Nettle: Analyzing Cases in Intractable Conflicts*. Edited by C. A. Crocker, F. O. Hampson, and P. R. Aall. Washington, DC: U.S. Institute of Peace Press: 99–121.

60. Kressel, K., and D. G. Pruitt. (1989). *Mediation Research*. San Francisco: Jossey-Bass.

61. Wolf, P. (1978). "International Social Structure and the Resolution of International Conflicts." *Research in Social Movements, Conflicts and Change*. Edited by L. Kriesberg. Greenwich, CT: JAI Press: 35–53.

62. Hedeen, T. (2004). "The Evolution and Evaluation of Community Mediation:Limited Research Suggests Unlimited Progress." *Conflict Resolution Quarterly* 22 (1–2): 101–33.

63. Bercovitch, J., and J. Langley. (1993). "The Nature of the Dispute and the Effectiveness of International Mediation." *Journal of Conflict Resolution* 37 (4): 670–91.

64. Bercovitch, J., and J. Karl Derouen. (2004). "Mediation in Internaliz4d Ethnic Conflicts: Assessing the Determinants of a Successful Process." *Armed Forces & Society* 30 (2): 147–79.

65. Rubin, J. Z., and B. R. Brown. (1975). *The Social Psychology of Bargaining and Negotiation*. New York: Academic Press.

66. Douglas, A. (1962). *Industrial Peacemaking*. New York: Columbia University Press.

67. Kochan, T. A., and T. Jick. (1978). "The Public Sector Mediation Process." *Journal of Conflict Resolution* 22 (June): 210–40.

68. Pressman, J. (2003). "Visions in Collision: What Happened at Camp David and Taba?" *International Security* 28 (2): 5–43; Malley, R. (2004, October 7). "Israel and the Arafat Question." *The New York Review of Books*: 19–23.

69. Kriesberg, L. (2015). *Realizing Peace: A Constructive Conflict Approach*. New York: Oxford University Press.

70. Rubin, J. Z., and B. R. Brown. (1975). *The Social Psychology of Bargaining and Negotiation*. New York: Academic Press.

71. Brookmire, D. A., and F. Sistrunk. (1980). "The Effects of Perceived Ability and Impartiality of Mediators and Time Pressure Negotiation." *Journal of Conflict Resolution* 24 (June): 311–27.

72. Kressel and Pruitt. (1989). *Mediation Research*. Such outcomes are not necessarily more just or fair.

73. Walton, R. E. (1968). "Interpersonal Confrontation and Third Party Functions: A Case Study." *Journal of Applied Behavioral Sciences* 4 (3): 327–50.

74. Kressel, K., and D. G. Pruitt. (1989). "Conclusion: A Research Perspective on the Mediation of Social Conflict." *Mediation Research*. Edited by K. Kressel and D. G. Pruitt. San Francisco: Jossey-Bass: 394–435.

75. Kriesberg, L. (2002). "The Relevance of Reconciliation Actions in the Breakdown of Israeli-Palestinian Negotiations, 2000." *Peace & Change* 27 (4): 546–71. On the importance of public engagement in a peace process, see Saunders, H. H. (1999). *A Public Peace Process: Sustained Dialogue to Transform Racial and Ethnic Conflicts*. New York: St. Martin's Press. For examples of public participation in different countries, see Fahr, E., and S. Gächter. (2002). "Altruistic Punishment in Humans." *Nature* 415 (Januarry 10): 137–40.

76. Khadiagla, G. M. (2002). "Implementing the Arusha Peace Agreement on Rwanda." *Ending Civil Wars: The Implementation of Peace Agreements*. Edited by J. Stephen, D. Rothchild, and E. M. Cousens. Boulder, CO: Lynne Rienner: 483–98.

77. Crocker, C. A., F. O. Hampson, and P. Aall, Eds. (1999). *Herding Cats: Multiparty Mediation in a Complex World*. Washington, DC: U.S. Institute of Peace Press; Kriesberg, L. (1996). "Coordinating Intermediary Peace Efforts." *Negotiation Journal* 12 (October): 341–52; Nan, S. A., and A. Strimling. (2006). "Coordination in Conflict Prevention, Conflict Resolution and Peacebuilding." *International Negotiation* 11 (1): 1–6.

78. McDonald, J. W. (1991). "Further Explorations in Track Two Diplomacy." *Timing the De-Escalation of International Conflicts*. Edited by L. Kriesberg and S. J. Thorson. Syracuse: Syracuse University Press: 201–20; Montville, J. V. (1991).

"Transnationalism and the Role of Track-Two Diplomacy." *Approaches to Peace: An Intellectual Map*. Edited by W. S. Thompson and K. M. Jensen. Washington, DC: U.S. Institute of Peace: 253–69; Chufrin, G. I., and H. H. Saunders. (1993). "A Public Peace Process." *Negotiation Journal* 9 (April): 155–77.

79. Kelman. (1995). "Contributions of an Unoffical Conflict Resolution Effort to the Israeli-Palestinian Breakthrough."

80. Ashrawi, H. (1995). *This Side of Peace*. New York: Simon & Schuster; Savir, U. (1998). *The Process: 1,100 Days That Changed the Middle East*. New York: Random House.

81. Wanis-St. John, A. (2010). *Back Channel Negotiations: Secrecy in the Middle East Peace Process*. Syracuse: Syracuse University Press.

82. Hume, C. (1994). *Ending Mozambique's War*. Washington, DC: U.S. Institute of Peace.

83. Zartman, I. W. (1989). *Ripe for Resolution: Conflict and Intervention in Africa*. New York: Oxford University Press; Zartman, I. W. (1991). "Conflict Reduction: Prevention, Management, and Resolution." *Conflict Resolution in Africa*. Edited by F. M. Deng and I. W. Zartman. Washington, DC: Brookings Institute: 299–319; Kriesberg, L., and S. J. Thorson, Eds. (1991). *Timing the De-Escalation of International Conflicts*. Syracuse, NY: Syracuse University Press.

84. Lund, M. S. (1996). *Preventing Violent Conflicts*. Washington, DC: U.S. Institute of Peace Press; Touval, S., and I. W. Zartman, Eds. (1985). *International Mediation in Theory and Practice*. Boulder, CO: Westview Press; Boulding, E., Ed. (1994). *Building Peace in the Middle East*. Boulder: Lynne Rienner; Carnegie Commission on Preventing Deadly Conflict. (1997). *Final Report of the Carnegie Commission on Preventing Deadly Conflict*. New York: Carnegie Corporation; Kriesberg, L. (1996). "Coordinating Intermediary Peace Efforts." *Negotiation Journal* 12 (October): 341–52.

85. Hume. (1994). *Ending Mozambique's War*.

86. Spencer, D. E., and H. Yang. (1992). "Lessons from the Field of Intra-National Conflict Resolution." *Notre Dame Law Review* 67 (5): 1495–517; Brinkley, D. (1995). "Jimmy Carter's Modest Quest for Global Peace." *Foreign Affairs* 74 (November/December): 90–100. International Alert, based in London, was established in 1985 by human rights advocates and others working in international development agencies and responding to ethnic conflict. See http://www.international-alert.org.

87. Zartman, I. W. (1991). "Conflict Reduction: Prevention, Management, and Resolution." *Conflict Resolution in Africa*. Edited by F. M. Deng and I. W. Zartman. Washington, DC: Brookings Institute: 299–319.

88. Keashly, L., and R. J. Fisher. (1996). "Complemenatity and Coordination of Conflict Interventions: Taking a Contigency Perspective." *Resolving International Conflicts*. Edited by J. Bercovitch. Boulder, CO: Lynne Rienner: 235–61; Stein, J. G., Ed. (1989). *Getting to the Table: The Process of International Prenegotiation*. Baltimore: The John Hopkins University Press.

89. Kressel, K., and D. G. Pruitt. (1989). *Mediation Research*. San Francisco, CA: Jossey-Bass; Bercovitch, J., and O. Elgstrom. (2001). "Culture and International Me-

diation: Exploring Theoretical and Empirical Linkages." *International Negotiation Journal* 6: 3–23.

90. Mitchell, C. R. (1995). "Asymmetry and Strategies of Regional Conflict Reduction." *Cooperative Security: Reducing Third World Wars*. Edited by I. W. Zartman and V. A. Kremenyuk. Syracuse, NY: Syracuse University Press: 25–57; Babbitt, E. F., and E. L. Lutz, Eds. (2009). *Human Rights and Conflict Resolution in Context*. Syracuse, NY: Syracuse University Press.

CHAPTER 9. NON-NEGOTIATED AND NEGOTIATED SETTLEMENTS

1. Galtung, J. (1969). "Violence, Peace, and Peace Research." *Journal of Peace Research* 3 (3): 168.

2. Megwalu, A., and N. Loizides. (2010). "Dilemmas of Justice and Reconciliation: Rwandans and the Gacaca Courts." *African Journal of International and Comparative Law* 18 (1): 1–23.

3. For a comprehensive review of this case, see Kluger, R. (1976). *Simple Justice: The History of Brown v. Board of Education and Black America's Struggle for Equality*. New York: Knopf.

4. The interesting and complex role that social media plays in shaping conflict behavior and conflict manifestation is explored in Zeitzoff, T. (2017). "How Social Media Is Changing Conflict." *Journal of Conflict Resolution* 61 (9): 1970–91.

5. Remnick, D. (1993). *Lenin's Tomb: The Last Days of the Soviet Empire*. New York: Random House. For an analysis of public opinion in the Soviet Union in the period of transformation, see Popov, N. (1995). *The Russian People Speak: Democracy at the Crossroads*. Syracuse: Syracuse University Press.

6. Stecula, D. A., and E. Merkley. (2019). "Framing Climate Change: Economics, Ideology, and Uncertainty in American News Media Content From 1988 to 2014." *Frontiers in Communication* 4 (6).

7. Kreutz, J. (2010). "How and When Armed Conflicts End: Introducing the UCDP Conflict Termination Dataset." *Journal of Peace Research* 47 (2): 243–50. Armed conflicts include wars, which are conflicts with one thousand or more battle-related deaths, and other conflicts with 25 to 999 battle-related deaths.

8. Maiese, M. (2003). *Negotiation Beyond Intractability*. University of Colorado, Boulder, Conflict Information Consortium: http://www.beyondintractability.org/essay/negotiation.

9. Lewicki, R. J., D. M. Saunders, and J. W. Minton (1999). *Negotiation*. New York: McGraw-Hill; Carnevale, P. J. (2004). *Negotiation in Social Conflict*. Buckingham: Open University.

10. Gulliver, P. H. (1979). *Disputes and Negotiations: A Cross-Cultural Perspective*. New York: Academic Press.

11. Fisher, R., W. Ury, and B. Patton. (1991). *Getting to Yes: Negotiating Agreement Without Giving In*, second edition. New York: Penguin.

12. This was a feature of Soviet intransigence in negotiations with the United States during the Cold War, which was often attributed to the inability of Soviet negotiators to deviate from strict instructions. See Mosley, P. E. (1951). "Some Soviet Techniques of Negotiation." *Negotiating with the Russians*. Edited by R. Dennett and J. E. Johnson. Boston: World Peace Foundation: 288.

13. Some of these matters are examined using data from India, China, Greece, Korea, the Netherlands, the United States, and elsewhere in Triandis, H. C., P. Carnevale, M. Gelfand, C. Robert, S. A. Wasti, T. Probst, E. S. Kashima, T. Dragonas, D. Chan, X. P. Chen, U. Kim, C. de Dreu, E. van de Vliert, S. Iwao, K.-I. Ohbuchi, and P. Schmitz. (2001). "Culture and Deception in Business Negotiations: A Multi-Level Analysis." *International Journal of Cross Cultural Management* 1 (1): 73–90.

14. Fisher, R., and W. Ury. (1981). *Getting to YES*. Boston: Houghton Miflin Company.

15. The Jimmy Carter Presidential Library contains a detailed description of the Camp David negotiations. See https://www.jimmycarterlibrary.gov/research/framework_for_peace_in_the_middle_east.

16. Zartman, I. W., and M. Berman. (1982). *The Practical Negotiator*. New Haven, CT: Yale University Press.

17. Zartman and Berman. (1982). *The Practical Negotiator*: 66.

18. Hopmann, P. T. (1996). *The Negotiation Process and the Resolution of International Conflicts*. Columbia, SC: University of South Carolina Press: 80; Sebenius, J. K. (1984). *Negotiating the Law of the Sea*. Cambridge, MA: Harvard University Press.

19. Kriesberg, L. (1992). *International Conflict Resolution: The U.S.-USSR and Middle East Cases*. New Haven, CT: Yale University Press.

20. Fisher, R. (1964). "Fractionating Conflict." *International Conflict and Behavioral Science*. Edited by R. Fisher. New York: Basic Books.

21. Kriesberg, L. (2015). *Realizing Peace: A Constructive Conflict Approach*. New York: Oxford University Press: 248–51; Parsi, T. (2012). *A Single Roll of the Dice: Obama's Diplomacy with Iran*. New Haven, CT: Yale University Press.

22. Tradeoffs in the context of complex environmental problems has been the subject of a large-scale MacArthur Foundation project called "Advancing Conservation in a Social Context: Working in a World of Tradeoffs." See www.tradeoffs.org. Also see "Bulletin: We Won!" (1989). *Review and Outlook, Wall Street Journal*: A14; Hirsch, P. D., W. M. Adams, J. P. Brosius, A. Zia, N. Bariolsa, and J. L. Dammert. (2011). "Acknowledging Conservation Trade-offs and Embracing Complexity." *Conservation Biology* 25: 259–64.

23. This is the basic premise of exchange theory. Blau, P. M. (1964). *Exchange and Power in Social Life*. New York: John Wiley. For applications to negotiations, see Raiffa, H. (1982). *The Art and Science of Negotiation*. Cambridge, MA: Harvard University Press.

24. Zartman, I. W., and V. Kremenyuk, Eds. (2005). *Peace versus Justice: Negotiating Forward-and Backward-Looking Outcomes*. Lanham: Rowman & Littlefield.

25. Manno, J. P. (1994). "Advocacy and Diplomacy: NGOs and the Great Lakes Water Quality Agreement." *Environmental NGOs in World Politics*. Edited by T. Princen and M. Finger. London: Routlege.

26. Nader, L. (1991). "Harmony Models and the Construction of Law." *Conflict Resolution: Cross-Cultural Perspectives*. Edited by K. Avruch, P. W. Black, and J. A. Scimecca. New York: Greenwood Press: 41–59.

27. Samore, B., Ed. (2015). *The Iran Nuclear Deal: A Definitive Guide*. Cambridge, MA: Harvard University: 1–67.

28. Galtung, J., C. G. Jacobsen, and K. F. Brand-Jacobsen. (2002). *Searching for Peace: The Road to TRANSCEND*, second edition. London: Pluto.

29. Fisher and Ury (1981). *Getting to YES*.

30. Haass, R. N. (1991). "Ripeness, De-Escalation, and Arms Control: The Case of the INF." *Timing the De-Escalation of International Conflicts*. Edited by L. Kriesberg and S. J. Thorson. Syracuse: Syracuse University Press.

31. Kriesberg, L. (1991). "Introduction: Timing Conditions, Strategies, and Errors." Edited by L. Kriesberg and S. J. Thorson. Syracuse: Syracuse University Press.

32. For a discussion of the hurting stalemate and a settlement formula, see Touval, S. and I. W. Zartman, Eds. (1985). *International Mediation in Theory and Practice*. Boulder, CO: Westview Press.

33. Hirsch, P. D., W. M. Adams, J. P. Brosius, A. Zia, N. Bariolsa, and J. L. Dammert. (2011). "Acknowledging Conservation Trade-offs and Embracing Complexity." *Conservation Biology* 25: 259–64.

34. "Transboundary Rivers and Crisis Prevention" at www.bicc.de/water/rivers.php.

35. Sneddon, C., and C. Fox. (2007). "Power, Development, and Institutional Change: Participatory Governance in the Lower Mekong Basin." *World Development* 35 (12): 2161–81.

36. Forester, J. (1994). "Lawrence Susskind: Activist Mediation." *When Talk Works: Profiles of Mediator*. Edited by D. M. Kolb. San Francisco: Jossey-Bass: 309–54.

37. Cohen, R. (1997). *Negotiating Across Cultures*. Washington, DC: U.S. Institute of Peace Press; Hall, E. T. (1959). *The Silent Language*. New York: Doubleday.

38. Binnendijk, H., Ed. (1987). *National Negotiating Styles*. Washington, DC: U.S. Government Printing Office, Department of State Publication.

39. Kriesberg, L. (2015). "Negotiating Conflict Transformations." *Handbook of International Negotiation: Interpersonal, International, and Diplomatic*. Edited by M. Galluccio. Cham, Switzerland: Springer: 109–22.

40. Provine, M. (1986). *Settlement Strategies for Federal District Judges*. Washington, DC:The Federal Judicial Center.

41. Lynch, J. (2001). "Beyond ADR: A Systems Approach to Conflict Management." *Negotiation Journal* 17 (3): 207–16.

42. O'Leary, R., and L. Bingham. (2009). *The Collaborative Public Manager: New Ideas for the Twenty-first Century*. Washington, DC: Georgetown University Press.

43. Lofland, J. (1993). *Polite Protestors: The American Peace Movement of the 1980's*. Syracuse: Syracuse University Press.

44. Sebenius, J. K. (1984). *Negotiating the Law of the Sea*. Cambridge, MA: Harvard University Press.

45. Leatherman, J. (2003). *From Cold War to Democratic Peace*. Syracuse, NY: Syracuse University Press.

46. See Kissinger, H. (1979). *White House Years*. Boston: Little, Brown. See also Smith, G. (1960). *Double Talk: The Story of the First Strategic Arms Limitation Talks*. New York: Doubleday; and Newhouse, J. (1973). *Cold Dawn: The Story of SALT*. New York: Holt, Rinehart and Winston.

47. Wanis-St. John, A. (2010). *Back Channel Negotiations: Secrecy in the Middle East Peace Process*. Syracuse: Syracuse University Press.

48. The Rhodesian Prime Minister Ian Smith led the opposition to black political participation in the 1960s. His son Alec describes the regular meetings of white and Black Christian leaders, which became known as the Cabinet of Conscience. It began to meet in 1975 and continued until Zimbabwe achieved independence in 1980. Alec Smith and Arthur Kanodereka, a Black resistance leader, traveled together and organized meetings attracting Blacks and whites. Smith, A. (1984). *Now I Call Him Brother*. Basingstoke, UK: Marsalls Paperbacks; Griffith, A. (1998). *Conflict and Resolution: Peace-Building through the Ballot Box in Zimbabwe, Namibia and Cambodia*. Oxford: New Cherwell Press. For the Rhodesian transformation, see Wiseman, H., and A. M. Taylor. (1981). *From Rhodesia to Zimbabwe: The Politics of Transition*. New York: Pergamon.

49. During and after World War I, secret diplomacy was widely viewed as bearing major responsibility for the war. President Woodrow Wilson, in the Fourteen Points, proclaimed the goal of "open covenants of peace, openly arrived at, after which there shall be no private understandings of any kind, but diplomacy shall proceed always frankly and in the public view." Morgenthau, H. J. (1950). *Politics among Nations*. New York: Alfred A. Knopf.

50. See Rubin, J. Z., and B. R. Brown. (1975). *The Social Psychology of Bargaining and Negotiation*. New York: Academic Press.

51. Beilin, Y. (1999). *Touching Peace: From the Oslo Accord to a Final Agreement*. London: Weidenfeld & Nicolson; Savir, U. (1998). *The Process: 1,100 Days That Changed the Middle East*. New York: Random House.

52. Kriesberg, L. (1992). *International Conflict Resolution: The U.S.-USSR and Middle East Cases*. New Haven: Yale University Press; Mitchell, C. R. (1990). "A Willingness to Talk." George Mason University, Center for Conflict Analysis and Resolution; Mitchell, C. R. (1991). "Ending Conflicts and Wars: Judgement, Rationality and Entrapment." *International Social Science Journal* 127 (February): 35–55; Kriesberg, L., and S. French. (1989). "Reactions to Soviet Initiatives." Paper presented at the annual meeting of the International Studies Association, London, March.

53. Dayan, M. (1981). *Breakthrough*. New York: Alfred A. Knopf: 38–54; also Patir, D., interview by author, Washington, DC, June 17, 1982.

54. Kriesberg, L. (1992). *International Conflict Resolution: The U.S.-USSR and Middle East Cases*. New Haven: Yale University Press.

55. Fisher, R. (1989). "Negotiating Inside Out: What are the Best Ways to Relate Internal Negotiations with External Ones." *Negotiation Journal* 5 (January): 33–41.

56. Cohen, R. (1997). *Negotiating Across Cultures*. Washington, DC: U.S. Institute of Peace Press.

57. Huthwaite Research Group and Huthwaite Inc. (1982). *The Behavior of Successful Negotiators*. Reston, VA: Huthwaite Research Group and Huthwaite Inc.

CHAPTER 10. POSTSETTLEMENT OUTCOMES

1. Simić, O., and I. Milojević. (2014). "Dialogues between Ex-Combatants and Youth in Serbia: A Constructive Use of War Experience." *Peacebuilding* 2 (3): 322–35.

2. Kasadha, J. (2020). "Digitizing Community Building and Reconciliation in Post-Conflict Communities: A Case of #Let'sTalkUganda in Northern Uganda." *Social Media + Society* 6 (2): 2056305120924785.

3. See Coser, L. A. (1956). *The Functions of Social Conflict*. New York: Free Press: 38, 95; see also Sumner, W. G. (1906). *Folkways*. Lexington, MA: Ginn; and Simmel, G. (1955). *Conflict and the Web of Intergroup Affiliations*. New York: Free Press.

4. Coser, L. A. (1956). *The Functions of Social Conflict*. Glencoe: Free Press, 38.

5. Solomon, F. (1965). "Civil Rights Activity and Reduction in Crime Among Negroes." *Archives of General Psychiatry* 12 (March): 227–36.

6. Hopmann, P. T. (1967). "International Conflict and Cohesion in the Communist System." *International Studies Quarterly* 11 (September): 212–36; Holsti, O. R. (1969). "External Conflict and Internal Cohesion: The Sino-Soviet Case." *Communist Party-States*. Edited by J. Triska. Indianapolis, IN: Bobbs-Merrill: 337–52.

7. While living in Germany in the summer of 1950 and the academic year 1956/1957, I heard many Germans express abhorrence at what the Nazis had done and bewilderment at their enthusiasm for Nazism. However, others denied awareness of the Holocaust at the time, and some even denied that it had happened on the scale revealed.

8. O'Connor, M. (1996). "Serves in Bosnia See No Peace for Their Dead . . . . And Are Angry at Leaders and Themselves." *New York Times*. January 18, A6.

9. The health of the British working class, however, improved during the war. See Winter, J. M. (1977). "The Impact of the First World War on Civilian Health in Britian." *Economic History Review* 30 (August): 487–507.

10. See Andrzejewski, S. (1954). *Military Organization and Society*. London: Routledge and Kegan Paul; Cutright, P. (1967). "Inequality: A Cross-National Analysis." *American Sociological Review* 32 (August): 562–78; Garnier, M. A., and L. Hazelrigg. (1977). "Military Organization and Distributional Inequality: An Examination of Andreski's Thesis." *Journal of Political and Military Sociology* 5 (Spring): 17–33; and Weede, E. (1992). "Military Participation, Economic Growth and Income Equality." *Defense, Welfare and Growth*. Edited by S. Chan and A. Mintz. London: Routledge: 211–30.

11. Weede, E. (1993). "The Impact of Interstate Conflict on Revolutionary Change and Individual Freedom." *Kyklos* 46 (4): 473–95.

12. Nincic, M. (1989). "Capital Labor and the Spoils of War." *Journal of Peace Research* 17 (2): 103–17.

13. Kriesberg, L. (1979). *Social Inequality*. Englewood Cliffs, NJ: Prentice-Hall: 58–65.

14. Stohl, M. (1976). *War and Domestic Political Violence: The American Capacity for Repression and Reaction*. Beverly Hills: Sage.

15. Winter, J. M. (1977). "Britian's Lost Generation of the World War." *Population* 31 (November): 487–66.

16. Phillips, D. K. (1980). "The Case for Veteran Preferences." *Strangers at Home: Vietnam Veterans Since the War*. Edited by C. R. Figley and S. Leventman. New York: Praeger: 348. Charles Moskos notes different bases for calculating the relative death rate in combat of African Americans, yielding different implications. Charles Moskos, letter to author, November 1996. Indeed, in military operations since Vietnam (1975–1995), Blacks comprised 15 percent of those killed in action, while they averaged 19 percent of active duty military personnel during that same period. See Moskos, C., and J. S. Butler. (1996). "Overcoming Race: Army Lessons for American Society." Paper presented at the symposium honoring Robin M. Williams Jr., Ithaca, NY, October.

17. Mehlum, H., K. O. Moene, and R. Torvik. (2002). "Plunder and Protection, Inc." *Journal of Peace Research* 39 (July): 447–59.

18. Koubi, V. "War and Economic Performance," *Journal of Peace Research* 42 (January): 67–82.

19. Melman, S. (1974). *The Permanent War Economy: American Capitalism in Decline*. New York: Simon & Schuster; DeGrasse Jr., R. W. (1983). *Military Expansion Economic Decline*. Amonk, NY: M. E. Sharpe; Lebow, R. N., and J. G. Stein. (1994). *We all Lost the Cold War*. Princeton, NJ: Princeton University Press.

20. Zunes, S. (2017). "Strategic Nonviolent Action: Waging Constructive Conflict against Authoritarianism." *Waging Conclicts Constructively: Concepts, Cases, and Practice*. Edited by B. W. Dayton and L. Kriesberg. Lanham: Rowman & Littlefield.

21. Swords, A. C. S. (2005). "The Power of Networks: Popular Political Education among Neo-Aapatista Organizations in Chiapas, Mexico." PhD dissertation, Cornell University.

22. Larry Dunn notes that this sometimes occurs in labor-management negotiations "where the rank and file accuse the leadership of caving in or selling out and they are left with two choices: not supporting a contract or blindly supporting it without understanding how that's the best they can get." Larry Dunn, email to Kriesberg, April 1997.

23. Wanis-St. John, A. (2010). *Back Channel Negotiations: Secrecy in the Middle East Peace Process*. Syracuse: Syracuse University Press.

24. Oppenheimer, M. (1969). *The Urban Guerrilla*. New York: Quadrangle/The New York Times: 71.

25. Weir, S. (1970). "U.S.A.: The Labor Revolt." *American Society, Inc.* Edited by M. Zeitlin. Chicago: Markham.

26. See the characterizations of the great subversive power of Jews articulated in Adolf Hitler's 1924 book, *Mein Kampf* (New York: Reynal and Hitchock, 1941).

27. Kriesberg, L. (1989). "Transforming Conflicts in the Middle East and Central Europe." *Intractable Conflicts and Their Transformation*. Edited by L. Kriesberg, T. A. Northrup, and S. J. Thorson. Syracuse: Syracuse University Press: 109–31.

28. Dobratz, B. A., and S. L. Shanks-Meile. (1997). *"White Power, White Pride!" The White Separatist Movement in the United States*. New York: Twayne; see also Bennett, D. H. (1995). *The Party of Fear: From Nativist Movements to the New Right*

in American History. New York: Vintage; and Barkun, M. (1994). *Religion and the Racist Right: The Origins of the Christian Identity Movement*. Chapel Hill, NC: The University of North Carolina Press.

29. Budd, E. C. (1967). "An Introduction to a Current Issue of Public Policy." *Inequality and Poverty*. Edited by E. C. Budd. New York: W. W. Norton & Co.: x–xix.

30. Femenia, N. A. (1996). *National Identity in Times of Crises: The Scripts of the Falklands-Malvina War*. New York: Nova Science.

31. Danner, M. (2005 September 11). "Taking Stock of the Forever War." *The New York Times Magazine*: 45–53, 68, 86, 87; Diamond, L. (2005). *Squandered Victory*. New York: Henry Holt.

32. Stohl, M. (1976). *War and Domestic Political Violence: The American Capacity for Repression and Reaction*. Beverly Hills: Sage.

33. For example, see Rummel, R. J. (1963). "The Dimensions of Conflict Behavior Within and Between Nations." *General Systems Yearbook* 8: 1–50; and Tanter, R. (1966). "Dimensions of Conflict Behavior Within and Between Nations, 1958–1960." *Journal of Conflict Resolution* 10 (March): 41–64. For a review and interpretation of the studies, see Stohl, M. (1980). "The Nexus of Civil and International Conflict." *Handbook of Political Conflict*. Edited by T. R. Gurr. New York: Free Press.

34. Wilkenfeld, J. (1969). "Some Further Findings Regarding the Domestic and Foreign Conflict Behavior of Nations." *Journal of Peace Research* 2: 147–56; Wilkenfeld, J., and D. A. Zinnes. (1973). "A Linkage Model of Domestic Conflict Behavior." *Conflict Behavior and Linkage Politics*. Edited by J. WIlkenfeld. New York: D. McKay: 325–56.

35. Mueller, J. E. (1973). *War, Presidents and Public Opinion*. Hoboken, NJ: Wiley & Sons.

36. Borker, S., L. Kriesberg, and A. Abdul-Quader. (1985). "Conciliation, Confrontation, and Approval of the President." *Peace and Change* 11 (Spring): 31–48.

37. Weede, E. (1993). "The Impact of Interstate Conflict on Revolutionary Change and Individual Freedom." *Kyklos* 46 (4): 473–95.

38. Schmeidl, S. (1997). "Exploring the Causes of Forced Migration: A Pooled Time-Series Analysis, 1971–1990." *Social Science Quarterly* 78 (June): 284–308; see also UN High Commissioner for Refugees at www.unhcr.ch.

39. Dugan, M. A. (1979). "The Relationship Between Pre-Independence Internal Violence and Nonviolence and Post-Independence Violence, External Belligerency, and Internal Governmental Repressiveness." Unpublished Ph.D. dissertation, Syracuse University.

40. Frank, T. (2004). *What's the Matter with Kansas?* New York: Henry Holt.

41. Fendrich, J. M., and E. S. Krauss. (1978). "Student Activism and Adult Leftwing Politics: A Causal Model of Political Socialization for Black, White, and Japanese Students of teh 1960's Generation." *Research in Social Movements, Conflicts, and Change*. Edited by L. Kriesberg. Greenwich, CT: JAI Press: 231–90; Park, B.-c. (1995). "Motivational Dynamics of Student Movement Participation in Contemporary South Korea." Unpublished Ph.D. dissertation, Syracuse University.

42. Mannheim, K. (1952). "The Sociological Problem of Generations." *Essays on the Sociology of Knowledge*. Edited by P. Kecskemeti. New York: Oxford University

Press: 276–322; Braungart, R., and M. M. Braungart, Eds. (1993). *Life Course and Generational Politics*. Lanham, MD: University Press of America.

43. Leggett, J. C. (1968). *Class, Race, and Labor*. New York: Oxford University Press: 90–91.

44. Cutler, N. E. (1970). "Generational Succes as a Source of Foreign Policy Attitudes." *Journal of Peace Research* 1: 33–47; Jeffries, V. (1974). "Political Generations and the Acceptance or Rejection of Nuclear Warfare." *Journal of Social Issues* 30: 119–36.

45. Kriesberg, L., and R. A. Klein. (1980). "Changes in Public Support for U.S. Military Spending." *Journal of Conflict Resolution* 24 (March): 79–111.

46. Goldstone, J. A., Ed. (1986). *Revolutions: Theoretical, Comparative, and Historical Studies*. San Diego: Harcourt Brace Jovanovich.

47. Skocpol, T. (1979). *States and Social Revolutions: A Comparative Analysis of France, Russia, and China*. Cambridge, England: Cambridge University Press: 176.

48. Eckstein, S. (1986). "The Impact of Revolution on Social Welfare in Latin America." *Revolutions: Theoretical, Comparative, and Historical Studies*. Edited by J. A. Goldston. San Diego: Harcourt Brace Jovanovich: 280–307; see also Lewis-Beck, M. S. (1979). "Some Effects of Revolution: Models, Measurement, and teh Cuban Evidence." *American Journal of Sociology* 84 (March): 1127–49.

49. Coser, L. A. (1967). *Continuities in the Study of Social Conflict*. New York: Free Press; Melman, S. (1956). *Dynamic Factors in Industrial Productivity*. Oxford, UK: Blackwell; Levine, R., and J. A. Gewschwender. (1981). "Class Struggle, State Policy, and the Rationalization of Production: The Organization of Agriculture in Hawaii." *Research in Social Movements, Conflicts and Change*. Edited by L. Kriesberg. Greenwich, CT: JAI Press: 4.

50. O'Leary, R., and L. Bingham. (2009). *The Collaborative Public Manager: New Ideas for the Twenty-First Century*. Washington, DC: Georgetown University Press; Nabatchi, T., and M. Leighniger. (2015). *Public Participation for 21st Century Democracy*. Hoboken, NJ: Jossey-Bass.

51. Mitchell, C. (2017). "Peaceful Separation: The Politics of Constructive Dissolution." *Waging Conflicts Constructively: Concepts, Cases and Practice*. Edited by B. W. Dayton and L. Kriesberg. Lanham: Rowman & Littlefield.

52. Wilkenfeld, J. (1969). "Some Further Findings Regarding the Domestic and Foreign Conflict Behavior of Nations." *Journal of Peace Research* 2: 147–56.

53. Brock Blomberg, S., and G. D. Hess. (2002). "The Temporal Links Between Conflict and Economic Activity." *Journal of Conflict Resolution* 46 (1): 74–90; Junne, G., and W. Verkoren, Eds. (2004). *Postconflict Development: Meeting New Challenges*. Boulder, CO: Lynne Rienner.

54. Human Security Report. (2009). "The Shrinking Costs of War." *Human Security Report*. Edited by A. Mack. Vancouver, Canada: Simon Fraser University.

55. Paris, R. (2004). *At War's End: Building Peace After Civil Conflict*. Cambridge, UK: Cambridge University Press; Licklider, R. (2001). "Obstacles to Peace Settlements." *Turbulent Peace*. Edited by C. A. Crocker, F. O. Hampson, and P. Aall. Washington, DC: U.S. Institute of Peace Press: 697–718; Henisz, W. J.,

B. A. Zelner, and M. F. Guillén. (2005). "The Worldwide Diffusion of Market-Oriented Infrastructure Reform, 1977–1999." *American Sociological Review* 70 (6): 871–97; Lyons, T. (2005). *Demilitarizing Politics: Elections on the Uncertain Road to Peace*. Boulder: Lynne Rienner.

56. Kriesberg, L. (2011). "Challenges in Peacemaking: External Interventions." *Peacemaking: A Comprehensive Theory and Practice Reference*. Edited by A. Bartoli, S. A. Nan, and Z. Mampilly. Santa Barbara: Praeger.

57. Bar-Siman-Tov, Y., Ed. (2003). *From Conflict Resolution to Reconciliation*. Oxford: Oxford University Press; Pouligny, B., S. Chesterman, and A. Schnabel, Ed. (2007). *After Mass Crime: Rebuilding States and Communities*. Tokyo: UN University Press; Porter, E. (2015). *Connecting Peace, Justice & Reconciliation*. Boulder: Lynne Rienner.

58. Lederach, J. P. (1997). *Building Peace: Sustainable Reconciliation in Divided Societies*. Washington, DC: U.S. Institute of Peace Press.

59. Millar, G. (2015). "Performative Memory and Re-victimization: Truth-telling and Provocation in Sierra Leone." *Memory Studies* 8 (2): 242–54.

60. See Kritz, N. J. (1995). "Germany (After Nazism)." *Transitional Justice*, volume II. Edited by N. J. Kritz. Washington, DC: U.S. Institute of Peace Press: 1–69. See also Auerbach, Y. (2004). "The Role of Forgiveness in Reconciliation." *From Conflict Resolution to Reconciliation*. Edited by Y. Bar-Siman-Tov. Oxford: Oxford University Press: 149–75.

61. Henderson, M. (1996). *The Forgiveness Factor*. London: Grosvenor Books; Minow, M. (1998). *Between Vengeance and Forgiveness*. Boston: Beacon Press.

62. Robinson, R. (2000). *The Debt: What America Owes to Blacks*. New York: Dutton: 201.

63. Ryback, T. W. (1996–97). "Dateline Sudentland: Hostages to History." *Foreign Policy* 105 (Winter): 162–78. In 1992, Czechoslovakia broke into the Slovak and the Czech republics through negotiations.

64. Thiessen, G. (1999). "Object of Trust and Hatred: Public Attitudes towards the Truth and Reconciliation Commission." *Wits History Workshop*. Johannesburg.

65. See, for instance, Aall, P. (2001). "What Do NGOs Bring to Peacemaking?" *Turbulent Peace: The Challenges of Managing International Conflict*. Edited by C. A. Crocker, F. O. Hampson, and P. Aall. Washington, DC: U.S. Institute of Peace Press: 365–83. See also Goodhand, J. (2006). *Aiding Peace? The Role of NGOs in Armed Conflict*. Boulder: Lynne Rienner.

66. Crocker, C. A., F. O. Hampson, and P. R. Aall (2004). *Taming Intractable Conflicts: Mediation in the Hardest Cases*. Washington, DC: U.S. Institute of Peace Press; Dayton, B. W. (2009). "Useful but Insufficient: Intermediaries in Peacebulding." *Conflict Transformation and Peacebuilding*. Edited by B. W. Dayton and L. Kriesberg. London: Routledge: 61–73.

67. Crocker, C. A. (1992). *High Noon in Southern Africa: Making Peace in a Rough Neighborhood*. New York: W.W. Norton.

68. Paris, R. (2004). *At War's End: Building Peace After Civil Conflict*. Cambridge, UK: Cambridge University Press.

CHAPTER 11. TOWARD CONSTRUCTIVE CONFLICT TRANSFORMATION

1. Bank, T. W. (2020). *COVID-19 to Add as Many as 150 Million Extreme Poor by 2021*. Washington, DC: World Bank Group.

2. Agency, T. U. R. (2021). *UNHCR: Conflict, Violence, Climate Change Drove Displacement Higher in First Half of 2021*. New York: UN High Commissioner of Refugees.

3. Palik, J., S. A. Rustad, and F. Methi. (2020). *Conflict Trends: A Global Overview, 1946–2019*. Oslo: Peace Research Institute

4. For an interesting discussion of the various explanations for the decline of international war, see Gleditsch, N. P., S. Pinker, B. A. Thayer, J. S. Levy, and W. R. Thompson. (2013). "The Forum: The Decline of War." *International Studies Review* 15 (3): 396–419.

5. Pinker, S. (2011). *The Better Angels of Our Nature: Why Violence Has Declined*. New York: Viking. For a critique of Pinker's thesis and discussion of alternative perspectives, see Grey, J. (2015). "Steven Pinker is Wrong about Violence and War." *The Guardian*.

Index

About the Authors

Bruce W. Dayton (Ph.D. 1999, Syracuse University) serves as Associate Professor and Chair of the Master of Peace and Justice Leadership, the Master of Diplomacy and International Relations, and Director of the CONTACT Peacebuilding Institute at the School for International Training in Brattleboro, Vermont, USA. Professor Dayton has been active in peacebuilding and conflict transformation work for over twenty years as a practitioner, a researcher, and an educator. His other books include *Perspectives in Waging Conflicts Constructively* (Rowman and Littlefield, 2017) and *Peacebuilding and Conflict Transformation* (2009), each co-authored with Louis Kriesberg. He has published multiple book chapters on peace and conflict studies as well as articles on conflict transformation and crisis leadership in the *Negotiation Journal, International Studies Perspectives, The Journal of Contingencies and Crisis Management*, and *International Studies Review*. Dayton's previous appointments include Associate Director of the Moynihan Institute of Global Affairs, Research Co-Director at the Program for the Advancement of Research on Collaboration and Conflicts, and Assistant Research Professor, all at the Maxwell School of Citizenship and Public Affairs at Syracuse University. Dayton also served for six years as Executive Director of the International Society for Political Psychology and as Associate at the Center for Policy Negotiation in Boston, Massachusetts, where he ran policy dialogues on pressing public policy controversies.

Louis Kriesberg (Ph.D. 1953, University of Chicago) is Professor Emeritus of Sociology, Maxwell Professor Emeritus of Social Conflict Studies, and founding director of the Program on the Analysis and Resolution of Conflicts (1986–1994), all at Syracuse University. In addition to over 160 book chapters and articles, his recently published books include *Overcoming Intractable*

Conflicts: New Approaches to Constructive Transformations, co-edited with Miriam F. Elman, Catherine Gerard, and Galia Golan (2019); *Conflict and Collaboration: For Better or Worse*, co-edited with Catherine Gerard (2018); *Perspectives on Waging Conflicts Constructively: Concepts, Cases and Practice,* co-edited with Bruce Dayton (2017); *Louis Kriesberg: Pioneer in Peace and Constructive Conflict Resolution Studies. Series: Pioneer in Arts, Humanities, Science, Engineering, Practice,* volume 1 (2016); *Realizing Peace: A Constructive Conflict Approach (2015); Conflict Transformation and Peacebuilding* (co-editor, 2009); *International Conflict Resolution* (1992); *Timing the De-Escalation of International Conflicts* (co-editor, 1991); *Intractable Conflicts and Their Transformation* (co-editor, 1989); *Social Conflicts* (1973, 1982); *Social Inequality* (1979); *Mothers in Poverty* (1970); *Social Processes in International Relations* (editor, 1968); and *Research in Social Movements, Conflicts and Change* (editor, volumes 1–14, 1978–1992). He was President of the Society for the Study of Social Problems (1983–1984), and he lectures, consults, and provides training regarding conflict resolution, security issues, and peace studies.

Milton Keynes UK
Ingram Content Group UK Ltd.
UKHW041644120923
428525UK00020B/179